THE LEGEND OF
GENERAL PARTS

PROUDLY SERVING A WORLD IN MOTION

THE LEGEND OF
GENERAL PARTS

PROUDLY SERVING A WORLD IN MOTION

Jeffrey L. Rodengen

Edited by Heather Lewin and Mickey Murphy
Design and layout by Ryan Milewicz and Dennis Shockley

WRITE STUFF

Write Stuff Enterprises, Inc.
1001 South Andrews Avenue
Suite 120
Fort Lauderdale, FL 33316
1-800-900-Book (1-800-900-2665)
(954) 462-6657
www.writestuffbooks.com

Publisher's Cataloging-in-Publication Data
(Prepared by The Donohue Group, Inc.)

Rodengen, Jeffrey L.
    The legend of General Parts : proudly serving a world in motion / Jeffrey L. Rodengen ; edited by Heather Lewin and Mickey Murphy ; design and layout by Ryan Milewicz and Dennis Shockley.

    p. : ill. ; cm.

    Includes bibliographical references and index.
    ISBN: 0-945903-79-0

1. General Parts (Firm)—History. 2. Automobile supplies industry—United States—History. I. Lewin, Heather. II. Murphy, Mickey. III. Milewicz, Ryan. IV. Shockley, Dennis G. V. Title.

HD9710.3.U544 G46 2006   338.4/7/629/287/2/0973
                                        2002116131

Completely produced in the
United States of America
10 9 8 7 6 5 4 3 2 1

Also by Jeffrey L. Rodengen

The Legend of Chris-Craft

IRON FIST:
The Lives of Carl Kiekhaefer

Evinrude-Johnson
and The Legend of OMC

Serving the Silent Service:
The Legend of Electric Boat

The Legend of Dr Pepper/Seven-Up

The Legend of Honeywell

The Legend of Briggs & Stratton

The Legend of Ingersoll-Rand

The Legend of Stanley:
150 Years of The Stanley Works

The MicroAge Way

The Legend of Halliburton

The Legend of York International

The Legend of Nucor Corporation

The Legend of Goodyear:
The First 100 Years

The Legend of AMP

The Legend of Cessna

The Legend of VF Corporation

The Spirit of AMD

The Legend of Rowan

New Horizons:
The Story of Ashland Inc.

The History of American Standard

The Legend of Mercury Marine

The Legend of Federal-Mogul

Against the Odds:
Inter-Tel—The First 30 Years

The Legend of Pfizer

State of the Heart: The Practical Guide
to Your Heart and Heart Surgery
with Larry W. Stephenson, M.D.

The Legend of
Worthington Industries

The Legend of IBP, Inc.

The Legend of
Trinity Industries, Inc.

The Legend of
Cornelius Vanderbilt Whitney

The Legend of Amdahl

The Legend of Litton Industries

The Legend of Gulfstream

The Legend of Bertram
with David A. Patten

The Legend of
Ritchie Bros. Auctioneers

The Legend of ALLTEL
with David A. Patten

The Yes, you can of
Invacare Corporation
with Anthony L. Wall

The Ship in the Balloon:
The Story of Boston Scientific
and the Development of
Less-Invasive Medicine

The Legend of Day & Zimmermann

The Legend of Noble Drilling

Fifty Years of Innovation:
Kulicke & Soffa

Biomet—From Warsaw
to the World
with Richard F. Hubbard

NRA: An American Legend

The Heritage and Values
of RPM, Inc.

The Marmon Group:
The First Fifty Years

The Legend of Grainger

The Legend of
The Titan Corporation
with Richard F. Hubbard

The Legend of Discount Tire Co.
with Richard F. Hubbard

The Legend of Polaris
with Richard F. Hubbard

The Legend of La-Z-Boy
with Richard F. Hubbard

The Legend of McCarthy
with Richard F. Hubbard

InterVoice:
Twenty Years of Innovation
with Richard F. Hubbard

Jefferson-Pilot Financial:
A Century of Excellence
with Richard F. Hubbard

The Legend of HCA
with Richard F. Hubbard

The Legend of Werner Enterprises
with Richard F. Hubbard

The History of J. F. Shea Co.
with Richard F. Hubbard

True to Our Vision
with Richard F. Hubbard

Albert Trostel & Sons
with Richard F. Hubbard

The Legend of Sovereign Bancorp
with Richard F. Hubbard

Innovation is the Best Medicine: the
extraordinary story of Datascope
with Richard F. Hubbard

The Legend of Guardian Industries

The Legend of
Universal Forest Products

Polytechnic University:
Changing the World—The First 150 Years

In It For The Long Haul:
The Story of CRST

Nothing is Impossible: The Legend of
Joe Hardy and 84 Lumber

The Story of Parsons Corporation

Cerner: From Vision to Value

New Horizons:
The Story of Federated Investors

Taking Care of Business:
Office Depot—The First 20 Years

TABLE OF CONTENTS

ACKNOWLEDGMENTS

AT THE TOP OF THE LIST OF THOSE WHO assisted in *The Legend of General Parts: Proudly Serving a World in Motion* is Ken Rogers, who devoted tremendous time and effort in the early stages of collecting and organizing photos and information. Although Ken was never an employee of General Parts, Inc. (GPI), he provided invaluable insight thanks to more than 50 years of experience working in the aftermarket supply field. His assistance during his retirement is duly noted and certainly appreciated.

The publication of this book would have been impossible without the dedicated assistance of GPI executives and associates. Vital to this effort was the time and cooperation extended by Joe Owen, GPI vice chairman, whose attentive and resolute guidance made it possible for our research and editorial teams to identify records and individuals crucial to the GPI legacy.

We are especially thankful to the former owners and CEOs of those companies that have joined GPI through mergers and acquisitions, several of which began in the 19th century. The time taken by each to furnish a brief history of their businesses is greatly appreciated.

Special thanks are also due to the GPI associates who assisted in the final stages of the book production process, including Michael Shields, Tina Davis, and Matt Davis in the GPI graphic arts department; Scott Ginsburg, Rachel Stroud, and Kathie Greeson in the photography department; and Linda Canipe, DeLisa Jones, Marsha Barlow Pettitt, and Ruby Beddingfield, administrative assistants.

To mention each and every person who has responded to requests for photos and information would be impossible, but without this cooperation, *The Legend of General Parts* could never have been completed.

Finally, special thanks are extended to the dedicated staff at Write Stuff Enterprises, Inc., who helped with the book. Thanks are due to Sam Stefanova, executive editor; Ann Gossy, Heather Lewin, Mickey Murphy, and Elizabeth Fernandez, senior editors; Sandy Cruz, vice president/creative director; Rachelle Donley and Dennis Shockley, art directors; Elijah Meyer and Ryan Milewicz, graphic designers; Roy Adelman, on-press supervisor; Martin Schultz, proofreader; Mary Aaron, transcriptionist; Connie Angelo, indexer; Amy Major, executive assistant to Jeffrey L. Rodengen; Marianne Roberts, executive vice president, publisher, and chief financial officer; Steven Stahl, director of marketing; and Sherry Hasso, bookkeeper.

THE ARENA

THE AUTOMOTIVE INDUSTRY, PERHAPS with the exception of the food industry, might well be considered the keystone industry of the 20th century in terms of America's economic—and thus national—growth and development. Throughout the century, motor vehicles have been essential in efficiently moving people and products, a function that is absolutely vital to the health of the American economy.

The 20th century truly was the key era of transportation development in the United States, and automotive vehicles were by far the leading mode of transportation. There were only 8,000 registered cars and trucks in the United States in 1900, but by the end of the century, there were 216,370,359 vehicles.

The automotive aftermarket is the segment of the industry that keeps these vehicles operational. General Parts Inc., founded in 1961, has earned an enviable position in the North American automotive aftermarket.

U.S. Vehicle Registration	
1900	8,000
1910	460,500
1920	9,329,161

'Horseless Carriages'

The first automobiles, known as "horseless carriages" in the early 1900s, presented Americans with a questionable and untested means of transportation. But with the development of better roads, along with a host of needed design improvements for comfort, most upper-income families in this era eventually purchased and drove automobiles.

Then, Henry Ford had a vision of building an automobile that would be affordable to the masses. His dream was fulfilled with the production of the Model T by his Ford Motor Company. The first production Model T Ford was assembled at the Piquette Avenue plant in Detroit on October 1, 1908. Over the next 19 years, Ford would build 15 million Model T automobiles, the longest run of any single model with the exception of the Volkswagen Beetle. From 1908 to 1927, the Model T would endure with little change in its design. "You can get the Model T in any color you want," Ford is said to have quipped, "as long as it is black."

The Assembly Line

Ford proved to be a manufacturing genius. Indeed, his innovative, moving assembly-line method of automobile manufacturing represented a major change at the time—one that was quickly imitated by manufacturers in numerous other industries across America and around the world.

Prior to Ford, automobiles were primarily sold by companies that did very little manufacturing within their vehicle assembly plants. Instead, they purchased vehicle components such as bodies and chassis, transmissions, and seats, and then assembled these components.

In the first 20 years of the 20th century, more than 1,900 different models of automobiles and trucks were marketed by approximately 50 different companies, including Pierce Arrow, Stutz, Mercer, Peerless, Auburn, Hupmobile, Moon, and Stearns. Ford, Buick, Cadillac, and Chevrolet are among the few survivors from these early days of

automobile manufacturing that remain in operation today.

In 1954, *The Saturday Evening Post,* which followed the American automobile industry with fervor for advertising reasons, released a poster titled, "Roll Call of Automobiles Sold in America During the Past 60 Years." The poster listed 2,594 different models. With this release, *The Saturday Evening Post* stated that only a dozen or so had survived.

What About Parts?

The owners of automobiles in the early days had one big problem—the limited availability of replacement parts. The assembly plants were primarily concerned with selling their models but had no workable plan for providing replacement parts for the components they assembled. Further, even those that had a plan would likely be out of business by the time replacement parts were needed.

The key components of vehicles assembled during these early days were Continental Red Seal engines and Spicer Brown Lipe transmissions and axles. Body and chassis builders were Cunningham, Briggs, Labaron, and Fisher. Champion was the preferred spark plug.

It was G. W. Yeoman, chairman of Continental Motors, who first recognized the need to have replacement parts readily available in the field for his Red Seal engines. He addressed the issue by establishing independently owned "parts stations" in 25 major cities from New York to Los Angeles. In 1925, 28 men representing these 25 locations met in Detroit and formed the first association of independent automotive parts distributors. They called it the National Auto Parts Association (NAPA).

NAPA members successfully developed mutual plans to increase operational efficiency, increase products, improve profitability, and deal with the competitive forces of the automobile manufacturers. Later on, NAPA members developed common marketing plans, pooled advertising funds, and in the mid-1960s introduced NAPA as a brand name for replacement parts. Today, NAPA is credited with being the first "program" distributor in the aftermarket.

U.S. Vehicle Registration	
1930	26,749,853
1940	32,453,233
1950	49,161,691

It was about this time that automotive vehicle manufacturers also developed an interest in becoming dominant players in selling replacement parts.

General Motors (GM) was the most aggressive in this area, understanding that its car dealerships alone could not provide all the parts demanded by the ever-increasing number of car owners. As early as 1918, GM's United Motors Service (UMS) division sold parts that were manufactured by its 13 manufacturing divisions to the independent aftermarket (brands as Delco batteries, Delco Remy ignition, Guide lighting, New Departure and Hyatt bearings, Rochester carburetors, and Packard wire and cables). GM's car dealers also sold these brands, and, consequently, the UMS and AC divisions were directly in competition with the GM car dealers.

New Challenges

The automotive aftermarket industry survived the Great Depression of the early 1930s with few failures. Indeed, it earned the reputation for being a depression-resistant business. While new-car sales dropped off, vehicle registration figures held their own through 1935, then climbed to a record 35 million in 1941.

World War II was the second major challenge facing the fledgling aftermarket industry. Vehicle production was discontinued midway through the 1942 model year as manufacturing was

diverted to military vehicles and support materials. Without new vehicle sales until 1946, along with a diversion of parts manufacturing, the automotive aftermarket was plagued with inadequate supply during the war years and for several years thereafter.

The major players among the traditional auto parts distributors of this era are too numerous to mention. Some were purely distributors with no involvement in ownership of the parts stores they served, and some owned their own parts stores. Some started as parts store owners buying direct from factories and later opened distribution centers to serve independently owned stores in addition to their own stores.

Some of these distributors specialized in paint and body shop supplies, engines, chemicals, heavy duty trucks, or marine or agriculture parts. Some specialized in machine shops. All were competitors trying desperately to get a piece of the gigantic aftermarket sales pie, which has been strong every year and valued at approximately $60 billion by the end of the year 2000.

U.S. Vehicle Registration	
1960	73,768,565
1970	108,435,903

The Golden Era of the '50s

The 1950s were great years for new-car sales. Registration increased 50 percent during the decade due to a population shift from the cities to the suburbs. The automobile had become the primary means to move people back and forth from home to work.

During this era, roads and highways were greatly improved. The interstate expressways were completed, making coast-to-coast motoring a new and enjoyable reality. Gasoline was plentiful and cheap. Service stations captured the lion's share of the vehicle repair business, even though oil companies tried to discourage them from any activity other than selling their products.

T.B.A. Programs

Since the early 1930s, T.B.A. (tires, batteries, and accessories) programs had been initiated by tire companies. They targeted the 200,000 gasoline service stations, which were capturing a good share of the tune-up and light maintenance business at the time. The tire companies forced oil companies to reconsider their position of being against service station repair and parts replacement work. Soon, T.B.A. programs were available from oil companies, also.

For its part, General Motors was discouraged with the parts business generated by its UMS division. In 1954, GM introduced a plan allowing its new car dealerships to wholesale parts previously sold only by independent distributors. Unpopular with car dealers and independent distributors, the plan was abandoned in 1957.

Around this time, Ford introduced a program called Motorcraft, an effort to sell electrical parts to independent distributors. Previously, such parts were available only from Ford dealers. Another manufacturer, Chrysler, discontinued buying from Autolite and began manufacturing electrical products in its own factories. Its success in the aftermarket, however, was minimal.

In 1958, General Motors made a decision to round out the coverage of its Delco-Remy ignition line to handle the needs of vehicles other than those sold by GM. This move allowed GM to sell the Delco-Remy line to fill the needs of oil and tire companies' individual T.B.A. programs. Ford joined the T.B.A. parade in 1961 with the purchase of Autolite.

Still searching for the key to success in the aftermarket, in 1961, General Motors announced that all its UMS lines, previously marketed under the names of their factories—Packard, Rochester, New Departure, and so on—would be packaged

under one name, Delco. An extensive ad campaign asked America to "Simply Say Delco."

In the early 1960s, Ford was selling parts in the aftermarket under three different brand names. Ford car dealers were selling Ford application parts under the Fo-Mo-Co label and non-Ford application parts under the Rotunda label. For the independent auto parts aftermarket distributors, the Autolite label was employed.

A $7 Billion Market

The automotive aftermarket remained largely unnoticed until mid-1962 when *Fortune* exposed its size to the world in an article titled, "The $7 Billion Aftermarket Gets an Overhaul." This influential article quickly attracted a large number of investors who wanted to get in on this huge, fast-growing industry. Mass merchandisers such as J.C. Penney, Sears, and Kmart not only set up automotive parts departments but also opened their own auto repair centers.

However, few of these companies seemed to understand that selling auto parts was not like selling other consumer products. This despite a key passage from the *Fortune* article:

> *The aftermarket's size has been governed, essentially, by these figures ($7 billion). But its special character has been determined by the American motorist, who has come to regard his automobile as something essential to his mobility, like, say, his left leg.*
>
> *On the comparatively rare occasions when his car fails him altogether, he sets up an anguished rumpus. Whether this betrayal occurs in metropolitan Chicago, in the outskirts of Flat River, Missouri, or in the Nevada badlands, he demands fast, efficient service.*
>
> *Whether he needs a new fuel pump for a 1960 Chevrolet or an engine bearing for a 1953 Dodge, he looks for one to be almost instantly available. He is not interested in the brand name of the essen-*

tial part, the function of which he does not pretend or even want to understand. He almost never asks about its cost. All he insists, vehemently, is that somebody fix his automobile, right now.

Clearly, the auto parts aftermarket was proving to be a unique one. The vast majority of vehicle repairs are performed by professional auto service technicians. Almost always, it is the technician—and not the automobile owner—who decides which parts to use. So, expensive mass media advertising of "X" brand auto parts directed to the car owner represented a questionable marketing expense. This has proved true up to the present day. As advanced technology increases with each model year, fewer and fewer car owners attempt their own repairs. But universally, they continue to demand that repair work be speedy.

Import Vehicles

Imported vehicles began making their entry into the United States marketplace during the 1960s. Prior to that, except for a limited number of isolated European cars with high price tags, very few imports had found their way to American shores. Then Volkswagen changed everything with its funny-looking little bug-like vehicle with a four-cylinder, air-cooled engine. Its price tag in 1961 was $1,450, and it could run on an unheard-of 40 miles on a single gallon of gasoline. Backed by an ingenious and highly effective advertising campaign, Volkswagen's "Bug" quickly took America by storm.

At first, the new German competitor was scorned by GM, Ford, and Chrysler, but Volkswagen's tsunami-like sales quickly got their attention.

General Parts Incorporated

The 1960s also marked the beginning of both General Parts Inc. and another aftermarket supplier, American Parts Company. Both of these

companies were started in the early '60s with visions of complete aftermarket marketing programs selling only through affiliated auto parts stores—General Parts eventually under the CARQUEST banner and American Parts under the Big A flag.

While NAPA and Big A were marketing names with jobbing store identification packages, it wasn't until 1965 that NAPA announced its first product with its own NAPA brand name. American Parts followed with its own Big A brands. General Parts' CARQUEST program originated in 1973, also with a marketing plan to offer products under the CAR-QUEST brand name. Most of the other aftermarket program groups continued representing individual manufacturers' brands.

U.S. Vehicle Registration	
1980	155,889,692
1990	188,655,462

The '70s

With three consecutive decades of vehicle growth—of 50 percent, 47 percent, and 44 percent—the automotive industry was flexing its muscles as the 1970s began.

American car manufacturers were preoccupied with the problem of Japanese automakers gaining market share in the United States. The Japanese presence had begun in the mid-'60s, and by 1970, approximately 10 percent of new cars registered that year were manufactured outside the country. Most of those were imported from Japan. By 1984, that number had increased to 26 percent, and the major Japanese vehicle companies had established manufacturing plants within the United States.

The Energy Crisis

During this era, the single event that had the greatest impact on the automotive aftermarket was the great energy crisis of 1974. Whether the fuel shortage was real or contrived, the long lines at service stations will long be remembered. The problem was so dramatic that it quickly got the attention of lawmakers in Washington.

For several years, imported automobiles had been traveling American highways in increasing numbers. Due to higher gasoline prices in Europe and Japan, these vehicles were engineered to get more miles per gallon than American cars. This was just one of the popular features of the imports that attracted American car buyers.

Also, by 1974, there was a growing concern among Americans that automobile exhaust emissions were polluting the air. Legislation calling for cleaner exhaust systems was already under consideration when the fuel crisis struck. Lawmakers began to work overtime to establish much stricter standards for cleaner emissions and fuel efficiency, to take effect with the 1980 models.

Improved Vehicles, More Parts

Automobile engineers were challenged to design a completely new automotive vehicle—one that was fuel-efficient and that offered clean emissions to meet government standards. Such vehicles required onboard computers needed to control fuel/air ratios for fuel efficiency and also to regulate emissions.

For parts distributors, the set of events triggered by the 1974 energy crisis created severe inventory problems. Already facing sharply increasing inventories due to the ever-growing import population, parts distributors now faced investments in additional inventory to service a completely new generation of domestic vehicles.

Some of the more expensive replacement parts for the new fuel-efficient, emissions-free vehicles of the '80s and '90s were front-wheel-drive axles, fuel injection parts, antilock brake parts, strut suspensions,

catalytic converters, rack-and-pinion steering, and a wide array of electronic emission and ignition parts.

The challenges facing distributors didn't stop with inventory concerns. Their primary customer base, professional auto technicians, were faced with learning new electronic and computer skills to match their mechanical skills. New forms of training were suddenly needed at the independent service repair centers. This training would continue throughout the balance of the century, because with each model year, more and more automotive systems would be controlled by electronics.

U.S. Vehicle Registration	
1999	216,370,359

Big Three Lose Market Share

Many significant events occurred during the last quarter of the 20th century. The vehicles registered at the end of 1999 equaled the number of U.S. citizens eligible for driver's licenses. Starting in the late 1970s, the "Big Three" U.S. vehicle manufacturers—Ford, General Motors, and Chrysler—began losing market share for automotive vehicle sales. The trend was created by two primary developments. First, the fuel crisis of the mid-1970s resulted in higher gasoline prices and this resulted in an increase in import sales. Import vehicles were already more fuel-efficient in response to higher fuel prices for almost every European and Asian country.

The second development was an improvement in the overall quality and design of vehicles manufactured by Asian companies.

The combination of these events created a notably favorable shift in attitudes of American consumers toward import cars and trucks.

The decline in overall market share by the Big Three might have been even more severe had they not introduced two new types of vehicles: minivans and sport utility vehicles (SUVs). These two vehicle types were well-received by a huge number of American vehicle buyers who replaced passenger cars with minivans and made SUVs their primary family vehicles.

Because of their popularity, the Big Three's attention to these new vehicle types created an opportunity for import manufacturers to make gains in passenger car sales in the United States.

An illusion was created that made the problem look worse when minivans and SUVs were classified and reported as "light truck" sales rather than "passenger car" sales; "light truck" vehicles were not required to meet the same strict Corporate Average Fuel Economy (CAFE) standards required by law. This classification, while beneficial to the Big Three, created an opportunity for import manufacturers to make further gains in passenger car sales in the United States.

If one looked only at "passenger car" share, the Big Three dropped from a 72.9 percent share in 1985 to a 48.4 percent share in 2002. The combined cars and light trucks share dropped from 75.9 percent in 1985 to 62.9 percent in 2002.

Of course, the Big Three understood that maintaining their share of the U.S. and worldwide markets was no longer realistic. A new global economy was emerging, spurred by the lifting of trade barriers and free trade initiatives such as NAFTA. New players were lining up to demand their own piece of the pie.

The pie, however, was growing larger. Even with a loss of market share as a percentage of the total, the Big Three continued to set new sales records in terms of total unit sales. This increase in new worldwide vehicle sales resulted in part by demands from consumers in developing countries who were able to purchase their own vehicles for the first time.

CARQUEST is Born

The new fuel-efficient and electronically controlled cars of the 1980s and 1990s dramatically

escalated consumers' costs, resulting in a large segment of middle-income families moving out of the new-car market. The average life of a car approached an all-time high of 10 years at the end of the 20th century, a trend that greatly favored the automotive aftermarket.

To take advantage of these developments, the CARQUEST marketing program began in 1973 by General Parts Inc., with Temple Sloan Jr. and Ed Whitehurst providing the marketing blueprint. Bobro Inc. of New York and Indiana Parts Warehouse of Indianapolis joined the program that December. In the next few years, many independent distribution companies joined the CARQUEST team.

Genuine Parts Company, of Atlanta, also was on the move at this time. By 2000, after acquiring other NAPA distribution companies, Genuine owned all NAPA companies except two. In 2003, that number was reduced to one.

American Parts Inc. (APS), with its Big A marketing program, also grew rapidly from its beginning in 1961 by acquiring some excellent independent distribution companies. For more than three decades, APS had long been a major factor in the auto parts aftermarket. But after being sold several times, it declared bankruptcy in the late 1990s.

Facing increased competition, most of the remaining independent distributors aligned with various marketing groups. In the 1990s, some of the marketing groups merged to create larger, more recognizable entities for buying purposes.

The Automotive Aftermarket Becomes Increasingly Complex and Challenging

Vehicles manufactured for about 10 years after World War II made only slight changes in body design and even fewer changes in component replacement parts. This was a blessing for the parts distributors as the number of stock keeping units (SKUs) increased very little during the late 1940s and the early 1950s.

But by the mid-1950s, with a great increase in the number of women drivers, auto manufacturers were challenged to make the driving experience easier, more enjoyable, and more comfortable. As a result, automatic transmissions, power steering, power brakes, and air conditioning—originally optional items—soon became standard equipment on most all passenger cars. Of course, each new advance came with additional parts that needed to be stocked.

Engine and brake efficiency were also improved, with alternators replacing generators and disc brake pads replacing brake shoes. Spin-on oil filters and the paper air filter extended the life of engines with improved filtration. All of these options increased sales opportunities for parts distributors but also greatly increased inventory investments.

The Advent of Retail Auto Parts Stores

Pure retail auto parts stores surfaced in the 1970s and 1980s, focusing on car owners who repaired their own cars. Their retail skills were normally more refined than the traditional auto parts jobber, and their store hours were similar to those of retailers of consumer products.

Set up in modern buildings located in high-traffic areas, these retail stores quickly took a great deal of business away from the large mass merchandisers. Growing rapidly, some of the chains began to merge in the 1990s. Among the most dominant before mergers were AutoZone, Advance, Western Auto, Checker-Shucks-Kragen (CSK), Pep Boys, O'Reilly's, Discount Auto Parts, Hi-Lo, and Chief.

The new generation of late '80s and '90s domestic vehicles with electronically controlled systems reduced the number of motorists willing or able to do their own repairs. This negative trend for the auto parts retailers caused them to shift their focus somewhat from the "do-it-yourself" customer to the professional auto service technician. This led to

more competition for the traditional auto parts distributor and jobber.

Vehicle Registration 2004	
U.S.	239,308,503
Canada	18,665,119

The Global Effect

With the advent of the global economy, availability of lower-priced auto parts became plentiful due to dramatic differences in off-shore labor costs when compared to U.S. labor costs. Also through worldwide sourcing, any level of quality became immediately available. These factors have made it easy for everyone in the aftermarket, including retailers, to set up second lines and lower pricing.

Additionally, the global economy has forced many U.S. manufacturing companies to move or establish off-shore manufacturing sites. Consequently, the variety of quality levels in auto parts is greater than ever. This has given do-it-yourselfers a wide choice of quality in the parts they install, and a wider range of high-quality options available for professional technicians.

Another trend took place in the past two decades that affected the aftermarket. There were approximately 200,000 gasoline service stations in the late 1970s, and most of these stations were performing auto service work. Starting in the 1970s and extending through the 1990s, oil companies began to find it more profitable to convert gasoline stations to convenience stores and to require motorists to fill their own gas tanks. Independent auto service shops opened at about the same rate that gasoline service stations closed. At the turn of the century, independent auto service shops were still in the No. 1 position for share of aftermarket auto service.

Additionally, muffler and brake specialty shops have experienced rapid growth during this era as have drive-in, quick oil change businesses primarily owned by oil companies. Environmental laws pertaining to the disposal of used motor oil helped to make the rapid oil change companies successful.

The size of the aftermarket attracted a large number of investors and entrepreneurs with a variety of plans for getting their own share of the market. For example, one company with profits made in petroleum from the Far East purchased several U.S. distribution companies but was unable to make them a success and eventually backed away from the automotive aftermarket.

Another investment group applied the "Wal-Mart" approach in California. With a membership card to their club, a consumer could buy auto parts, supplies, tires, and accessories at greatly reduced prices. This concept also failed. These ventures continued throughout the last quarter of the 20th century, but with each new failure, there seemed to be two new hopefuls waiting in the wings to try out their own schemes.

The car manufacturers, while temporarily sidetracked by redesigning their vehicles to meet the new government standards for fuel efficiency and emissions control, revised plans to increase their share of replacement parts in the automotive aftermarket. In some cases, their efforts in this regard came under investigation. For example, some vehicle manufacturers have attempted to withhold diagnostic and repair information from vehicle owners and independent aftermarket repair shops. Indeed, as this book goes to press, this effort is still continuing. It is being challenged by proposed legislation, which, if passed, would make this practice illegal.

As the year 2000 approached, General Motors spun off its parts manufacturing companies under a separate public company called Delphi. General Motors remained a major stockholder and the No. 1 customer of Delphi, both as an auto manufacturer and as an aftermarket parts customer through AC-Delco and its Service Parts Organization, which sup-

plied parts to GM car dealerships. Delphi's original marketing plan included the development of a line of auto parts for car makers. These would be marketed under the Delphi brand name and would be sold in the global aftermarket. On October 8, 2005, Delphi Corporation and its 38 U.S. subsidiaries filed for Chapter 11 bankruptcy protection.

Ford Motor Company likewise spunoff its manufacturing companies into a separate public company called Visteon. This firm also is on a mission to compete in the independent aftermarket. While Visteon faced many of the same problems as Delphi in terms of competing in the global economy, it was able to avoid filing for Chapter 11 bankruptcy protection with help from Ford. A number of non-performing Visteon companies were placed in an LLC (limited liability corporation) holding company and managed by Ford Motor Company. This allowed a

TOP AUTOMOTIVE AFTERMARKET MANUFACTURERS

OTHER THAN DELPHI AND VISTEON, THE largest automotive aftermarket manufacturers at the end of the century included:

- Dana Corporation, having acquired Spicer, Perfect Circle, Victor, Wix, Weatherhead, Clevite, and Echlin. This latter firm had previously acquired Borg Warner, Raybestos, Beck Arnley, and Aimco from ITT. In 2004, Dana sold Wix, Raybestos, and Beck Arnley to Cypress, an investment company. That company was named Affinia.
- Standard Motor Products, having acquired Four Seasons, EIS Brakes (which it later traded to Cooper Automotive in exchange for Murray/Everco). Guaranteed Parts, Sorenson, Champ Service Line (later sold to Motormite which had acquired Dorman), Philco, Federal Parts, and Hayden. In 2003, Standard acquired Echlin and Borg Warner, the engine controls division of Dana Corporation.
- Federal Mogul Corporation, having acquired Carter, TRW's aftermarket division; Sealed Power; Dietz; Signal-Stat; Turner Newell; Fel-Pro; and Cooper Industries Auto-

motive Division. Cooper had previously acquired Moog, Wagner Brakes and Lighting, Abex, Ferodo, Lee, Gibson, Rolero Omega, Belden, Champion Spark Plug, Anco, and Precision U-Joint.
- Tenneco acquired Monroe Ride Control and Walker Exhaust.
- Gates Rubber Company, one of the nation's largest privately held companies, was acquired by Tomkins and began an aggressive acquisition plan, which included Stant, Trico, Tridon, Edelmann, and Bridge.
- Arvin Industries, which had acquired Maremont, Gabriel, Strong Arm, and Purolator prior to being acquired by Meritor (formerly Rockwell) in 1999. The surviving company is identified as Arvin-Meritor. Late in 2004, Arvin-Meritor announced its intention to sell the aftermarket manufacturing operations of filters, exhaust, and ride control products. This was done in early 2006.
- UIS Inc. acquired Airtex, Wells Manufacturing, Neapco, Pioneer, and Champion Laboratories. In 2003, UIS was acquired by The Carlyle Group, which sold NEAPCO and Pioneer in 2006.

downsized Visteon to reorganize and concentrate on its core business.

GM's AC-Delco division accelerated its plan to round out its coverage on all makes and models and to select approximately 100 exclusive AC-Delco independent distributors who will agree to inventory and distribute all AC-Delco brand product lines.

Extended Warranties

Another event of this era involved new-car warranties, which started in 1979 with an extended warranty policy being offered as an optional purchase by the car buyer. Later, car manufacturers offered extended warranties with the cost built into the price of the car. Almost immediately, new-car dealers became consumed with warranty repairs. Extended warranties quickly became an enormous expense for the car manufacturer. This led to car manufacturers insisting on better quality in O.E. (original equipment) parts that would perform throughout the extended warranty period.

Needless to say, extended warranties and longer-lasting O.E. parts had an adverse effect on the independent aftermarket sale of replacement parts.

New-car leasing became popular in the 1990s. This idea by the car manufacturers was just another ploy to gain a share of the parts aftermarket. But by the end of year 2000, the trend of leasing private vehicles had waned.

The "Supercar"

In the mid-1990s, the U.S. Council for Automotive Research (USCAR) was organized to coordinate joint automotive industry/government projects. One of the projects is the development of a "supercar" for the 21st century. Goals for the supercar include tripling the current corporate average fuel economy (CAFE) rating to more than 82 miles a gallon, while producing low emissions.

The most obvious trend of all during this era was the move toward business consolidation among both parts distributors and parts manufacturers. Public companies especially were faced with pressures to keep their stock prices attractive to the investment community. Mergers and acquisitions were ways to show revenue growth, and efficiencies in consolidating synergies proved to be a great way to improve profits.

Consolidations

Like the top manufacturing companies supplying the automotive aftermarket, the automakers also consolidated their operations. In 1987, Chrysler acquired American Motors. In May 1998 came a surprise announcement of the merger of Chrysler Corporation and Daimler-Benz AG of Stuttgart, Germany, maker of Mercedes-Benz cars and trucks. Ford got into the merger mode in 1990 with the acquisition of Jaguar and again in 1999 with the acquisition of AB Volvo car operations and the purchase of the Land Rover Sports Utility vehicle operations from BMW.

Also in the late 1990s, Ford acquired a chain of 1,600 auto repair centers in Europe and a large recycler of used auto parts in Florida. In 2002, however, both of these companies were sold.

Among parts distributors, one of the most aggressive firms for acquisitions and mergers was a private company, General Parts Inc. (GPI). This book relates GPI's highly successful operations and strong growth since it was founded in 1961. It also preserves the history of the companies that merged into or were acquired by GPI. And it is designed to reflect the development of the singular GPI culture.

—Authored by Joe Owen,
Vice Chairman, General Parts Inc.

NATIONAL ADVISORY COUNCIL
DENVER, COLORADO — AUGUST, 1968

Serving on manufacturers' advisory councils fed Temple Sloan's passion to learn—a passion that has been reflected throughout his career in the automotive aftermarket. These photos show Sloan (circled) at distributor council meetings—the Gates National Advisory Council, Denver, in 1968 (top photo); and the McQuay-Norris Distributor Sales Council, St. Louis, in 1966 (bottom photo). In both photos, Sloan clearly is the youngest person in the room. He always made it his business to associate with older and more seasoned businesspeople in order to benefit from their expertise. Executives shown in the Gates photo at top are, standing, left to right: Loyd Bixler, Bob Higgins, John Duke, Jack Williams, Dick Hedgpeth, Roy Miller, Moore McKinley Sr., Temple Sloan Jr., Craig Stevenson, and Dick Phillips. Seated, left to right: Bob McAllister, Jack Ketchum, Barney Lyons, Dick Martin, Denham Taylor, and Wayne Bull. Shown in the McQuay-Norris photo at bottom are, left to right: Bob Sirotek, Nolan Wright, Frank Enterline, Bob Jacobson, Cope Hughes, Bill Myers, Lorrie Lee, Arlie Hibits, Temple Sloan Jr., Gene Vining, Joe Wilkinson, and Bob Sass.

CHAPTER ONE

THE START

1958–1969

Hell, Calton, sell him the land for $12,000. I just want to see the boy get started.

—A. E. Finley, renowned Raleigh entrepreneur,
during negotiations with Temple Sloan Jr. concerning
the purchase of a parcel of land for the site of General Parts
Incorporated's first newly constructed warehouse.

TEMPLE SLOAN JR. AND HIS younger brother, Hamilton, were raised in a family in which business was often discussed, entrepreneurship practiced, excellence encouraged, and principles and integrity taught by example from both parents. Before entering college, it was their objective to enter into—and succeed in—the world of business.

O. T. Sloan Sr.

The two boys came from strong stock. Their father, O. T. Sloan Sr., spent a 50-year career with Macks Stores Inc., overseeing and operating 94 highly successful 5-, 10-, and 25-cent stores, with the company listed on the American Stock Exchange. He retired as president and CEO in 1976.

He joined the company as an employee at its first store in Sanford, North Carolina. He later moved to Dillon, South Carolina, to open Macks' second store. It was there that he met his wife-to-be, Thelma Hamilton. Shortly after Sloan Sr.'s move to South Carolina, the two principal stockholders retired. O. T. Sloan Sr. then moved back to Sanford to start building the Macks' chain of stores.

Along the way, he joined Charles M. Reeves as a one-third investor in Reeves' start-up company focused on consumer finance. This company became Provident Finance Company, and in later years, was merged into a South Carolina bank, which later merged with Wachovia Bank & Trust Company.

Having grown up on a farm during the Depression, Sloan's hobby was buying and selling tobacco farms and timberland. The life story of his father had a tremendous emotional impact on young Sloan. His father was always Sloan Jr.'s most trusted adviser and severe critic, but he had the unique faith and courage to allow his son to learn by making mistakes.

Charlie Reeves also had a strong early impact on Sloan Jr.'s business career, by giving him his first real job during the summers of 1958 and 1959. This occurred while Sloan was attending Duke University from 1957 to 1961. Following Sloan Jr.'s marriage to Carol Carson in April 1958, O.T. Sloan Sr. advised his son that, if he was old enough to get married, he was old enough to support himself. He would only provide the funds necessary to complete his son's education but would not cover his and Carol's living expenses.

A lesson that Sloan Jr. never forgot was given to him by his father at this time. Sloan Sr. said to his son, "You are leaving home with a good name,

According to Temple Sloan Jr., shown on a short warehouse break, "You must enjoy what you do."

Left: Carol Sloan, Temple Sloan Jr.'s wife. Sloan met Carol Carson, his wife-to-be, while both were students at Duke University. By the time he graduated in 1961, they had two children.

Below: A. C. Burkhead Jr. was the manager of the original General Parts Warehouse Company, which eventually became a part of General Parts Inc. Burkhead became a key employee of GPI.

with good credit, and a good education. Only you can either build on them or mess them up." Sloan Jr. took this advice to heart.

Opening a Loan Business

In 1959, Reeves encouraged Sloan Sr. to open a small loan office in Elizabeth City, North Carolina, so he could go into business with his son. He did. Thereafter, two days a week, Sloan Jr. would leave Duke after classes, drive four hours to the Elizabeth City office, make loans, collect payments, and supervise a staff of four employees. He would then drive back to Duke for his classes the next day.

Right from the start, the loan business begun by Sloan Sr. and his son thrived. After several months of operation, it got a further boost when Sloan Sr. swapped some of his First Provident stock for five different loan offices in North Carolina. These were located in Wilson, Kinston, Greenville, Goldsboro, and Dunn.

The Sloans merged the two separate loan companies, forming a new entity known as the Southern Credit Company. This company provided Sloan Jr. with additional valuable experience in managing people and raising money.

The new company's early credit relationships were with Commercial Credit Company and Branch Banking and Trust Company, both located in Wilson, North Carolina; and with the Chatham Bank in Siler City, North Carolina, which later became part of First Union and Wachovia Bank in Raleigh. Southern Credit's loan operations proved highly successful, ultimately providing the capital for General Parts Inc.

General Parts Warehouse

In the mid-1950s, an entrepreneur by the name of Frank Baber made the decision to leave NAPA and open his own auto parts warehouse, which he named Genuine Parts Warehouse. The new company was operated by A. C. Burkhead Jr., purchasing agent at Brown's Auto Supply, an 11-store NAPA auto parts group also founded by Baber. In 1958, First Provident acquired Brown's.

Following a legal confrontation—along with an eventual monetary settlement—with Genuine Parts Company of Atlanta, a NAPA firm, involving the name "Genuine," Burkhead renamed the company General Parts Warehouse. Soon thereafter, Brown's Auto Supply and General Parts Warehouse were cited by the Federal Trade Commission for a rules infraction regarding "vertical integration." As a result, Brown's was ordered to immediately sell General Parts Warehouse.

In 1960, Reeves persuaded the Sloans to absorb General Parts Warehouse into their Southern Credit Company in order to resolve the issues with the Federal Trade Commission. However, serious conflicts between Brown's Auto Supply and General Parts Warehouse quickly arose from Brown's lack of profitability and a major overstocking situation at its various stores. This ultimately led to the withdrawal of Sloan Sr.'s investment in First Provident.

In 1961, when the Sloans refused to sell General Parts Warehouse, now known as General Parts Inc. (GPI) back to Brown's, the latter company opened its own auto parts warehouse in Sanford, calling it United Parts Warehouse. The Sloans severed their business relationship with Reeves due to these issues. It is ironic that at a later date, General Parts passed on the purchase of Brown's and of United Auto Parts Warehouse. The stores eventually were sold to various interests, some of which are CARQUEST stores today. United itself was liquidated.

Mac Graham

During the spring of 1960, Sloan Jr. and A. C. Burkhead

Left: The first home for General Parts' warehouse was located in this building on Rock Street in Sanford, North Carolina.

Bottom left: Mac Graham was one of GPI's first employees. He spent 42 years with the company, eventually retiring as corporate secretary.

agreed that it was time to add another person to assist with the day-to-day operations of the warehouse. Burkhead recommended hiring Mac Graham, a former employee of Brown's. Graham had worked in inventory with A. C. Burkhead for about two years, and at the time working as a furniture salesman for a company located next door to the Brown's Auto Parts Store.

Temple Sloan Jr. met with Graham in front of the Sprott Brothers Furniture Store and hired him on the spot. It was, to say the least, an informal meeting, with both men discussing the job while leaning casually against a parking meter.

Graham became an important addition to General Parts and spent 42 years with the company, working as operations manager, as the company's first technology manager, and as corporate secretary. Today, Graham continues to help General Parts on a semi-retired basis.

Move to Raleigh

By the summer of 1961, Sloan Jr. had graduated from Duke University. Following an unsuccessful attempt to merge with Southern Sales Company in Durham, it was decided to move the Sanford operation to Raleigh, North Carolina. Sloan was convinced the new company should be located in Raleigh to achieve success.

Around this time, the Sloans agreed they should consolidate their capital into one business, so they sold the six loan companies to Liberty Loan Company of St. Louis, Missouri, controlled by the August Busch family. Sloan Jr. turned down an offer from Liberty's president to move to St. Louis and become his administrative assistant. He was offered three times his salary—a very tempting offer for a man who by this time was the father of two children—but Sloan Jr. had big plans for General Parts, and he was sure he could make the business a success.

The move to Raleigh in 1961 kindled Sloan Jr.'s interest in real estate, something that remained with him throughout his business career. Following an unsuccessful attempt to locate a suitable property to lease, Sloan decided to build a new facility in Raleigh. He located a piece of property then owned by A. E. Finley, a renowned Raleigh entrepreneur. Finley was introduced to Sloan Jr. by W. C. Calton, a Finley partner. Calton eventually became a good friend of Sloan Jr.'s.

After learning of his needs, Finley asked Calton what the property was worth. Calton replied that the land was valued at $20,000. Finley said, "Hell, Calton, sell him the land for $12,000. I just want to see the boy get started." From that day forward, Sloan Jr. became not only a strong admirer of Finley but also began to carefully study him as the model of a successful—and generous—businessman.

Upon this plot of land, located on South Saunders Street in Raleigh, General Parts constructed a new 20,000-square-foot building in 1962.

A Well-Connected Individual

Harold Makepeace, a neighbor of Sloan Sr., played a key role in helping to get General Parts' first new warehouse built. He introduced Sloan Jr. to Seby Jones, a partner at Davidson and Jones, the Raleigh general contracting company that was eventually selected to handle construction. He also introduced Sloan Jr. to Ray Long, the president of Raleigh Federal Savings and Loan. Long gave Sloan Sr. a 100 percent loan for the warehouse project, which General Parts ended up leasing.

Seven years later, in 1968, the property was sold by Sloan Sr.—who had not invested a dime of his own money in the project—for more than $200,000. This large profit provided another valuable lesson to Sloan Jr. concerning the value of excellent credit.

Through his association with Seby Jones, Sloan Jr. met Roddy Jones, Seby's son, who was driving a truck for his father on construction projects. The young Jones and Sloan Jr. would later become partners in many real estate and other business ventures, including the founding of Highwoods Properties with Steve Stroud and the development of the

---

GPI's 20,000-square-foot warehouse in Raleigh, North Carolina. This facility, located on South Saunders Street, opened in 1962.

Southern Equipment Company—later doing business as the Ready Mixed Concrete Company—with George Turner.

The '60s

In January 1961, Sloan Jr.'s fledgling company was ready to move into its new Raleigh warehouse. Sloan could not imagine how it would ever utilize all of the building's space. At the time, the company distributed only about 13 product lines. Among these were Fitzgerald gaskets, Merit exhausts, McQuay-Norris chassis and engine parts, Purolator filters, Gates fan belts and radiator hoses, Wells ignitions, Wagner brake shoes, and EIS brake hydraulics. Hastings, a North Carolina auto parts company, provided a strong line of remanufactured products for General Parts. Sloan often remarked that had it not been for Harry Hastings, the founder of Hastings Inc., General Parts may not have survived the early years.

The Company Begins to Expand

Bill Norris was the first person hired for the new Raleigh warehouse. He arrived from an employment office on a Tuesday and was hired immediately.

Recognizing the importance of sales to a start-up company, Sloan immediately started a search for experienced salesmen. First hired was Shorty Britt, a 5-ft-1-in dynamo with a strong sales background and an enthusiasm for asking for the order. A year later, Willie Rushing from Florence, South Carolina, was added to the GPI sales team. Rushing had spent several years as an outside

salesman for a tough General Parts competitor in Charlotte, North Carolina.

To round out the sales force, Robbie Harrison was hired. Harrison gained his sales experience as an outside salesman for Spartan Automotive in Spartanburg, South Carolina. (This company was merged into GPI in March 2003.)

With vast experience and broad contacts, these three GPI warehouse salesmen were arguably the finest automotive parts sales team in North Carolina. Together, they were largely the key to General Parts' impressive early sales growth. All three spent the remainder of their careers with GPI, "asking for the order," up to and including the days upon which they individually retired.

In October 1962, Mary Pope, a part-time service station bookkeeper, was recruited to be General Parts' bookkeeper, although her first day unexpectedly involved unloading an entire truck of tail pipes. She quickly found that working at General Parts would challenge her powers of concentration. "I was constantly being interrupted by Temple Jr., who was always bumming cigarettes, Cokes, and coffee," she said. Pope retired as a full-time associate in 1992 but still works one day a week just to be sure, according to Sloan, that someone at General Parts is paying attention to the details.

"Can I Borrow Some Money to Take You to Lunch?"

Pope's experience with Sloan was not atypical. Indeed, according to company lore, Sloan was always in need of some little thing, often small amounts of money. One well-circulated story recalls a time when

Sloan, who was in Goldsboro, North Carolina, calling on customers, had to pawn his watch so he could buy enough gasoline to drive home. Many other times, he would borrow money from his customers so he could buy them lunch.

But Sloan and General Parts must have been doing something right, because, from its earliest days, the business was growing. This was no surprise to Arthur F. Page, a manufacturer's sales agent and close friend of Sloan's. Page noted:

What could General Parts do that others were not doing, or paying much attention to? The customer always came first. If a special order was received, it was shipped—and shipped quickly. And General Parts was the only warehouse that I knew of—or still do—which double-checked the zeroes on any order before the order was shipped.

Mac Graham and Bill Norris, who was the warehouse manager for many years, were wonders at finding items that had been zeroed but nevertheless were in stock somewhere. Later, General Parts paid a weekly bonus to the parts picker who had the fewest mistakes. I don't know of any other warehouse that did things like General Parts did for their customers.

Page credits General Parts employees' strong orientation to customer service to the good example set by Sloan. He said:

Far left: The first Raleigh warehouse worker was Bill Norris. He was immediately hired when he interviewed with GPI and began work the same day.

Left: Willie Rushing joined GPI's sales team along with Shorty Britt and Robbie Harrison. These three sales professionals played a large part in GPI's early success.

Right: Shorty Britt (standing) and Robbie Harrison.

It always seemed that Temple could draw [very] good people to him. This is not surprising. You did not have to know him very long to know that he was a straight arrow. If he told you something, he would do exactly that. If you wanted to work for him or do business with him, you had to be the same way.

Plus, he was always a highly focused worker. Let me provide an example. One day, not too long after the warehouse moved to South Saunders Street in Raleigh, Mr. Sloan Sr. stopped by to see Temple. He was on his way back from a New York buying trip, and he was immaculately dressed, as always.

Mr. Sloan Sr. and I were standing in the office by the door going into the warehouse, when Temple Jr. came by, almost at a run, working hard, as usual. He spoke to his dad but did not stop to talk. One shirtsleeve was undone and turned up, and the

Above: Shown, left to right, are Mary Pope, General Parts' first bookkeeper, with Alida Baker and Harriet Camak, GPI secretaries.

Left: Manufacturer's agent Arthur Page was impressed with the special attention GPI paid to getting its orders perfect. At GPI, "the customer always came first," said Page.

other was unbuttoned and flopping. He had on a pair of tweed pants that looked as if they belonged to a suit. The pants legs were round as stovepipes and kind of sprung at the knees.

Mr. Sloan Sr. looked at him, and after Temple had gone into the warehouse, he turned to me, and said, "Arthur, I could take him to Nowells Clothing Store and buy him the best outfit they have, but in three days he would look just like he does now."

New Products

In 1964, with help from Tom Perry of Atlanta, GPI joined the Automotive Warehouse Distributors Association (AWDA). While attending the AWDA annual meeting in Kansas City, Sloan made several important contacts with manufacturers that would become important to GPI's growth in future years, including Ed Gammie, vice president of Victor Manufacturing & Gasket.

Returning to Raleigh and still weighing the pros and cons of offering the Victor gasket line, Sloan was approached by Clyde Hill, Victor's regional representative, a resident of Beaufort, North Carolina. "Do you pay your bills, and do you have any customers?" was the first question Hill asked. Sloan was impressed by Hill's direct, take-no-prisoners approach. Shortly thereafter, Sloan changed GPI's gasket line to Victor, a move that greatly enhanced the company's sales growth for many years. Also among the key product lines added in this era was Ramco Piston Rings. Charlie Watkins of Ramco was instrumental in this addition.

At a subsequent AWDA meeting, Sloan Jr. met Jim McGovern, vice president of Raybestos Brakes. This proved to be the beginning of a long, successful relationship. The change to Raybestos Brakes was made after McGovern came to Raleigh to call on his largest Raleigh-based customer, S.M. "Bee" White at Motor Bearings and Parts. He received White's approval for General Parts to become a Raybestos distributor.

One major step in adding key product lines was a change to Guaranteed Ignition. The North Carolina factory representative for Guaranteed was Ed Whitehurst, a native of New York and a former representative for Willard Batteries. He was responsible for selling Sloan on the change to Guaranteed.

Not all manufacturers, however, were willing to add GPI to their customer list. For example, AC-Delco refused to sell to General Parts unless it bought all of their product lines. When Sloan refused to do so, the AC-Delco general manager warned him at an AWDA meeting in Kansas City that GPI would be unable to survive without AC-Delco parts.

Among other manufacturers that refused to sell their products to General Parts in the early years were Champion Spark Plug Company, Timken Bearings, Hastings Filters, Casite Chemicals, Walker Exhaust, and Trico windshield wiper products.

Strong Sales and Earnings

With its powerful work ethic, its emphasis on customer service, and a range of new product lines, sales rose quickly for GPI. By the end of 1963, sales were $801,000, an increase of 23 percent over the previous year. Earnings increased 186 percent from the previous year. A year later, sales rose to $1.03 million, an increase of 28.6 percent, while earnings increased 100.1 percent.

Adding a Sales Manager

With A.C. Burkhead handling the buying, Mary Pope handling the paperwork, and Mac Graham and Bill Norris looking after the internal operations, Sloan spent his time—indeed, a great deal of it—calling on customers, looking for new customers, monitoring expenses against income, and working constantly to improve the product offering.

Shortly after making the switch to Guaranteed Ignition, Whitehurst and Sloan Jr. visited a key customer prospect to make a presentation. After the presentation, Whitehurst rode to dinner with the prospect's father, while Sloan Jr. rode with the prospect. Despite all this, the sale was not finalized. A few days later, during a conversation between Ed and Temple concerning the unsuccessful meeting, Whitehurst suggested that perhaps Temple was just too young to sell to some of the older, more established accounts. "Maybe you need a sales manager with a bit more age and some gray in his hair," he advised. Sloan immediately offered Whitehurst the job of sales manager for GPI, effective January 1, 1966. This proved to be the beginning of a highly profitable 16-year partnership.

Let's Take a Trip!

As competition grew more intense, General Parts began employing travel incentives for customers, which was becoming a general practice in the industry. Trip destinations included Grand Bahamas, Acapulco, Bermuda, and Paradise Island.

On the first trip to Bermuda, Shorty Britt, who was on the chartered plane along with the GPI customers, whispered to the flight attendant shortly after take-off that the engine on his side of the plane didn't seem to be working. Sure enough, it wasn't. The plane immediately returned to Charlotte, and another chartered plane was assigned to quickly ferry the GPI crowd to Bermuda.

The brief delay didn't create any concerns amongst the customers, but there was apprehension when Ed Whitehurst noticed that the pilot boarded the plane with an ESSO road map in his hip pocket. Fortunately, everyone aboard arrived safely in Bermuda slightly after midnight. This particular trip will be remembered not only as entertainment for GPI's customers but also as a honeymoon for Ed and Sarah Whitehurst. "It was just another one of Ed's great jobs of planning," commented Sloan.

Sharing the Wealth

In 1968, GPI's board of directors approved a profit-sharing plan for employees, the forerunner of today's GPI Employee Stock Ownership Plan (ESOP). It was the hope of management that the plan would

Guaranteed Ignition's Ed Whitehurst told Temple Sloan Jr. he was far too young to effectively manage GPI's sales efforts. Sloan immediately offered Whitehurst the job of GPI sales manager, which he accepted. Whitehurst spent 16 years with GPI.

TEMPLE SLOAN JR.

IN THE INTERVIEW THAT FOLLOWS, JOE Owen, vice chairman of General Parts Inc., describes the personality and management style of O. Temple Sloan Jr., founder, chairman, and CEO of General Parts (GPI) through 2004. The interview was conducted by Jeffrey Rodengen, founder and CEO of Write Stuff Enterprises, Inc., publisher of the *Legend of General Parts Inc.*

Rodengen: Joe, I think you would agree that the *Legend of General Parts* would not be complete without a close-up look at the founder, Temple Sloan Jr. I know that you have been in an excellent position in recent years to discuss Temple's management style.

Owen: Well, first, let me mention that Temple is somewhat uncomfortable being in the limelight. So you better keep this feature well-hidden in your desk drawer in Fort Lauderdale until right before the book is ready to go to press, or else it is likely to be deleted. Temple is a genuinely modest individual.

Rodengen: Do you believe that modesty is an important characteristic for a CEO?

Owen: It certainly is, especially when it's natural, sincere, and real. There's nothing counterfeit about Temple Sloan Jr.

Rodengen: But isn't that type of personality a bit unusual in a person who has achieved so much success? Many CEOs, I believe, have some problems with overblown egos.

Owen: Temple has always maintained complete control of his ego. I have worked closely with him for 23 years and have never seen him in any situation where his ego got in the way. Modesty is just a natural part of his personality.

Rodengen: Would you identify Temple's other leadership qualities?

Owen: They are numerous. One of the most visible is Temple's constant drive to improve, never allowing complacency to sneak in. He is quick to acknowledge good performance but also quick to remind everyone that things can always be done better. Also, Temple is a very courageous individual. A good example of this is when he started GPI. Seldom does a college student start his or her own business before they graduate from college, but Temple did. At the age of 21 and in his senior year at Duke University, Temple started GPI in his hometown of Sanford, North Carolina. He did so with a minimum of automotive parts knowledge—but with a maximum of moxie.

Rodengen: Yes, I can see that would be a very brave move.

Owen: That's for sure. While a student at Duke, Temple met and married Carol Carson. By the time Temple graduated in 1961, he and Carol had two children. So, starting up a brand-new and untested business, while at the same time being responsible for a family of four, represents, I believe, the epitome of courage.

Rodengen: Tell us more about his management style.

Owen: Temple is a strong leader. This begins with his unquestionable integrity. No matter what the occasion, he always seems to find the right way to do the right thing. He has never compromised his integrity, that of General Parts Inc., or of any of the firm's associates.

provide employees with additional security for their retirement, along with protection in the event of death or disability and that it would help increase operating efficiency.

With the seams bulging on the original 20,000-square-foot GPI warehouse, it was time to consider a larger building. A new location on Atlantic Avenue was acquired, and a new building with more than double the square footage of the previous distribution center was built.

Charlie Maurer, a specialist in material handling and warehouse layout, was hired by GPI for the construction. Maurer's organization has since engineered all of GPI's distribution centers. In December 1968,

Rodengen: Would you call Temple a workaholic?
Owen: I've never been around anyone who works harder than Temple. His work ethic, combined with his numerous other leadership qualities, sets a challenging example for every GPI associate.
Rodengen: What else is unique about Temple Sloan Jr.?
Owen: Temple possesses a remarkable hunger to always learn more about his business—and about life. In the early '60s, as he was struggling to establish his new company, he continually searched for new opportunities to associate with successful businessmen, individuals he could learn from. He was a member of several manufacturers' and distributors' advisory councils. Almost always, he was the youngest council member. He was always highly active in AWDA [Automotive Warehouse Distributors Association] so he could stay abreast of the latest developments in the business. Temple has always believed that he could learn something from everyone he met, and this attitude continues to the present day.
Rodengen: How does Temple get along with others?
Owen: His people skills are terrific. Plus, he sincerely cares for people. This is a primary reason why he created the company's employee stock ownership plan and set GPI up to offer stock to key supervisory associates. It also helps explain GPI's joint venture plan, which has been such a key to GPI's success.

Rodengen: What about Temple's business acumen?
Owen: I think Temple possesses the most clairvoyant financial mind of anyone I have ever known. This is why he has always been in such strong demand to serve on corporate boards. For example, he currently is chairman of the executive committee on Bank of America's board. He also serves on the Lowe's board and continues to serve as chairman of the board of Highwoods, a public real estate company he co-founded years ago.
Rodengen: Have you overlooked anything?
Owen: Besides GPI, Temple has been a principal owner in several other businesses. So he is always very busy. But he nevertheless unselfishly finds time to devote to civic activities, including the Boy Scout program.
Rodengen: Anything else about Temple you would like to mention?
Owen: I would only say that Temple has very little tolerance for procrastination. Plus, he is a super salesman in every respect.
Rodengen: Is Temple "all work and no play"?
Owen: Not at all. When Temple finds a little extra time, he likes to spend it fishing, hunting, and riding his horses at his ranch in Montana.

GPI Vice Chairman Joe Owen describes GPI founder and Chairman O. Temple Sloan Jr. as an executive of rare courage, special integrity, and expert business acumen.

the move to the new Atlantic Avenue location was completed, setting the stage for greatly improved efficiency and customer service in 1969 and beyond. A grand opening was held for the new warehouse facility in April 1969. The event was officiated by Raleigh Mayor Pro Tem William Law, O. Temple Sloan Jr., and Ed Whitehurst.

Program Distribution

With Whitehurst responsible for sales, Sloan Jr. could focus his energies on building a stronger product offering and on other management tasks. However, he always enjoyed customer contact and continued to stay in close touch with the market.

Raleigh Mayor Pro Tem William Law cuts a fan belt during the grand opening of General Parts' warehouse. With him are O. Temple Sloan Jr., left, and Ed Whitehurst, right.

Within the automotive aftermarket's three-step distribution scheme—manufacturer to wholesaler to parts store—General Parts played an absolutely vital role. Whitehurst and Sloan understood, however, that GPI's ultimate success depended on the success of the individual auto parts stores it routinely supplied. They determined that each of these stores had some pressing needs: assistance in financing, inventory management, daily delivery of orders, merchandising and advertising assistance, complete product offerings, help in accounting, and other miscellaneous needs.

For GPI to be able to afford to offer all of these important services, it was clear that it would need full and complete support from the stores—that is, a commitment from the store owners to purchase all of their major lines from General Parts. The industry terminology for this mutual support was "program distribution."

NAPA and Big A

Within the industry, the leaders in program distribution during this era were Genuine Parts Company's NAPA program and American Parts' Big A program. Sloan and Whitehurst carefully studied these two successful programs.

Thanks to Sloan's active AWDA involvement, he quickly developed friendships with many other independent auto parts distributors throughout the industry. He made it a point to listen to those from whom he could learn and to exchange ideas with anyone, even competitors. These valuable industry associations confirmed for Sloan Jr. and Whitehurst that program distribution offered GPI

the best opportunity to grow. Therefore, during the last two years of the 1960s, the two GPI executives began building up the company's own strong customer base by addressing individual stores' key needs—but always in exchange for total support.

In doing so, they worked diligently to transform the company into a full-fledged program distributor-type firm.

By the end of the 1960s, it was becoming clear to Sloan and Whitehurst that a larger company was a necessary attribute to achieve their goals and to gain the respect of the major manufacturers. This meant that GPI needed to either grow rapidly or join with other carefully selected independent distributors to build one unified program. As the decade of the 1970s approached, this idea became the forerunner and foundation of today's CARQUEST program.

Starting a business from the ground up takes courage, determination and hard work by everyone involved. GPI was no exception. In this regard, Temple Sloan Jr. would always be quick to give credit and special thanks to a number of parts store owners who believed in GPI and supported it with their business purchases in exchange for quality products and great service. They included these North Carolina companies: Bill Cotten who owned City Auto Parts in Sanford; Ed McIntyre, Ed's Supply in Biscoe; Tom and Francis Townsend, Townsend Auto Parts, Wallace; Pee Wee Beasley, Tractor and Auto Supply, Dunn; Felix Bell, Mt. Olive Auto Supply, Mt. Olive; Doug Waller, Bladen Auto Parts, Elizabethtown; Red Wall, Wall Auto Parts, Raleigh; J.R. Creech, Creech Auto Parts, Four Oaks; Paul Humphrey, Paul's Auto Parts, Richlands; Joe Dunn, Brown's Auto Supply, Siler City; Bill Dildy, Brown's Auto Supply, Asheboro; Fred Brown, Service Auto Supply, Mooresville; and Bill Blackburn, B&D Auto Parts, Elkin.

Special thanks should also be extended to certain key manufacturer executives and sales people who worked hard and believed in GPI's future. These

Right: A message for all salespeople.

Below: General Parts Inc. moved its Raleigh distribution center from the location on South Saunders Street to a much larger facility at 2319 Atlantic Avenue in December 1968.

"Every morning in Africa,
a gazelle wakes up knowing
it must run faster than the fastest lion
or it will be killed.

Every morning in Africa,
a lion wakes up knowing
it must outrun the slowest gazelle
or it will starve to death.

It doesn't matter whether you are a lion
or a gazelle; when the sun comes up,
you had better be running."

CARQUEST
AUTO PARTS

include Arthur Page of the N.A. Williams Company, a manufacturer's sales agency; Phil Costello of McQuay Norris; Harry Hastings of Hastings Rebuilders; Ed Gammie, Jesse Corbitt, and Clyde Hill of Victor Gaskets; Jim McGovern, Earl Stanford, and Leroy Handsel of Raybestos; Charlie Watkins of Ramco; Skip Stivers of AP Exhaust; and Jack Williams of Gates.

Among those in the parts distribution business who spent valuable time in coaching Temple Sloan Jr. during the '60s were Marty Larner, owner of Indiana Parts Warehouse, Indianapolis; and Tom Perry, owner of the Thomas S. Perry Company, Atlanta.

Strong Sales at End of Decade

The '60s came to a close for GPI with tremendous results. In 1969, sales exceeded $3 million. The number of GPI employees increased right along with the firm's booming sales. An enthusiastic team of 44 associates approached the new decade with pride in what they had accomplished and a determination to find even better ways to grow sales and improve customer service. GPI was clearly becoming a major force to be reckoned with in the North Carolina automotive aftermarket. Its game plan was working.

The individuals shown above all played key roles in the successful development of General Parts Inc. (GPI) during the early 1970s. Left row, top to bottom: Ed Whitehurst, Mary Pope, Willie Rushing, Bill Norris; middle row, top to bottom: Temple Sloan Jr., Mac Graham, R.D. Carson, Ken West, Bill Turbeville; right row, top to bottom: Ham Sloan, A.C. Burkhead, Robbie Harrison (on left) and Shorty Britt, Harry Evans.

CHAPTER TWO

EXPANSION, ACQUISITION, AUTOMATION
1970–1973

We have a unique company. It is a huge partnership that is built on trust and respect for each other. GPI is not a social club ... it is a big business in a very competitive industry. It is important to recognize that we control our own destiny. Our success will require teamwork, dedication, sacrifice, and hard work.

—Temple Sloan Jr., chairman and CEO,
General Parts Incorporated

THE 1970S WERE A difficult decade for business in general and a momentous one for the automotive and the aftermarket industries in particular. It was during these lean years that the nation first learned of the term "stagflation," that is, stagnant economic conditions accompanied by roaring inflation rates in the double digits.

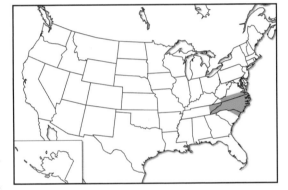

In addition to these severe economic difficulties, the nation was being roiled by dramatic international and national events. In 1973, the Yom Kippur War was launched in the Middle East; and America, a longtime ally of Israel, sent billions of dollars in wartime aid to the country. In retaliation, the oil-producing Arab nations of OPEC announced they would not sell oil to countries supporting Israel and promptly raised prices by 400 percent. The price of a barrel of oil immediately spiked—despite the fact there was no actual shortage—and the price hikes were quickly passed along to consumers.

Heading into 1974, American consumers were forced to deal with long lines at the gas pumps and supposed "spot-shortages" while unscrupulous gas companies gouged prices. The economic effect of this oil hysteria was devastating. The already weakened economy, in decline since 1971 under President Richard Nixon's wage and price controls, nosedived.

"With the oil crisis, if you couldn't get gas, you couldn't drive," commented Temple Sloan Jr. "So people didn't need repairs made to their cars. The only good thing about the oil crisis was that it didn't last too long. If it had lasted a long time, it would have been a disaster."

Nevertheless, the situation was bad enough. Americans were forced to squirm in front of their television sets during the early 1970s as the Watergate drama and subsequent hearings unfolded a story of intrigue and deceit at the highest levels of the American government. This was compounded by the deteriorating situation in Vietnam, a war that America had yet to admit it had lost even as it evacuated the American Embassy in Saigon, leaving behind crowds of desperate Vietnamese.

Americans were beset with worries about the war, energy problems, a floundering economy, high unemployment, and a crisis of confidence in their government. Nor did things improve significantly as the nation moved into the second half of the

This map shows the extent of GPI's sales and marketing reach during the early 1970s.

decade. Indeed, in 1977 and 1978, due to economic mismanagement and another spike in oil prices, the nation was again plunged into a fierce recession, the second in less than a decade.

GPI Stays Strong

In contrast to this national pall, General Parts, Inc., entered the decade of the 1970s with a flourish, establishing sales and earnings records each year. Its market penetration continued to improve at a rate exceeding that of the industry. Increased earnings reflected close control of costs resulting from rising interest rates. In 1974, sales passed the $1 million per month mark in April. GPI was definitely on a roll. In the four-year period, 1970 through 1973, GPI sales increased 228 percent and earnings increased 422 percent.

Indeed, as the company moved into the 1970s, its prospects looked highly promising, despite poor economic conditions that would confound so many other business sectors. This was due in large measure to the excellence of the management team and the company's highly experienced and hard-working employees. But GPI was also fortunate to be in the right business for these austere times.

Automobiles, of course, have long been central to the U.S. economy. Back in the '50s, General Motors' president, "Engine" Charlie Wilson, who was secretary of defense in the Eisenhower administration, famously remarked: "What's good for General Motors is good for America." With one out of six U.S. workers employed directly by the automobile industry or involved in some manner, even tangentially, many Americans had no reason to doubt the wisdom of Wilson's sentiment.

"Whip Inflation Now" buttons represented the federal government's efforts during the mid-1970s to control costs. Because of double-digit inflation, GPI switched over to the LIFO ("last-in, first-out") inventory accounting system in early 1975 to avoid higher taxes that otherwise would accrue due to the inflated value of the company's inventory.

The auto industry obviously wasn't limited to carmaking. Each car on the road depended on hundreds of separate parts. As a result, the replacement parts industry represented a whopping $17 billion in sales. Additionally, between 1970 and 1978, the number of cars on the road increased nearly 30 percent.

Part of this increase was because new cars were not necessarily replacing older models. With the economy sagging, car owners were holding onto their cars longer and thus repairing them more often. Further, the trend toward smaller cars resulted in additional auto repair business. Conventional wisdom held that as the size of automobiles and trucks downsized, the lighter, major components of the smaller vehicles would work harder to do the same job. Thus, the increased wear and tear would result in an accelerated repair cycle.

Many of the smaller autos were among a rising tide of foreign imports, primarily Japanese. The influx of new car makes and models with new lines of repair parts to be stocked and sold represented further growth opportunities for aftermarket suppliers.

"We were almost recession-proof because people needed their cars to get to work. Also, transportation was needed to get children to school, and businesses needed to transport their products," said Sloan.

A Switch to LIFO

During inflationary periods, such as the 1970s, many American companies switched their inventory valuation methods from what is termed FIFO (first-in, first-out, signifying that the first unit that made its way into inventory is the first unit sold) to LIFO (last-in, first-out, signifying that the last unit that makes its way into inventory is sold first). This was done to reduce the taxes levied on the increased value of newer inventories. Temple Sloan Jr. explains how and why GPI switched to LIFO.

In 1974, inflation was hovering around 18 to 19 percent. The value of our inventory had risen tremendously, which meant we would have to pay taxes on "paper profits."

We had heard about LIFO accounting but weren't certain of its value. One morning in Chicago, I met with Bob Holwell who was president of Gates Rubber Company. This is in February 1975, and we still hadn't filed our tax return for 1974. I asked Bob if he was familiar with LIFO. He said that Gates Rubber Company had switched to the LIFO system back in the 1930s and that there was no way they could have remained a privately held company if it hadn't been for LIFO because of all the price increases that had taken place over the years, and all those dollars, the millions of dollars on taxes they had been able to defer.

Bob made our decision easy, and we ultimately ended up with $7 or $8 million in LIFO reserves. If you look at the size of our company then, that was a great deal of money—approximately 30 to 40 percent of our typical yearly revenue. I always buy Bob a drink every time I see him.

Industry Challenges

While the industry enjoyed advantages compared to American business in general, numerous challenges confronted aftermarket parts suppliers during the '70s. One key factor was the fragmented nature of the business itself. The aftermarket parts industry was not easily conquerable, even by the automobile manufacturers who provided many of the parts. The market was highly diffuse with numerous outlets and thousands upon thousands of separate parts numbers. Increasingly, the parts-supply business was being carved up into ever smaller subsegments such as the under-the-hood segments, tires, batteries, DIY, and engine components. Stocking and inventory control presented major challenges.

Competition for the most profitable market segments intensified when mass merchandisers such as Sears and Kmart began moving into the aftermarket business in a major way, capturing sales with discounts that standard parts suppliers often found impossible to match. Also, new specialized service

Left: Bob Holwell, president of Gates Rubber Co., explained the benefits of the LIFO accounting system to Temple Sloan Jr.

Right: R. D. Carson joined GPI in 1970 to oversee the firm's telephone sales activities.

Below: Hamilton Sloan joined GPI's management team in 1970. Placed in charge of internal operations, he quickly introduced numerous new methods and techniques that improved GPI efficiency and customer service.

retailers, such as Midas Mufflers, were making sizable inroads into the most specific auto parts business segments; and companies such as Pep Boys and Discount Auto Parts were offering DIYers just about any part they needed to fix their own cars.

Each of these disparate trends represented a threat to the independent auto mechanic and in turn eroded sales at the parts jobbers who were the main customers of parts distributors such as GPI.

Hamilton Sloan Joins GPI

In late 1970, Hamilton ("Ham") Sloan, Temple Sloan Jr.'s younger brother, joined General Parts in what would be an important event in his life, and a very important event in GPI's future growth and development. Ham Sloan immediately took command of internal operations and began to greatly improve efficiency and customer service, accomplishments that he continued to embellish until his early retirement nearly three decades later in 1999. Temple Sloan Jr. described his brother's contributions to the company.

Having attended Duke University, spending four

years in the United States Coast Guard, and a brief career in the department store business, my brother Ham elected to join the General Parts management team to oversee internal operations. Burkhead, Graham, Whitehurst, and I were delighted to have Ham join us in shaping the company during the important decade of the '70s. From his first day, he has been instrumental in the growth and success of the company.

Jobber Advisory Council

In order to stay in complete contact with jobbers, GPI organized the "Jobber Advisory Council," with the first meetings held in late February 1970. "The Advisory Council enabled us to bring in a group of our best customers and listen to them and let them tell us what was important to them," said Sloan.

The jobbers were enthusiastic about the meetings and appreciated GPI's interest in them and their opinions. The Jobber Advisory Council meetings proved highly successful—and hugely popular with jobbers. They eventually became known collectively as the "Owner's Conference."

"They were CARQUEST without the name and the program," said Sloan.

Indeed, from this first small Jobber Advisory Council acorn in 1970, a mighty oak known as CAR-QUEST, with more than 3,500 auto stores across the country, would eventually grow.

With its strong sales, GPI routinely plowed its earnings back into the company in order to remain competitive and to grow. It did so through expansion, improvement of services and support, increased benefits for employees, and acquisitions.

W.N.C. Parts Distribution Acquired

In March 1972, GPI completed its first acquisition: W.N.C. Parts Distribution Inc. in Asheville, North Carolina. Sloan described why GPI acquired the firm.

W.N.C. was located in the mountains. The discussion we had at the time was whether we should go to Charlotte, but the problem was that Charlotte was loaded with competition. We had a chance to acquire this company, it was a niche market, and that was the reason we made the move.

For more about WNC's history, see chapter 12.

Expansion

In addition to its acquisition activity, GPI was moving ahead full speed in expanding its internal operations. In 1970, after less than two years in operation, the new distribution center in Raleigh was expanded, making it one of the largest automotive replacement parts distribution centers in the Southeast. The company expanded the facility again in 1973. Sloan sent a letter late that year to the company's customers announcing the expansion.

GPI stays in business for one reason only—we pay attention to our customers and keep in stride by continually seeking ways to improve our service to you. Growth means much more than dollars and cents— as your business increases, so does our need for more warehouse space and personnel. In 1962, GPI started with 20,000 square feet in Raleigh. By 1969, we had progressed into a 45,000-square-foot distribution center. That was about five years ago, and at that time, we felt we had ample space—but expansion is here again! Construction of an additional 14,000 square feet, plus decking, is almost completed, which will bring us to 81,000 square feet [in Raleigh]

TRANSITIONS

1970—**R. D. Carson,** manager of telephone sales team; **Carol R. Jamison,** to direct store financing program; **Ken West** and **Dennis Massey,** both to purchasing department.

1972—In loving memory of **Mose Zuzulin** who passed away.

1973—**E. Parker Hyman Jr.** promoted to field sales manager; **Martha Merrill** appointed director of advertising and promotion; **Donald E. Robinson** promoted to field sales manager.

GPI's new facility in Columbia, South Carolina, was occupied in January 1974. After expansions were maximized, it was replaced with a 109,000-square-foot facility in 1997.

by December 1. This facility will house our 19-hour-a-day warehouse operation, 24-hour-a-day computer center, and round-the-clock telephone service.

In 1973, with the rest of the country mired in a deep recession, GPI announced plans to build a third distribution center, this one located in Columbia, South Carolina. It opened in January 1974. The 29,000-square-foot distribution center project was placed under the management of W. S. "Willie" Rushing, a district manager with the company.

"Willie was a local icon," said Sloan. "He knew everyone who ever sold an auto part in South Carolina. He convinced us that we should open from scratch in Columbia and move our South Carolina business out of Raleigh into that new facility." Rushing served as general manager and sales manager of the new facility when it opened.

All of this expansion did not occur at the most fortuitous of times, however. "We opened Columbia just in time for the gas crisis. That gas crisis was about as big an interruption in the business world as any we had ever seen. Plus, that's when the explosion of inflation really started. So our timing couldn't have been much worse. But things have a way of working out, and they did," Sloan said.

By the end of the year, the company's three warehouses would measure 149,000 square feet in total. A year later, more expansions were made to Asheville and Columbia. The rapid growth of GPI

continued to spur the development of additional warehousing space in order for the company to continue providing superior customer service.

Automation Advances

When GPI developed its distribution centers, it always invested in the most efficient and effective equipment available. For example, all such facilities were fully air-conditioned, which provided a pleasant work environment for associates. These operational procedures were under the watchful eye of Ham Sloan.

Additionally, the company was careful to stay abreast of developments that might improve support and related services for all of its operations. This included the way that it managed inventory and other essential data, which inevitably led to important decisions about emerging technology. Unfortunately, computers remained a mystery to most of the business world during the early '70s. And this was no different at GPI, according to Temple Sloan.

In those days computers scared you to death. I mean they were huge investments for what you got, but what you got was better than a group of people sitting in a room pushing pencils. Automation was more of an efficiency objective. It really had little impact on our customers because we didn't interface our computer systems with our customers until the late '70s. Everything regarding computers concerned improving our internal efficiency.

During the period 1970–1973, GPI's sales increased 228 percent and earnings increased 422 percent.

This CARQUEST illustration depicts the strong partnership that exists between CARQUEST and its distributors, jobbers, and dealers.

CHAPTER THREE

CARQUEST CREATED

*We knew we wanted an identity program but I was nervous about making
this ambitious and risky move. I kept saying, "We can't afford to do it,"
and Ed Whitehurst kept saying, "You can't afford not to do it."*

—Temple Sloan, Jr.

IN THE 1970s, INDEPENDENT warehouse distributors and jobbers began to form their own marketing groups in order to remain competitive. They were compelled to do so because of the movement into the DIY marketplace by big retailers such as Sears, Kmart, and Woolco, along with the emergence in the aftermarket industry of new specialty service suppliers such as Midas Mufflers and retail companies such as Pep Boys and Discount Auto Parts.

These new marketing groups were similar in function to NAPA, which was the largest network and the blueprint for industry players to pattern themselves. NAPA had trail-blazed in this area, even introducing its own NAPA-branded product lines. American Parts, another warehouse distributor, had unveiled its own umbrella marketing group called Big A. It would soon market a line of Big A-branded product lines.

As NAPA and American Parts had shown, it was no longer enough to merely be able to supply parts quickly (although this was still very important). To be truly effective competitors, warehouse distributors, and independent jobbers needed to join together in umbrella organizations of their own that shared promotional and advertising expenses and promoted the independent service technician.

The groups worked most effectively when independents joined with warehouse distributors like GPI to build a recognizable brand.

At first, there were many such marketing groups, and like any industry, it would take a while for a clear leader to emerge. GPI, as it turned out, would play a starring role in this shakeout.

The Birth of CARQUEST

During the late 60s and early 70s, GPI had focused its marketing efforts on targeted customers, offering a complete package of services to jobbers who would commit a major portion of their purchases to the company. Coupled with a strong financing program, GPI began to build on this strategy. As a result, numerous new stores were opened. In the early seventies, Ed Whitehurst, GPI vice president of sales, began to discuss the need for a strong identification program to complete this marketing package. He envisioned a branding program similar to those NAPA and American Parts had developed.

Whitehurst proved to be a persuasive advocate for the new program. "We knew we wanted an

Ed Whitehurst was a strong advocate of a new marketing program at GPI.

identity program," said Sloan. "But I was nervous about making this ambitious—and risky—move. I kept saying, 'We can't afford to do it.' But Ed kept saying, 'You can't afford *not* to do it.' You always worry about what would happen if you had gone left instead of right. But at the end of the day, we did what he suggested, and the results speak for themselves.

"I often look back and wonder if Ed Whitehurst had not been so persistent in pushing me to go forward with our identity marketing program, what would have been the fate of GPI," Sloan continued. "I really know the answer: We would not be here today."

What to Call It?

When looking for a name for their new entity, Whitehurst originally suggested "Conquest" during a meeting with Sloan and Dave Hutson, from Martin Fromm & Associates. Hutson, an account manager with Fromm, the advertising agency that was helping to roll out the new marketing campaign, immediately took Whitehurst's suggestion a step further and suggested "CARQUEST." Unanimously, the three men agreed on this name for the new program.

The next task was to come up with a logo for the new CARQUEST program. It was soon decided the same red, white, and blue colors be used for the CARQUEST logo that GPI incorporated in its own GPI logo. The Fromm agency designed the original CARQUEST shield. "Ed and I, we would go out and ride up and down the roads at night and pick out which signs stood out the best, and it was always red, white, and blue, which was used for ESSO, now EXXON. We liked those colors best and decided to go with them," said Sloan.

So, in early 1973, when the CARQUEST logo was finalized with the help of Martin Fromm Associates, GPI began to market the CARQUEST Program in the Carolinas. The first auto parts stores completely identified as CARQUEST were established in the summer of 1973. In late 1973, two other respected auto parts distributors, Bobro Products, Inc. in the Bronx section of New York, and Indiana Parts Warehouse (IPW) in Indianapolis, agreed to follow the CARQUEST plan started in the Carolinas by Sloan and Whitehurst within their own respective markets of New York and Indianapolis.

Joe Hughes of IPW described how his firm became a part of the new marketing organization.

Temple and I had been good friends since about 1960. He asked myself and Dan Bock from Bobro to join him for a meeting in Las Vegas because he had a great idea that he wanted to talk to us about. He proceeded to discuss a new marketing program he believed would benefit us all. Up until that point, neither Dan nor I had spent any money on advertising. So at first, the program didn't seem like it would fit either one of us. For IPW, we had a very successful business in Indiana. I remember saying, "I don't know if we need something like this because we have a good program going for ourselves. We're making good money." But we both went home and told Temple we'd think about it. He called me a month later, and I said we'd go with him on it. For me, I knew Temple, and I knew Ed Whitehurst, and I knew how hard they worked. I figured I'd go along with them because these two guys will make anything a success.

Opposite: This letter concerning the original design of the CARQUEST logo was sent in January 1973 to Temple Sloan Jr. from Bill Fromm, president of the advertising agency that developed it.

Below: From left to right, Dan Bock, Joe Hughes, and Temple Sloan Jr. admire the first CARQUEST logo.

Advertising / Marketing / Public Relations

January 19, 1973

Mr. O. Temple Sloan, Jr.
GENERAL PARTS, INC.
2319 Atlantic Avenue
Raleigh, North Carolina 27602

Dear Temple:

Enclosed is a layout on the trade name Carquest. I like it not only because it is eyecatching but because it uses the red, white and blue motif that we started with GPI.

In addition to the sig we have incorporated it into a sign and have marked the white area at the bottom as the imprint area for the jobber's individual name.

Although we have had to spend a great deal more time than I would have liked to come up with a solution for a name and graphics, after looking at this, I am thoroughly convinced that it was well worth it and I think that we are on a great identification symbol.

Please let me hear from you at your earliest convenience with your comments.

Kindest personal regards,

Sincerely,

MARTIN FROMM & ASSOCIATES

WILLIAM M. FROMM
President
WMF/mh
Enclosure

    cc: Ed Whitehurst
        Larry Hedlund
        Martin Zander

Martin Fromm and Associates / 633 East 63rd Street / Kansas City, Missouri 64114

Not long after the commitment of Bobro Products Inc. and IPW, the decision was made to hire the Pitluk Group Advertising Agency in San Antonio, Texas, as the official CARQUEST advertising agency. Louis Pitluk was a college roommate of Dan Bock of Bobro Products. He had also worked for the Straus-Frank Company in Texas. The professionalism of Louis Pitluk and his advertising firm proved instrumental in CARQUEST's early success.

Originally, CARQUEST was designed to develop a recognizable merchandise program for wholesale customers in the aftermarket industry. It was meant to be identifiable to both professional and walk-in customers. The program included identification and point-of-sale promotional elements within the store. It also involved newspaper, radio, and TV advertising. Direct mail was used to allow automotive service centers to participate in special promotions.

The CARQUEST program was designed to help auto parts jobbers improve their market share; and also, through branding, help them gain a portion of the rapidly growing DIY market. It was hoped that CARQUEST would also help blunt the advantage gained by prominent national retailers like Kmart, Woolco, and Fedmark, which had all recently entered the DIY retail market and were rapidly taking away large chunks of business, especially in the area of fast-moving parts.

First CARQUEST Customer

Bill Cotten, of City Auto Parts in Sanford, North Carolina, the town where Temple Sloan was raised, was GPI's first full-line jobber. In the summer of 1973, Cotten and City Auto Parts agreed to put up the first CARQUEST sign. He would remain a CARQUEST and GPI loyalist for nearly three decades, owning four CARQUEST stores when he retired.

CARQUEST Program Formally Introduced

By early 1974, GPI was ready to introduce CARQUEST to the industry at large. For its venue, it chose the 1974 ASIA show (now known as the Automotive Aftermarket Products Expo), an event described by *Warehouse Distributor News.*

Martha Merrill, of GPI's CARQUEST advertising and promotions department.

A unique automotive aftermarket parts marketing program was introduced by three leading distributors during the February 1974 ASIA Show. The program unites and includes the manufacturer, warehouse distributor, and wholesaler in a joint venture investment featuring continuing, consistent automotive parts marketing together with sales promotion and a business development program. An estimated 200 wholesalers in many of the regions served by these distributors are expected to be involved in the CARQUEST network by the end of 1974.

One of the unique parts of the program is its multistage marketing concept, which will market and merchandise sales at every level through the entire pipeline—manufacturer, warehouse distributor, parts stores, and the auto service dealer. All CARQUEST marketing programs are being developed and produced by the Pitluk Group, an advertising/ marketing and public relations agency located in San Antonio, Texas.

In talks with manufacturers, CARQUEST leaders emphasized the need for active manufacturer support in planning for special marketing and merchandising events and programs. The first promotion is scheduled for April 1974.

CARQUEST's introduction to GPI's customer base was greeted with much excitement and high hopes. The comments of Jack Williams, president of the Gates Rubber Company, in a 1977 interview with *Automotive Aftermarket News* were typical of the response.

"CARQUEST and its affiliated warehouse distributors, jobbers, and dealers provide a means for all of us to combat the inroads into the traditional market being made through the very aggressive television, newspaper, and radio advertising promotions of the mass merchandiser and rubber company chain stores," said Williams.

Sloan confidently predicted that 200 jobbers would join the network by 1975 and that the CARQUEST name would begin to spread.

A Singular Organizational Plan

The CARQUEST organization that Sloan helped create was set apart from the other marketing groups that were forming. Sloan characterized its special framework:

What made CARQUEST so unique was the desire to attract premiere independent auto parts distributors as members; those with a strong desire to grow and be successful and those that would most likely be compatible in problem solving. Two important issues were declared up front in CAR-QUEST bylaws. First, it was declared that distribution members would not compete with one another and the second was that each member, regardless of size, would have an equal vote.

The original CARQUEST partners also decided to plan, organize, and implement marketing activities through committees comprised of members. This plan enabled the organization's important marketing activities to remain well-grounded, and thus responsive to trends within the marketplace.

In addition to CARQUEST's egalitarian approach, the organization was able to secure new stores quickly due in part to an extremely forward-thinking—and highly effective—financing program GPI was already employing on behalf of its own customers. Sloan

BEER WITH ICE; PICCOLA VENITZIA

THE UNOFFICIAL DRINK OF CARQUEST is "Beer with Ice." Joe Hughes pioneered this tradition, but Art Lottes continues to carry it on in a most hearty fashion. It has been said that before the Sheridan Hotel at the Atlanta airport was torn down, if you ordered a beer with ice, someone there would ask you about Joe Hughes.

The unofficial restaurant of choice for the CARQUEST board of directors has been, and continues to be, Piccola Venitzia, located in Astoria, New York.

describes the program, which was first set up for GPI customers and expanded for CARQUEST customers.

During the late 1960s and 70s, GPI developed a formalized financing plan, which enabled the company to sponsor over 100 new stores. One of our strategies for growth was to finance the opening of new stores by independent owners. In other words, Mr. "X" wanted to go in business,

Bill Cotten (below), owned the very first CARQUEST store, City Auto Parts in Sanford, North Carolina (Below right).

but he might have only a fraction of the money needed. Therefore, we would arrange the financing for him on favorable terms with the bank—indeed, much more favorable than he could get anywhere else. Then we would stretch his repayment term out over five to seven years so he could get his business started and build the business. We would cosign and get buy-back agreements.

The program was set up through Carol Jamison, who was our banking officer at First Union National Bank, now known as Wachovia. Carol eventually came on board at GPI to organize this program and run it. Jamison, while also serving as CFO for GPI, was in charge of it during most of the 1970s, which resulted in significant growth for the company.

This program worked extremely well. If you look back at our sales figures for those years, you will see the addition of 50 stores in one year, 25 stores the next year, 35 stores the following year, and so on. Just about all of those stores were financed through those special programs. Indeed, most of our biggest customers operating in the Carolinas today we helped finance. And the program is still going extremely strong.

ALSTON AND BIRD

THE CARQUEST CORPORATION HAS always utilized the law firm of Alston and Bird, located in Atlanta, Georgia. When CARQUEST was being formed, O. Temple Sloan Jr. called Wilton Looney, CEO of Genuine Parts Company in Atlanta, to see if he could recommend a law firm. "Use ours," Looney said. So, for more than 30 years, CARQUEST and NAPA have used the same law firm. "We understand there is a 'Chinese Wall' between the NAPA and CARQUEST guys at Alston and Bird," said Temple Sloan Jr.

On the CARQUEST side of this "wall" was John Train and Marty Elgison both of whom have been a great help to GPI.

In March 1976, CARQUEST signed three well-established warehouse distributors: Sussen Inc., Cleveland; Illinois Auto Electric Co., Elmhurst, Illinois; and Parts Distributors Warehouse Inc., Memphis. Shown, left to right, are William Fording, sales manager, Sussen; Robert Sirotek, president, Illinois Auto Electric; Herman Markell, president, Parts Distributors Warehouse; and Dan Bock, CARQUEST president. With the addition of these firms, 10 CARQUEST warehouse distributors were operating throughout the United States east of the Mississippi by the mid-'70s.

CARQUEST Network Quickly Expands

The CARQUEST program proved to be hugely popular with auto parts distributors from the start. The goal to attract high-quality membership was aided by the early success in doing just that. With GPI, IPW, and Bobro as cornerstones, strong companies like Strauss Frank in Texas and PDW in Memphis/Nashville Tennessee both came aboard in 1976. Parts Warehouse Company, a strong Michigan distribution, joined in 1977 and was followed in 1978 by General Trading Company, a well-recognized distributor in Minnesota, Wisconsin, and the Dakotas.

Success follows success.

INDY RACE CHAMP SERVES AS CARQUEST NATIONAL SPOKESPERSON

SINCE ITS INCEPTION CARQUEST HAS been a natural tie-in sponsor for all types of highly visible sports promotions. This is why, in 1976, Johnny Rutherford, famous race car driver, three-time winner of the Indy 500 (1974, 1976, and 1980) and CART national champion in 1980, was hired as national spokesperson, handling all radio and TV commercials and also appearing in all institutional advertising.

In addition to the Rutherford connection, CARQUEST has sponsored ACC basketball games over TV stations throughout North and South Carolina and has a radio sponsorship with the North Carolina Sports Network that is carried over 49 stations and on the South Carolina Sports Network over 21 stations. On the national level, CARQUEST advertising has appeared in national publications such as *Hot Rod*, *Car Craft* and *Mechanics Illustrated*.

O. Temple Sloan Jr., left, with three-time Indy 500 champion Johnny Rutherford, who spoke at the December 1977 CARQUEST Raleigh meeting.

A "WHO'S WHO" OF AUTO PARTS DISTRIBUTORS

THE EARLY CARQUEST MEMBERS REPresent a true "Who's Who" of wholesale auto parts distributors. In addition to General Parts Inc., Raleigh, North Carolina; Bobro, Products, Bronx, New York; and Indiana Parts Warehouse, Indianapolis, Indiana, they include:

- Avro Warehouse Sales, Buffalo, New York (owned by Seymour Hesch)
- Borden-Aieklen Auto Supply, New Orleans (owned by Joseph Greiner)
- The Kay Automotive Warehouse of Philadelphia, Pennsylvania (owned by Herbert Lipton)
- Sussen Inc, Cleveland, Ohio (owned by Dan Sussen)
- Parts Distributors Warehouse (PDW), Memphis, Tennessee (owned by William Lowenberg) Note: PDW had a branch warehouse in Nashville, Tennessee, doing business as S&S Parts Distributors
- Illinois Auto Electric, Elmhurst, Illinois (owned by Robert Sirotek)
- Straus-Frank Company, San Antonio, Texas (owned by David Straus)
- Chancelor and Lyons, San Francisco, California (owned by Mort Schwartz)
- Parts Distributors Inc. Waltham, Massachusetts (owned by Charles Roazen)
- Parts Warehouse Company, Bay City, Michigan (owned by Sam and Bob Rogers)
- General Trading Company, St. Paul, Minnesota (owned by Carl Pollad, Murphy Handmaker, and Paul Christian)
- A.E. Lottes Company, St. Louis, Missouri (owned by the Lottes family)
- Hatch Grinding Company, Denver, Colorado (owned by the Kornafel family)

By the end of 1975 there were six CARQUEST companies with 14 distribution centers servicing more than 350 auto parts stores. Within a year, there would be more than 500 auto parts stores bearing the CARQUEST identification, serviced by more than 22 distribution centers and 12 participating companies. By the end of 1975, sales to CARQUEST companies already accounted for 69 percent of GPI's total sales. In 1976, 17 new CARQUEST auto parts stores were opened, 73.3 percent of GPI sales came from CARQUEST, and there were already more than 1,000 stores participating in the program. In 1977, 19 new stores were added and 10 independent stores joined the program. In 1978, 15 new auto parts stores were opened and 11 new customers joined the network. In 1979, 13 new CARQUEST stores and 12 independent customers were added. At the end of the decade, GPI served 190 CARQUEST stores in Virginia and the Carolinas, and one in Georgia. GPI's sales to these 190 stores represented 90.4 percent of its total revenue.

One key reason for CARQUEST's popularity with its customers was the heady success it was having with its auto parts sales. Ed Whitehurst told the *Carolina Financial Times* that sales at CARQUEST stores went up between 25 percent and 30 percent in a single year, far outstripping the industry average of 12 percent to 14 percent.

"CARQUEST is synonymous with the future," said Dan Bock, president of Bobro Products and cofounder of CARQUEST, in *Automotive Aftermarket News*. Bock continued:

The future growth of our customer, the parts jobber, is related to his ability to compete effectively through the next decade. The challenges

1979 CARQUEST
BOARD OF DIRECTORS

D.M. Bock
Bobro Products Inc.
Bronx, New York

Rudolph G. Flashner
Borden-Aicklen Auto
Supply Co. Inc.
New Orleans, Louisiana

I.H. Handmaker
General Trading Co.
St. Paul, Minnesota

Seymour Hesch
Avro Warehouse Sales Inc.
Buffalo, New York

Joe Hughes
Indiana Parts
Warehouse Inc.
Indianapolis, Indiana

Louis J. Baumer
V.P./Executive Director CARQUEST
National Headquarters
Memphis, Tennessee

Peter Kornafel
Hatch Grinding Co.
Denver, Colorado

Herbert Lipton
Kay Automotive Warehouse Inc.
Philadelphia, Pennsylvania

A.E. Lottes Jr.
A.E. Lottes Co.
St. Louis, Missouri

Herman P. Markell
Parts Distributors Warehouse Inc.
Memphis, Tennessee

Lee Meriwether
Automotive Central Inc.
Montgomery, Alabama

Charles Roazen
Parts Distributors Inc.
Waltham, Massachusetts

Robert G. Rogers
Parts Warehouse Company
Bay City, Michigan

Mort Schwartz
Chanslor & Lyon Co. Inc.
Brisbane, California

Robert L. Sirotek
Illinois Auto Electric Co.
Elmhurst, Illinois

O. Temple Sloan Jr.
General Parts Inc.
Raleigh, North Carolina

David Straus
STRAFCO
San Antonio, Texas

Daniel C. Sussen
Sussen Inc.
Cleveland, Ohio

that confront the parts jobber are tough ones. Will the DIYers market continue to go the mass retailer route, or will the parts store be able to change its marketing practices quickly enough to regain that all-important phase of the business? The jobber of the future must compete and must solve other distribution problems that he will face, such as the parts explosion ... and increasing costs, to name a few. But to succeed, the warehouse distributor and the jobber must work as a team. Alone, there is no way—together we can do it! For our company, that means CARQUEST.

Temple Sloan, quoted in the same article, was also highly enthusiastic concerning CARQUEST.

Our company's affiliation with CARQUEST has been the most significant marketing step in our 16-year history. Through CARQUEST, we developed a unique marketing teamwork, involving all four steps

---

In 1977, Temple Sloan, president of GPI, welcomes Samuel L. Rogers, president of Parts Warehouse Company, center, and Robert G. Rogers, executive vice president of Parts Warehouse, right, to the CARQUEST team. Parts Warehouse Co. was a leading parts distributor in Michigan.

of distribution—manufacturer, warehouse distributor, jobber, and service dealer—to reach the motoring public. The strength of each has been combined to tell our story, one of quality, service availability and competitiveness.

Sloan had hit the nail on the head. GPI's arrangement with CARQUEST had proven remarkably lucrative for the firm. Indeed, by 1979 the ratio of CARQUEST sales as a portion of GPI sales had grown to an astounding 90 percent. And through CARQUEST, its presence across the country was even more impressive. Of course, that was Sloan's and his CARQUEST cofounders' original plan. He explained it this way:

The whole concept of developing CARQUEST as it evolved was that if we were going to make it a national organization to compete with NAPA and American Parts, or American Parts System as it was known back in those days, we had to figure out how to have a national presence. To get that national presence, our objective was to hook up with strong, regional companies in a format similar to a co-op. That's just what we did.

Warehouse Distributor News

In 1977, *Warehouse Distributor News*, an aftermarket trade publication, reported 21 program distribution groups. Listed alphabetically, they were: APS, Auto Partner, APW Full Circle, Autopro, Autowize, Bumper-to-Bumper, CN Parts System, Car Care Man, CARQUEST, CAPS, Full-Line Associate, GTC Auto Parts, Gold Star, Green Light, I-Way Auto Parts, Mr. Automotive, NAPA, Parts Plus, Parts Post, Pro-Am Partshop, and Quickparts.

A Momentous Decade

CARQUEST's stunning start-up led to a remarkably successful decade for GPI. "It should be emphasized just how important the decade of the 1970s was in the development of GPI," said Joe Owen, who joined GPI in 1983. "This era could well be referred to as the building of the 'launching pad' for the rapid growth in the 1980s and beyond."

And well it should be. The executives at GPI had demonstrated a strong degree of foresight and vision in developing and then bringing to life the highly successful CARQUEST concept. But their timing also proved to be highly fortuitous. And there was one additional element that also played its part. "One of our employ-

The CARQUEST Annual Membership Meeting, circa 1977.

ees once asked me to describe the plan we had to get so big," said Sloan. "I told him it was called 'luck and hard work.'"

JOHNNY RUTHERFORD SAYS:
CARQUEST WILL GIVE YOUR BUSINESS THAT EXTRA LIFT.

Yes, Johnny Rutherford, two-time Indy 500 winner, is now promoting name-brand parts and professional service at competitive prices for independent CARQUEST service stations and garages. Why not climb aboard and watch your profits rise? You'll get free point-of-sale materials to let motorists know you're providing expert installation of the specials Rutherford offers on radio, TV, and in the newspapers. All you do is buy the advertised specials from your CARQUEST jobber and promote them to your customers. You'll not only make bigger profits by moving more merchandise and making more installations, but you'll be adding more and more customers with each promotion.

So go with the pros. Get in the Winner's Circle with CARQUEST and Johnny. Contact your local CARQUEST jobber or mail the coupon for complete information, but do it now while it's fresh on your mind.

You've got everything to gain, and nothing to lose because CARQUEST will give you that extra lift.

Winner's Circle

CARQUEST

MAIL TO: Johnny Rutherford
100 Richmond, San Antonio, TX 78205
Please send me complete details on the CARQUEST program

Name _____

Address _____

City _____

State_____ Zip _____

Use reply card—refer to AAN-3050

During the '70s, racing great Johnny Rutherford performed very effectively as a CARQUEST spokesperson, as evidenced in this full-page CARQUEST "Winner's Circle" ad that was published in *Automotive Aftermarket News*.

CHAPTER FOUR

SINGING THE CARQUEST SONG

1974–1979

Our ESOP has never owed any money. All the stock has gone into the ESOP at the book value and has been treated as a benefit plan for our people, not as a financing tool for the company.

—Temple Sloan Jr.

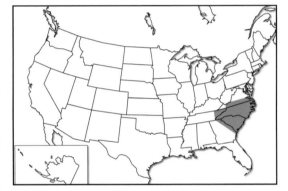

THE YEAR 1974 WAS A significant year for GPI as it represented the first full year for its new marketing program, CARQUEST. The balance of the decade was spent selling the CARQUEST concept to the existing GPI customer base and to new potential customers as well.

Temple Sloan Jr., Joe Hughes, and Dan Bock spent a lot of time presenting the CARQUEST program to independent auto parts distributors to build the program nationwide. This effort was joined with each new member and almost immediately, CARQUEST became a dynamic force in auto parts distribution.

1974 also was perhaps the most significant and memorable year in the history of the automotive aftermarket because of the gasoline crisis. The effects of the energy crisis reshaped the future of the entire automotive industry and for our nation. It created high inflation and high interest rates, both detrimental to the economy. It led to a record high unemployment and a severe recession in 1974 and 1975. U.S. vehicle manufacturers rushed to produce a whole new generation of fuel-efficient automobiles with cleaner exhaust emissions mandated by the federal government to meet the 1980 deadline.

The excitement generated by the CARQUEST program permeated throughout GPI and its customer base. No longer was GPI just another parts distributor with a variety of manufacturer's brands. No longer were GPI wholesale customers just another auto parts store with the same manufacturer's brands as their competition. With CARQUEST they could distinguish themselves with their own exclusive brand that would be dedicated to high-quality standards.

At the end of 1974, after one full year with CARQUEST, GPI was serving 82 CARQUEST Auto Parts stores, which represented 59% of their total sales. By the end of 1979, GPI was serving 190 CARQUEST stores representing 90% of their total sales. Their goal was to reach 100%, which was achieved in 1988.

Temple Sloan Jr. was quick to credit GPI's rapid growth in the late 1970s to the sales team under the leadership of Ed Whitehurst combined with elevated customer service under the leadership of Ham Sloan and Mac Graham. The Whitehurst-led sales team of Dennis Fox, Don Robinson, Willie Rushing, and Bill Turbeville combined with the

This map shows the extent of GPI's sales and marketing reach during the late 1970s.

General Parts, Inc.

P.O. Box 26006 2319 Atlantic Ave. Raleigh, N.C. 27611 828-0967

To: GPI SALES FORCE

DATE: May 1, 1974

Your company's sales for the month of April exceeded $1,025,000, a booming 38% increase over April 1973, and the first time ever our sales have exceeded one million in a single month. CONGRATULATIONS to each of you on an excellent performance.

The feedback on the CARQUEST Program is great, and it is helping our customers and GPI. With continued effort, we can make May even better.

Keep up the hard work.

"Together, we can work wonders."

Sincerely,

O. Temple Sloan Jr.
President

awda   AUTOMOTIVE DISTRIBUTION CENTER

On May 1, 1974, despite a difficult business climate, Temple Sloan announced that GPI had exceeded $1 million in monthly sales for the first time.

internal service and operations team of R.D. Carson, George Montague, and John Brian, along with the purchasing group led by A.C. Burkhead and Ken West, worked in harmony to produce remarkable results in a difficult business climate.

As this success spread throughout the industry, parts distributors became interested in learning more about CARQUEST. From only three members at the end of 1974, just five years later there were 16 CARQUEST distributors serving 1,336 CARQUEST Auto Parts stores.

The Automotive Warehouse Distributors Association (AWDA) annual meeting became an important venue for independent parts distributors

to learn about the numerous marketing groups being formed. Temple Sloan Jr. along with Joe Hughes, Dan Bock, David Straus, Mort Schwartz, Sam and Bobby Rogers, Pete Kornafel, and Art Lottes, who were all AWDA members, spent many hours in the bars at AWDA meetings discussing the virtues and values of CARQUEST. Their enthusiasm was contagious.

Through these meetings and other AWDA functions, Temple developed friendships and business relationships that later would lead to discussions

AWDA NETWORKING

IN ADDITION TO BUILDING HIS OWN company, O. Temple Sloan Jr. has been a longtime promoter of the auto parts industry as a leader in the Automotive Warehouse Distributors Association (AWDA). And while the AWDA has worked to advance the automotive business, Sloan has made valuable connections over the years that he has used to help build GPI and CARQUEST.

Sloan had been a member of the board of governors for eight years and during that time served in almost every association office or position. In 1976, at the age of 37, he was elected chairman of the board of governors for AWDA, becoming the second-youngest elected chief executive.

"AWDA has proven to be extremely valuable for us," Sloan said. "This is where I met all the people who later became a part of CARQUEST.

"My brother Ham was likewise active in AWDA affairs, advancing through the chairs to chairman in 1988. His AWDA activities centered on internal operations where he shared ideas and procedures. These were very beneficial to GPI's success."

concerning mergers and acquisitions that have played a vital role in GPI's growth.

In 1975, Avro Warehouse Sales, Buffalo, New York; Borden Aicklen Auto Supply, Inc., New Orleans, Louisiana; and Kay Automotive Warehouse Inc., Philadelphia, Pennsylvania; became CARQUEST members.

In 1976, Chanslor & Lyons, California; Illinois Auto Electric, Elmhurst, Illinois; Parts Distributors Inc., Waltham, Massachusetts; Parts Distributors Warehouse, Memphis, Tennessee; Straus Frank Company, San Antonio, Texas; and Sussen Inc., Cleveland, Ohio, became CARQUEST members.

Sloan Keynotes AWDA's 30th Convention

Temple Sloan has delivered some truly memorable keynote addresses on behalf of AWDA. In 1977, during AWDA's 30th annual convention, in the make-believe Roman Empire setting of Caesars Palace, Las Vegas, AWDA brought in bands, balloons, badges, and even clowns to help celebrate 30 years of progress, success, and influence in the automotive aftermarket.

It was AWDA's Diamond Anniversary, and AWDA Chairman Sloan quickly got the attendees' undivided attention with a not-so-casual and definitely not run-of-the-mill keystone speech. Indeed, his 1977 address has gone down in the records of AWDA and the aftermarket industry as not only a genuine masterpiece but a continuing contribution to GPI's viability in the automotive aftermarket.

During his speech, Sloan discussed various disparate trends that had been negatively impacting AWDA members in recent years—the introduction of heavy aftermarket parts discounts by mass merchandisers such as Sears and Kmart, plus the arrival of relatively new industry players such as Midas Mufflers, Pep Boys, and Discount Auto Parts. These all represented a threat to the independent auto mechanic and in turn eroded sales for the jobbers who were the main customers of AWDA firms such as GPI.

Any time sales growth slows, internal competition intensifies. We've seen it firsthand ... between suppliers of mufflers, rubber goods, ignition, and other lines. With fewer service station outlets, jobbers—who are being sold at

Temple Sloan Jr., delivers the keynote address at AWDA's 30th annual convention, held at Caesars Palace in Las Vegas in 1977. *(Photo courtesy of* Southern Automotive Journal*).*

warehouse distributor prices—are selling the larger and often smaller dealers at jobber prices. These practices do not generate a savings to the consumer; they just destroy the economics of our industry at a time when profits are so badly needed by the warehouse distributor and the jobber.

Sloan went on to warn his industry against the incursion of mass merchandisers and others who only sold the fast-moving product lines such as brakes and mufflers, which accounted for anywhere between 20 percent and 50 percent of industry sales. These new companies, he pointed out, were skimming the cream from everyone else in the industry and destroying margins for warehouse

ESOP

GREAT COMPANIES DEPEND ON GREAT people. This is one of the reasons that GPI has thrived over the years. Indeed, during the economically troubled 1970s, when thousands of companies nationwide were closing their doors, the hard work and dedicated efforts of GPI employees enabled the company not only to weather those tough times, but to excel and pull ahead of its competitors.

"We had a group of people that had a passion, and they weren't going to lose. That took us through a lot of dark days," said GPI CEO and Chairman O. Temple Sloan Jr.

Understanding that its employees were the key to its success, GPI has made a commitment to provide its workers and management with competitive salaries and excellent benefits. One notable example is the Employee Stock Ownership Program (ESOP) that GPI instituted in 1976, the 15th anniversary of the company's founding.

The company-funded profit-sharing plan was available for all GPI employees who qualified after one full year of service. The fund was established for three key reasons: to promote the future economic welfare of GPI employees, to develop in employees an increased interest in the successful operation of GPI, and to encourage employee savings.

The program was very generous. For example, employees are not required to deposit money in the plan. Instead, each year, the company's board of directors determines the company's distribution to the fund on the employees' behalf. The ESOP fund then purchases General Parts shares of stock for each eligible employee.

Now Valued at More Than $209 Million

"General Parts converted an earlier profit-sharing plan for its employees into the ESOP on December 31, 1976. At the time there was $248,100 in the fund, and there were 83 members," said Sloan. "At the end of 2005, it was worth over $209 million with 11,903 participants and has paid out $85 million in benefits. Our ESOP owns approximately one third of the company.

"The stock market was terrible back in those days," he continued. "Your money would earn from 2 to 4 percent a year, but our company was growing back then around 15 to 20 percent each year. So the ESOP was a great deal. Plus, Ham and I agreed that we needed a way to retain people if we wanted to continue to grow. That's why we never used the ESOP as a financing tool.

"There have been some abuses of ESOPs over the years where the owner goes out and gets a stock appraised at two times book, and then enables the ESOP to borrow a lot of money, buy the stock back, but then they've got to pay the loan back," Sloan explained. "The wheels run off the wagon and you've got a disaster. Well, we never did any of that. Our ESOP has never owed any money. All the stock has gone into the ESOP at book value and has been treated as a benefit plan for our people, not as a financing tool for the company."

Considering such a valuable benefit, it is not surprising that retention rates for General Parts employees have consistently remained strong over the years.

"There is a terrific book called *My Years with General Motors*, by Albert P. Sloan [no relation to Temple Sloan], the legendary former CEO of General Motors, in which he described GM's pay plans and how the company always made sure to defer enough money so that top employees would not want to leave," said Sloan. "One of his statements in the book was that, 'We never lost a man that we didn't want to lose.' That's a pretty strong statement when you think about a company that big. Well, for us, the ESOP was planned with that thought in mind. And it has worked."

GPI's ESOP's Earnings on its Investments

Year	Earnings	Year	Earnings	Year	Earnings	Year	Earnings
1977	30.0%	1984	21.2%	1991	15.3%	1998	14.2%
1978	25.3%	1985	16.1%	1992	14.1%	1999	13.3%
1979	23.0%	1986	19.1%	1993	17.6%	2000	11.3%
1980	18.6%	1987	16.7%	1994	18.0%	2001	11.4%
1981	17.8%	1988	15.1%	1995	15.6%	2002	13.2%
1982	17.6%	1989	11.7%	1996	13.7%	2003	15.0%
1983	20.1%	1990	13.4%	1997	11.6%	2004	14.2%
						2005	17.4%

distributors that stocked every product line, both fast and slow, but could not command the same high-volume price breaks. In effect, this meant that warehouse distributors were subsidizing sales for the mass merchandisers. Sloan's remarks were describing a situation that shortly led to the introduction of private brands by distributors.

During his 1979 keynote address to the AWDA, Sloan stressed the importance of the warehouse distributor and jobber.

Today the warehouse distributor is stronger than at any time in the association's 30-year history. They are financially stronger, operating from modern, computerized facilities with highly educated, well-trained management and operating personnel, and [are] providing a level of service and expertise to the automotive jobber that totally amazes the sophisticated outside observer.

The complexity of supplying tens of thousands of parts numbers, which is the greatest strength of the warehouse distributor and jobber distribution, will be—and is already—the greatest challenge to our future success. We must be capable of managing our financial assets and earn the necessary profits to cope with the tremendous inventory investments that will be necessary to maintain our position of strength.

Sloan went on to outline a clear vision of what the warehouse distributor must do to survive in an increasingly complex and competitive industry. He said that jobbers should be committed to marketing products and services through

PRESIDENT'S CLUB

AS AN INCENTIVE FOR SALES AND operations excellence, the GPI President's Club was initiated in 1977. To achieve President's Club status, sales and operations managers had to achieve a measured level of performance. Each year's winners were taken on a long weekend trip with their spouses. The first President's Club trip was to Williamsburg, Virginia, and the winners were R. D. Carson, Harry Evans, Dennis Fox, Martin Havens, Grady Dunn, Steve Palmer, and Spencer Scott.

Winners for 1978 were Harry Evans, Jerry Taylor, Bill Turbeville, Ed McIntosh, and Buddy Pearce. In 1979, winners were Harry Evans, Martin Havens, Buddy Pearce, Grady Dunn, George Montague, Willie Rushing, Bill Turbeville, John Brian, Gary Goldston, Ernie Hendley, Randal Long, and Steve Palmer.

GPI – PROUD OF OUR PAST

THE FOLLOWING APPEARED IN THE October 1979 edition of GPI's newsletter, "The GP EYE."

Ask shipping and receiving supervisor Bill Norris how GPI has changed in the 18 years he's been here and he shrugs, "we're not so different. Our old customers are still with us. We've just grown."

Quintupled is more like it, but it didn't come easy, President O. Temple Sloan was still a Duke University student in 1961 when he invested in General Parts' first distribution center, a 20,000 square foot warehouse on South Saunders Street, Raleigh.

Unknown to him, the inventory was 50 percent obsolete. "It wasn't a very smart way to go into business," but he remembers feeling a desire to succeed, a willingness to learn and the ability to work hard.

An Automotive Warehouse Distributors Association (AWDA) plaque was awarded to Temple Sloan Jr., in appreciation for his service as first vice chairman in 1976 and as chairman of the AWDA in 1977. Shown (left to right) are Martin Fromm, president of AWDA; Temple Sloan Jr., 1977 AWDA chairman; and Dunbar Abston, first vice chairman and incoming 1978 chairman of AWDA. Fromm also presented the 6th annual AWDA Scholarship Memorial award to Temple Sloan Jr. This award was established as a memorial to deceased association leaders. Funds help support students in automotive parts management at the University of Southern Colorado and are given in honor of the scholarship recognitions within the AWDA.

warehouse distributors. Second, while recognizing the many distribution channels in the industry, Sloan emphasized the destructive power of pricing competition by newcomers.

Regarding the predatory trade practices of mass merchandisers, Sloan stated that a number of effective ways to fight back existed, including the branding of product lines by warehouse distributors, the way NAPA was doing. By doing this, the traditional aftermarket would command loyalty among its cus-

tomers. He also called upon manufacturers to treat warehouse distributors and mass merchandisers equally in terms of pricing to prevent them from destroying the aftermarket that "keeps America's vehicles running."

A major building expansion of the Asheville and Columbia distribution centers was completed during 1977, plus further expansion of the internal storage and conveyor system. This was done to

GPI MANAGEMENT TEAM

Heading GPI's Management Team in the Late 1970s

O. Temple Sloan Jr.
PRESIDENT AND DIRECTOR

C. Hamilton Sloan
EXECUTIVE VICE PRESIDENT

Edward Whitehurst
VICE PRESIDENT OF SALES

Malcolm Graham
SECRETARY

John Gardner
TREASURER

Asheville Distribution Center

Dennis A. Fox
SALES MANAGER

R. D. Carson
OPERATIONS
MANAGER

Columbia Distribution Center

William J. Turbeville
SALES MANAGER

George H. Montague
OPERATIONS
MANAGER

Raleigh Distribution Center

Don Robinson
SALES MANAGER
EAST

R. S. Palmer
SALES MANAGER
WEST

T. John Brian
OPERATIONS
MANAGER

Corporate Staff

Joel B. Mullen
DIRECTOR
OF PERSONNEL

Barbara D. Perkins
CONTROLLER

Mary E. Pope
ASSISTANT
SECRETARY

Kenneth F. West
DIRECTOR
OF PURCHASING

Michael Deal
ASSISTANT
TREASURER

Left to right: Mac Graham, Temple Sloan, Ham Sloan, John Gardner, and Ed Whitehurst.

The new Raleigh, North Carolina, distribution center and offices, circa 1979.

assure that customer service levels remained the same as business increased.

In 1977, Parts Warehouse Company, Bay City, Michigan, became a CARQUEST member. In 1978, General Trading Company, St. Paul, Minnesota, became a CARQUEST member. In 1979, Hatch Grinding Company, Denver, Colorado, and A.E. Lottes Company, St. Louis, Missouri, became CARQUEST members.

GPI Moves Corporate Offices and Distribution Center

The rapid growth of GPI required larger facilities to continue providing superior customer service. In Raleigh, the Atlantic Avenue location could not be considered adequate for projected

IN APPRECIATION

THE EXCELLENT MANAGEMENT TEAM and outstanding employees at GPI were the primary reason for the company's success during the 1970s.

The operations team was devoted to providing top-flight service to the parts stores. This group, under the leadership of Ham Sloan was made up of Mac Graham, R. D. Carson, Hersey Hall, Bill Norris, John Brian, Paul Holliday, and George Montague.

The sales team was led by Ed Whitehurst with assistance from Shorty Britt, Robbie Harrison, Willie Rushing, Dennis Fox, Don Robinson, Bill Turbeville, Randal Long, Hilton Winders, Grady Dunn, Jody Joy, David McCollum, Lynn Linker, Ken Oliver, Phil Corbin, Sam Glover, Gary Goldston, Ed McIntosh, Steve Palmer, Spencer Scott, Harry Evans, Ernie Hendley, Jerry Taylor, and Marty Havens.

On the administrative staff, the pioneers of this era were A. C. Burkhead, Mary Pope, Ken West, John Gardner, Joel Mullen, Barbara Perkins, Mike Deal, Martha Merrill, Alida Baker, and Harriet Camak.

Customers

In addition to the previously mentioned customers who helped General Parts Inc. through the 1960s, the following should be recognized for their help in the 1970s: Nat Cannady and Dewey Roland, Wholesale Auto Parts, Raleigh, North Carolina; Slick Gibbons, Clarendon Auto Parts, Manning, South Carolina; Dusty Boozer, Sunrise Auto Supply, Newberry, South Carolina; Prentiss Yarborough, Yarborough Auto Parts, Florence, South Carolina; Jimmy Liles and Phil Flies, CARQUEST of Beauford, Beauford/Richland, South Carolina; Junior Anderson and Jim Cook, Murphy Auto Parts, Murphy, North Carolina; Eddy Caldwell, Eddy's Auto Parts, Lincolnton, North Carolina; Pete Bush, Ace Auto Parts, Easley, South Carolina; Frank, Fred, and Ronnie James, James Brothers Auto Parts, Brevard, Skyland, Waynesville, and West Asheville, North Carolina; Claude Steele, Center Parts Company, Lancaster, South Carolina; Tom, and Frances Townsend, Townsend Auto Parts, Wallace, North Carolina; and Bill Cotten, City Auto Parts, Sanford, North Carolina.

TRANSITIONS

1974—William J. "Bill" Turbeville promoted to sales manager, Columbia Distribution Center; **Joel B. Mullen** joins staff as personnel director.

1976—Randal Long joins sales team, Raleigh Distribution Center; **R.D. Carson** appointed operations manager, Asheville Distribution Center; **John Gardner,** CPA, joins as controller.

1977—John Gardner, promoted to treasurer; **Kenneth F. West** promoted to director of purchasing; **Steve Palmer** promoted to western division sales manager, Raleigh Distribution Center.

1979—Joel B. Mullen joins as personnel director; **John Brian** joins the company as operations manager, Raleigh Distribution Center; **Barbara Perkins** joins as controller; **Charles Deck** joins as company pilot; **David McCollum** joins as sales representative, Columbia Distribution Center; **Temple Sloan Jr.** elected president of CARQUEST; **Joe Hughes** elected vice president of CARQUEST; **Herm Markell** elected secretary-treasurer of CARQUEST. Also, in 1979, **Martin L. Larner,** founder and chairman of the board of Indiana Parts Warehouse, died at the age of 74. Larner served on many key AWDA committees, as well as on its board of governors. He was a wonderful friend of the Sloan family, GPI, and CARQUEST.

Top left: Randal Long joined GPI in 1976. Left: John Gardner was promoted to treasurer in 1977. Above: In memorium, Martin L. Larner, who died in 1979.

growth and relocation planning started in 1978. Therefore, in the fall of 1979, a new 104,000-square-foot distribution center was completed in North Raleigh at 2635 Millbrook Road on a beautiful 12-acre site. A state-of-the-art conveyor system and double-decking afforded 150,000 square feet of storage capacity. The new facility also included corporate offices and the brand new computer center.

The new facility was occupied in October 1979. Ham Sloan and Mac Graham were responsible for building design as well as planning the physical relocation from Atlantic Avenue. GPI Raleigh customers immediately enjoyed the benefits of increased efficiency and GPI associates were proud to be a vital part of an improved working environment.

The late 1970s was spent in fine tuning and growing the CARQUEST program into a nationwide association of the strongest distribution companies devoted to developing a closed customer base of the finest CARQUEST Auto Parts store. At the same time GPI, like all other businesses, struggled to control expenses in a business climate consumed with high interest rates, high unemployment, abnormal inflation, and the aftershock of the worst fuel crisis in U.S. history.

During the period 1974 through 1979, GPI's sales increased 176%, and its earnings increased 190%.

Of all companies acquired or merged into General Parts Inc., the one with the longest history was General Trading Company (GTC) in St. Paul, Minnesota. GTC began in 1855 as a retail iron store known as Nicols & Dean.

CHAPTER FIVE

CARQUEST EXPANDS RAPIDLY

1980–1984

I went to Raleigh with a true intent to help Temple [Sloan] find Ed's [Whitehurst] replacement. However, I was immediately impressed with Temple and Ham Sloan and their enthusiasm for the parts business, their work ethic, and their ambition. The longer I stayed, the more I liked what I saw.

—Joe Owen, GPI vice chairman

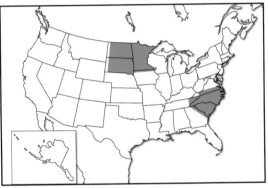

GPI's marketing area in 1980.

NET SALES TOOK A dramatic jump during the early 1980s. This was particularly impressive because of the overall poor business conditions plaguing the national economy at the time: record inflation, unprecedented high interest rates, and high unemployment. These negative business factors all took a heavy toll on virtually every U.S. business sector, including the replacement auto parts industry. They forced car owners to readjust their spending priorities in light of their shrinking disposable incomes. Preventive maintenance on America's vehicle fleet was postponed indefinitely and repairs were often made only when breakdowns occurred.

Additionally, cash flow of individual auto parts stores was severely impacted by the record high interest rates being charged by banks and other lending institutions. This troubling factor, plus inflation, negatively impacted individual store operators' inventory levels and also increased their operating costs. Auto parts stores were forced to return inventory to satisfy their payables. Considering these and related negative circumstances, CARQUEST's steady growth during this difficult economic period takes on even more of a luster.

However, for the most astute observers, including Temple Sloan and his savvy and seasoned GPI management team, it was clear that numerous optimistic factors had the potential to positively impact the automotive replacement parts market for years to come. Total vehicle population was 160 million vehicles, an increase from 50 million in 1970. The average age per car was approaching seven years, the highest since World War II. In 1983, miles driven over the previous year were up four percent; and reduced inflation had driven gas prices down to approximately 55 cents per gallon in 1972 dollars.

And these trends continued to improve yearly. Vehicle growth remained robust, between two percent and four percent per year. Plus, the average age of vehicles on the road moved from seven to seven and one-half years—a figure up 31 percent over the previous 10 years.

CARQUEST's sales growth was expected to stay strong, due to the proliferation of small vehicles and the growing foreign car population, excellent growth markets for the immediate future. Of course, any improvement in the current economy and a corresponding reduction in interest rates were also expected to result in an improvement in replacement parts sales.

Although GPI's sales were strong in 1980, the company's earnings growth slowed due to the overall high interest rates of the period, plus an increase in income tax rates. On the plus side, effective management enabled GPI to retire all short-term bank debt prior to the end of the year.

There was no question that the previous years had been challenging. As a result, General Parts decided its employees, customers, and suppliers deserved special recognition, according to Temple Sloan.

As we conclude our second decade, a special thanks is extended to our loyal customers, suppliers, and employees and to the continuing confidence and support of our company and investors. We approach our third decade with confidence and enthusiasm, but with the awareness of the economic climate in which we currently operate.

General Trading Company Acquired

On July 1, 1980, General Parts made its first acquisition outside the Carolinas—General Trading Company (GTC). Located in St. Paul, Minnesota, the highly regarded firm enjoyed a rich and respected history, beginning in 1855 as a retail iron company.

GTC had been a CARQUEST member since 1977, and was serving approximately 90 CARQUEST stores in Minnesota, North Dakota, South Dakota, and Wisconsin. The company generated a reasonable profit for the six months following the merger, and those results were reflected in GPI's 1980 financials. Significant expense reductions and improved operating efficiencies followed the acquisition's conversion to GPI's

General Trading Company (GTC), headquartered in St. Paul, Minnesota, was General Parts' first acquisition outside the Carolinas. GTC started out as an establishment supplying iron for use in the manufacture of nails, plowshares, sled castings, and related products.

distribution center computer system in the fourth quarter. The start-up cost and computer conversion expense for GTC was written off in 1980.

Around this same time, plans were implemented for a contemporary 100,000-square-foot distribution center, to be located in Lakeville, a Minneapolis suburb. The new facility was scheduled for completion in the spring of 1981.

"Why Reinvent the Wheel?"

What turned out to be an important key to General Parts Inc.'s success over the years was Temple Sloan's strong drive to constantly improve. One of his favorite expressions was, "Why reinvent the wheel?" For every company merged into GPI, a search was always conducted for those things that the merged company might be doing *better* than GPI. With the GTC merger, GPI discovered that they had an important management position known as "director of finance" that was

Ain't hardly no business

been got around here

what ain't been went out after.

Temple received this inspirational card from an elderly retired salesman who offered it as a simple reminder to salesmen to ask for the order.

held by a key member of the GTC team, Don Annala. An important aspect of Annala's responsibility was working with the company's customer base, and helping the CARQUEST Auto Parts store owners better understand their financial statements and the importance of financial management. It was obvious that financially sound independent stores would lead to a stronger customer base for GPI.

Immediately, GPI created the same position in the Carolinas; and in 1981, two directors of finance were hired to join the corporate staff—Glenn Ellis and Bonner Mills. Finance directors have since played a valuable role in GPI's overall success. For more about GTC's history, see chapter 12.

CARQUEST Goes to the Races

One high-profile aspect of CARQUEST's savvy marketing over the years, along with its very effective public relations posture, was its strong identification with NASCAR (National Association for Stock Car Auto Racing), an increasingly popular attraction not just in the South, where it had been a mainstay activity for years, but also in the Northeast, Midwest, and West.

As part of its overall NASCAR marketing activities, Temple Sloan served as the Grand Marshal for the 1980 CRC NASCAR Darlington (South Carolina) Rebel 500 racing classic. More than 670 CARQUEST and GPI racing fans enjoyed the event along with 60,000 NASCAR fans. The Columbia distribution center's George Montague, operations manager, and Bill Turbeville, sales manager, coordinated CARQUEST's and GPI's participation in the event with help from other GPI operations and sales managers. CARQUEST customer Mike Young, owner of Wholesale Auto Parts in South Boston, Virginia, enjoyed the honor of dropping the green flag to officially start the race.

In 1983, more than 1,100 customers and other friends of CARQUEST and General Parts attended the Darlington event for the seventh straight year. "It's a really nice thing GPI does for us," said "Slick" Gibbons, owner of Clarendon Auto Parts, Manning, South Carolina. "It's nice to meet owners of other CARQUEST Auto Parts stores who share things in common with me."

In the spring of 1984, Joe Hughes, president of IPW, a founding member of CARQUEST, con-

Left: CARQUEST has long enjoyed a close and profitable relationship with NASCAR. This team of CARQUEST employees and representatives played an active role at the 1980 CRC NASCAR Darlington Rebel 500 race classic, held in Darlington County, South Carolina, near the quaintly named Pee Dee River. From left to right: Richard Childress, NASCAR driver; Steve Palmer, GPI Raleigh sales manager; Miss CRC; Don Robinson, GPI Raleigh sales manager; Dennis Fox, GPI Asheville sales manager; and Bill Turbeville, GPI Columbia sales manager.

vinced CARQUEST's board of directors to sponsor Timberwood Racing's entry in the Indianapolis 500 at a cost of $60,000. The CARQUEST driver was Jerry Sneva, brother of Tom Sneva, winner of the previous year's race. On Thursday, May 10th, during a practice run, Sneva crashed into the wall, thus ending CARQUEST's first—and only— entry in the Indianapolis 500 race classic. Still, CARQUEST continued to align itself with NASCAR and other race classics, a highly effective marketing and promotional practice that continues to the present day.

A 20-Year Anniversary

Sales in 1981 increased almost $10 million over 1980. This growth was impressive considering the basic demographics of the aftermarket industry. While the automotive parts aftermarket remained stronger than any other segment of the automotive industry, the average auto parts store was, in effect, a small business, which typically had to borrow from banks in order to maintain adequate inventories. (The industry profit structure did not support interest rates at the unprecedented high levels experienced in 1979 and 1980.) In

CARQUEST's alignment with NASCAR and other motor sports was well received by their customer base.

The Lakeville distribution center, a new 100,000-square-foot facility near Minneapolis, opened in 1981. R.D. Carson (inset) took over operations when it opened.

1980, the prime interest rate hit an all-time high of 21 percent. That, coupled with inflation, necessitated the reduction of the typical auto parts store inventory, so as to maintain liquidity.

The company's capital base, stockholders' equity, and reserves grew appropriately. Also on the plus side, for the second year in a row, no short-term debt remained outstanding at the end of the year. There was improvement in operating earnings while net earnings reflected the total write-off of moving expenses incurred in May 1981 during the relocation from St. Paul to the new Lakeville, Minnesota, distribution center.

The physical challenges of such a move were enormous, yet with 100,000-plus square feet and the new central conveyor system, the Lakeville distribution center was built to deliver maximum efficiency. Distribution was handled through distributor center delivery trucks and contract carriers, providing overnight delivery to CARQUEST Auto Parts stores in the upper Midwest.

1982—A New Year Dawning

In 1982, the financially strong CARQUEST store owners enjoyed another excellent growth year. Still, many owners were victims of the then-unprecedented high inflation and high interest rates. Plus, the unemployment rate in numerous CARQUEST markets was over 20 percent at the time.

GPI's net earnings for 1982 represented the ninth consecutive year of increases. Working capital increased and there was no short-term debt outstanding.

1982 was the first year since 1978 where GPI's operating costs were not impacted by a major facility change. GPI was successful in reducing cost as a percent of sales in every major expense category. The development and improvement of operating systems, with an emphasis on man-hour production and delivery efficiency, were major achievements during the year. The impact of those efforts on costs

O.T. Sloan Sr.
1909–1981

THE UNEXPECTED DEATH OF O.T. Sloan Sr. on February 14, 1981, was a major shock to his sons, Temple Sloan Jr., Hamilton Sloan, and their families, and all those within and outside the company who loved and respected him.

Sloan Sr. was never active in General Parts, Inc. Being a retailer at heart, he was never enthused with the wholesale business; however, for 20 years, he served as chairman of the GPI board of directors. His business experience and leadership skills provided strong guidance, sage advice, and counsel. His respect for people and his down-to-earth wisdom made his advice invaluable. Truly, GPI was a significantly stronger and more successful company as a result of his contribution.

A Tribute to the D.C. and Store Delivery Drivers

THE KEY TO MANAGING A SUCCESSFUL auto parts store is having the right replacement part at the point of repair quicker than the competition. With hundreds of thousands of different replacement parts needed, including the challenge of inventorying and stocking every single one of them, it becomes absolutely necessary for parts stores to rely on regional distribution centers regarding availability.

Also, parts stores must always be sure that their own inventories are specifically tailored to cover the most-needed part numbers. To do this with a reasonable investment, a store must extend the coverage rather than have stocking depth for every stocking part number. To accomplish this, the store must replenish the inventory they sell on a daily basis.

Therefore, buying daily from a well-stocked distribution center allows the individual stores not only the daily replenishment of inventory sold, but also the daily availability of slow-selling, non-stocking part numbers. This is why General Parts, Inc. is committed to daily delivery of parts to all CARQUEST Auto Parts stores, even though it is the most costly of any service offered.

In an effort to get the merchandise to the stores as quickly as possible, the GPI distribution centers (D.C.s) receive daily orders electronically, process them within hours, and deliver those orders that same night.

This is why GPI associates responsible for night delivery from D.C.s to CARQUEST stores are very carefully selected—and are trusted and respected, not only by GPI but by customers as well. Each driver has keys to the stores on his or her route and delivers while the store owners sleep. Drivers are well trained in areas of safety and security, and are resolute in insuring that they make their deliveries on schedule. Indeed, it is rare when inclement weather ever delays a delivery. GPI drivers' dedication, determination, and team spirit are extremely important to customers and GPI. They perform a truly number one service so the job they do cannot be understated.

At the store level, delivery of parts to the individual automotive technicians is equally important. Availability and fast service is expected by service repair centers because their customers insist on having their vehicles repaired quickly. JV (joint venture, i.e., GPI-controlled CARQUEST Auto Parts stores) store drivers are likewise trained in safety and customer service. They are in constant, face-to-face contact with their customers—more than any other store associates—and the worth of the individual stores is measured by their individual actions.

From left to right: A GPI store delivery driver goes over the details of a parts order with a CARQUEST store owner; Raleigh distribution center drivers, circa 1978, from left to right, include Wes Linn, George Nagy, Kert Glover, Don Glover, Neil Harris, Tommy Allen, Larry Webb, and Earl Wiggins; and, armed with keys to the individual stores on their routes, GPI D.C. delivery drivers make nightly deliveries.

Dan Bock retired from CARQUEST in 1996.

was expected to be even greater in 1983.

At the same time, CARQUEST's marketing program continued to mature and provide customers with programs and services necessary to maintain and expand their competitive positions. During 1982, sales to CARQUEST Auto Parts stores represented 95.5 percent of General Parts' total sales.

Additionally, GPI's management team continued to grow in experience and performance, guaranteeing a strong group of young people to lead the company in the years ahead. Total employees at this time numbered 240.

Bock Picked as President of CARQUEST

Nationally, the CARQUEST organization continued to rapidly expand. By the end of 1982, there were 16 member companies serving over 1,700 independently owned CARQUEST Auto Parts stores. Total CARQUEST members' distribution center sales exceeded $400 million for the first time in the history of the program.

In 1982, Dan Bock and his brother Jay made a decision to sell their CARQUEST Distribution Center, Bobro Products Inc., located in the Bronx Borough of New York City, to the Stockel Family who owned White Plains Automotive in White Plains, New York. Ray Stockel and his brother Stanley merged Bobro Products into their company and named the new company BWP Distributors Inc. Ray and Stanley Stockel were blessed with sons—Neil, Irwin, Andy, and Jon— who worked in White Plains and learned the parts business from the ground up. The Stockel sons proved to be extremely capable of managing the new BWP entity.

Bock was immediately hired by the CARQUEST board of directors to be president of CARQUEST. The organization's main office was moved from Memphis, Tennessee, to Tarrytown, New York, where it remained until Bock retired in 1996.

90 Million Older Cars

By the end of 1982, the number of registered vehicles in the United States was 159,509,825, an increase of 0.6 percent over 1981. This was the lowest percentage of registration growth in many years. The annual average growth in the 10 previous years was 3.4 percent. More than 90 million cars in the United States were more than three years old, and their new-vehicle warranties had expired.

Improving Economic Indicators

As the 1980s rolled on, falling inflation rates, interest rates, and fuel costs had a major impact on consumers' spendable income, resulting in past-due, preventive maintenance to be performed by many car owners. Because of the cost of new car ownership, many potential new car buyers continued to operate their older cars.

With the industry projecting a rate of older automobiles being scrapped that was below the rate of new car sales, the future looked bright; plus, car population was expected to grow about 1.5 percent annually. Also, lower fuel prices would result in a continued increase in the number of miles driven annually. Miles driven, of course, has a direct correlation to the wear factor of parts. Only in 1973, 1974, and 1979 had the industry experienced a decrease in miles driven, and that was due to interruption of fuel supply and sharply increased fuel prices. These and related factors led GPI to expect steady market growth for the balance of the 1980s.

Valley Motor Supply—Motor Parts Warehouse

In 1983 General Parts Inc. acquired a majority interest in Valley Motor Supply Company (VMS), located in two Montana towns, Havre and Billings. This acquisition introduced a store management partnership plan to GPI that was later defined as a "joint venture."

This joint venture, or "JV," ownership structure was set up on behalf of company-owned auto parts stores that offer store managers and key associates the opportunity to invest in their individual stores and thus become partners with GPI in store ownership. This JV plan, formalized through GPI's Joint Venture

GPI's First 20 Years

THE FOLLOWING IS BASED ON A WRITE-UP from the 1982 GPEYE Special Edition of GPI's first 20 years of operations:

Most of GPI's employees could recite a synopsis of the historical facts surrounding the founding of GPI. Statistics had a way of becoming very non-personal. The purpose of the *EYE* feature (No. 1, Vol. 4, January 1982) was to take one back in time, allowing the reader to experience the flavor of GPI's beginning as it had been revealed through the experiences of a special group of people, the 20-year employees. These included Temple Sloan, A.C. Burkhead, Robbie Harrison, Mac Graham, Bill Norris, Shorty Britt, and Mary Pope.

Temple Sloan, a 22-year-old native of Sanford, North Carolina, with ambitious goals and enthusiasm for life, didn't sit back and wait for opportunity to knock on his door. His graduation from Duke University signaled the beginning of a successful business venture in the highly competitive field of automotive parts distribution. Lacking experience, but possessing an abundance of perseverance, charisma, and energy, Temple entered the parts business by purchasing a very small warehouse in Sanford, North Carolina.

A.C. Burkhead, another Sanford native, provided the missing ingredient—experience in the parts business. In 1961, A.C. joined Temple and formed the company's purchasing department. In fact, A.C. was the purchasing department.

"I priced and extended every purchase order," A.C. recalled. "That was necessary then to see if we could afford to buy the stock we needed! From day to day, I was scared. I had faith in Temple, but we didn't have any customers."

Shorty Britt and Robbie Harrison were the first GPI salesmen entrusted with the responsibility of seeking out the customers that the struggling company so desperately needed. Together they saturated North Carolina with a GPI sales campaign designed to deliver more than mere promises.

"We beat the bushes and pounded on doors," Shorty remembered, "and soon we were acquiring several new customers a week." Long hours on the road covering thousands of miles paid off. Orders began to trickle in. In the early days, a sparse crew of order pickers, including Temple Sloan and two drivers, ensured prompt delivery. Soon something more precious began coming in—repeat orders.

In need of a warehouse manager, A.C. told Temple about Mac Graham, a young man employed at a Sanford furniture company. Recalling that fateful interview, Mac said, "Temple and A.C. interviewed me on a street corner. I was out of place in the furniture business anyway, so I took the job."

Soon Mac Graham would become an integral part of the new distribution warehouse.

Clockwise from top left: Temple Sloan Jr.; Shorty Britt (standing) and Robbie Harrison; Mac Graham; and Ed Whitehurst.

Temple's next venture was to relocate the young auto parts business from the Sanford area to South Saunders Street in Raleigh, North Carolina. He secured the funds to build a 20,000-square-foot brick warehouse late in 1961. In January 1962, the warehouse officially opened for business under the name General Parts, Inc.

The encouraging spurt of growth required more personnel, and Mac Graham hired Bill Norris as the first warehouseman to work in the new South Saunders Street facility. Bill and Mac vividly remembered the day of the move. "The parking lot was unpaved, it was raining hard, and trucks heavy with automotive parts quickly sank into the mud," said Mac. "Rockwell was next door," recalled Bill. "We borrowed a tractor to pull trucks out of the mud. Then we brought truckloads of slabs to cover the parking lot in order to unload the trucks." Soon the staff was moved in, facing the January cold without heat or light fixtures. Temple, Bill, A.C., and Mac strung lights in the warehouse so orders could be pulled.

Occasionally Bill joked that he wasn't sure if he was a warehouse man or serving time—in his spare moments he became chief landscaper, raker of rocks, and seeder of the lawn.

In the fall of 1962, Mary Pope was working as a bookkeeper for a local Texaco service station. Encouraged by a friend to apply for a position at General Parts, Mary soon found herself doing a little bit of everything. "Temple hired me for bookkeeping and other office duties, putting up stock, and I even did maintenance work including plumbing!" she recalled. The fiery redhead soon earned a reputation as a hard worker, demanding excellence from others, and herself. She quickly learned all that Temple and Mac taught her and became a valuable asset to GPI.

Repeatedly, businessmen would come in to see Temple Sloan, president of GPI. Invariably, A.C. would be mistaken for Temple. "I was the one with the tie," A.C. laughed. "Temple would be in the warehouse with his sleeves rolled up pulling parts. We always had to go look for him."

It was precisely that attitude, sleeves rolled up and working the parts bins, that created the success of General Parts. Temple Sloan never sat in a big office with his feet propped up and removed from his people. Working side-by-side with his employees, learning and managing every aspect of the business, he earned the respect of all within GPI and made General Parts a respected competitor in the aftermarket auto parts sector.

With each passing day, A.C.'s confidence in General Parts grew. "I was so sure we were going to make it that I went into debt to buy a Volkswagen and an organ," A.C. said.

The characteristics of Temple, A.C., Mac, Shorty, Robbie, Bill, and Mary, together with long hours and hard work, nurtured General Parts through its infancy. They worked together like a family. While each was assigned specific areas of responsibility, all joined to complete each task necessary for the business to succeed. "There wasn't one of us who didn't feel like walking out at times," Mac said, "but we stuck it out."

Clockwise from top left: Bill Norris; Temple Sloan Jr. congratulates Robbie Harrison, (seated), and Shorty Britt (right), as they proudly display their Bulova Accutron watches, which were engraved and presented at a company-wide sales meeting in recognition of their many years of significant contributions to General Parts; and A.C. Burkhead (right) and Mary Pope.

The General Idea

WHO CAME UP WITH THE GREAT idea to name the company newsletter *The General Idea*? This was Penny Long, GPI's personnel coordinator in Lakeville, Minnesota. "'*The General Idea*' just came to me one day and it seemed to best fit the purpose of the newsletter," said Long.

Martha Merrill was the first publisher of *The General Idea*, which proved to be a tremendous communications tool for GPI.

Store Division, quickly became key to the growth and success of GPI's own controlled auto parts stores.

VMS consisted of a small distribution center in Havre; a larger distribution center in Billings, 36 auto parts stores in Montana, Wyoming; and northwest South Dakota; and two industrial welding supply companies known as Valley Welders Supply. It was recognized as the dominant auto parts company in the region.

GPI's 1983 annual report reflected the consolidated balance sheets of both companies—GPI and VMS. Only two months' income was included from VMS. The impact of VMS' operations on GPI's 1983 earnings was insignificant, as GPI would have reported approximately the same earnings had the acquisition not occurred.

The next year, a huge step forward for all of the auto parts stores served by VMS was taken with the introduction of J-CON computers. Prior to this introduction, neither VMS company stores nor their independent customers were computerized. Following extensive training, J-CON immediately provided VMS stores with all of the advantages being enjoyed by GPI customers in the Midwest and in the Carolinas. For more about Valley's history, see chapter 12.

TRANSNET

In 1983, GPI began a new, more efficient method of purchasing. Some of its manufacturers had begun using a newer and faster system of handling purchase orders called TRANSNET. The TRANSNET system was developed by manufacturers primarily as a way to cut their costs of time and paperwork in processing orders. With computers communicating back and forth, significant efficiency was added to the entire supply cycle, which resulted in a savings to the manufacturer—and to GPI.

CARQUEST—Pierre South Dakota

In late 1983, another significant event in GPI's history occurred. Sloan received a phone call from Ham Kjelland, owner of Prairie Auto Supply in Pierre, South Dakota. Kjelland was one of the largest CARQUEST independent customers served by GPI's Lakeville, Minnesota, distribution center. Kjelland told Sloan that he had decided to sell his business. He also mentioned that one of GPI's largest competitors had made him an offer.

Sloan's immediate question to Kjelland was, "Have you signed anything?" When it was determined that he had not, Sloan quickly invited himself to Pierre to discuss options; and in particular, ways to prevent losing this valued business. Since GPI negotiations were underway to acquire VMS in Montana, Sloan was familiar with a partnership plan used by VMS involving store managers as shareholders.

Temple Sloan, Ron Wehrenberg, and Don Annala flew to Pierre. Their first plan was to determine whether there was a person working for Kjelland who would be a good candidate to manage the business, and become a partner with GPI. Luckily Kjelland had already selected a key employee, the general manager, as the best person to play this important role. His name was Duane Cromwell—and he became GPI's first JV partner of a CARQUEST Auto Parts store.

In 1994, for health reasons, Cromwell turned over the general manager's responsibility to Clayton Boyle, who was the company's full-time salesman. He continued to work until he retired in 2001. Cromwell's health remained in decline and he died in 2004. Upon his death, GPI lost its first JV partner, a loyal associate, and a good friend.

GPI Scholarships

In keeping with its dedication to education, GPI made a decision in 1983 to begin awarding annual scholarships to the sons and daughters of people in these key categories: CARQUEST Auto Parts storeowners, employees of CARQUEST Auto Parts stores, and professional automotive technicians. Additionally, high school students who were members of Future Farmers of America (FFA) also were eligible. From 1983 through 2005, 494 GPI scholarships were awarded. Years later, in 2003, GPI also established the Founder's Scholarship Program.

"You Make the Difference"

"You Make the Difference," the chosen theme for GPI in 1983, highlighted CARQUEST'S 9th annual marketing meeting, held in February. More than 300 GPI-CARQUEST Auto Parts store owners and their key personnel once again made these annual meetings a memorable success for GPI customers served by the three Carolina distribution centers and the Lakeville, Minnesota, distribution center.

Sloan concluded each meeting with a brief review of the fundamentals needed to develop a situation in which everyone could grow. "Competition will be even greater and the personal commitment each of us makes during this period will determine how we can make the difference, not only in our personal lives but in day-to-day business practices," Sloan commented.

Joe Owen Joins GPI

In December 1982, Ed Whitehurst, GPI's vice president of sales and marketing, informed Sloan that he had decided to retire within the next 12 months. Whitehurst had been the focal point of GPI's strong growth over the years. He was the driving force behind the development of CARQUEST's highly effective marketing program, the conversion of the GPI customer base, and the integration of General Trading's customers into the GPI organization.

Sloan and his brother Ham had not expected Whitehurst to retire at age 58, and they did not have an immediate replacement for him on the GPI team. This made it necessary to go outside of GPI to find a new marketing and sales leader.

Through AWDA, Sloan had developed a friendship with Jack Creamer who possessed a vast knowledge of active aftermarket professionals. Sloan had heard that Joe Owen, a highly respected industry veteran, had left Genuine Parts Company, but he had never met him. Sloan knew that Jack Creamer was friendly with Owen, so he asked

Above: In 1984, the CARQUEST logo was redesigned (right). The original style (left) had been in use since 1973.

Left: Prairie Auto Supply, Pierre, South Dakota, became GPI's first joint venture store in 1983.

Left: Joe Owen joined GPI as senior vice president of sales and marketing.
Below: Logo for CARQUEST Cornerstones, a series of management tips and techniques bulletins for CARQUEST store owners.

Creamer to call him to see if he would come to Raleigh and assist GPI in the search for Ed Whitehurst's replacement. Creamer made the call. Owen then flew to Raleigh to visit with Sloan and his brother.

After two days observing all aspects of General Parts Inc.'s operations, Owen suggested that he, himself, be considered for Whitehurst's replacement. Years later, Owen described those two days.

> I went to Raleigh with a true intent to help Temple find Ed's replacement. However, I was immediately impressed with Temple and Ham and their enthusiasm for the parts business, their work ethic, and their ambition. The longer I stayed, the more I liked what I saw. I knew that I would enjoy being a part of growing GPI and CARQUEST. And, you know what? It's been even more exciting and enjoyable than I thought.

Years later, Sloan remembered his initial meeting with Owen.

> I had heard a lot about Joe Owen from others in the industry, all good. I really knew we could not match the level of income Joe had when he was with GPC, but I thought we had a chance to sell him on a bright future with GPI. It worked, and I believe it was one of my best selling jobs ever.

In October 1983, Joe Owen who spent 31 years with Genuine Parts Company (NAPA), joined General Parts, Inc. as senior vice president of sales and marketing and a corporate director. A brief biography of his 31 years with NAPA is as follows:

> In June 1952, one week after graduating from high school, Joe Owen got a part-time job with the NAPA warehouse in Memphis, Tennessee, while attending Memphis State University. After three years at Memphis State, he received a bachelor's

degree and one year later, in 1956, he received his master's degree.

> After college, Joe became a full-time employee at Genuine Parts Company and throughout his career he held every position of leadership from distribution center general manager to division vice president to group vice president responsible for all GPC's auto parts distribution throughout the United States. In 1968, he was selected as GPC "Man of the Year." In 1974, Joe was appointed to the NAPA board of directors and in 1976 and 1977, served as president of NAPA and chairman of the NAPA board of directors.

Master Installer Rebate Program

In 1984, sales increased 15 percent, but varied significantly by geographical area, mostly reflecting economic conditions. South Carolina and the Midwest turned in the strongest overall sales growth. The western Dakotas and eastern Montana were severely depressed due to an extended drought, which echoed the "Dust Bowl" period of the 1930s. Net income improved 41.5 percent. Operating earnings of all divisions improved during the year, and major project expenses were absorbed into the 1984 operating results.

To assist CARQUEST Auto Parts stores to compete with distribution centers and/or manufacturers who sell direct to auto service centers, GPI designed a program in 1984 known as the Master Installer Rebate Program. The program, which continues to the present day, rebates CARQUEST stores on sales to approved auto service centers. The rebates supplement the store owners' profit margins and allow them to be competitive. The Master Installer program has proven extremely effective in keeping CARQUEST stores competitive.

CARQUEST Cornerstones

In 1984, GPI introduced *CARQUEST Cornerstones*, a series of formalized management tips, in bulletin format, to assist CARQUEST store owners. *Cornerstones* bulletins

included fundamentals of managing an auto parts store in such key areas as sales, marketing, merchandising, advertising, expense control, accounts receivable, computer utilization, security, machine shop operation, inventory control, cash flow, and people management. By the end of 2004, 178 *CARQUEST Cornerstone* bulletins had been released.

Hamilton Sloan Receives AWDA Award

Ham Sloan, executive vice president of General Parts, was named the 1984 recipient of the AWDA Memorial Scholarship Award during the 37th Annual

Ham Sloan was given the 1984 AWDA Memorial Scholarship Award.

Conference of the Automotive Warehouse Distributor Association.

Sloan had been recognized in the past for his betterment of business education for AWDA-sponsored events. He has been highly active in AWDA and served as chairman of the Warehouse Operations Committee, 1981–1984; was a

NOTABLE EVENTS 1980–1984

1980—General Trading Company (GTC) is acquired, the first such acquisition made outside of the Carolinas.

1980—Eleven stores started; the year ended with a total of 291 CARQUEST Auto Parts stores being served by GPI.

1981—New 100,000-square-foot Lakeville, Minnesota, distribution center opens.

1981—In spite of a continuing increase in part numbers required to service the new generation of domestic vehicles, GPI maintained exceptional order-fill rates. During the year, each of the four distribution centers inventoried more than 75,000 different part numbers.

1982—CARQUEST's main office is moved from Memphis, Tennessee, to Tarrytown, New York.

1982—Sixteen member companies were serving more than 1,700 independently owned CARQUEST Auto Parts stores.

1983—A majority interest is acquired in Valley Motor Supply Company (VMS).

1983—Prairie Auto Supply, Pierre, South Dakota, becomes GPI's first JV auto parts store with Duane Cromwell as a joint venture partner.

1983—New more efficient method of purchasing, known as TRANSNET, is implemented at GPI.

1983—The Columbia Distribution Center further expanded its facility with a 14,000-square-foot addition. After the addition, Columbia's storage capacity exceeded 66,000 square feet.

1983—The CARQUEST membership was strengthened with the addition of Fremont Electric Company in Seattle, Washington.

1984—CARQUEST reached a new milestone, supplying more than 2,000 CARQUEST Auto Parts stores nationwide.

1984—Automotive Distributors Inc., Kansas City, Missouri, owned by Dan Myers, joined CARQUEST, bringing the total membership to 16.

TRANSITIONS

1980—Jesse "Shorty" Britt and **Robbie Harrison** both retired. Britt was GPI's very first salesperson and Harrison was the company's third. Britt joined the firm in 1961, Harrison a year later.

A.C. Burkhead, GPI's first employee, retired after 20 years of service managing the GPI purchasing department. Formerly honored during the company's Christmas festivities, A.C. was reminded of his colorful past as Temple paid homage to this dedicated associate and friend.

"In the beginning, A.C. taught me all I knew about the parts business. We've come a long way together," said Temple.

1981—Promotions and new additions: **Hersey Hall** to operations manager, Asheville, North Carolina; **Bill King** joined GPI as manager, human relations; **Joel Mullen** to operations manager, Raleigh, North Carolina; **R.D. Carson,** who had served as operations manager of the Asheville distribution center since 1974, was selected to move to Minnesota and assume responsibilities as vice president of operations for GTC's new distribution center in Lakeville.

As expected, Carson provided the internal leadership that was needed for improving efficiency and service to the CAR-QUEST Auto Parts stores located in the Midwest.

1982—Promotions: **Dennis Fox** named vice president, sales, the Carolinas; **John Gardner** to director of finance, corporate.

1983—New additions: **Tina Davis,** graphics designer, corporate; **Howard Hobbs,** finance director, S. E. Region; and **Rick Cox,** controller, S.E. Region. **Temple Sloan III** graduated from the University of Wyoming and quickly joined GPI in Raleigh to begin his chosen career working in the automotive aftermarket. His first two assignments were in distribution center operations and purchasing.

1983—December marked the retirement of **Ed Whitehurst,** along with **Willie Rushing**—

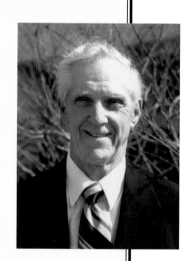

Clockwise from top left: A.C. Burkhead; Temple Sloan, III; Ed Whitehurst; and R.D. Carson.

two associates who had spent the majority of their automotive careers with General Parts Inc. Since 1966, Whitehurst had been instrumental in organizing all of GPI's sales and marketing activities, and in the original formation of the CARQUEST marketing program. In a letter Whitehurst sent to all GPI employees, he mentioned the "tremendous development and growth of the company, its customers and many of the GPI suppliers" that he had witnessed over his 18 years with GPI. Whitehurst planned to stay involved with GPI by participating in future marketing developments and other opportunities. He would also continue as a member of the board of directors and in an advisory position.

In his 20 years with GPI, Willie Rushing, who joined GPI as the company's second salesperson, one year after Shorty Britt, worked in various key capacities, including serving as Columbia's vice president/sales manager from 1973 to 1979. In 1979, Rushing reduced his workload by taking on the role of sales representative. He was instrumental in building up the South Carolina customer base. His hard work and dedication to service served as an example of the commitment that is required to be successful in the automotive aftermarket.

GPI's history will reflect that both Whitehurst and Rushing made numerous contributions to GPI's success. Their unrelenting determination, their hard work,

and their desire to be the best made them true pioneers in GPI's early years of growth and development.

In 1983, **Chuck Douglas** (37) and **Sherman Haagen-sted** (30) also retired.

1983—Jesse D. "Shorty" Britt, GPI's first sales representative, died on October 10, 1983. He brought many innovations and meant much to GPI. He has been fondly remembered as a co-worker, a teacher, a salesman, and most importantly, a friend. "In his own way, Shorty was a pioneer. He made the hard decision to join GPI when it was not the thing to do," said Sloan. "There was no security, no experience, no history and no customer base. There was just a belief that service, honesty, dedication, sincerity, and hard work could build a company and develop a dream."

1984—Promotions for the year: **Bill Ball** to regional manager, Valley Motor Supply Co. (VMS); **Allen Dedman** to controller, VMS; **Tony Dyba** to regional manager, VMS.; **Jim Hall** to vice president, purchasing, VMS.; **Dennis Peterson** to vice president, operations, VMS; **Chuck Romee** to president, VMS; **Searl Stroup** to vice president, VMS; **Roger Troutman** to president, Valley Welders Supply Inc. Also in 1984, **Chuck Keene** retired with 38 years of service.

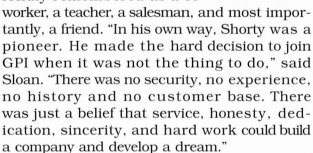

Clockwise from above left: Willie Rushing; Jesse D. "Shorty" Britt; Allen Dedman; and Chuck Romee. *(Chuck Romee photo courtesy of Cetrone Studio.)*

The Asheville distribution center underwent a full modernization of all offices in 1984.

member of the board of governors, 1982–1984; served as the 1985 AWDA secretary; and chaired the AWDA Education Committee in 1985.

Facility Upgrades

In keeping with a determination to stay ahead of the curve in upgrading facilities to assure a high level of customer service, several projects were completed in 1984. In Montana, the Havre distribution center was closed. All VMS customers would be serviced from the 74,000-square-foot Billings, Montana, distribution center. To accommodate this closing, major expansion and remodeling of the Billings Distribution Center was introduced. This included a 4,000-square-foot office addition, 12,000 square feet of additional mezzanine, 1,000 new storage bins, expanded bulk capacity, and development of a new fully automatic sort station and staging system. VMS' general offices were moved from Havre to Billings.

Additionally, plans were finalized at the Asheville distribution center for a 5,700-square-foot expansion of the mezzanine, with completion expected during the first half of 1985. A complete remodeling of the offices was also completed during 1984. Facility upgrades were directed by Ham Sloan, assisted by Mac Graham.

CARQUEST Owner Conferences

In mid-1984, Joe Owen introduced a new management program: CARQUEST owner conferences, which were held in all of GPI's markets. Those conferences provided an opportunity for the managers of each auto parts store to meet with management from their individual GPI distribution centers to discuss problems and develop solutions for everyone's benefit. The conferences, scheduled throughout the fall and winter in locations convenient to auto parts stores within a 40-50 mile radius, were well received by GPI's CARQUEST store owners. Indeed, these owner conferences became annual events for each GPI distribution center management team. Eventually, they were considered so valuable that no excuses were accepted for failure to hold these important meetings.

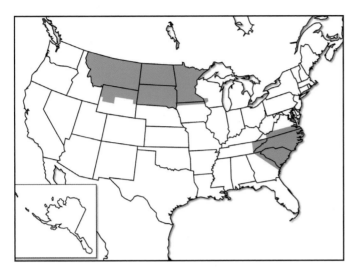

GPI's marketing area in 1984.

CARQUEST's 10th Anniversary Marketing Conference

The year 1984 marked CARQUEST's 10th anniversary. All GPI/CARQUEST customers were invited to attend the 10th anniversary CARQUEST marketing conference which was held in Myrtle Beach, South Carolina, in March. The conference showcased CARQUEST's 1984 marketing plan, as well as the effectiveness of various advertising media. CARQUEST's 1984 television, radio, and outdoor billboard advertising was spotlighted during the conference. Customers were also able to visit display booths set up by GPI's manufacturer suppliers. Ronnie James, a co-owner of J & J Auto Parts Stores in western North Carolina, spoke to some 650 fellow representatives and GPI personnel. "What CARQUEST means to me" was his topic. "[The] program was designed to be as exciting as it was informative," explained Martha Merrill, GPI's advertising/promotion director.

Annual Sales Conference in Billings

In 1984, a major presentation outlining the overall CARQUEST program was the highlight of the annual sales conference, held in Billings, Montana in February. The presentation was delivered by GPI President O. Temple Sloan Jr., GPI Senior Vice President–Sales and Marketing Joe

Owen, and CARQUEST Corporation President Dan Bock. Other conference presentations spotlighted CARQUEST's history and the functions of the CARQUEST corporate office. CARQUEST's advertising program was presented by Louis Pitluk, president of The Pitluk Group, CARQUEST's advertising agency.

It was also in 1984 that CARQUEST formed the Dealer Committee which was later renamed the Professional Markets Committee. This committee was instrumental in changing the name of those who serviced vehicles from "mechanics" to "technicians," and helping to unify the CARQUEST membership into a focused marketing direction, with the professional auto service technician as the prime customer. That direction has not changed over the years.

Beneficial Factors Positively Impact the Aftermarket Industry

During 1984, miles driven in America increased nearly 4.5 percent, a rate of growth not seen since the 1960s. This had a positive effect on the aftermarket business. Another major influence was a decrease in fuel cost by over $.08 per gallon. Total vehicle population also continued to grow, to 169 million. By 1984, there were more than 137 million vehicles on America's roads, with 81 percent of these more than three years old, representing the prime automotive replacement parts market.

Imports continued to be a growing factor in the aftermarket, representing 17 percent of the passenger car and light truck market. Japanese vehicles, which comprised 76 percent of the import total, had an average age of five years. All those factors, coupled with an improving economy, lower interest rates, and lower inflation, would result in continued growth opportunities for GPI for years to come.

During the period 1980–1984, GPI's sales increased 224 percent and earnings increased 246 percent.

SOME OF THE MANY WHO HELPED

Hersey Hall

Tim Pfeifer

Danny
Durham

Judy Miller

Hilton
Winders

Mike Hedge

Dee Stoll

Arnold
Jenkins

Paul Holliday

Mike Norris

Carolyn
Peebles

Ron Girard

Ruth Sawyer

Bonner Mills

Ken Oliver

Mike Jamison

Jody Joy

Marie Dodd

Dennis
Massey

Dick
Wehrenberg

Phil Corbin

Roger
Hastings

Gary
Knewtson

Donna
Southern

Harriet
Camak

Grady Dunn

Rachel Stroud

Tom Hubal

Bill Carter

Don Robinson

Gerhart Just

Jo Ann
Pleasant

Mike Mills

David
McCollum

Dave Wibben

Joe Kappel

Bill Turbeville

Ed McIntosh

Myers
Pendergraft

Russ Kelly

Jim Cochran

Don Grover

Carter Smith

Sam Glover

George
Montague

Faye O'Daniel

Joel Mullen

John Brian

CARQUEST understands that its loyal, long-term associates are a competitive strength. All are challenged to realize their full potential, and all are guided by a core purpose: "To be a positive influence on the lives we touch, while proudly serving a world in motion." It's the CARQUEST Way.

CHAPTER SIX

DRAMATIC INCREASES IN SALES

1985–1989

We decided to contact the only person in America to whom we would even consider selling our company ... the founder of CARQUEST and president of General Parts Inc., Temple Sloan.

—Sam Rogers and Bob Rogers, owners of
Parts Warehouse Company (PWC)

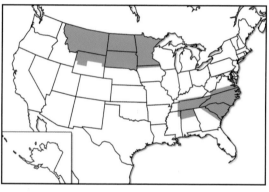

IN 1985, THE U.S. AUTO-motive parts aftermarket failed to show any growth, impacted by a decline in the number of vehicles in the three- to 10-year age group, due to low new car and truck sales during the early 1980s. Growth was further affected in the Midwest and Northwest by serious agricultural problems, the most severe drought in 50 years, and a slow down in energy, mining, and timber activity. However, the introduction and reinforcement of strong marketing programs was instrumental in keeping GPI's customers growing and profitable. Sales for the year increased a healthy 6 percent.

For the first time, however, net earnings were down, 11 percent from 1984. This was due to the fact that financial reporting was presented in a new format from previous years. Since the acquisition of Valley Motor Supply Company (VMS) in 1983, a substantial portion of GPI equity had been stated as minority interest. General Parts was dedicated to employee participation in equity ownership of the VMS operating companies. To further emphasize the common interest of the investors, GPI utilized a format that combined the traditional stockholders' equity and minority interest into investors' equity. These new accounting procedures negatively affected GPI's bottom line.

GPI Acquires CARQUEST Member in Nashville

All the stock of S & S Parts Distributions Warehouse Inc., located in Nashville, was acquired by GPI on September 1, 1985. S & S Parts Distributions Warehouse had a strong history. Parts Distributors Warehouse (PDW) of Memphis was formed in 1955 by William Loewenberg. PDW purchased S & S Sales Company, Nashville, in September 1960. In 1981, Bert Berry and Richard Murchison, long time PDW and S & S employees, purchased the company. S & S had been a CARQUEST member since 1976. For more about S & S' history, see chapter 12.

An Important Restructuring

When General Parts acquired General Trading Company (GTC) in 1980, the acquisition continued to operate under the General Trading Company name. In late 1983, when General Parts became the majority stockholder in Valley Motor Supply (VMS), it continued to operate under the Valley name and also that of Motor Parts Warehouse, a Division of

GPI's marketing area in 1985.

Valley Motor Supply Company. In early 1985, in an attempt to simplify the structure of GPI, management decided to create company divisions and rename some of the operations.

General Parts Inc. would officially continue to be the primary corporate entity, and its headquarters would remain in Raleigh, North Carolina. Additionally, there would be three separate automotive divisions. The Southeast Division, headquartered in Raleigh, consisted of CARQUEST distribution centers in Raleigh and Asheville, North Carolina, and in Columbia, South Carolina. Dennis Fox was appointed president of the Southeast Division.

The Midwest Division consisted of the CARQUEST distribution center located in Lakeville, Minnesota. Ron Wehrenberg was appointed president of the Midwest Division. Wehrenberg's team included Ron Anderson, sales manager, Terry Langhorst, controller, and Don Annala, director for finance.

The Northwest Division was headquartered in Billings, Montana, and consisted of the CARQUEST distribution center in Billings, a sizable number of auto parts stores in Montana, Wyoming, and South Dakota, and a welding supply company. The auto parts stores continued to do business as CARQUEST Valley Motor Supply Company and the welding supply company operated as Valley Welder's Supply Inc. Chuck Romee was appointed president of the Northwest Division as well as president of Valley Motor Supply Company. Allen Dedman served as controller.

Purchasing and personnel management for General Parts Inc. were located at corporate headquarters in Raleigh with Ken West directing purchasing and Bill King directing personnel. With several years of experience in parts warehouse operations, Mike Hollingsworth assumed the position of operations manager for GPI's largest distribution center.

Corporate Office Addition Near Completion

The completion date for the new addition to the GPI headquarters building in Raleigh was projected for the early fall 1985. The 2,000-square-foot structure would house the corporate offices, with additional space provided for the Southeast Division and for an audiovisual studio.

Security Department Formed at GPI

In February 1985, GPI formed a Security Department, with Dick Goldberg as director. "My primary responsibility will be to develop and maintain a loss prevention and safety program to protect the company's assets," said Goldberg, a former Federal Bureau of Investigations professional.

In my 23 years with the FBI, I dealt with individuals from all walks of life: college presidents to presidents and executives of large corporations. But never did I see leaders or executives who were more caring and supportive of their people than the management of GPI.

Security at GPI became increasingly important with the growth of the company, especially regarding JV store growth. During his tenure, Goldberg set impressive new standards for GPI security.

More than 2,200 CARQUEST Auto Parts Stores

Nationally, more than 2,200 CARQUEST Auto Parts stores made up the CARQUEST team during this period. Three new parts distribution companies joined the CARQUEST organization in 1985, bringing the total membership of this type of firm to 19. New members were Muffler Warehouse Inc. in Pocatello, Idaho, owned by the Albano family—Keith, John, and Bill; Service Parts Warehouse Corporation in Albany, Georgia, owned by Paul Keenan; and World Supply Corporation, Lemont, Illinois, owned by Ben Roscrow. Additionally, Chanslor and Lyon, one of the oldest CARQUEST members, was acquired by Cardis.

President's Club Rings

In 1985, GPI added an extra incentive for achieving President's Club status by awarding a new President's Club ring to those who were recognized as President's Club winners for two consecutive years. Once a ring was awarded, a diamond was inserted for each year that the President's Club was achieved thereafter.

Joe Owen assured Temple Sloan Jr. not to worry about the added expense because he felt that few rings would likely be awarded due to the difficulty of earning President's Club status during two consecutive years. But Owen was proved wrong concerning the number of rings that eventually would be earned. He underestimated the extra incentive that wearing the GPI ring would create among GPI associates.

Sloan always enjoyed reminding Owen of his "low-cost" ring and diamond incentive enhancement plan.

Still, both men liked to see GPI associates successfully achieve their goals and develop pride in wearing their President's Club rings. From 1985 through 2005, GPI has awarded 579 rings and 644 diamonds.

A Special Thanks to Carol Sloan

One of the primary reasons that the President's Club continued year after year to be a successful incentive plan for GPI was because of the high quality of travel incentives that were made available for winners and their spouses. A special expression of gratitude is due Carol Sloan for her dedication and hard work for well over 20 years in making these four-day trips always superb incentive attractions.

The JV Concept

By the mid-1980s, it was becoming clear that growth opportunities for GPI would depend, in large part, on the company's ability to acquire and profitably manage auto parts stores. With two years experience in Montana observing and fine-tuning the VMS JV (joint venture) concept,

Above: In 1985, GPI began awarding handsome President's Club rings to associates who had been recognized as President's Club awardees for two consecutive years. Single diamonds were added to rings for winners for each year thereafter.

From far left to right: Dennis Fox; Ron Wehrenberg, Ken West, Bill King, Mike Hollingsworth, and Dick Goldberg.

GPI's management was convinced that this ownership approach was sure to become an important part of the company's future.

It was clear that the success of the GPI joint venture program would require a strong management structure, supported by experienced store people. Also, GPI's top management would need to possess a comprehensive understanding of store management. A step in this direction was taken in 1985 when Temple Sloan III was sent to Montana to spend over a year working in the GPI CARQUEST-Valley store in Bozeman. This experience would serve him—and more importantly, GPI—well in the years to come.

1986—and Sales up 54 Percent!

In 1986, sales at General Parts took a huge leap forward—a whopping 54 percent increase! Investors' equity grew, driven by strong earnings and newly invested capital. Associates made substantial investments of new capital in the operating units, illustrating the dedication of the associates to equity participation.

Parts Distributors Warehouse Joins GPI

On April 1, 1986, GPI announced the merger of Parts Distributors Warehouse (PDW) into General Parts, Inc. PDW located in Memphis, Tennessee, was owned by Bobby Webb and Herman Markell. It had been a CARQUEST member since 1976.

Markell remained as president of PDW. Webb retired at the time of the merger. Webb's brother, David, stayed on as vice president of sales. For more about PDW's history, see chapter 12.

Parts Warehouse Company Joins GPI

Three months later, GPI again was blessed with an opportunity to expand the company by merging with one of the premier existing CARQUEST members, Parts Warehouse Company (PWC), located in two Michigan cities: Bay City and Lansing. PWC was owned by Sam Rogers and his nephew, Bob Rogers. Sam Rogers stayed on as chairman and remained active in the business. Elected to GPI's board of directors, Bob Rogers was able to share his expertise on special projects. The two Rogers men made it clear

they were not interested in any other company but GPI taking over their operation.

We decided to contact the only person in America to whom we would even consider selling our company ... the founder of CARQUEST and president of General Parts, Inc., Temple Sloan.

"Sam Rogers and Bob Rogers will forever be remembered for recognizing and developing talented people," said Sloan. Heading a long list of former PWC associates now holding or who have held important positions within GPI are Wayne Lavrack, Fred Kotcher, Rick Guirlinger, Scott Ginsburg, Ken Karber, Dave Pruden, Danny Haag, Mike Najdowski, Andy Kennell, Peter Hafford, Norm Ferguson, and Tom Ferguson. For more about PWC's history, see chapter 12.

In December 1986, Motor Services Inc., of Glendive, Montana, also was acquired. Motor Services Inc. was an established and successful eight-store jobbing chain located in Eastern Montana and North Dakota. Four stores were merged with existing Valley Stores, while four represented new markets for the Valley group.

Maintaining Company Infrastructure

While focused on steady acquisitions, General Parts, Inc. remained committed to the expansion and upgrading of its various facilities. Such work had taken place at the Memphis and Bay City distribution centers. Indeed, with the exception of Nashville, where a new distribution center was being planned, all distribution centers were highly modern, conveyorized, and efficient. Additionally, during this period, a scheduled plan to modernize all JV CARQUEST Auto Parts stores was introduced.

Continued CARQUEST Growth—
But Overall Market Growth Slows

By the end of 1986, there were a total of 2,263 CARQUEST Auto Parts stores served by 18 different CARQUEST distribution companies. Automotive Warehouse Inc (AWI) of Honolulu joined the CARQUEST program during 1986. Ken Kaminaka, CEO of AWI, joined the CARQUEST board of directors.

In 1986, GPI merged with Parts Warehouse Company, a Michigan firm owned by Sam Rogers (left) and his nephew, Bob Rogers.

The independent automotive replacement parts market had shown no real growth for more than two years. This was due to there being fewer vehicles in the three-to-10-year age group on the road. The drop in the prime repair-age vehicle population resulted from lower than normal new car and light truck sales during 1980, 1981, and 1982. Industry data showed that 81 percent of the service market originated from vehicles that were over two years old. This illustrated the major impact of the drop in prime repair-age vehicles.

Despite these short-range indicators, however, the long-range outlook for the industry appeared promising. One indicator: the prime repair age vehicle population began to grow during 1987. Plus, America's total vehicle population experienced

BEING BIG IS OK—BUT BEING *BEST* IS BETTER

IN THE SEPTEMBER 1986 EDITION OF *THE General Idea*, the following message was delivered to GPI associates.

"My big brother just got bigger," was the explanation used by one of the better CARQUEST Auto Parts store owners in Michigan to describe the recent merger between General Parts and Parts Warehouse Company of Bay City, Michigan.

"Bigger, indeed. The three acquisitions of GPI since September 1, 1985, have almost doubled the size of our company. We have been very fortunate to join hands with three distinct companies with which GPI shared a lot in common. Each were well managed and respected companies within our industry. Each were CARQUEST members with identical marketing philosophies. Each had a good solid base of loyal CARQUEST Auto Parts stores. Each used the same computer system as GPI; and most importantly, each were wealthy with good, dedicated people.

"Yes, we are fortunate at GPI to grow under such favorable conditions. But let's be warned that being big does not necessarily guarantee success. There are numerous big companies within our industry which have failed. All it takes to be big is to buy other companies. All that's needed to buy other companies is money. And there are an unlimited number of sources for borrowing money.

"So being big is not difficult. But dedicated people make companies successful. People who enjoy being a part of a winning team. People who get personal satisfaction from doing their best. People who realize that service is the only thing that separates us from our competition. People who realize that our CARQUEST Auto Parts stores pay our salaries and keep us in business. These are the type of people we discovered at Nashville, Memphis, and in Michigan; and this is what convinced us that these mergers were right."

strong growth during 1986—the third consecutive year. Also, miles driven continued to increase due to lower fuel costs.

Overall, General Parts' strong sales performance throughout its various markets illustrated the aggressive and competitive position of GPI and CARQUEST Auto Parts stores.

1987

In 1987, growth and consolidation were in order for the company as recent major acquisitions were successfully merged into GPI's operating and marketing programs. Consolidated sales established new records with an increase of 25.1 percent.

Every GPI division enjoyed sales increases, and the Central, Midwest, Michigan, and Southeast Divisions all set new sales records. Those achievements were made in spite of a decision to eliminate $4 million in sales to accounts in Michigan and Tennessee that did not fit GPI's long-term marketing objectives. Growth rates far exceeded the industry average and resulted in substantial improvement in market share.

During this year, there were 230 GPI associates with equity positions. Net income as a percent of beginning investors' equity was 15.6 percent.

Technician's Advisory Council

In 1987, GPI undertook an important marketing step to focus on the primary customer of the CARQUEST Auto Parts stores—the professional auto service technician. To better understand the true needs of this important target customer, GPI instituted a Technician's Advisory Council consisting of carefully selected and highly successful auto service shop owners. Annual two-day council meetings were scheduled to be held with the goal that CARQUEST Auto Parts stores would become better suppliers by having a more complete understanding of technicians' needs. Annual meetings would serve as constant reminders to the auto service segment that "CARQUEST listens."

Later, the entire CARQUEST membership adopted this plan. This was developed into a national program in which annual awards would be given to the most outstanding auto service businesses. These awards are known as the "Excellence Awards."

Store Inventory Management Improved

With the population of automotive vehicles exploding due to new energy-efficient domestic vehicles and the growing number of import models, managing inventories at the store level became more important than ever. To address this issue, GPI developed plans to improve inventory management at the individual store level. Computer programs provided a means to improve accuracy in part-number classification.

Two systems were introduced to implement store inventory classification and management at the individual store level. A "Base Inventory Profile" (BIP) was developed as the primary blueprint of a store's stocking plan, with all parts listed by part number based on that particular store's needs. The blueprint would serve as an invaluable guide for annual store inventory control. It would also serve as a guide to implement another new plan known as "Automatic New Number" (ANN). With this plan in place, a store's inventory was automatically updated with new part numbers as they became available throughout the year from manufacturers.

General Parts, Inc. Marks 25th Anniversary

"GPI's success in a rapidly changing technical marketplace is directly dependent upon our dedicated people," said Temple Sloan Jr., upon the occasion of General Parts' 25th anniversary in 1987. "They have already made General Parts one of the top 10 [firms] in the business, and it is because these people continuously challenge the 'status quo' that makes General Parts what it is today and will be tomorrow."

An Orlando Getaway

CARQUEST Auto Parts stores from GPI's 21-state marketing areas gathered in Orlando, Florida, from October 15 through 18, 1987, at the Stouffer Orlando Resort, for GPI's first company-wide business management seminar.

Almost 300 people from around the country attended such events as the "1950's Party," com-

MEMORABLE AIRPLANE CRASH

BY JOE OWEN

ONE OF THE MOST UNFORGETTABLE moments occurred in Miles City, Montana, on January 7, 1987. Temple and I were negotiating the purchase of several parts stores in eastern Montana.

The owner of the stores along with myself, Temple, Jim Russell, general manager of our recently acquired Valley Motor Supply Company in Montana and Wyoming, and Bill Ball, one of our regional store managers, leased an Aero Commander two-engine airplane in Billings. It was a quick way to visit all store locations. Little did we think about the risk of having only one pilot until later.

As we approached our first stop, Miles City, there was fog with about a 400-foot ceiling. Landing in Miles City is not electronically assisted and good visibility was important. The pilot of our leased Aero Commander took an unnecessary risk to land under these conditions. As we broke through the 400-foot ceiling,

we discovered that we were misaligned with the runway. The logical thing to do was to make another attempt.

The pilot shoved the throttle forward and the plane's engines stalled. We fell approximately 400 feet but in a semi-glide. We were fortunate that the ground was a frozen wheat field. As we hit, the left landing gear was torn off rather than digging into softer ground, which would likely have flipped the plane. Instead, the frozen ground caused a series of ground loops for 200 to 300 yards before coming to a stop. The plane was totaled due to undercarriage and landing gear damage.

Thankfully, none of us was seriously injured. Bill Ball promised God that he would never fly again as he subsequently walked in a circle with a 12-foot diameter, 30 feet from the crash. Needless to say, we had some trouble getting Bill to board another plane the next day. That was the last time either Temple or I have boarded a plane with only one pilot.

Temple Sloan, Joe Owen, Jim Russell, general manager of Valley Motor Supply Company, and Bill Ball, CARQUEST regional store manager, were passengers on a business trip when this Aero Commander twin-engine plane crash landed in Miles City, Montana.

THE MOST IMPORTANT CARQUEST MEETING EVER HELD

BY JOE OWEN

THE CARQUEST PROGRAM ORIGINATED IN 1973. The key elements involved distribution through only CARQUEST Auto Parts stores and selling only the proprietary CARQUEST-branded products.

The first priority was to build a membership consisting of the best distribution companies that could be assembled, each with a primary marketing area that would not overlap with another CARQUEST member. This was not an easy task and the original pioneers spent the first 10 years collecting quality members who agreed with the concept.

During this period, General Parts also worked to eliminate all line accounts in order to be ready for the next step—our CARQUEST brand of products. Not every member worked diligently in that direction, however, and in the mid-1980s, most of the 18 CARQUEST companies still had a sizable percentage of their sales volume in business to non-CARQUEST accounts.

A band-aid approach was agreed to in 1981. The idea was to develop an alternative brand name that was proprietary to CARQUEST but could be sold to both CARQUEST and non-CARQUEST line accounts. This move bought some time for some of the members to eliminate their line account business. The name chosen for this new line was

Proven Valu. Only miscellaneous lines—for example, hose clamps, gas and oil caps, thermostats, and so on—were introduced in Proven Valu. But GPI/CARQUEST Auto Parts stores were impatient with this approach, and wanted CARQUEST to move on and develop its own identity with CARQUEST-branded products.

In early 1987, GPI lost a CARQUEST Auto Parts store to a competitor. Temple and I visited the auto parts store to determine why the owner had made a decision to change. He told us he was tired of waiting for us to provide CARQUEST-branded product lines. He wanted his own identity. He didn't want to be just another auto parts store in his market with a combination of different factory brands. How could we argue? We firmly agreed with his logic.

During our plane ride back to Raleigh that evening, Temple and I agreed that we couldn't continue without a CARQUEST plan to move forward to the next marketing level. The next day we requested Dan Bock, president of CARQUEST Corporation, to assemble an ad hoc committee consisting of several but not all owners of CARQUEST member companies to discuss this important issue.

The meeting was quickly arranged and held at the Marriott Southeast Hotel in Denver, Colorado,

plete with a life-size façade of Arnold's Diner, '50s music, photographs, and a dinner. The Friday morning business management seminar featured remarks by Temple Sloan Jr., Joe Owen, Scott Ginsburg, and motivational speaker Jerry Wilson. Roger Miller, CARQUEST spokesperson and popular celebrity and singer, entertained the guests and volunteered for photos.

Fochtman Stores Acquired

In the fall of 1987, in an unusual transaction that took place in the northern part of the lower peninsula of Michigan, the Fochtman family—36 individual family member shareholders—agreed to sell their 11-store chain, which had borne the family name for over 40

on May 6, 7 and 8. Those invited were Dan Bock, president of CARQUEST; Neil Stockel, BWP-New York; Pete Kornafel, Hatch-Denver; Seymour Hesch, Avro-Buffalo; Ken Johnsrud, Cardis-California; David Straus and Roger Pritt, Strafco-Texas; Joe Hughes, IPW-Indiana; and of course, Temple Sloan Jr. and Joe Owen, both of GPI. All were advised to come prepared to discuss the future of CARQUEST and plan to stay as long as necessary.

The meeting lasted a full three days (and three nights). During this time, a clear direction was agreed on regarding the marketing future of CAR-QUEST. This included a mission statement, a target date for all members to eliminate non-CAR-QUEST business, and a calendar for converting every major product line to CARQUEST-branded products with first, second, and third options as to the selected manufacturer.

A regular quarterly meeting had already been scheduled to take place about a month later in Colorado Springs, Colorado. It was decided that the entire Colorado meeting would be devoted to presenting the new plan to those CARQUEST members who did not attend the meeting at the Denver Marriott.

This plan, which was carried forward in Colorado Springs following a CARQUEST board meeting, was unanimously adopted by all members present.

The mission statement drafted for CARQUEST approval by ad hoc committee:

- Establish CARQUEST Auto Parts stores as the most recognizable supplier of quality products and services to the aftermarket nationwide.
- Make a total commitment to provide the most complete service, supply, and mar-

keting programs to enable CARQUEST jobbers to effectively compete on a profitable basis.
- Each CARQUEST distributor pledges to commit its total marketing efforts and direction to achieve 100 percent distribution through CARQUEST jobbers and support CARQUEST programs and products in a unified fashion.
- Move with practical speed toward CARQUEST- branded product lines.

The calendar for product line conversions was followed to the letter and completed as scheduled. Among application lines, only engine parts and spark plugs were left off the list for CARQUEST-branded products.

Without a doubt, the 1987 three-day, three-night meeting at the Marriott in Denver will be remembered as the most important CARQUEST meeting ever held.

Of course, the easy part was completed during the meeting. The tough part fell immediately on the shoulders of Dan Bock, and his well-trained, hard-working office staff, including Tom Kirby, Mike Leach, Dan O'Connell, and Tom Easton. These experienced staffers worked closely with various CARQUEST committees and with Dan Bock's leadership, the mission statement became reality—and on schedule.

In 1988, the most significant marketing news of the year was a move toward the new CARQUEST-branded product lines. CARQUEST windshield wipers, on the design drawing board a year prior, were introduced in 1988 and achieved record sales results. Wiper products were supplied by Trico, the leading original equipment manufacturer.

years, and to dissolve the family-owned warehouse. For more about Fochtman's history, see chapter 12.

Growth Cycles

During 1987, GPI believed that the automotive parts aftermarket would be returning to a

growth cycle during the next four to five years. The total vehicle population continued to grow around 2 percent per year and miles driven were up 4 percent in 1987. The three- to 11-year-old vehicle population returned to an upward trend in 1987; the five- to nine-year-old group demonstrated that there would be a strong growth trend during 1988.

1988

Another outstanding year for GPI was 1988, with sales increasing 19.2 percent from the previous year. Each operating division enjoyed significant sales increases. Intentional elimination of stores and sales volume that did not meet long-term marketing objectives continued, with $2.8 million being trimmed from sales as a result.

Inflation during the year was around 3.5 percent. The vast amount of sales growth resulted from an increase in unit sales as GPI continued to improve its market share—an outstanding achievement in a mature market. In this regard, company sales more than doubled industry sales for the same period. The increase represented the 26th consecutive year of sales increases—*every single year since the company's inception*. The year 1988 was also another record profit year for GPI.

General Parts, at year-end, had 293 associates holding equity positions in GPI and related companies. Net income as a percent to beginning investors' equity was 17.1 percent.

Also, operating efficiencies continued to improve in the distribution centers and joint venture stores, making a major contribution to the company's increased earnings. GPI's management well understood what side its bread was buttered on and continued to emphasize training at all distribution levels, a major company objective.

Kentucky Jobbers Supply
Joins General Parts/CARQUEST Family

GPI's strong push to acquire respected companies continued unabated. In this regard, negotiations for the purchase of Kentucky Jobbers Supply (KJS), based in Lexington, Kentucky, were completed on March 28, 1988. This brought to 12 the number of distribution centers within the General Parts organization. The purchase of KJS also brought 34 company stores and 25 indepen-

GPI's distribution center delivery fleet plays an important role with nightly deliveries to all CARQUEST auto parts stores. This service enables CARQUEST to get the right part to the point of installation quickly.

HAM SLOAN'S AWDA LEADERSHIP APPRECIATED

HAMILTON SLOAN WAS PRESENTED a plaque of appreciation from the Automotive Warehouse Distributors Association (AWDA) at the group's annual convention in Las Vegas in November 1988. Ham served the association as chairman in 1988. David O'Reilly, incoming chairman for 1989, made the presentation.

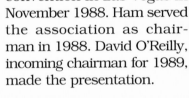

dent jobbers into the GPI organization. For more about KJS' history, see chapter 12.

CARQUEST TECH-NET

Formed in early 1984, the CARQUEST Dealer Committee was concerned about the growing number of new generation domestic vehicles since 1980. These were equipped with onboard electronics to increase fuel efficiency and produce cleaner exhaust, both mandated by the government following the 1974 energy crisis. To service these vehicles, independent auto service technicians would need to develop electronic skills to match their mechanical skills. This would mean extensive training and assistance.

The committee discovered that Automotive Data Systems Inc., a fledgling company in Huntington Beach, California, founded by an automotive veteran, Leith Tecklenburg, could be of major assistance in this area. Tecklenburg's concept was to collect and store technical service information in a computer and then sell the information by subscription. He staffed his company with highly trained automotive technicians who would be able to communicate with subscribers by phone, assisting them with complicated auto service problems.

Two CARQUEST dealer committee members, Joe Owen, committee chairman, and Neil Stockel, president of CARQUEST member BWP in New York, met with Tecklenburg to develop the CARQUEST TECH-NET program. The plan became an instant success when it was introduced to all CARQUEST Auto Parts stores. During the first three months of operations, more than 1,400 auto service shops enrolled in the new program.

In 1988, GPI placed its first long-term debt with a group of insurance companies. It enhanced the balance sheet, positioning the company to pursue the growth that was to follow.

Joint Venture Store Participation Up

Continued growth and development of the Joint Venture store plan was a critical part of GPI's

Far left: The TECH-NET staff of 12 highly trained automotive technicians utilized a massive computer database of diagnostic information by vehicle year, make, and model. This information was used to assist hundreds of professional automotive service technicians who subscribed to this service through their CARQUEST auto parts store.

Left: Leith Tecklenburg.

long-term plan for the 1990s. Participation in joint venture stores was increased to 160 by the end of 1988, up from 112 at the end of 1987. In each division, store management structure along the joint venture model was already in place. Further, joint venture operating procedures had been developed for the future.

The joint venture plan included computerization of all stores, development of a company-wide billing schedule and a computerized inventory management system, which permitted automatic inventory update and adjustment. In addition, training offered to management and sales teams was intensified. And the result? GPI's objective of developing an outside sales program in every joint venture store was achieved by the end of the year.

The markets where most of the 160 GPI JV stores were concentrated were Montana, Wyoming, Michigan, and Kentucky. Mike Hedge was responsible for the JV store in Montana and Wyoming. Wayne Lavrack was responsible for the Michigan JV

stores. Russell Huffman was responsible for the JV stores in Kentucky.

CARQUEST
Distribution Membership
On the Increase

Nationally, the CARQUEST Distribution Membership increased with the addition of Parts Wholesalers, Inc. in Bangor, Maine. John Darling, owner,

---

GPI's corporate management staff in the late 1980s. Shown left to right are Hamilton Sloan, vice chairman; John Gardner, treasurer; Joe Owen, president; Temple Sloan Jr., chairman and CEO, and Mac Graham, secretary.

Opposite: CARQUEST promoted its new TECH-NET service with this print advertisement that ran in various trade publications when the service was instituted.

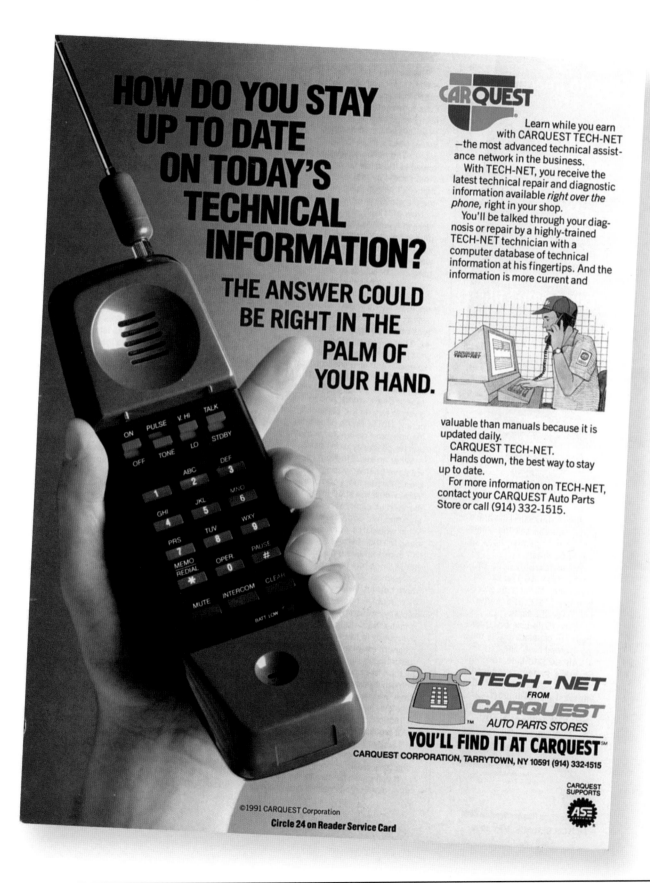

Right: GPI's distribution center located in Jackson, Mississippi.

Below left to right: Trey Dickerson, Rosina Sumerall, Roy Williams, and Wallace Clay. *(Rosina Sumerall photo courtesy of Olan Mills.)*

and Earl Seymour, vice president and general manager, were welcomed by the CARQUEST board of directors.

Key Indicators

Miles driven were up 3.5 percent in 1988. The average age of passenger cars remained at 7.6 years versus 5.6 years in 1970 and 6.6 years in 1980. Sales of light trucks stayed strong, representing one out of every three new vehicles sold.

1989

During 1989, net sales increased 10.5 percent, which again exceeded the industry growth rate. Operating income grew 7.4 percent over the prior year. All moving and start-up costs for facilities were expensed in the current year.

Seizing the Moment

The ability to recognize and capitalize on new business opportunities has long been a defining business characteristic of GPI. A good example of this took place in 1989. A Parts Plus distributor in Memphis, Tennessee, with a branch distribution center in Jackson, Mississippi, acquired a Green Light program distributor in Fort Smith, Arkansas, which also owned a distribution center in Jackson, Mississippi. A number of cities in south Mississippi had Parts Plus auto parts stores competing with Green Light auto parts stores. As a result of this single acquisition, the Green Light program was discontinued, presenting GPI with the opportunity to quickly convert 30 auto parts stores to CARQUEST.

The closing of the Green Light Distribution Center in Jackson, Mississippi, presented GPI with experienced personnel to staff a new GPI CARQUEST distribution center in that city. This pool of talent included Trey Dickerson, Rosina Sumerall, Roy Williams, Jimmy Sumerall, Jerry Moorehead, Gerald Harrison, Kevin Sharp, and Ed Graham. GPI hired these former Green Light distribution center employees, who worked diligently as CARQUEST team members for five months before the GPI Jackson distribution center building was finished. They were assisted by Wallace Clay who was assigned to

NEW NASHVILLE DISTRIBUTION CENTER

GROUNDBREAKING FOR GENERAL PARTS' new 60,000-square-foot distribution center in Nashville took place in early August 1988. The facility, equipped with state-of-the-art material-handling equipment, was planned to replace an existing distribution center that had served its usefulness. Located on a five-acre-plus site on Brick Church Pike, the new distribution center was fully occupied in February 1989.

Ham Sloan, GPI's vice chairman of the board, said, "As General Parts continues its growth and expansion into new markets, the firm has dedicated its efforts to provide the finest warehouse distribution services available in the automotive aftermarket to serve GPI's CARQUEST Auto Parts stores. The investment in modern facilities and equipment offered continues proof of GPI's commitment to employee associates and auto parts stores customers. Keeping CARQUEST as the leader in the automotive parts aftermarket will always be the primary goal at General Parts."

GPI's Nashville distribution center was completed and fully occupied in 1989.

the Jackson area by the CARQUEST Memphis distribution center.

These activities were directed by Temple Sloan III who was sent to Jackson as sales manager in early 1989. Construction began for a new 55,000-square-foot Jackson, Mississippi distribution center, scheduled to open in the fall of 1989. The modern distribution center would permit further market share penetration into central and southwest Mississippi, western Alabama, and eastern Louisiana.

Working from the new distribution centers in Nashville, Tennessee, and Jackson, Mississippi, represented an important strategic move for GPI for the future. This permitted the installation of modern inventory handling systems that were more conducive to the recruitment of top caliber personnel. Also the new distribution centers strengthened GPI's ability to expand market share in the dynamic middle Tennessee and south Mississippi markets.

During 1989, several associates retired, and a sizable amount of capital stock was redeemed. By the end of the year, there were 372 associates holding equity positions in GPI companies. Net income as a percentage of beginning investors' equity was 14 percent.

New Product Lines

Significant events took place in 1989 which further solidified GPI's strong market position for the

SLOANS HONORED

TEMPLE SLOAN AND HAM SLOAN, BOTH former chairmen of the Automotive Warehouse Distributors Association (AWDA), were named as 1989's "Automotive Men of the Year" by AWDA. Pete Kornafel, Hatch Grinding Company Inc., Denver, Colorado, made the presentation. He was the 1988 recipient of the AWDA Award. The award was made during AWDA's 42nd Annual Conference at the Las Vegas Hilton Hotel.

The award inscription saluted the Sloans for their personal and corporate contributions "as role models for the automotive aftermarket, and for generously sharing their experience and knowledge to help others succeed and improve the industry." The Sloan brothers were the first co-recipients in the history of the Automotive Man of the Year Award.

Temple Sloan was first elected to the AWDA board of governors in 1970 and was the association's treasurer from 1971–1972.

He later proceeded through the officer chairs and served as AWDA chairman in 1977. Sloan chaired numerous AWDA committees, including the conference planning committee, and was then a trustee of the AWDA University Foundation.

Temple Sloan received the AWDA Memorial Scholarship Award in 1977 and was honored that year with the Automotive Aftermarket Education Award from Northwood University, Midland, Michigan.

Ham Sloan had been a member of the AWDA board of governors since 1981. He was elected to proceed through the association's officer chairs in 1984 and served as AWDA chairman in 1988. Ham Sloan also chaired the warehouse operations committee, academic advisory council, and conference planning committee, and had been chancellor of the AWDA University. He was honored by AWDA with its Memorial Scholarship Award in 1984. He received Northwood University's Automotive Replacement Education Award that same year. He also was a trustee for the AWDA University Foundation.

In 1986, at the 38th annual conference of AWDA, Ham Sloan was appointed vice-chancellor of AWDA University. Two years later, he was presented with a plaque of appreciation from AWDA at the group's annual convention in Las Vegas in November.

Left to right: Temple Sloan Jr., Pete Kornafel, of Hatch Grinding Company, Denver, and Ham Sloan. The Sloan brothers were jointly presented with the 1989 Automotive Men of the Year awards from Kornafel, the 1988 award winner.

Left: Temple Sloan III was sent to the Jackson, Mississippi, distribution center in 1989 as sales manager.

Below: By the mid-1980s, CARQUEST was offering a wide variety of its own branded auto parts and products.

1990s. Two major product lines were introduced under the CARQUEST label: CARQUEST filters, supplied by the Wix Division of Dana Corporation; and CARQUEST chassis parts, supplied by Moog. Both received strong market acceptance by CARQUEST Auto Parts stores and their installer customers. Also, CARQUEST hose clamps, caps, and thermostats were converted to the CARQUEST brand. Additional planning and groundwork was completed to convert CARQUEST temperature control, brakes, and shock absorbers. Customers continued to encourage the acceleration of additional product lines to the growing CARQUEST brand.

Nationally, the CARQUEST program grew with the addition of PSC Distributing Inc. of Phoenix, Arizona. PSC filled a major territory void in the Southwest for the distribution of CARQUEST products. Brothers Jim and Tom Eaton, owners of PSC, were welcomed by the large CARQUEST membership.

Within this membership, one significant merger took place in 1989. Avro Warehouse Sales in Buffalo, New York, owned by Seymour Hesch, merged with Sussen Inc. of Cleveland and Columbus, Ohio. Sussen Inc. is owned by Dan Sussen.

CARQUEST Brand Explained

At an annual GPI sales managers' meeting held in Raleigh, North Carolina, in late 1989, Sloan closed the meeting with an astute explanation of the

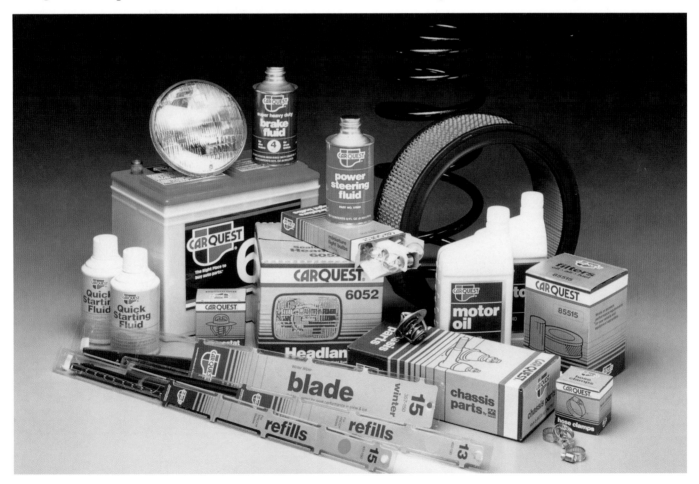

GPI/CARQUEST marketing direction and the importance of CARQUEST branded products. The following are excerpts from his address:

For GPI and the CARQUEST Auto Parts store to be successful, there must be a partnership between the two parties. It must be profitable for both—or neither will succeed. The CARQUEST product is the "glue" that holds this partnership together ...

CARQUEST products provide CARQUEST jobbers with their own marketing identity at both the installer and the fleet level. With the consolidation of manufacturers, industry brands have become hopelessly over-distributed in every market ...

Few manufacturers have control over their product line once it leaves their building. With our own brands, we can control the flow through those who have marketing integrity ...

CARQUEST products enables the CARQUEST distribution center to offer CARQUEST products with a competitive marketing strategy for the jobber without destroying profitability, a tragedy being witnessed daily in this industry ...

Another important area is efficiency in advertising where our budget is not being spent on advertising brands stocked by our competitors ...

And another key benefit is exclusive factory manpower, whose full-time efforts are dedicated to helping sell more CARQUEST products only through CARQUEST jobbers ...

CARQUEST brands will be demanded by the professional installer and will become synonymous with quality ...

Our immediate challenge is choosing the right suppliers to be our partners in the development of the CARQUEST brand and the CARQUEST marketing strategy. These are suppliers who are up to date in the world of engineering and manufacturing, and who have the financial and ownership stability to be our partners for the balance of this century. They must have management teams that possess an excellent understanding and dedica-

Above: CARQUEST's red, white, and blue corporate ID colors make the stores immediately recognizable across the country—and memorable with customers.

Left: In late 1989, Temple Sloan Jr. explained CARQUEST's business and marketing strategies to GPI sales managers at a meeting held in Raleigh, North Carolina.

tion to the traditional aftermarket, and more importantly, the CARQUEST marketing strategy ...

Commitment begins at the top. If those of us here today are not 100 percent committed to implementation of the CARQUEST mission statement, selling only through one customer, the CARQUEST jobber, we will not be successful.

National Accounts

In 1989, GPI took another giant step to enhance sales—to identify large chains of auto repair centers with a program to supply their needs through CARQUEST Auto Parts stores. This program, identified as "National Accounts," would include auto or truck repair centers with operations in two or more states. National account development was a "door opener" and a special sales opportunity for every CARQUEST Auto Parts store. The growth of National Accounts continued to expand each year.

Excellent progress was made in store identification and modernization, which made the CARQUEST Auto Parts stores easily recognizable with their red, white, and blue colors.

A record number of salesmen were trained with the CARQUEST SalesQuest Program, while store personnel were trained with the Counter-Pro Program. Tom Easton was added to the CARQUEST headquarters staff. He would contribute greatly in the training needs of GPI and members of the CARQUEST team.

The "Tahoe Bonanza"

In September 1989, the "Tahoe Bonanza," a four-day GPI CARQUEST get-together, was held in Lake Tahoe, Nevada. Attending were independent GPI CARQUEST store owners for fun, relaxation, and business at the High Sierra Hotel. This activity also involved a late show at Harrah's South Shore Room, featuring Sammy Davis Jr., and the great performer's last stage performance.

The occasion celebrated a decade of remarkable growth for CARQUEST. By the end of 1979, GPI was serving 190 independent CARQUEST stores in four states. By the end of 1989, GPI was serving more than four times that number: a grand total of 844 CARQUEST Auto Parts stores in 23 states, including 179 joint venture stores. CARQUEST's strong growth paralleled that of GPI itself. The continuing confidence of investors, suppliers, and customers had allowed GPI to grow rapidly. GPI had always maintained that short-term results must sometimes be given up in order to position for long-term growth and success—and this is how the company had operated from its earliest days. Of course, this is much easier to do being a private company.

Above: GPI—not all work and no play. Shown, left to right, Joe Hughes, president and CEO of Indiana Parts Warehouse, a CARQUEST member located in Indianapolis; Dan Bock; and Temple Sloan Jr. At the time of the photo, Bock was serving as president/executive director of CARQUEST. He is the former CEO of Bobro Inc., Bronx, New York. GPI, Bobro, and Indiana Parts Warehouse were the first three members of CARQUEST.

Below left: GPI's marketing area in 1989.

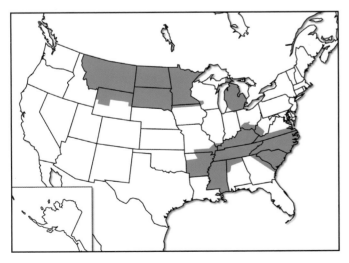

The year 1989 brought to an end the most exciting decade in General Parts' 28-year history, a 10-year period when sales increased 7.7-fold. Operating earnings increased 8.4-fold, investors equity grew 7.9-fold, and the average return on investors equity was 15.7 percent. And the company was well positioned to continue this growth into the future. Indeed, development of the management team, operating systems, and marketing programs would enable GPI to enter the 1990s well positioned to continue its outstanding performance.

> **During the period 1985–1989, GPI's sales increased 169 percent and earnings increased 72 percent.**

TRANSITIONS

1985—Promotions and new additions: **John Anthony** joined GPI as sales manager, Nashville D.C.; **R. D. Carson** to corporate-operations systems & procedures; **Mike Deal** to operations manager, Nashville; **Hersey Hall** to vice president/operations manager, Billings, Montana; **Paul Holliday** to operations manager, Lakeville, Minnesota; **Randal Long** to product manager, purchasing department, Raleigh; **Jim Russell** to president, Northwest Division, Valley Motor Supply.

1985—**Chuck Romee,** who had served as president and general manager of the Valley Organization, semi-retired on December 31. His leadership and service were deeply appreciated by all his associates and all who knew him. He would continue as an advisor and chairman of Valley Welders Supply, a division he headed for over 20 years. Other retirees for 1985: **Al Carlson** (33), **Dean Coddington** (28), and **Harlan Klima** (35).

1986—Promotions and new additions: **Bob Goodman** to vice president, operations, Bay City, Michigan; **Rick Guirlinger** to treasurer, Bay City; **Hersey Hall** to vice president, operations, Memphis; **Roger Hastings** to controller, Southeast Division; **Janet Higgins** to Southeast Division regional accounting; **Frederic C. Kotcher** to vice president, sales, Bay City; **Wayne Lavrack** to general manager, JV stores, Michigan; **Gary Ljunggren** to operations manager, Billings; **Betty Moore** to controller, Memphis; **Bruce Nicholson** joined GPI as director of finance in Memphis; **Temple Sloan III** to director of purchasing, Memphis.

1986—**Bert Berry,** president of S & S Parts Distributors Warehouse (PDW), Nashville, Tennessee, died on February 17 at the age of 58. Berry had been president of S & S since April 1981. Prior to that, he had been sales manager for 21 years with PDW of Memphis. Since the merger with GPI just five months prior, Berry had worked diligently to make the transaction seamless. Employees and customers who knew him missed Berry's sparkling personality, friendship, zest for living, and high integrity.

1986—Retirees: **Jerry Knutson** (29) and **Harry Evans** (35).

1987—Promotions and new additions: **Pat Basgall** to operations manager, Michigan; **Scott Ginsburg** to corporate director of advertising; **Peter Hafford** to divisional purchasing manager, Michigan; **Mike Hedge** to vice president and general manager, Valley Store Operations; **Kirby Matlick** to regional director of finance, Raleigh; **Phil Porter** to GPI JV store division, Asheville; **Temple Sloan III** to divisional purchasing manager, Central; **John Turcotte** to divisional purchasing manager, Northwest; **Mark Walley** to senior J-CON manager, Memphis; **Brian**

Wiggs to divisional purchasing manager, Southeast; **Rick Young** to corporate manager, J-CON services. Retirees: **Jim Farrar** (31); **Dewey Myhre** (43); **Thomas Owens** (39); **Si Stroup** (40) **Gerald Tanner** (41).

1988—Temple Sloan Jr. was elected chairman, **C. Hamilton Sloan,** vice chairman, and **Joe Owen** president of General Parts Inc. by the board of directors on April 1. **Joe Owen** was selected by Northwood University to receive the Automotive Aftermarket Education Award. Other promotions: **R. D. Carson** was elected vice president of D.C. operations, corporate; **Jim Downs** to president, Valley Welders Supply; **Rick Guirlinger** to corporate controller. Retirees: **Tony Dyba** (37), **Rex Gifford** (32), **James Hilen** (45), **Jim Norman** (40), **D.O. Taylor** (43), **Roger Trotman** (29), and **Harry Chute** (20).

1989—Charles Shaw, an 18-year veteran in the automotive aftermarket, joined GPI. He had spent 12 years with AP Parts Company in distribution center management and was vice president of operations for Mid-American Industries, coordinating the activities of several distribution centers. In his new capacity with General Parts, Shaw would be involved with operations and report directly to R.D. Carson.

1989—Fred Kotcher, vice president of sales for the Michigan Division, was promoted to president of that division. Kotcher began his career in the automotive aftermarket in 1971 when he went to work for Republic Automotive Parts Inc. as corporate controller and rose to the position of president of the firm's warehouse group. He left Republic in 1984 and moved to Bay City, Michigan, with Parts Warehouse Company as executive vice president and general manager.

1989—Promotions and new additions: **Ron Adkins** to sales manager, Valley Welders; **George Couch** joined GPI JV store division, S. E.; **Grady Dunn** to operations manager, Lexington; **Danny Durham** to operations manager, Asheville; **Dennis Fox** to president of southeast division, Memphis; **Rosina Sumerall** to operations manager, Jackson; **Danny Haag** to controller, Michigan; **Victor Hymel** to controller, Memphis; **John Kahut** to operations manager, Nashville; **Ken Oliver** to sales manager, Columbia D.C.; **Mark Schnarr** to sales manager, Nashville D.C.; **Temple Sloan III** to sales manager, Jackson D.C.; **Al Wheeler** to sales manager, Memphis D.C.

1989—Retirees: **Betty Moore** (25), **Bob Goodman** (20), and **Wilbur Franklin** (21).

In loving memory of the following additional associates who passed away during the period: **Robert Brurud, Bud Gleson, Paul Johnson, Clarence Littrell, Leander Petrey, Jr.,** and **Duke Seal.**

> Retiree information shows years of employment after names. This may include time spent at acquired companies.

Opposite page, clockwise from far left: Chuck Romee, Bert Berry, and Hersey Hall.

This page: Charles Shaw (left) and Fred Kotcher.

SOME OF THE MANY WHO HELPED

Mike
Najdowski

Ashton Wells

Rosina
Sumerall

Kevin Wilson

Ralph Wells

Jerry Berryhill

Jim Roth

Andy Kennell

John
Michutka

Mark Walley

Dick Egan

Jack Boyle

Delisa Jones

Orville Parrish

Tommy
Thomas

Doug
Blanchard

John
Weinmann Sr.

Peggy Gregory

Mike Long

Socorro Williams

Tim Wood

Barbara Stephens

Mickey White

John Hill

Trey Dickerson

Gary Goldston

Kenny Hinson

Gary Chelgren

Annette Perry

Jerry Dickey

John Anthony

Joe Kneer

Tom Ferguson

Sylvia Warrell

Jerry Gran

Frank Howard

Jerry Briggs

Chris Birmingham

Ronald Williams

Howard Hobbs

Don Davis

Jan Gardner

Pat Basgall

David O'Daniel

Mark Roth

Bob Creed

Rick Cox

Bob Goodman

By 1990, CARQUEST stores were providing a full range of quality products, offered in attractive, customer-friendly settings.

CHAPTER SEVEN

BREAKING RECORDS

1990 – 1994

Our products are visibly the best! Our marketing programs are now visibly the best! Our advertising is visibly the best! Our training is visibly the best! And yes, our sales force is visibly the best!

—Temple Sloan Jr.

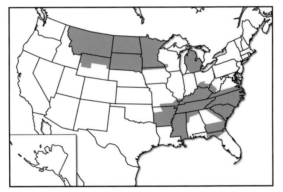

GPI'S SUCCESS DURING the 1980s was a tremendous confidence builder for continued company growth throughout the 1990s. The aftermarket industry was in a state of major flux during the early '90s, but none of the new developments required major marketing changes for GPI/CARQUEST. Indeed, maintaining marketing consistency was a definite advantage for every distribution segment within CARQUEST.

Anticipating the Market

A primary aftermarket advantage is being able to project well ahead which mix of vehicles will make up the current market for any given year. Of course, this requires careful observation on the part of aftermarket suppliers and distributors. In this regard, GPI has always considered it important to pay close attention to vehicle production and registration statistics each year. It utilizes various resources to handle this most effectively.

Since 1983, GPI has subscribed to *Ward's Reports*, a Detroit automotive statistical publication. *Ward's* is recognized as the most comprehensive and accurate information available regarding automotive vehicle production, sales, and registration figures worldwide. GPI also sub-

scribes to *Lang Reports* for aftermarket statistics.

According to *Lang*, the growth in U.S. households with motor vehicles has been steadily increasing. In 1960, 80 percent of households had vehicles, and by the end of 1990, that figure had grown to 91 percent. Additional *Lang* information indicated that there was one vehicle per 3.2 people in 1960 and one vehicle per 1.6 people in 1990. Also, *Lang* reported that the increase in annual miles driven during the decade of the 1980s averaged 2.6 percent per year.

By utilizing *Ward's*, *Lang*, and other informed sources, GPI looks for trends in vehicle models every year and then makes adjustments to have the right replacement parts stocked at the time they are needed.

An Experienced Management Team

The '90s began with a GPI management team that had gained valuable experience through numerous successful acquisitions and mergers.

This map shows the extent of GPI's sales and marketing reach during 1990.

They also quickly became more expert in effectively managing their chain of auto parts stores that was growing by leaps and bounds as a result of GPI's highly successful joint-venture store program. Additionally, GPI constantly improved its efficiency and productivity through information technology advances made during the 1980s—and was committed to continue to do so for the future.

Also, GPI was dealing from another position of strength: the widespread acceptance of CARQUEST's branded products during the late 1980s by GPI's target customers, the professional auto service technicians. This created confidence, pride, and enthusiasm at every CARQUEST level. This was a huge plus for CARQUEST as it entered the 1990s.

GPI AVIATION

IN 1990, MIKE WHITE JOINED GPI TO manage its aviation arm, replacing Charlie Deck who retired after 12 years of service. An amazing professional pilot, Deck set the standard for Mike White and the GPI flight department.

Today, White continues to manage the aviation activities of GPI, which includes two airplanes, a Citation 10 and a Beech 400-A, and five of the very best pilots. In addition to White, other pilots are Jim Webb, David Perry, John Brusso, and A. J. Johnson. Safety is the number one issue in flying at GPI where no one argues with GPI pilots.

In 1990, Mike White (left) replaced Charlie Deck as head of GPI's aviation operations.

Additionally, auto parts purchase decisions were becoming more straightforward because of significant consolidation among manufacturers, a trend matched by that of distributors. As a result, GPI made a growing percentage of its purchases during the '80s from just 10 vendors. This trend was expected to continue in the 1990s. The excellent relationships GPI had forged with key suppliers during the 1970s and 1980s would prove to be invaluable assets for the company as it prepared to meet the challenges during the 1990s and beyond.

1990

The 1990s began with record sales and earnings performance. Sales reached an increase of 13.3 percent over 1989. GPI stores did well across the board, with record results at the new Jackson, Mississippi, Distribution Center and Joint Venture stores. Sales grew 8.1 percent for the Joint Venture Store Group, while sales to independent CARQUEST Auto Parts stores grew 6 percent. Additionally, each company segment beat industry performance.

The year 1990 also set a new record for earnings. Operating income increased 16 percent while net income grew 22.7 percent. All acquisition and startup costs were expensed against 1990 operating results. LIFO reserves were increased and the capital base grew 17.4 percent.

Service Parts Warehouse and Keenan Auto Parts Join GPI Family

On June 1, 1990, GPI negotiated the final details of the merger of Service Parts Warehouse and Keenan Auto Parts of Albany, Georgia. The merger brought an additional 65 CARQUEST Auto Parts stores and the 13th distribution center into the GPI organization. Additionally, 250 employees joined the ranks of GPI, swelling the employment count to more than 2,200.

Service Parts Warehouse and Keenan Auto Parts stores joined the CARQUEST marketing program in 1985. They had been a driving force in the Georgia market, serving auto parts stores within a 125-mile radius of Albany. For more about Keenan's history, see chapter 12.

During 1990, GPI undertook the capital reorganization of Valley Motor Supply Company (VMS) and most of its subsidiaries. In the transaction,

Valley investors traded their various VMS stocks for GPI stock. This had no effect on total investors' equity—but the move allowed the investors to earn a more typical GPI return. By the end of 1990, 420 associates held equity positions in GPI companies. Net income as a percent of beginning investors' equity was 14.79 percent.

Pacific Wholesalers Inc.

In 1990, CARQUEST's board of directors unanimously approved and welcomed Pacific Wholesalers Inc. of Portland, Oregon, into the CARQUEST family of distribution companies. Pacific was owned by Chris Winters and Charles Troutman.

Diversified Automotive Distributors
Buys Automotive Distributors

During 1990, the CARQUEST membership had a change of ownership. Dan Myers, president of Automotive Distributors Inc., the CARQUEST member in Kansas City, Missouri, announced the sale of their company to Diversified Automotive Distributors Inc., owned by Marty Brown. CARQUEST's board of directors were pleased that Brown elected to retain the CARQUEST program affiliation.

Annual CARQUEST Automotive
Technicians Advisory Council

In 1990, CARQUEST held its annual Automotive Technicians Advisory Council in Huntington Beach, California, headquarters of TECH-NET. The meeting lasted two days, with six highly qualified and successful technicians offering professional input. Their input assured CARQUEST that its programming was properly targeted to meet the needs of the professional installer.

That same year, CARQUEST developed an interior design program for its Auto Part stores. The modern design concept for the stores provided an easy, inexpensive way to upgrade store interiors creating an inviting appearance.

Giant steps were made in converting product lines to the CARQUEST brand. CARQUEST chose Gabriel as shock absorber vendor, Arvin-Maremont for exhaust products, and Murray for air-conditioning parts. In each case, quality was the primary focus

for selecting these vendors to supply CARQUEST.

CARQUEST developed a leasing program to make large equipment sales easier for CARQUEST Auto Parts stores. The first "Value Sale" of tools and equipment took place in 1990.

GPI's Joint Venture Stores group continued to grow during 1990 with 226 stores, including Keenan Auto Parts. Growth consisted of 46 acquisitions (30 from Keenan), and six new openings. At the same time, five stores closed. Success in this increasingly important area came from hard work as store managers and store salespeople spent a record number of hours training in the areas of sales, finance, and supervision.

GPI's stores' sales force expanded to 210 full- and part-time outside salesmen. Continuing development of the Joint Venture Stores would be a vital element of growth strategy for the coming years.

CARQUEST Welcomes Sronce Automotive

In 1990, GPI finalized the merger of Sronce Automotive Supply of Asheville, North Carolina, into its Joint Venture Store Group. John Sronce managed the business, which had been founded by his father in 1942. Sronce Automotive Supply had earned a strong reputation for service and honesty and was the largest parts store in Asheville. The Sronce facility was 13,000 square feet including 5,500 square feet of display area. GPI welcomed the 29 Sronce employees and John Sronce was named manager for all the GPI JV stores in Asheville.

Industry Trends

The energy crisis of the mid-1970s created a new automotive technology, starting with new car production in 1980. The technology was electronic with onboard computers to control fuel-air ratios for better fuel efficiency. For each succeeding model year, multiple onboard computers were used to control an increasing number of automobile systems.

The new generation of fuel-efficient vehicles of the 1980s, along with an increase in imported vehicles, created an inventory explosion. Many automotive-parts distributing companies had a hard time managing the additional dollar investment required to support these larger inventories. National automotive companies such as Sears,

Firestone, Goodyear, and KMart also found it difficult to stock the right parts in their inventory at the time they were needed.

Additionally, advances in technology made it progressively more difficult for the automobile owner to do their own repairs (DIY). Even the professional technicians faced an uphill battle learning the complex electronic technology to supplement their mechanical skills.

None of this took GPI by surprise. Indeed, the company's market forecasts had been right on target: there had been 12 consecutive years of domestic automobile production with increasingly complicated electronic technology.

Service, Service, Service

At a 1990 annual GPI management meeting, Sloan delivered a challenge to the management team: "Service at all levels will be more important than ever. We are dealing in thousands more parts in our inventories, so having the right part at the right place quickly will be increasingly difficult. However, we have no choice but to do this better than our competition if we are to grow and prosper."

1991—GPI's 30th Year

The year 1991, GPI's 30th year, was a time of excellent achievement in a difficult economic environment.

Consolidated sales grew 14.5 percent, a new record. By the end of the first quarter of 1991, GPI experienced a sales decrease of 4.5 percent on comparable operating units. Following the end of the first Persian Gulf War, sales recovered and grew significantly in the final three quarters. The sales increase for the Joint Venture Group was 3.4 times the industry's growth rate. Sales growth to independent CARQUEST Auto Parts stores was nearly 4 percent, while the industry's sales were down .25 percent in 1991. The aftermarket, while not totally escaping the impact of the economic recession, did not suffer the significant sales decreases

A DEFINITION OF GPI

WRITTEN IN 1991, THE FOLLOWING description of GPI appeared on the inside cover of the company's annual report for several years.

"General Parts Inc. ... a unique partnership of associates dedicated to growth through outstanding service to our customers."

This definition of GPI is probably as good as can be done with one sentence. But is one sentence enough to explain our company? Yes, it is a unique partnership ... unique and exciting. And yes, our people are dedicated ... dedicated to being the best in service to our customers.

But it does take more than a sentence to reinforce the fact that GPI's complete formula for success has been the quality of its people. We are in an industry that demands quality in product and quality in service, and it must begin with quality in people.

All key associates are direct shareholders in GPI and/or the JV stores. All GPI people are shareholders through the "GPI ESOP [Employee Stock Ownership Plan]." Each shareholder is directly involved in our operations every day. This ownership structure is an extraordinary advantage, which allows us to keep our focus on long-term results.

It has long been a GPI principle that people want standards against which they can measure themselves. Management's job is to provide these standards and then get out of the way. This atmosphere attracts motivated people and provides an environment of non-destructive competition.

As GPI has grown through mergers with other companies, we have been blessed with a wealth of added talent. This is not by accident because the quality of the people is the first asset examined in any prospective merger.

Certainly, the common thread that runs in all GPI people is the burning desire to be the best. As long as this fire is kindled, GPI's success will be guaranteed.

experienced by other industries. In light of the weak 1991 economy, GPI was pleased with its own sales performance and market share increases.

Company net income was up 27.1 percent over 1990. In keeping with historical accounting practices, all acquisition costs and startup expenses for new operations were expensed in 1991.

Vehicle Statistics, Plus
Key Events and Indicators for 1991

In 1991, there were 188 million registered vehicles in the United States, of which 45 million were trucks. Foreign models represented 29.5 percent of all cars and trucks. The growth in foreign models was projected to continue increasing, and GPI's suppliers were challenged to provide complete availability of parts for all foreign vehicles.

Some key events and indicators for 1991:

• Operation Desert Storm was a success with Iraqi forces driven out of Kuwait
• Average income: $29,943
• Average new car cost: $16,850
• Average new house cost: $120,000
• A gallon of gas cost $1.12
• Minimum wage: $4.25

GPI's Significant Developments in 1991

GPI expanded the internal decking of the Chicago Distribution Center by 17,200 square feet, providing a total of 74,200 square feet of storage space, plus a significant addition of new bins, racks, and expanded conveyor systems. The distribution center was converted to GPI's computer system and steps were taken to add 20,000 part numbers to bring inventories in line with GPI's standard coverage.

The company expanded the Asheville, North Carolina, Distribution Center by 21,000 square feet and constructed totally new offices there. It added new storage bins and racks and expanded the conveyor system. The larger, updated facility gave the company the capacity to handle significant growth in western North and South Carolina.

The annual CARQUEST Technicians Advisory Council was held again in Huntington Beach, California. Attendees also visited the CARQUEST

A SALUTE TO THE TROOPS

IN THE MARCH 1991 *GENERAL IDEA*, Temple Sloan Jr. made the following statement of gratitude for the U.S. military in the Gulf War:

The price of peace and freedom is very high. Today, as I write these lines, 78 members of the GPI family are serving in the Middle East. They are the sons and daughters of our associates, or even associates themselves who have been called from the reserves. They are always in our thoughts and prayers. They represent the "best of the best" in American spirit and patriotism. Please join all of us at GPI in expressing our tremendous pride and support for all the troops of Operation Desert Storm.

TECH-NET facility. GPI President Joe Owen and CARQUEST Marketing Manager Dan O'Connell hosted the group, consisting of some of the finest automotive technicians in America.

Varied types of training continued to be a high priority at GPI/CARQUEST. New seminars were developed at a record pace and presented to Joint Venture store personnel and to independent CARQUEST Auto Parts store employees and owners.

The entire year was spent in the introduction of the exciting CARQUEST-branded brake systems program. The new brake parts line, which took two years to plan, received an excellent reception by CARQUEST Auto Parts stores and professional service technicians from coast to coast. CARQUEST selected EIS, a division of Standard Motor Products, as the vendor.

Including the CARQUEST brake product line, there were 28 product lines under the CARQUEST brand by 1991, and 75 percent of GPI's application line sales were made under the CARQUEST label.

GPI's JV Store Division successfully pioneered a new concept called "Super Stores," which appeared to be the wave of the future for many of the metropolitan markets. Super Store inventories included much more inventory coverage.

Indiana Parts Warehouse

April 1991 marked the merger of Indiana Parts Warehouse (IPW), headquartered in Indianapolis. IPW was one of the very first CARQUEST members and played an important role in the development of the CARQUEST program. Indiana Parts Warehouse operated three distribution centers serving 23 company-owned stores and 58 independently owned CARQUEST Auto Parts stores.

Joe Hughes, president of IPW, said, "Everyone at IPW is happy to join forces with our longtime friends at GPI, and we are certain that by working together, we will continue the success of CARQUEST in the state of Indiana."

"Over the years, as members of CARQUEST Corporation, everyone at GPI has worked closely with our friends at IPW, so we are certain that this new venture will provide us with the opportunity to achieve our mutual goals to the greater benefit of both companies," said Sloan.

The "President's Message" column in the June 1991 edition of the *General Idea*, reported on the IPW merger.

The people within IPW are genuinely dedicated to the service aspect of the business. This is a tribute to Joe Hughes' leadership. There is nothing artificial about Joe Hughes. He is a believer in fairness, truthfulness, and honesty—and it reflects throughout the IPW organization.

For more about IPW's history, see chapter 12.

World Supply Corporation

September 30, 1991, marked the completion of the acquisition of World Supply Corporation, located in Lemont, Illinois, in the southwest suburbs of Chicago. World Supply joined the CARQUEST distribution organization in 1985. Sloan was enthusiastic about the merger.

"World Supply has contributed greatly to the CARQUEST Corporation and has an outstanding record of customer service. Ben Roscrow, Jeff Lundh, John Martens, and their management team have built an outstanding company, and we are pleased to have the opportunity to continue our growth together," said Sloan.

Roscrow, owner of World Supply, said, "The merger with GPI will strengthen World Supply's position in the marketplace. World looks forward to growing together with such a respected organization as GPI."

For more about World Supply's history, see chapter 12.

After the World Supply Corporation acquisition, GPI acquired Whitlock Enterprises, a six-store operation in the western suburbs of Chicago. GPI was grateful to Bill Whitlock for his trust and for his continued help in merging his company with the Chicago team.

HR-1790
Design & Protection Bill

In 1991, U.S. Congressman Dick Gephardt of Missouri introduced legislation known as HR-1790. If enacted, it would have provided original equipment parts manufacturers with a 10-year protection provision on their new products. This meant that no one else would be permitted to manufacture replacements for the protected parts for the first 10 years. Such a law would have enabled original equipment manufacturers to monopolize the replacement parts market.

For the first time, all members of the aftermarket industry came together against this pending legislation. They were determined to prevent car and truck manufacturers from achieving through law what they had been unable to accomplish in an open and competitive market. This advocacy worked and HR-1790 became yet another failed attempt by vehicle manufacturers to unfairly control the automotive aftermarket.

1992

During 1992, GPI's consolidated sales increased 32 percent, setting another company record. Stores and distribution centers that GPI operated in 1991 and 1992 experienced growth of 7.8 percent. Sales to independently owned CARQUEST Auto Parts stores increased 7.1 percent, while Joint Venture Auto Parts stores' sales grew 11.4

percent, more than double the industry's growth rate of 3.6 percent.

Net income at GPI registered a remarkable 27.6 percent increase, establishing another new record for GPI. Consistent with past practice, $677,000 of acquisitions, startups, and moving costs were expensed in 1992. Those non-recurring expenses resulted from the move to the new Indianapolis Distribution Center and from several acquisitions.

ESOP Change

In 1992, GPI formulated an important change in the company's Employee Stock Ownership Plan (ESOP). Sloan announced that after the 1992 plan year, the company's contributions to the ESOP would amount to 10 percent of the pretax profits.

"Our aim is to more closely tie ESOP contribution with the company's performance. Not only will our GPI associates benefit from the growth in value of the ESOP investment in company stocks, but their efforts will be directly rewarded by the company's annual profit performance," Sloan said.

Also that year, GPI associates were informed of a new 401K savings plan. This allowed associates to increase their retirement funds by making pretax payroll contributions. The plan was made available to all associates.

Distribution Center Expansions

Although in operation less than two years, the Jackson Distribution Center was already pinched for space—sales grew 17.4 percent in 1991 and were up another 25 percent for the first two months of 1992. To meet this growing demand, GPI added 14,000 square feet to the distribution center, bringing total square footage to 70,600 square feet.

To allow for the increased number of stock-keeping units (SKUs) in the Chicago Distribution Center, an additional 20,000-square-foot mezzanine and bins were added. In Raleigh, a 20,000-square-foot expansion and internal modernization was completed for the distribution center there.

Other distribution center changes: consolidation was completed for three smaller facilities, two in Indianapolis and one in South Bend, Indiana. They joined to become the new 92,000-square-foot Indianapolis Distribution Center. It contained an additional 17,000 square feet of fully mechanized mezzanine, and housed a new CARQUEST Joint Venture store. The new facility greatly improved

In 1992, GPI built and opened a huge, state-of-the-art, 92,000-square-foot distribution center in Indianapolis.

operating efficiencies, inventory management, and the level of service to CARQUEST Auto Parts stores.

Taylor Parts Inc.

In September 1991, GPI announced that it planned to acquire Taylor Parts Inc., effective January 2, 1992, an apt way to ring in the new year. Taylor Parts operated 36 company-owned stores, a cleaner and equipment division, and two distribution centers. It served independently owned ALL-PRO Jobbers. The company was the largest independently owned automotive parts distributor in Alabama. During the conversion, GPI purchased two auto parts stores, closed one, and sold one. All CARQUEST identification and product line changeovers were completed quickly and the company's previous computer systems were replaced by GPI's J-CON System. The acquisition could not have been completed efficiently without a tremendous effort by both GPI and Taylor Parts' management and employees.

Sloan said, "Taylor Parts is a premier company with an outstanding record of customer service and is a highly respected company within our industry. Jimmy Taylor, Lee Meriwether, and the entire management team have built an outstanding organization, and we are pleased to have the opportunity to join them."

With the merger, GPI established a new operating division with O. Temple Sloan III appointed as division president. For more about Taylor Parts' history, see chapter 12.

Industry Changes

As GPI expanded and prospered, the aftermarket industry was going through its own series of changes. This included increased inventory investment resulting from the continued increase in the number of parts. All levels of distribution were challenged to generate enough sales volume to sustain the added investment in inventory.

Additionally, sales by the well-financed retail chains added substantial pricing pressure to aftermarket retailers and distributors. For the most part, the chains inventoried only the fast-selling replacement parts, and they did so at heavily discounted prices. Because of their retail structure, most chains could not contend with the sizeable investment asso-

ciated with slower-moving parts and products, or with costly services such as delivery, accounts receivable, and training. Of course, that pattern was always subject to change if the DIY market continued to decline.

CARQUEST Marketing

Year after year, CARQUEST routinely fine-tuned its key marketing programs in order to remain competitive within the estimated $85 billion automotive products aftermarket. This included installer pricing programs so the CARQUEST Auto Parts stores would be able to favorably compete with two-step specialists.

For GPI, the year 1992 represented the first full year selling its CARQUEST Brake Program. The program was a huge success with a sales increase on brake products of 21.4 percent. With CARQUEST-dedicated factory sales representatives working exclusively with CARQUEST Auto Parts stores, and concentrating their efforts at the professional technician level, this product line would continue to show healthy increases.

Division Realignment

With the addition of Taylor Parts in Andalusia, Indiana Parts Warehouse in Indianapolis, and World Supply Company in Chicago, GPI needed to reorganize its divisions. This was done in December 1992.

Temple Sloan III moved to Andalusia, Alabama, as division president of the Southern Division. This included GPI distribution centers in Albany, Georgia, Andalusia, and Montgomery, Alabama. Orville Parrish, a longtime employee of Keenan Auto Parts, was appointed personnel manager for the division.

Dick Egan was named division president of the Central Division, which included the Lexington, Kentucky, and Indianapolis distribution centers. Judy Brim, who had been office manager and assistant controller in Lexington, was appointed controller.

Ron Wehrenberg was named president of the newly reorganized Midwest Division. In addition to the Lakeville, Minnesota, Distribution Center, Wehrenberg would also be responsible for the Chicago Distribution Center.

Those moves brought the GPI/CARQUEST family to seven divisions, including 16 distribution centers serving nearly half of the United States.

CLEANER & EQUIPMENT

JUST AS THE VALLEY Motor Supply acquisition introduced GPI to the welding supplies business, the year 1992 introduced GPI to the cleaner and equipment business.

Walter Ray Fowler, who passed away in October 2004, was a pioneer in the development of Taylor's Cleaner and Equipment Division. He spent more than 50 years in the business and was recognized throughout the United States as one of the most knowledgeable professionals within the industry. Additionally, Fowler was a professional salesman and enjoyed selling equipment as much as a golfer enjoys making birdies.

The cleaner part of the business involves the sale of pressure washers and various chemical solutions. This side of the business is primarily conducted in the Andalusia, Alabama, headquarters and in the Montana branch. The Cleaning Division exclusively distributes Alkota pressure washers in these two markets along with CARQUEST-branded cleaning chemicals and assorted manufacturers' brands in all markets.

Alkota has also customized four different commercial-grade pressure washers under the CARQUEST brand for drop-shipping in all GPI Cleaner and Equipment markets.

When Taylor merged with GPI, cleaner and equipment sales were just under $1 million from Andalusia, Alabama, alone. By the end of 2005, sales were more than $35 million from 11 locations including Andalusia, Raleigh, North Carolina; Denver, Colorado; Des Moines; Billings, Montana; Bay City, Michigan; Portland, Oregon; Bakersfield, California; Cleveland, Ohio; Houston, Texas; and Marshfield, Wisconsin.

The Cleaner and Equipment Division continued its rapid growth with record sales in 2005. Locations were added to the Denver, Colorado, and Bakersfield, California, distribution centers. Another was added to Phoenix, Arizona, in early 2006. The Cleaner and Equipment Division has 12 locations serving CARQUEST stores around the country.

Hoke Smith, who for several years worked with Fowler, is general manager of the GPI Cleaner and Equipment Division. He reports to John Taylor, regional JV vice president. Smith is assisted by Harold Barrow, Dan Studstill, Molly Robertson, and a staff of knowledgeable associates.

CARQUEST stores throughout the United States and Canada have enjoyed supplementing their parts with cleaner equipment sales needed by professional auto service technicians. The Cleaner and Equipment Division has played a vital part in GPI's success.

Hoke Smith was in charge of GPI's Cleaner and Equipment Division.

The realignment included the reduction of one accounting office and the consolidation of seven purchasing offices into four.

At the same time, GPI increased its directors by three with Fred Kotcher, Chuck Henline, and the addition of O. Temple Sloan III.

State-of-the-Art Machine Shops

In 1992, GPI/CARQUEST Auto Parts stores' machine shops were expanding to service all types of engines for cars, trucks, diesels, lawn mowers, stationery engines, and so on. In order to handle work on so many different engine types, the shops needed to offer the latest technology. But technology alone was not enough. The shops needed to feature efficient layouts, hazardous chemical waste control, cleanliness, and most important of all, highly professional personnel.

Gar Odor

To plan this out correctly, GPI had spent a huge amount of time during the previous 18 months evaluating the GPI stores' machine shops and directing a large effort to upgrade all of the shops nationally by the end of 1992. Gar Odor, a machine shop expert, headed up this important task for GPI.

Odor was—and remains—a legend in the automotive aftermarket, with more than 60 years of experience. He received his start at the entry level with the Merrill Company in Spencer, Iowa, in 1942. After serving in the military for 20 months during World War II, Odor returned to the Merrill Company and at age 24 was managing one of Merrill's parts stores. From there, he worked his way up to general manager in 1968. Odor was responsible for the management of 20 parts stores, 50 salesmen, and 50 machinists. Every store had a machine shop.

Gar Odor, a respected industry expert, set up the GPI/CARQUEST Auto Parts stores' machine shops.

Odor's knowledge and passion for automotive machine shops is unparalleled. Since 1991, when he joined GPI, Odor's contributions in shop operations have been numerous and valuable.

GPI Training

Training had always been a high priority at GPI/CARQUEST and this continued to be the case in 1992. Students graduated in record numbers from a wide range of training programs. The improved skills resulting from these programs would pay dividends as GPI and CARQUEST moved forward. Additionally, the format for the annual jobber weekend conferences were weighted heavily toward seminars to further educate and train students—and CARQUEST customers unanimously applauded the new format.

Two Famous Names

CARQUEST continued to expand its national accounts with huge retailers such as Kmart and Montgomery Ward being served by the CARQUEST Auto Parts stores. Those two important new customers, together with Sears and Firestone, added valuable sales volume for GPI.

Pacific Wholesalers Inc.

On August 26, 1992, GPI finalized its merger with Pacific Wholesalers Inc., of Portland, Oregon. Pacific Wholesalers Inc. (PWI) was the largest independently owned automotive parts distributor in Oregon. A CARQUEST member and a CCI customer with J-CON, Pacific served 66 CARQUEST Auto Parts stores in Oregon, Washington, and Northern California. For more about PWI's history, see chapter 12.

Northern Industries Inc.

The same day that GPI closed its deal with PWI, it also completed the acquisition of Northern Industries Inc., of Marshfield, Wisconsin. Northern was the largest independently owned automotive replacement parts distributor in Wisconsin and a strategic addition to the GPI family. Northern operated distribution centers in Madison, Marshfield, and Green Bay, Wisconsin, and two Welding Supply locations in Wausau and Green Bay.

THE ONLY CONSTANT IS CHANGE

THE FOLLOWING WAS TAKEN FROM A speech delivered by Joe Owen to various CARQUEST Auto Parts store owners during numerous annual marketing conferences in 1993.

Change is nothing new in our industry, or any other industry. It's as certain as death and taxes. Change must not be used as a basis for excuses. It should be looked at as an opportunity. Technology change in automotive vehicle production will continue to dictate the kind of parts we sell.

Today we sell rack and pinion, half-shafts, CV joints, map sensors, electronic-control modules, anti-lock brake parts, gas-charged struts, micro V-belts, fuel injectors, catalytic converters, and timing belts. We were not selling any of these 20 years ago. But remember, 20 years

ago, we were selling disc brake pads, ball joints, automatic transmission parts, power steering hose, alternators, and air conditioning parts—all of which we were not selling 20 years before.

Guess what: 20 years before that, we were selling ring gears and pinions, rear-axle shafts, generators (not alternators), transmission cluster gears, king bolt sets, and drilled brake lining in sets which were riveted on brake shoes by installers. Back then, piston rings were actually stocked and replaced by auto repair shops.

Now, for those of you who had grandparents in this business ... 20 years prior to that, retailers sold leaf springs, ignitors, magnetos, and "snubbers," which were the shock absorbers of that period. And yes, no doubt, 20 years from today, we will be selling replacement parts which we are not selling or have even heard of today.

To handle this, a new division headquartered in Marshfield, Wisconsin, was formed with Don L. Komis continuing to serve as president. Northern's entire management team remained with GPI, including Chuck Harwick, vice president, sales, Dave Lockwood, treasurer, and Don Kohlbeck, general manager, stores.

The Marshfield Distribution Center was organized to service 90 stores in Wisconsin and the upper peninsula of Michigan. The changeover to CARQUEST product lines and programs met with an excellent reception. In early 1994, the Green Bay Warehouse was converted to a joint venture super store. For more about Northern Industries' history, see chapter 12.

On October 31, 1992, a letter of intent was issued outlining the possible acquisition of assets of the Cardis Corporation, a CARQUEST member in central and northern California. After extensive due diligence, including visits by management members to more

than 100 California CARQUEST Auto Parts stores, the intent was withdrawn on December 8, one week prior to the contract date. GPI could not satisfy itself regarding the economic viability of the project within an acceptable period of time. It felt the risk was too great, particularly in light of other recent acquisitions.

Auto Parts Wholesale (APW), owned by the McMurtrey family and headquartered in Bakersfield, California, was interested in joining CARQUEST and acquiring the assets of the Cardis Corporation. This interest grew once GPI made the decision to turn down the Cardis acquisition. In 1993, APW simultaneously acquired Cardis assets and was welcomed as a new member by the CARQUEST board of directors. Combined with the Cardis locations, APW would now be serving 260 CARQUEST stores, with 30 stores owned by APW. The McMurtreys did an expert job merging the remains of Cardis into their company.

Excellence Award

In 1992, CARQUEST's Professional Markets Committee voted to participate in the Technicians Advisory Council concept begun by GPI in 1987. At that time, it was decided to add a feature to the council that each year would recognize the most outstanding automotive service repair center in the United States. Every CARQUEST Auto Parts store was allowed to submit candidates based on rigorous qualification standards. Industry magazine editors performed as judges to determine the top 10 finalists who would serve on the CARQUEST Technicians Advisory Council for the current year. The award was acclaimed as the "Excellence Award."

CARQUEST
National Sales Conference

Held in Scottsdale, Arizona, the first National Sales Conference was, according to CARQUEST chairman, Neil Stockel, a key meeting in the history of CARQUEST. Sloan addressed the CARQUEST associates and owners during the meeting.

Our theme for our National Sales Conference this weekend has been "Team CARQUEST: Visibly the Best."

Yes, our products are visibly the best! Our marketing programs are now visibly the best! Our advertising is visibly the best! Our training is visibly the best! And yes, our sales force is visibly the best.

Industry leaders and suppliers love to tell us how wonderful CARQUEST is doing. They say things like "you are doing so much better than the others." When I hear such comments, I shudder. To me, in far too many cases throughout our company and your companies, our sales performance tells us loud and clear, we are not doing as well as we should, but even more important, as well as we must!

There is a downside to being "visibly the best." Unfortunately, it sends a wrong message to some of us. If we are this good, if we are the best ... then we can relax and coast awhile. Are too many of us guilty of believing our own headlines? The history books are full of companies who failed or are failing after reaching the top and resting on their laurels.

It's all right to demonstrate pride in being visibly the best, but only if it is blended with a strong determination and the consistent effort required to remain the best.

The marketplace allows you no slack, no time to relax and enjoy your achievements. There is some-

SAM ROGERS HONORED

GPI ASSOCIATES, CARQUEST SUPPLIERS, and Michigan Division customers came together at a gala reception in Bay City, Michigan, on December 2, 1992, to celebrate the 75th birthday of Sam Rogers, chairman of the Michigan Division.

The following day, employees of the Bay City Distribution Center joined in to wish Sam "Happy Birthday" at a party during the lunch hour. The highlight of the celebration was an announcement of the Sam Rogers Northwood Institute CARQUEST Scholarship Fund, made jointly by O. Temple Sloan Jr., GPI

chairman, and Dr. David Fry, president of Northwood Institute.

The fund was set up to provide scholarships for the children of employees of CARQUEST distribution centers and CARQUEST stores, as well as children of CARQUEST-dedicated factory sales personnel who pursue a career in the automotive aftermarket through the two- or four-year programs offered by Northwood Institute.

Northwood Institute has campuses in Midland, Michigan, and Cedar Hill, Texas, that offer the Automotive Aftermarket studies program.

one working every hour of every day to take your place, because they also have a desire to be the best.

Success is not a matter of chance. Success is a matter of choice.

As a member of the CARQUEST sales team, you must consider yourselves true professionals, the best at what you do. But to be the best, to continue to grow in this market, both today and tomorrow, you must continue to develop yourselves through both personal and professional growth.

Personal growth is your self-esteem, your self-confidence. But for you to be successful, your self-esteem and self-confidence must be built on a solid foundation of skills and knowledge. The whole purpose of this weekend, a huge investment, was to assist you in the further development of your professional skills and knowledge.

You can be sure, the business world is tough. It is highly competitive, it is unforgiving, it takes no prisoners, and it is filled with constant change. It could care less about what you did yesterday or last year. It requires that we do our very best everyday, today, and again tomorrow.

I urge you to take what you have learned in the past three days ... take it back to your company and your territory. Help us achieve our goal of becoming the fastest-growing, most dynamic marketing force in the industry.

Vehicle Statistics for 1992

By 1992, the number of registered vehicles in the United States had grown to 190.4 million, of which 61.3 million were trucks. Foreign models represented 26 percent of the population of cars and trucks, and their impact on the aftermarket was projected to grow. The domestic fleet of cars and trucks reached an average of 8.6 years, versus 6.3 years for foreign models.

In 1992, miles driven increased 3.1 percent, the 12th consecutive year of increase with the rate of growth substantially ahead of 1991. Stable fuel prices contributed to the continuing increase of motor vehicle travel.

For the year 1992, the "Big Three" U.S. vehicle manufacturers, Chrysler, General Motors, and Ford, had a 71.4 percent market share of new car and light truck sales in the United States. This broke a two-year trend of losing market share.

Consumer acceptance of mini-vans, pick-up trucks, and sport utility vehicles (SUVs) was the reason for the increased market share.

Ward's Reports listed the following vehicle types as the top 10 sellers in 1992:

1. Ford Taurus	6. Ford Ranger*
2. Honda Accord	7. Ford Escort
3. Ford Explorer*	8. Honda Civic
4. Toyota Camry	9. Chevrolet Lumina
5. Dodge Caravan*	10. Chevrolet Cavalier

*Classified as light trucks ...
29 percent of the top 10 vehicle types

S-2237

Vehicle manufacturers tried again in 1992 to use legislation to further their own cause with U.S. Senate bill S-2237, introduced by Senator William Roth of Delaware. Unofficially known as the "clunker bill," S-2237 would eliminate from the road all cars manufactured before 1980. The Big Three U.S. car manufacturers were behind the bill. Like HR-1790, it also failed to pass.

An Added $100 Million in Sales

GPI began its fourth decade with the acquisition of Taylor Parts Inc., of Andalusia, Alabama. Prior to 1992, there had been no indication that GPI would have an opportunity to merge with the CARQUEST member in Portland, Oregon, and Northern Industries Inc. of Marshfield, Wisconsin. The Alabama, Oregon, and Wisconsin acquisitions would add a whopping $100 million to GPI's annual sales.

1993

There was no question that GPI was on a roll during the early 1990s. But even the most ambitious executive at the company would not have predicted that sales would double in four years. Yet this is exactly what happened. In the four-year period from 1990 to 1993, sales growth increased more than 200

EVOLUTION OF GPI'S PAINT AND BODY SHOP BUSINESS

FOR THE FIRST 20 YEARS, GPI WAS A parts distributor to independent parts stores without any ownership in parts stores. The only major automotive paint manufacturer with a program for warehouse distributors was Sherwin-Williams, so GPI's paint line was the Acme brand from Sherwin-Williams. Eventually, the Acme brand was discontinued by Sherwin-Williams and replaced with the Sherwin-Williams brand.

Every other major paint manufacturer sold directly to parts stores rather than through auto parts distributors. The dominant brands were PPG, Dupont, and BASF. Even though there were no profit margins for distribution centers on Dupont, PPG, and BASF paints, GPI's distribution centers maintained inventories of these lines so that their JV stores would have daily access and eliminate the need for stores to buy direct from the paint manufacturers.

It wasn't until GPI began aggressively pursuing the acquisitions of automotive distributors and auto parts stores that they inherited paint inventories supplied by PPG, Dupont, and BASF. With very few exceptions, stores stocked only one paint line and, with very few exceptions, collision and refinishing shops used only one primary brand. Consequently, with each new store acquisition, GPI continued marketing the paint brand that was in place. An exception to this rule occurred in Raleigh, North Carolina, where GPI's JV stores' primary line was PPG. With the acquisition of Raleigh-based CJS that stocked Dupont, both lines were combined in a state-of-the-art facility on Market Street, which also included a paint training center.

Starting about this time, the face of body shops changed dramatically. Due to advanced technology in the new paint products, along with more stringent environmental and safety laws,

---

percent, operating income increased 225 percent, and net income at 290 percent nearly tripled!

It would be difficult to recall a more exciting and successful year in the history of GPI. Each of the operating divisions achieved record sales and earnings in 1993. At the same time, GPI employees had never been more productive. Distribution centers and CARQUEST Joint Venture store sales grew 11.1 percent compared to an industry growth of 4.3 percent. Sales to independently owned auto parts stores grew 6.9 percent. Consolidated sales increased 23 percent.

Operating income increased 33 percent and net income grew 47 percent. Acquisitions, startups, and moving expenses incurred in 1993 were expensed in the amount of $893,000. These expenses arose from the consolidation of the Andalusia and Montgomery distribution centers, consolidation of

purchasing and accounting offices, and acquisitions in Iowa and Washington.

Competition Stays Strong

Competitive pressures continued throughout 1993. Normal price increases in product lines were erased by pricing compression in a marketplace that was challenged by erratic distribution practices. This, coupled with price competition on maturing products, front-wheel drive, and under-hood electronics resulted in the lowest-priced replacement parts for motorists of any year in recent history. Fortunately, this all occurred in a year when demand was good.

The professional automotive service technician continued to win an increasing share of the auto repair market as technology became more complex each year. CARQUEST continued to focus its efforts

small shops fell by the wayside and larger, better financed, and more sophisticated collision/refinishers emerged.

With almost every GPI acquisition involving stores, there was an established automotive paint business. GPI's volume grew with each addition. To coordinate marketing, Jim Purvis was moved to Raleigh in 1997. Purvis established a GPI advisory team consisting of PBE (paint, body and equipment) talent within the company. The advisory team assisted in establishing a departmentalized store blueprint and a marketing and identification program for CARQUEST Automotive Refinish Supply (CARS).

In 2000, Kevin Nelson was moved to Raleigh as national PBE sales manager. In 2003, Nelson was instrumental in organizing an annual company-wide recognition program. It was called the CARQUEST Collision Center Excellence Award, and it was set up to recognize outstanding PBE customers. Nelson also was responsible for directing 75 PBE salesmen within the JV group.

With help from Pete Royal and Joe Jackson at Dupont, GPI developed five PBE training centers. These were located in Billings, Montana;

Raleigh, North Carolina; Lexington, Kentucky; Baton Rouge, Louisiana; and Anchorage, Alaska.

By the end of 2005, PBE sales volume in GPI locations in the United States and Canada was more than $175 million. Of the 583 JV stores selling paint, 35 were stand-alone locations and 272 were departmentalized stores that featured separate paint departments located within the stores with separate staffs and separate phones.

Within GPI distribution centers, 11 now stock Dupont, six stock PPG, four stock BASF, and 16 stock Sherwin-Williams, primarily for independent CARQUEST Auto Parts stores.

By the end of 2005, GPI's PBE business in its U.S. stores grew by 7 percent. PBE sales then represented 7 percent of the JV store group's total volume. As *The Legend of General Parts* goes to press in 2006, GPI's goal is to have PBE represent 10 percent of total sales volume within the next two years. In Canada, the sale of PBE included a 9.6 percent increase in JV stores in 2005 and represented 16 percent of the total, gaining 1 percent from 2004.

The paint and collision market continues to play an important role in GPI's growth.

to make the CARQUEST Auto Parts stores the number one supplier to the professional segment of the auto service market.

Automotive Jobbers Warehouse and GPI Merge

Effective March 29, 1993, Automotive Jobbers Warehouse (AJW) of Portland, Oregon, merged with the Pacific Division of GPI. The company planned to eventually phase AJW into the GPI/CARQUEST Portland Distribution Center.

AJW was a division of Burns Brothers Inc., which also owned a group of truck stops and a tire chain manufacturing company. According to Bruce Burns, president of Burns Brothers Inc., the decision to exit the auto parts business was based on economics. "We wanted to select a company with the strength and management philosophy that would benefit our customer

base. GPI was exactly that kind of company," said Burns.

"We are pleased that Jack and Bruce Burns selected GPI. AJW has an excellent reputation for serving the needs of auto parts stores under the CAPS and Pronto marketing programs. We have seen nothing but quality from their people and their customer base," said Sloan.

Jack Burns and his brother started Burns Bros. Inc. in 1946. AJW was formed in 1969 from a previous division, Burns Brothers Tire and Supply, which had been started in 1950. Tom Moffenbeier, AJW sales manager, was the only management member to join GPI after the merger.

Maintaining the Edge

During 1993, a number of adjustments were made in various CARQUEST product lines to keep

In 1993, GPI built and opened a new 98,500-square-foot distribution center in Montgomery, Alabama.

CARQUEST Auto Parts stores in a strong position to combat all forms of competition. Quality, service, and competitive pricing were the cornerstones of GPI's marketing thrust. Strong master installer programs by the CARQUEST Auto Parts stores, coupled with well-defined Bravo product lines aimed at price shoppers, proved to be the winning combination.

During the year, major subsidiaries were merged into GPI, greatly simplifying the company's corporate structure. This included the merging of Joint Venture

CARQUEST PRODUCTS

IN JANUARY 1993, CARQUEST'S BOARD OF directors unanimously approved Joe Owen's plan to start up a supply company for a single product line that would consolidate all of the miscellaneous service and supply items into one catalog, one numbering system, and one packaging scheme. The company would be built from the ground up. Every CARQUEST member would jointly own the company and its board of directors would be made up of representatives from each CARQUEST member.

Jim McWilliams was appointed president and general manager. He had 18 years of experience in managing two competitive service line companies. GPI veteran Dick Egan was selected to assist McWilliams.

The development of the CARQUEST service line was an exciting venture and step-by-step evolution. An important marketing tool, it offered total flexibility for the procurement of products.

CARQUEST Products Inc. (CPI) began operations in the spring of 1993. Each CARQUEST member was equally invested, and the company supplied only CARQUEST distribution centers.

CPI immediately became the supplier for several application product lines such as motor mounts, coil springs, power steering hose, transmission filter kits, and oil pumps. This allowed the company to generate profits from the very beginning. Since its inception, the company has set sales and profit records each year.

CPI is located in New Castle, Indiana. The company site initially featured a 50,000-square-foot building. After three years, it became obvious that more space would be needed, so in early 1997 a 50,000-square-foot addition was undertaken. In 2000, the CPI building again doubled its size with a 100,000-square-foot addition for a total of 200,000 square feet.

CPI represents a remarkable CARQUEST success story, thanks in large part to the management team: Jim McWilliams, Todd Hack, Dick Egan, Bill Kindig, Mike Low, Jay King, Bob Hamilton, Barney Barnhart, Doug Ireland, Kathy Vallerie, and Bennie Maynard. In 2002, CARQUEST Products received the Outstanding Performance Award by the CARQUEST Corporation.

Also, a new equipment division was launched under the direction of Wayne Hubanks and

Parts stores, welding companies, Capital Computing Inc., and VMS Properties Inc.

In Wisconsin, the huge transition from the Redcar program to the CARQUEST marketing program was virtually completed during 1993. The Marshfield Distribution Center was serving 90 new CARQUEST Auto Parts stores in Wisconsin and the upper peninsula of Michigan. The Madison pick-up warehouse was converted to a Joint Venture super store and the Green Bay Distribution Center to a pick-up warehouse.

In its first full year in Portland, Oregon, GPI was successful in adding 26 new CARQUEST Auto Parts stores, including nine Joint Venture stores, which brought the Oregon Joint Venture Store Group to 13. Acquisition of Burns Brothers' Automotive Jobbers Warehouse resulted in 13 of the new customers.

Portland was then servicing 60 CARQUEST Auto Parts stores. To meet increased sales, GPI planned to build a new and larger distribution center in Portland during 1995.

On December 16th, 1993, GPI completed the consolidation of two Alabama distribution centers into one new 98,500-square-foot distribution center in Montgomery, Alabama. The new facility housed the Southern Division's accounting offices and a new CARQUEST Joint Venture store. Incorporated in the distribution center were several new material-handling systems involving "fast pick" zoning and bar code sorting systems designed to enhance productivity. Sales to Montgomery-serviced customers grew 29 percent in 1993 and positive growth was projected for years to come.

supported with an all-new leasing program. This placed CARQUEST Auto Parts stores in a much stronger competitive position to increase their market share in equipment sales.

Hack Appointed CPI President and General Manager

Jim McWilliams elected to take a well-earned retirement at the end of 2004. Todd Hack, a well-qualified candidate to replace McWilliams, accepted the challenge and completed his first year as president and general manager in 2005. Hack had served several years on the CARQUEST product and marketing staff.

Jim McWilliams was the first president of CARQUEST Products Inc.

The year 2005 ended with CPI establishing its 13th consecutive sales record with a 7 percent increase.

With a renewed customer service approach, the majority of CPI's growth came from sales improvements from existing product lines. CPI also introduced new lines, including a complete line of OEM replacement headlamps, taillights, and mirrors, garage exhaust hose, and expanded offerings of professional quality air tools, and an increased sourcing role in the CARQUEST temperature control line.

By providing service line products that are sourced worldwide from more than 200 manufacturers, CPI has fully rounded out the CARQUEST product offering. This allows CARQUEST stores to reach virtually any market. CPI products include supplies for shop, safety and emergency, towing, lighting, lifting, and maintenance; plus numerous accessories and tools.

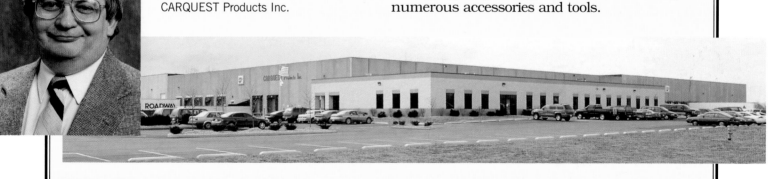

Throughout 1993, GPI made significant changes and expansions of its material-handling systems to improve efficiencies and increase storage capacity in the Portland, Chicago, Belle Plaine, and Albany distribution centers. These major reworkings and consolidations would result in substantial cost savings in the years ahead.

Additionally, late in the year, GPI began work on the expansion of the Raleigh corporate offices, expected to take approximately six months to complete.

GPI's Merger with
Motor Supply Warehouse Company

The Motor Supply Warehouse Company of Belle Plaine, Iowa, operated with a business philosophy that almost perfectly matched that of GPI. The Blanchard family and their associates had built this business on total quality—quality people, quality service, quality products, and quality programs. This was a tribute to the leadership of Beryle Blanchard.

When the opportunity arose for a merger with Motor Supply Warehouse, GPI could not pass it up. The merger was consummated on April 1, 1993. The conversion from the firm's "Bumper to Bumper" program to the CARQUEST Marketing Program, including identification, computer systems, and marketing materials, together with product conversion, was planned to be completed by the first quarter of 1994.

Wayne Wickwire and Douglas Blanchard continued as sales manager and operations manager, respectively. They were joined by Gene Ford as Joint Venture general manager, having merged his three stores into GPI. Ford later served as sales manager of the GPI distribution center in Des Moines and retired in early 2006.

At the time of the merger with GPI, Motor Supply Warehouse Company had grown substantially and was serving 16 of their own parts stores and 65 independent auto parts stores. For more about Motor Supply's history, see chapter 12.

Merger with Fremont Electric

On December 1, 1993, GPI announced a merger with Fremont Electric, a CARQUEST member in Seattle. Fremont had been a CARQUEST member since 1983. At the time of the acquisition by GPI, Fremont operated a distribution center and 10 company-owned CARQUEST Auto Parts stores. Fremont employed more than 170 people and supplied 65 CARQUEST Auto Parts stores that were independently owned.

The firm's management team—Moore M. McKinley Jr., Buz McKinley, Gary Pratt, and Jim Bigelow—had served on various CARQUEST committees and contributed greatly in developing CARQUEST programs. These executives and all key personnel remained in place to assure Fremont's continuing growth.

At the same time, GPI was negotiating to either purchase or build a new distribution center in the Seattle area to increase capacity and improve efficiency in order to serve the entire state of Washington. For more about Fremont's history, see chapter 12.

More Salespeople and More Training

Maintaining its focus on the professional auto service trade through CARQUEST Auto Parts stores, GPI continued to expand its sales force and intensify training. As of December 31, 1993, GPI employed 376 full-time and part-time salespeople in its JV Store Division. In a drive to strengthen the company's sales efforts, GPI added sales managers for JV stores in certain key markets. These positions were already in place for the Chicago, Kentucky, Carolinas, Georgia, and Michigan store groups. And with sales continuing to grow, GPI's management team made plans to add more store sales managers in 1994.

GPI completed several strategic auto parts store acquisitions in 1993. On April 1, GPI acquired four Louisiana auto parts stores from Larry and Doris Watts. Larry Watts began his career in the automotive parts industry in 1959.

On May 1, the GPI Southern Division acquired three CARQUEST Joint Venture stores in Louisiana. Two of the stores in New Orleans were known as Al's Auto Parts. Al Gomez was the part owner and operator of the stores. He remained as manager for GPI's New Orleans marketing area.

Williams Auto Parts
Joins the GPI Family

In 1993, Williams Auto Parts of Decatur, Madison, and Huntsville, Alabama, merged with

TEMPLE SLOAN HONORED

ON JUNE 3, 1993, AT THE CAROLINA Country Club in Raleigh, North Carolina, more than a thousand friends, family, and associates gathered to witness the presentation of the Boy Scouts of America's Distinguished Eagle Award to O. Temple Sloan Jr.

The Distinguished Eagle Award is one of scouting's most prestigious awards. Only three have been presented in the history of the Occoneechee Council, located in Raleigh. The award recognizes former Eagle Scouts who have contributed their time and efforts in continuous support of the Boy Scouts of America program in their adult life.

The presentation included a review of the numerous achievements that Sloan had made, not only to scouting but also to his community, church, and the automotive industry.

The portion of the plaque explaining why Sloan was chosen for this award reads as follows:

Because O. Temple Sloan Jr. earned the rank of Eagle Scout as a member of the Boy Scouts of America 40 years ago, on November 17, 1952; and because as an Eagle Scout he has contributed to serve his God, country, and fellow man, following the principles of the Scout Oath and law.

Joe Owen, also a former Eagle Scout, was asked to say a few words about Sloan. Following are a few excerpts from his comments.

This might well be the toughest assignment I've been faced with—to try to tell you within the time span allotted to me today about Temple Sloan's accomplishments within the automotive parts industry. Not to mention the time that would be needed to describe to you the degree of respect that he commands today within our industry.

Perhaps the most remarkable is Temple's founding of General Parts in 1961— remarkable because he started it by purchasing a small auto parts warehouse with about 50 percent of the inventory already obsolete. What made this more remarkable is that Temple is a Duke graduate and Duke is supposed to turn out smarter people.

But seriously, I think this was a clear indication of the rare courage and determination instilled in Temple Sloan at a very early age—and I sincerely believe that his years as a Boy Scout nourished these characteristics.

You know, I am convinced that if Temple had been around when God was trying to decide how many hours should make a day, he would have convinced him that it should be 48 instead of 24. And if he had, I can promise you that Temple would work 40 of the 48.

They asked me to take only a few moments so I will conclude with just two comments. First, Temple's success is positive proof that Duke does in fact graduate smart people. Second, Temple Sloan's character is the most perfect example of what the Boy Scouts of America's mission is all about.

GPI. Williams Auto Parts was established in 1936 as a family-owned jobbing store. J. W. Williams founded the company and then hired his first employee, E. J. Briscoe. Williams died in 1940 and Briscoe took over the day-to-day operations of the company. Williams' son Jimmy later joined in a partnership. In the 1950s, the partners saw an opportunity to begin one of the first re-distribution warehouse operations in the area.

Jimmy Williams retired in 1981 and Bill Briscoe, son of E. J. Briscoe, was named president of the company. Bill Briscoe had been active in the company since 1970. There was little doubt regarding the secret to the Williams' tradition: professional and highly knowledgeable parts people able to solve any problems their customers might experience.

Additional Changes

Lakeville, Minnesota, introduced the newest Joint Venture Store acquisition in Aberdeen, located in central North Dakota. CARQUEST's Aberdeen store had a machine shop, a large paint business, and a staff of 14 employees. Store manager Tim Jung and his associates were excited regarding the new relationship.

In August, Coastal Auto Parts joined the GPI/CARQUEST team with five stores. Solomon "Mutt" Prather began the business sometime before 1973 with one store and three employees. He, his wife Lorraine, and his sons ran the business for many years. Joel Prather became manager of the city stores. His brother, Allan stayed on to manage the main store in Panama City, Florida. Thirty additional Coastal associates joined the GPI JV Store team.

Two Davis Auto Parts stores owned by Alex Davis and his brothers in Greenville, South Carolina, joined the Mid-Atlantic Division. Meanwhile, the Chicago Joint Venture Store Group was expanded to 18 stores by adding four stores, including three from Al Mackey's Northbrook Auto Parts.

The many important Joint Venture transactions during 1993 were successfully completed. Equally important, a number of experienced managers and inside and outside salespeople joined the GPI/CARQUEST team. Market share was significantly advanced in the cities where JV Store acquisitions were made. Every company GPI acquired was successful, professionally operated, and well

established with highly service-oriented employees perfectly fitting the "GPI mold."

Division Realignment

GPI completed the realignment of its operating, accounting, and purchasing divisions in the first quarter of 1993. The realigned operating divisions of GPI were as follows:

- The Asheville Distribution Center was moved from the Southeast Division to the Mid-Atlantic Division. Chuck Henline's division included Raleigh, Asheville, and Columbia.
- The Jackson Distribution Center was moved from the Southeast Division to the Southern Division. Sloan III's division would include Albany, Jackson, and the soon-to-be consolidated Andalusia and Montgomery.
- Ron Wehrenberg was named chairman of the Midwest Division and would continue to contribute to GPI, concentrating on JV Store development and various training activities.
- Dennis Fox would move to Lakeville, Minnesota, as the president of the Midwest Division.
- Stepping into Fox's shoes as Southeast Division president was Al Wheeler. His division included Memphis, Nashville, and Lexington.
- Rounding out the divisional restructuring, Indianapolis became a part of the Michigan Division, which was renamed the Central Division. It included Bay City, Lansing, and Indianapolis.

With the acquisition of the Fremont Electric Company in Seattle, a new Pacific Division was formed to include Oregon and Washington, headed by Chris Winters.

It is not uncommon for businesses to stumble when they attempt to acquire firms or merge with other firms. Such activities often fail because of differences in company culture, business practices, operating philosophies, and so on. This has never been the case for GPI. The reason—

GPI's employees, who have established a record throughout the industry for professionalism and adaptability. Of the many moves, realignments, and divisional promotions put into action during 1993, most were filled with current GPI associates from companies that joined GPI through previous mergers or acquisitions.

In 1993, CARQUEST introduced an engine controls product line. Supplied by Standard Motor Products, the product line consisted of ignition and emission parts, carburetor repair kits, and wire and cable. CARQUEST bearings and seals, supplied by Federal-Mogul Corporation, and CARQUEST water pumps, supplied by Airtex Automotive Division, were released in late 1993.

An all-new CARQUEST clutch kit program was introduced later in the year. The complete kits included an original equipment clutch assembly, clutch disc, release bearing, and alignment tool. CARQUEST selected AMS Automotive as its supplier. CARQUEST named the Gates Rubber Company as the supplier for the CARQUEST belts and hose product line, with an introduction targeted for the fall of 1994.

By the end of 1993, GPI's sales of CARQUEST, PV, and Bravo-branded products represented 86 percent of all applications parts sales. The only major application product lines remaining to be introduced with a CARQUEST label were engine parts and spark plugs. Neither had been included in the mandated CARQUEST Mission Statement of 1987.

Favorable Indicators

By 1993, domestic automobiles and light trucks on the road had an average age of 8.9 years, while foreign cars and trucks had an average age of 6.6 years. As this on-the-road fleet aged and the aftermarket mix changed, GPI/CARQUEST was in an excellent position to continue to increase sales.

In 1993, miles driven went up by 2.4 percent, the 13th consecutive year of such increases. Stable fuel prices contributed to a continued increase for motor vehicle travel.

SUVs

Although mini-vans and SUVs entered the market in the late 1980s, it was the 1993–94 models of the larger SUVs that really caught the eye of the American vehicle buyer. These vehicles were classified as "light trucks" and were not required to meet the same government C.A.F.E. miles-per-gallon standards as passenger cars. These factors did not impair the public's strong desire to own this type of vehicle.

Consequently, truck registration as a percentage of total vehicle registration jumped from 24 percent in 1993 to 32 percent in 1994. In an eight-year period prior to 1994, light trucks averaged 23 percent of total vehicle registration. In an eight-year period after 1994, light trucks averaged 38 percent of total vehicle registration. Clearly, more of the general public increasingly saw the SUV as the prototypical family vehicle.

Industry Assessment from *Ward's Reports*

Ward's Reports made the following assessment regarding the U.S. auto industry for 1993:

All signs were go for the U.S. auto industry in 1993. Passenger car sales rose moderately, truck sales soared to record highs, and vehicle output reached its highest level since 1989. The U.S. Big Three automakers gained market share back from the Japanese for the second consecutive year.

With the increase in SUV sales by U.S. manufacturers and with SUVs being classified as "light trucks," the U.S. Big Three vehicle manufacturers had an outstanding 83.1 percent of market share of new light truck sales in the United States during 1993. Combined passenger car and light truck sales manufactured by the Big Three was 72.9 percent, the highest figure since 1988.

GPI's rapid growth during the early 1990s was exciting for all involved. And without the remarkable effort and dedication of GPI's management, staff, and associates, that success would not have been possible. Of course, with all of GPI's merger activities, there remained much to be accomplished to integrate the new companies completely. But through it all, GPI remained fully focused on its customers, anticipating and responding to their needs while facing a highly competitive, rapidly changing marketplace.

1994

GPI's 33rd year marked a continuation of the outstanding growth records established during the early 1990s. Sales grew 22.3 percent. During the first half of the 1990s, sales increased 157 percent.

Sales volume benefited from severe cold weather in the upper Midwest during the first quarter, the continued aging of the vehicle population, and a strong economy in most of GPI's markets. Net sales to independent auto parts stores grew 6 percent and store sales for the Joint Venture Store Group were up 7.3 percent. Comparatively, the industry's growth rate for 1994 was 4.4 percent.

Operating income reached a new high in 1994, supported by a 23.5 percent increase over 1993, while net income rose 21.4 percent. During the first half of the '90s, operating income grew 177 percent, and net income was up 256 percent. GPI continued to expense moving, acquisition, and startup expenses in the current year.

In the first quarter of 1994, NAFTA (the North American Free Trade Agreement) was phased in, thus removing trade barriers among the United States, Mexico, and Canada.

During 1994, despite new competition, GPI/CARQUEST Auto Parts stores continued to prosper and increase in numbers while, within the industry, the total number of auto parts stores rapidly declined. To stay on top, GPI routinely monitored all competitive factors on a daily basis to fine-tune its marketing program.

GPI's careful attention to markets—with extra emphasis on selected markets—has always been the key to the company's strong sales successes. As a result, GPI has continually moved sales forward at a record pace and routinely performed at more than double the industry average.

Remaining Focused

In addition to its constant and careful industry and market review, GPI also made sure that its business practices always fully supported its marketing base. Many other distributor firms have not always followed this rule. Indeed, many engaged in sales programs that were organized directly for installers, thus bypassing the jobbing stores. GPI, however, continued to advance market share by selling only through CARQUEST Auto Parts stores. GPI's primary focus continued to be professional automotive technicians whose needs were—and continue to be—best served through GPI/CARQUEST Auto Parts stores.

Key Industry Markers

In 1994, for the second consecutive year, there were no overall price increases on inventory evaluations, which reflected the competitive nature of the automotive aftermarket.

GPI's management team produced a record performance for both sales and earnings in established operating units, and absorbed several significant acquisitions. Considerable time and effort was invested in merging systems applicable to recent acquisitions. The back-to-back, record-setting sales numbers for 1993 and 1994 were a tribute to the efforts of the GPI team as a whole and to a fully dedicated effort by everyone in the company.

Additional Investments and Expansions

GPI continued to make significant investments in facilities and material-handling equipment to improve efficiencies and customer services. During 1994, the company consolidated its Green Bay, Wisconsin, Distribution Center with the expanded Marshfield Distribution Center. GPI expanded the Nashville Distribution Center and mezzanine and conveyor expansions were made in the Jackson, Montgomery, and Baton Rouge distribution centers. A new distribution center was under construction in Lexington, Kentucky. Also under construction were a new 106,700-square-foot Chicago distribution center and a new Seattle distribution center.

Corporate Headquarters Addition

In 1994, after about six months of work, GPI completed the new addition to its corporate offices, which began in the fall of 1993. The construction consisted of a two-story, 12,000-square-foot office addition.

All of the newly organized divisions at GPI presented a large challenge to the company's finance managers—Mike Najdowski, Steve Joyner, Beverly Moretina, Rob Saxby, Hines Johnson, Bruce Nicholson, David Sharer, Kirby Matlick, Dan Walsh, Kevin Sharp, Terry Goshorn, Bonner Mills, Roger Byrd, and Todd Rasmussen. Their expertise and astute financial adjustments contributed greatly to the restructuring of operating divisions within GPI.

New Moves

In 1994, GPI implemented two important organizational changes—the addition of regional training managers and the splitting of the inventory management/gross profit management position into two separate positions. Management exhib-ited a high degree of confidence that both of those changes would show positive results in 1995.

GPI initiated a profit bonus plan in 1994 with non-management Joint Venture Store personnel. In the spring of 1995, the first bonus checks in the amount of $628,000 were presented to JV Store CounterPros, delivery associates, and salespeople for their extra efforts.

Also in 1994, Fred Howard, a Raleigh Distribution Center associate employed in the corporate printing department, displayed his unique talent as an artist by painting a colorful mural of a beautiful, classic automobile on the wall of the lunchroom at the Raleigh Distribution Center.

Top: The expansion of GPI's corporate headquarters was completed in 1994.

Left: This handsome and colorful mural of a classic car graces the lunchroom of the distribution center in Raleigh, North Carolina. Raleigh employee Fred Howard, a highly talented artist in his spare time, spent many hours creating this mural, which became a big hit with distribution center employees.

Business Goes Where It's Invited And Stays Where It's Cared For.

He spent many long hours at this task, but the work was worth it and the mural quickly became a highly popular decorative addition with all Raleigh employees.

CARQUEST: The First 20 Years— A Brief Look Back

In March 1974, during the Automotive Service Industry Association show (ASIA) that was held for a week in Chicago, CARQUEST, a unique automotive parts marketing program, was introduced by three leading distributors. Final plans for the 12-state CARQUEST marketing program were reviewed by Temple Sloan Jr., president of GPI; Joe Hughes, president of Indiana Parts Warehouse; and Dan Bock, president of Bobro Products in New York.

During the conference, Sloan discussed his hopes and expectations concerning CARQUEST.

The year 1974 promises to be one of the most critical in the history of the automotive aftermarket, a year which will have far-reaching consequences for the future of all of our companies. The energy shortage, merchandise shortages, a changing vehicle population, and a rapidly changing marketplace create a difficult course to chart.

What you see this morning is the result of more than two years' work. It involved an in-depth analysis into the future of the automotive aftermarket, our customers, independent wholesalers, and distribution centers such as Bobro, Indiana Parts Warehouse, and GPI Inc. These questions are positive but involved. The one word that affects each of us is "change."

Today you will see the start of a program to ensure the future success of our customers. It is not complete but it is the foundation. It is strong, for without a strong foundation we cannot build for the future. One thing is certain: It is bold, exciting, and challenging.

At the annual CARQUEST meeting in 1994, Sloan discussed the first 20 years of CARQUEST.

Opposite: A popular maxim that GPI has promoted and displayed in its offices over the years.

Success is not accomplished without some failures and false starts along the way. But through it all, the CARQUEST members held together, reacted to change, and created change.

We never lost sight that the CARQUEST Auto Parts store must be a winner, or there would be no CARQUEST.

While the number of jobbers in America dropped from 31,000 to 21,000, the CARQUEST Auto Parts store population has grown to 3,000 strong, 14 percent of the total auto parts store population.

Key dates from 1972 to 1974 in the history of CARQUEST include development of the CARQUEST concept; the famous "bar" story; a false start; combined sales of less than $25 million; Pitluk becoming our ad agency; the Chicago breakfast of March 1974; and Marty Larner's gray hair.

Stories for 1974 include the product committee and first products—CARQUEST oil, Proven Valu brand (Straus Frank), CARQUEST thermostats, caps, clamps, and the first hard parts.

In 1983, Dan Bock sold to the Stockel family and became president of CARQUEST, establishing the Tarrytown, New York, office and developing the professional staff.

The year 1986 brought the training committee and our own training director. GPI has the finest training program within the industry. Over 4,000 people went through the program in 1993.

The year 1987 was the most important date, the most important meeting ever. Three days and nights in the Denver Marriott, then to Colorado Springs. The membership vote was unanimous—all 18 members.

The result was the CARQUEST Mission Statement. It recognized the change that was coming and what CARQUEST had to do to be a winner in the 1990s.

In the last 20-year period, we have spent nearly $250 million developing the quality image of the CARQUEST name. This required a total commitment from all of us, the CARQUEST distribution centers, and the CARQUEST Auto Parts stores.

I wish to identify some people who have possibly made the most significant contributions to the success to the CARQUEST program. It's always dangerous to mention names and everyone's opinion may be different from mine, but here is my list:

- *Ed Whitehurst—if he had not continued to push in 1972 and 1973, we might not be here tonight.*
- *David Straus—led Straus Frank into CARQUEST in 1976. His membership doubled the size of CARQUEST and introduced CARQUEST to Lamont Dupont. David was always a voice for progress.*
- *William "Uncle Willie" Loewenberg—"Sell the jobber first." He built pride in the CARQUEST program.*
- *Joe Owen—focused on the professional automotive service technician as the number one customer for our future. He also was the architect of today's CARQUEST Master Installer Marketing Program.*
- *Ken Rogers—worked behind the scenes to sell Nat and Larry Sills on supplying us the CARQUEST brand, a $100-million relationship today.*
- *Joe Hughes—our rock-solid foundation, he always was behind the scenes and would not let us waiver. Our treasurer for most of the 20 years.*
- *Dan Bock—our sales manager since 1983. He has been our cheerleader, always positive, always keeping us together as a team during times of challenge. He provided recruitment and leadership skills for the CARQUEST staff, including Tom Kirby, Tom Easton, Mike Leach, and the entire team. Special thanks to the Stockel family for buying Bobro, which gave us Dan to be our leader. He has carried us to heights beyond our dreams.*
- *And Pete Kornafel—always there with sound advice.*

There are many more in this room tonight whose unselfish contributions brought us here tonight.

There is no doubt tonight that we are bragging a little! But what the hell—after 20 years of blood, sweat, and tears, plus 20 years of successes and failures. We are here, we are still growing, we are still winning, 3,000 auto parts stores' strong. We have earned one night to celebrate, to thank each other, and to dedicate ourselves to the future. Let us toast to 20 years.

Neil Stockel, president of BWP, the CARQUEST distribution member in New York and chairman of CARQUEST, added these remarks:

CARQUEST did have many highlights in 1993. Distribution center sales reached a record $750 million.

Helping the growth this past year were seven new CARQUEST lines. We introduced remanufactured power steering products by Atsco, a complete flasher program by Ideal, bearings and seals by Federal Mogul, remanufactured distributors and wiper motors by CARDONE, engine controls by Standard Motor Products, new clutch kits by three different vendors, Westling and A1 Clutch, and new water pumps by Airtex.

What makes it all work is the dedication to teamwork, a team made up of manufacturers, CARQUEST distribution center members, and a CARQUEST office staff that refuses to let any minor detail fall through the cracks.

Other highlights in 1993 came in training and education. This year, between our training department in Tarrytown and all the training directors at the distribution centers, CARQUEST trained over 4,000 people for a total of 10,000 hours.

CARQUEST also earned the prestigious Excellence in Training Award presented by the Automotive Training Managers Council, which recognized CARQUEST for the best training program in the automotive service business.

For those of you who are not aware, in the last five years a CARQUEST member has walked away with the AWDA Automotive Man of the Year Award three times. In 1988, Pete Kornafel was honored; in 1989, Ham and Temple Sloan; and in 1992 Art Lottes III. Just mentioning those four people in the same breath shows the strength of leadership that CARQUEST possesses.

Yes, CARQUEST has come a long way in 20 years, and I'm sure that 20 years from now our market will have changed again, even more dramatically. But it's my bet that no matter how drastic the change may be, CARQUEST will be Number One.

CARQUEST Brand Sales Up

In 1994, approximately 80 percent of GPI's total sales volume was from the sale of parts with specific vehicle applications. That year, 88.4 percent of that volume was sold in CARQUEST, Bravo, or Proven Valu brands, proof that those brands were now widely accepted by customers in the automotive aftermarket.

O.E.M. Warehouse and Skaggs Auto Parts

O.E.M. Warehouse and Skaggs Auto Parts agreed to merge with GPI effective April 30, 1994. The announcement was made jointly by Ken Dunlap, president of O.E.M./Skaggs, and Temple Sloan Jr., chairman of GPI Inc.

O.E.M. Warehouse, a Spokane, Washington, distributor of automotive parts and supplies, had served the automotive aftermarket in eastern Washington, Idaho, and western Montana for 45 years. The company owned four auto parts stores in Spokane and one in Moses Lake, Washington, doing business under the name Skaggs Auto Parts.

O.E.M. and Skaggs Auto Parts had an outstanding record of service. Ken Dunlap, Don Castle, and their management team had built a solid company. GPI's management looked forward to the new merger arrangement. "The merger with GPI will strengthen our company. Don, myself, and our people look forward to working with such a respected organization as GPI," said Ken Dunlap.

In 1994, the Seattle team was occupied with its merger activities; changing over to new computer, purchasing, and accounting systems; converting the

This map shows the extent of GPI's sales and marketing reach during 1994.

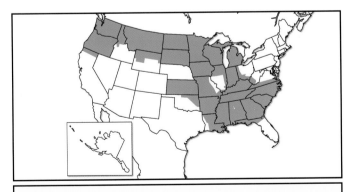

During the period 1990–1994, GPI's sales increased 157 percent and earnings increased 256 percent.

Yakima Distribution Center into Seattle's first JV Super Store; and integrating the Skaggs acquisition.

Plans were progressing to move the Seattle Distribution Center to its new 84,000-square-foot distribution center location, scheduled for April 1995. A portion of the existing distribution center would become the new Fremont Super Store. The new distribution center would permit expansion of product coverage to better serve the Washington CARQUEST Auto Parts stores. Moore McKinley's guidance and strong support helped make 1994 a very successful year for GPI.

Service Parts Warehouse and 688 Parts Service

On February 1, 1994, GPI merged with 688 Parts Service Inc./Service Parts Warehouse of Baton Rouge, Louisiana. George Tricou's company was the dominant parts distributor in the Baton Rouge market. Nineteen 688 Stores and 18 independent jobbers were converted to the CARQUEST marketing program.

Aubrey Weil, with his store management and sales team, led the successful conversion of the 688 Stores Group. In addition, a total reorganization of the Baton Rouge Distribution Center, including bin capacity, mezzanine and conveyors, plus re-roofing and air conditioning, took place. Changes to the distribution center enabled GPI to expand inventory coverage, thus improving service and efficiencies to the new CARQUEST customers. The New Orleans Joint Venture Group would be serviced from the expanded Baton Rouge Distribution Center. For more about SPW and 688's history, see chapter 12.

Diversified Automotive Distributors Inc.

October 1, 1994, marked GPI's merger with Diversified Automotive Distributors Inc. (DADI), Kansas City, Missouri. Martin Brown, chairman of DADI and Temple Sloan Jr., chairman of GPI, announced the merger.

The assets of DADI, formerly known as Automotive Distributors Inc. (ADI), were purchased by Brown in 1989. ADI had been a CARQUEST distributor since 1984.

"Marty Brown, Sue Weland, and their management team have built an outstanding company and we are pleased to have the opportunity to continue

TRANSITIONS

1990—Wayne Lavrack, general manager of Joint Venture stores in GPI's Michigan Division, was promoted to the newly created post of corporate vice president of all Joint Venture stores within GPI's five divisions. Lavrack, a seasoned veteran of the auto aftermarket, joined CARQUEST and the Michigan division in 1976. He was picked for this important position based on his proven performance in the Michigan Division. Under his leadership, the Michigan JV stores always produced outstanding results. In December, Lavrack and his wife Sue, and their children, Melanie, 18, Jeremie, 15, Lane, 13, and Brock, 8, moved to North Carolina. Other promotions: **Judy Brim** to controller, Lexington Group, **John Cuomo** to director of accounting, Albany, **Allen Dedman** to president of the Northwest Division, **Dick Egan** to sales manager for both Michigan Distribution centers, **Janet Higgins** to controller, Mid-Atlantic Division, **Ken Karber** to general manager, Michigan JV Store Group, and **Lenore Swenson** to controller, Northwest Division.

1990—GPI announced in 1990 the retirement of **Jim Hall.** Jim spent 40 years with Valley Motor Supply Company, Montana, and will be long remembered for his management contributions. Other retirees: **Olen Baucom** (21), **Eliose Cason** (24), **Jim Cason** (20), **Harvey McDaniel** (30), and **Dennis Peterson** (40).

1991—Promotions: **Roger Byrd** to finance director, Nashville/Lexington, **Don Davis** to operations manager, Nashville Distribution Center, **Trey Dickerson** to sales manager, Jackson Distribution Center, **Dick Egan** to president, Central Division, Indianapolis and Lexington, **Robert Ford** to general manager, Memphis JV Group, **Hersey Hall** to operations manager, Lexington Distribution Center, and **John Kahut** to sales manager, Albany Distribution Center.

1991—Two legendary south Mississippi auto parts associates retired in 1991—**Roy Williams** (40) and **Wallace Clay** (30). Between the two, they amassed more than 70 years of parts experience. Both greatly deserve their retirement. Other retirees: **Neale Browning** (20), **Ester Chernavage** (27), **Dan Connors** (29), and **Joe Mclendon** (45).

From top left clockwise:
Wayne Lavrack, Hersey Hall, Roy Williams, Wallace Clay, and Jim Hall.

1991—In memoriam: Friends and associates of GPI mourned the passing of **Alida Baker,** who died March 7 and **Robbie Harrison** who died November 29. Baker was executive secretary to senior GPI managers since 1971. Harrison who retired in 1980, was the second salesman hired by GPI and was instrumental in the early success of the company. His passion for taking care of customers was unsurpassed.

1992—John Martens joined GPI as general manager, Chicago JV Store Group. Promotions: **Judy Brim** to controller of the newly formed Central Division, **Linda Canipe** to executive secre-

tary, Corporate, **Tom Cantwell** to sales manager, Chicago Distribution Center, **Don Davis** to operations manager, Nashville Distribution Center, **Dick Egan** to president of the Central Division, **Tom Ferguson** to sales manager, Bay City Distribution Center, **Dennis Fox** to president, Midwest Division, **Mike Hedge**

to general manager, Albany JV Stores, **Chuck Henline** to president, Mid-Atlantic Division, **Fred Kotcher** to corporate vice president,

Purchasing & Administration, **Shipman Northcutt** to sales manager, Memphis Distribution Center, **Braxton O'Neal** to JV Store inventory coordinator, **Kim Patch** to general manager, Lakeville JV Stores, **Jim Roth** to sales manager, Lansing Distribution Center, **Robert Saxby** to finance director, Michigan Division, **O. Temple Sloan III** to president of the Southern Division, **Dan Studstill** to operations manager, Montgomery Distribution Center, **Rick Van Zant** to operations manager, Memphis Distribution Center, **Barney Watson** to sales manager, Raleigh Distribution Center, **Ron Wehrenberg** to chairman, Midwest Division, and **Al Wheeler** to president, Southeast Division.

1992—Herman Markell was honored for exceeding the 1,000-mark for graduates from CounterPro, SALESQUEST, Cold Call Selling, and the new customer service task force.

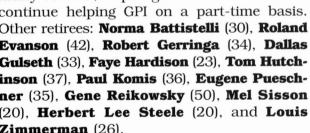

1992—After 30 years of devoted service, one of the true legends of GPI elected to officially retire. **Mary Pope** was one of the first five employees hired by Temple Sloan Jr. in 1962. She joined the company as a bookkeeper and was outstanding in that capacity and in just about anything else that needed to be audited and controlled. Although she formally retired, Pope agreed to continue helping GPI on a part-time basis. Other retirees: **Norma Battistelli** (30), **Roland Evanson** (42), **Robert Gerringa** (34), **Dallas Gulseth** (33), **Faye Hardison** (23), **Tom Hutchinson** (37), **Paul Komis** (36), **Eugene Pueschner** (35), **Gene Reikowsky** (50), **Mel Sisson** (20), **Herbert Lee Steele** (20), and **Louis Zimmerman** (26).

From top left clockwise: Alida Baker, Mary Pope, Linda Canipe, and Robbie Harrison.

1992—In memoriam: **Willie Rushing,** a GPI retiree, died October 13 at the age of 71. A year after GPI was founded, in 1962, Rushing joined the company as a sales representative for the Raleigh Distribution Center, working the North and South Carolina markets. He was instrumental in the growth of sales and new business. In 1974, when the Columbia Distribution Center was opened, Rushing was appointed sales manager. After serving in that capacity for four years, Rushing decided to semi-retire, working as a part-time salesman.

1993—New addition: **Tom Moffenbeier** joined GPI as sales manager, Portland Distribution Center. Promotions: **Ron Adkins** to president, Valley Welders, **Dale Dockter** to president, Northern Welders, **Dan Fochtman** to JV general manager, Indiana, **John W. Gardner** to vice president, Finance, **Rick Griffin** to sales manager, Asheville Distribution Center, **Richard E. Guirlinger** to corporate treasurer, **Arnold Jenkins** to JV general manager, Columbia Distribution Center, **John Kahut** to sales manager, Marshfield Distribution Center, **Stan Marks** to sales manager, Nashville Distribution Center, **Guy Martin** to sales manager, Albany Distribution Center, **David McCartney** to operations manager, Albany, **Don Robinson** to vice president, sales, Montgomery Distribution Center, **John Weinmann Sr.** to operations manager, Marshfield, and **Ralph Wells** to vice president, market development, Southern Division.

1993—**Charles A. "Chuck" Harwick** retired at the end of 1993, having served Northern Industries for 37 years. His leadership and guidance led to a very successful conversion of Northern's customer base to GPI/CARQUEST. GPI would continue to benefit from his counsel. Other retirees in 1993: **Kenny Freeman** (37), **Lynn Hadley** (24), **Betty Harp** (31), **Reed Roberts** (36), and **Shirley Smith** (29).

1993—In memoriam: **Beryle Blanchard,** president and founder of Motor Supply Company in Iowa, passed away in

From top left, clockwise: Willie Rushing, Charles A. "Chuck" Harwick, and Beryle Blanchard.

Opposite page: Jim Russell.

our growth together," said Sloan. "DADI looks forward to growing together with such a respected organization as GPI," said Brown. For more about DADI's history, see chapter 12.

First CARQUEST Store Joins GPI's JV Group

On February 24, 1994, Bill Cotten merged his four City Auto Parts stores into GPI's JV Stores division. Davis Harris, Bill's son-in-law, became a joint venture partner. Harris started buying from GPI in October 1962. Cotton recalled his early days with GPI.

Mac Graham would call for our order every day at 2:00 PM. A.C. Burkhead who lived in Sanford, North Carolina, would deliver the order to my house on his way home.

We were moving from our original location the weekend before Easter in 1969. I looked up and there was Temple. He had come by to get me to play golf, not knowing that we were moving. This was Saturday at about 1:00 PM.

We worked until late in the evening and planned to try and finish on Sunday. Well, when we arrived on Sunday morning there were about

the spring. Temple Sloan said, "We are most appreciative of his confidence in guiding the merger of our two companies. He will be missed."

1994—New addition: **Ron Ballard** joined GPI as sales manager, Columbia Distribution Center. Promotions: **Hersey Hall** was promoted to field operations manager and assigned to the corporate staff in Raleigh. Hall joined GPI in 1977 after serving six years in the army as a helicopter pilot. He started as assistant of operations in Columbia, South Carolina. He has accepted operations challenges throughout the company with stints in Asheville, North Carolina; Billings, Montana; Memphis; Lexington, Kentucky; and Raleigh, North Carolina. Other promotions: **Jerry Berryhill** to operations manager, Asheville, **Royce Bugg** to inventory control manager, Lexington, **Jon Cockerham** to JV general manager, Seattle, **Tina Davis** to corporate manager of Graphics & Promotions, **Danny Durham** to vice president, Operations, Montgomery, **John James** to operations manager, Seattle, **Phil Leding** to operations manager, Memphis, **Jeff Lundh** to vice president and general manager, Chicago Group, **Guy Martin** to operations manager, Baton Rouge, **Bubba McDonald** to JV general manager, Montgomery, **O. Temple Sloan III** to president of South Central Division, **Hoke Smith** to JV general manager, New Orleans, Mobile, and Baton Rouge, and **John Taylor** to vice president, JV Stores, Southern Divison.

1994—Retirees: On April 29, **Jim Russell** retired with over 25 years of service. Russell spent many years managing the Sheridan, Wyoming, JV Store, consistently producing sales and profit records. Russell also spent several years as president of GPI's Northwest Division. His contributions to the success of GPI in the Northwest were numerous and his retirement was richly  deserved. Other retirees in 1994: **Duane Cromwell** (34), **Emma Davis** (30), **Clif Franklin** (24), **Don Gradowski** (39), **Jack Hagie** (23), **Kenneth Hoehn** (34), **Virginia Kerby** (24), and **Herb Masoll** (43).

In loving memory of the following additional associates who passed away during this period: **Olin Burgess, Jerry Falkenhagen, Art Gregory, Doug Johnson, Tommy Johnson, Laverne Kandt, Dehava Knapp, Sandra Maxwell,** and **Herbert Steele.**

> Retiree information shows years of employment after names. This may include time spent at acquired companies.

10 or 12 GPI people from Raleigh to help. That was typical of Temple and GPI. They were always there to help whatever the problem or task might be.

In 1994, in addition to Baton Rouge, Seattle, and Spokane with their strategic store acquisitions, six stores were acquired in Ocala, Florida, two Rex Auto Parts Stores in Benton Harbor, Michigan, from Rex Watkins Sr., and six stores were acquired in the greater Chicago area.

By the end of 1994, GPI was serving 1,654 CARQUEST Auto Parts stores in 31 states including 531 joint venture stores. GPI had grown impressively during the first half of the decade, a trend that would continue.

SOME OF THE MANY WHO HELPED

Craig Flournoy

Jeff Fletcher

Bob Greathouse

Ron Ballard

Scott Compston

Dennis Weiland

Dave Pruden

Tom Brown

Brad Carter

Dan Conroy

Don Frankfather

Karl Hauer

Dale Morris

Dan Owczarzak

Stan Marks

Frankie Underwood

Sandy Macomber

Susan Howard

Al Haines

Tom Moffenbeier

Gary Ljunggren

Vic Hymel

Mike Mizelle

Paul May

Christina Irving

Jon Wehling

Gerry Ligon

Ed Wortman

Michael Shields

Randy Pisciotta

Troy Matherne

Jerry Sharpee

Jerry Dickey

Peter Wertz

Kenny Faulkner

Tony Bridges

Rolanda Holland

Danny Rains

Mike Buss

Brian Harper

Lisa Creech

Peggy Bella

Doug Buscher

Mark Miller

Beverly Moretina

Bruce Nicholson

Frank Aukland

Dan Walsh

Glen Avery

Phil Porter

Roger Smith

Diane Ellison

Wes Rice

Scott Halford

Penny Bullock

John Chachere

John Attenweiler

Dave Murley

Bob Wusterbarth

Millie Alford

Darrin Schmitt

Mike Pughes

Dede Geary

CARQUEST operates one of the most efficient parts delivery systems in the industry, ensuring that needed items always get to the CARQUEST stores in a timely fashion.

CHAPTER EIGHT

WINNING BIG

1995–1998

The one who wins is the one who prepares to win.

—Joe Hughes, former owner of Indian Parts Warehouse
and one of the first three members of CARQUEST

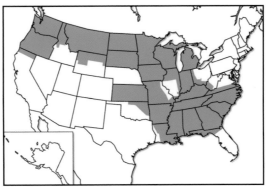

DURING THE FIRST half of the 1990s, GPI had been busy with numerous companies acquired, many new facilities built and old ones expanded, and with sales taking off like a rocket. As the company entered the second half of the decade, it began to take a more measured approach by consolidating its operations, restructuring the management team's responsibilities, improving reporting and internal systems, and updating and installing operating systems. It would not take long, however, for GPI to resume its breakneck pace in acquiring more companies and expanding its marketing reach.

Sales Stay Strong

Even with substantial time and effort now focused on housekeeping necessities, GPI's sales continued to climb in 1995, a year when the automotive aftermarket experienced its smallest growth in more than 50 years. During the year, GPI's sales grew 11.2 percent. Again, GPI outperformed its competitors and continued to drive market share in the mature aftermarket. Operating income grew 13.6 percent and net income, negatively affected by interest expense, grew 6.9 percent. With sales strong, GPI reached several major financial goals in 1995, including being recognized as an investment grade company by the National Association of Insurance Commissioners and by Fitch Investor Service, a ratings bureau.

GPI continued to build new facilities and expand old ones to meet the increasing demand. Major expansions and investment in GPI/CARQUEST distribution centers were authorized during 1995. The company replaced outdated or overcrowded facilities with new modern distribution centers in four key markets. It constructed and occupied new distribution centers in Seattle (91,000 square feet), Chicago (115,000 square feet), Portland, Oregon (105,000 square feet), and Lexington, Kentucky (100,000 square feet). GPI's two largest distribution centers, Raleigh, North Carolina, and Lakeville, Minnesota, both underwent major bin system expansions of more than 1,000 bins each, as well as the installation of advanced bar code sortation systems for improved order-handling efficiency.

The Baton Rouge, Louisiana, and Albany, Georgia, distribution centers underwent major

---

This map shows the extent of GPI's sales and marketing reach during 1995.

remodeling with new loading dock equipment, sortation systems, and air conditioning installed in the warehouse areas. GPI associates at these facilities appreciated these much-needed improvements. Most important, the improved facilities would make for better customer service and operating efficiency.

These extensive projects were accomplished with minimum disruption to the CARQUEST Auto Parts stores, thanks to the efforts of all GPI personnel.

More Growth and Restructuring in 1995

GPI's first full year in Baton Rouge resulted in a growth of 8.3 percent in the Joint Venture Store Group and an earnings growth of 56 percent. The remodeling and reorganization of the Baton Rouge Distribution Center, including the expanded inventory coverage, was completed in 1995, a major accomplishment for the entire Baton Rouge team.

In 1995, GPI expanded the Joint Venture Store Group in Kansas City, going from 11 to 18 locations. Two stores were added to the Kansas City Metro Group, along with major entries into the Kansas cities of Lawrence and Topeka.

Due to continuing growth in Joint Venture Store sales, along with opportunities for growth

Above, from left to right: GPI distribution centers in Chicago; Lexington, Kentucky; Portland, Oregon; and Seattle, Washington.

Below: All GPI distribution centers operated from a common footprint designed for maximum efficiency. Shown here is a view of the DC shipping area where daily shipments to CARQUEST stores are assembled.

within the independent CARQUEST Auto Parts stores, GPI decided to restructure nine divisional management organizations into three new management groups:

- Joint Venture Store Group, headed by Wayne Lavrack who was promoted to group vice president. Four division vice presidents were named to lead the JV Stores Divisions: Allen Dedman, John Taylor, John Martens, and Hoke Smith. Each vice president would be assisted by three general managers, 15 regional managers, and approximately 150 auto parts stores in their respective divisions. In addition, Al Wheeler was named vice president, sales, for Joint Venture Stores.
- The CARQUEST independent auto parts stores base was placed into regions, to be headed by Dennis Fox, group vice president, supported by four regional vice presidents responsible for sales growth through independent CARQUEST Auto Parts stores and for acquisitions for the JV Store Group. Heading the four regions were Norm Ferguson, Chuck Henline, Jeff Lundh, and Chris Winters.
- C. Hamilton Sloan, vice chairman, was to head the Operations Group, supported by R.D. Carson and Charles Shaw, vice presidents responsible for the operation of 21 distribution centers.

While the old divisional structure had served GPI well since 1980, the new alignment recognized the talents of the different members of the team and refocused their efforts on their strengths.

New CARQUEST Product Lines

In 1995, GPI developed plans for the introduction of the new CARQUEST gasket product line supplied by Victor-Reinz, to be released to the field in early 1996. Also, CARQUEST announced a new branded line of welding supplies in late 1995. By this time, the full range of CARQUEST-branded product lines was nearly complete.

In 1995, important store acquisitions included City Auto Parts of Bristol, Virginia, and Blountville, Tennessee. Tony Harlow and Henry Millard joined GPI as stockholders, continuing to expand the company stores by offering outstanding customer service. Brack's Automotive in Coeur D'Alene and Bonners Ferry, Idaho, were added in mid-year, led by Stan Parks.

Western Auto Parts Joins GPI

Decades ago in Minot, North Dakota, Mose Zuzulin, son of Russian immigrants, began in the auto wrecking business with an original outlay of $135 saved while working in the threshing fields of North Dakota in the 1920s.

When Zuzulin died in 1972, it was announced that arrangements had been made to sell his business, the Western Auto Supply Company/United Auto Stores Company, to its employees, the people who managed the stores and warehouse. With the financial guidance of Warren Anderson, a prominent Fargo CPA who also became a stockholder, the buyout occurred with 15 individual employees buying shares.

Nels Gilberg, manager of the Grand Forks store was elected president of Western Auto Supply Company/United Auto Stores Company. In 1987, the company became affiliated with the Road Pro Program. In 1988, all of the stores were united under the Western Auto Parts name. On October 2, 1995, GPI welcomed Western Auto Parts to the GPI/CARQUEST family.

Midwest Acquisitions

Late in the fourth quarter of 1995, Randy Russell and Mark Augustine brought their three

MURF HANDMAKER

LONG-TIME GPI FRIEND AND ADVISOR, I.H. "Murf" Handmaker died April 1, 1995, in Tucson, Arizona, following a long battle with heart disease. He was 86 years old.

With his brother, Handmaker founded Automotive Supply Company in Pennsylvania. In 1944, he moved to Tucson and built Complete Auto Supply, an 11-store group. In 1973, Handmaker and Carl Pohlad, a Minneapolis banker, bought General Trading Company in St. Paul, Minnesota, which in 1978 became a CARQUEST Member.

The story has been told that in January 1980, Handmaker took Temple Sloan Jr. into a bar in the Marriott Hotel in Atlanta, Georgia, and convinced him to purchase General Trading Company when interest rates were 20 percent.

large stores in Laurence, Kansas, and Topeka, Kansas, to the GPI Joint Venture Stores Group; plus, eight auto parts stores were added in the Chicago Joint Venture Group.

Industry Trends in 1995

During 1995, the automotive aftermarket continued to consolidate at every level. Larger manufacturers acquired smaller manufacturers, and larger warehouse distributors acquired smaller warehouse distributors. Many small jobber stores went out of business, as a result of the growing inventory requirement and increased competition.

Overall, two-step competitors—automotive parts distributors who sold direct to auto service repair shops, thus bypassing auto parts stores—continued to multiply, although some were closing, some were going out of business, and some were being acquired. Many of the two-step operations were moving much too rapidly and loading inventories into facilities without proper planning. The predictable result: a lack of profitability. GPI/CARQUEST Auto Parts stores' Master Installer rebate concept continued to be an effective marketing approach to compete with the two-step distributors.

General Parts saw no reason to make any major changes in its marketing direction. The company continued to fine-tune its actions to keep CARQUEST Auto Parts stores in a strong competitive position. The GPI distribution centers were constantly challenged to keep their service level to the stores at an all-time high. This was absolutely necessary in allowing the CARQUEST stores to serve their customers better than the competition.

Most Popular Models for 1995

Ward's Reports listed the following as the top 10 new vehicle types in the United States for 1995:

1. Ford F Series (truck)	6. Toyota Camry
2. Chevy C/K (truck)	7. Ford Ranger (truck)
3. Ford Explorer	8. Honda Civic
4. Ford Taurus	9. GM's Saturn
5. Honda Accord	10. Ford Escort

Moving Into a New Year

As GPI prepared to enter the new year, Temple Sloan Jr. looked back in an address to associates on what the company had accomplished recently.

We enter 1996 with confidence that we have the management team, structure, marketing programs, and facilities to take GPI into a successful future. Our restructure has been enthusiastically received within our company, and we are confident of our future growth in sales and earnings.

GPI associates know that our ability to out-serve the competition in supplying auto parts to professional service technicians through CARQUEST Auto Parts stores will determine our future.

Our solid growth, in light of industry performance, illustrates the dedication and ability of all GPI associates. We are appreciative regarding their successful efforts on the company's behalf. Plus, the faith our investors and suppliers routinely place in us, along with the service they provide, helped us to achieve another record year.

1996: GPI's 35th Year

The year 1996 marked the completion of 35 years of operation by GPI in the automotive parts aftermarket. During this period, GPI experienced rapid sales growth and enjoyed a profit each and every year, a record for which every GPI associate has always been proud. This exemplary achievement was a testimonial to all GPI employees—their teamwork, performance, pride, and commitment.

GPI's Management: Deserving of Credit

Throughout its history, GPI's executive management had always made sure to extend much deserved credit and recognition to the company's associates for GPI's unbroken run of annual sales and profitability increases. But until *The Legend of General Parts*, little had ever been written about the leadership of the company, which had always modestly shunned the limelight.

During its first 35 years of operations, GPI's management had accomplished some remarkable feats: prospering when so many other companies recorded only lackluster performance, or even slid backwards; outperforming the industry average every year without fail; convincing numerous respected warehouse distributors to follow GPI's lead in utilizing the new CARQUEST marketing program; and getting both warehouse distributors and auto parts stores to join GPI in an associate/partnership relationship and/or a merger/acquisition association.

The motivator has been GPI's people in leadership positions with a vested interest in the company. This continued in 1996 with these highlights:

- Merger with Sussen Inc. (Cleveland, Columbus, and Buffalo), a CARQUEST member
- Merger with Hatch Grinding (Denver and Albuquerque), a CARQUEST member
- Acquisition of The Equipment Company (Kansas City)
- Acquisition of PSC Distributing Inc. (Phoenix), a CARQUEST member
- Achievement of the company's first $200 million sales quarter
- Founding of the GPI Management Institute
- Sales growth of 20.2 percent, the largest single year's sales growth in GPI's history
- Net income up 6.1 percent over 1995, a worthwhile achievement due to integration and startup costs of acquisitions, along with the growth in interest cost

The new acquisitions were profitable from day one, even after deducting startup costs. Indeed, the companies acquired would make significant contributions to sales and profits in 1997 and in the years ahead.

Market Trends for 1996

Market trends for 1996 continued along the same course as during 1995. More aftermarket participants clearly understood that the pace of technology change for new cars was speeding up. As a result, with each new model year, it was becoming increasingly difficult for do-it-yourselfers to handle their own repair work. Auto parts stores, which had depended on the DIY market for 100 percent of their sales, found themselves in a declining market.

As a result, the larger stores had to spend more time diversifying their customer bases to include professional automotive service technicians. At the same time, many of the smaller chains and stores were put up for sale, with some even closing up for good. Joe Owen commented on this situation to JV store managers.

If we are winning today's battles for customer loyalty based on price, we have achieved an incredibly hollow victory. Because, as profit margins continue to be squeezed in a consolidating industry, those cus-

MOORE M. MCKINLEY JR.

THE YEAR 1996 MARKED THE PASSING of Moore M. McKinley Jr., who built one of the largest wholesale automotive parts distribution systems in the Northwest. He died in September at the age of 65. He was honored at his memorial service as a highly personable individual whom people liked to be around. Temple Sloan Jr. and Joe Owen both commented that they never heard anyone ever say an unkind word about McKinley.

Prior to the GPI merger in 1993, McKinley was the owner and president of Fremont Electric.

He expanded this firm into a major wholesale auto parts dealer, with operations in Washington, Oregon, Idaho, and Alaska.

Shortly after the GPI merger, Moore was instrumental in the GPI merger with O.E.M. Warehouse and Skagg's Auto Parts in Spokane and eastern Washington.

McKinley was an outstanding salmon fisherman. A photo showing him catching a 66-pound king salmon appeared in the first issue of *Sports Illustrated*. He also was an avid pheasant hunter and trained Brittany Spaniels.

McKinley was survived by his wife Ann, two daughters, and his son, Buz, who served previously as a sales manager for GPI in Seattle.

---

tomers will only stay until the next hungry and willing supplier gives them an even lower price. In order for us to stay profitable and at the same time distinguish ourselves from our competitors, there is only one practical approach—offer an unmatched, high-quality, customer-driven level of service. And remember that there is a cost for this type of service.

Vehicle Manufacturers

While focused on selling cars and trucks, new car manufacturers were still trying to increase their parts sales. Ford and Honda were experimenting with off-site, strategically located service centers in major markets. Chrysler was using a mobile van service where Chrysler technicians would repair Chrysler products in the owners' own driveways.

Two major U.S. parts manufacturers, Dana Corporation and Federal-Mogul Corporation, were trying to develop the retail distribution of auto parts in foreign countries. Both eventually withdrew, sold their retail companies, and abandoned this distribution approach.

Accounting Advances

For GPI, the ongoing project of centralizing store account receivables processing and credit management into the regional accounting offices was completed during the first half of 1996. Bad debt expense declined to .23 percent of sales, down from .27 percent in 1995. While GPI maintained satisfactory reserves, the company was determined to continue reducing bad debt expense and exposure.

Distribution Center Expansions; National Account Business Up

In 1996, GPI completed a 35,000-square-foot expansion of the Lakeville, Minnesota, Distribution Center. To accommodate anticipated growth, it launched five major material-handling and bin-system expansion projects in distribution centers in Chicago, Buffalo, Cleveland, Denver, and Albuquerque.

Additionally, GPI continued expanding its national account business. CARQUEST's three full-time national account salesmen developed several new national account customers.

GPI and Sussen, Inc. Merge

Effective January 26, 1996, GPI and Sussen, Inc., merged. Sussen, Inc., had been a CARQUEST member since 1976. The merger announcement was made jointly by Daniel C. Sussen Sr., chairman of Sussen, and Temple Sloan Jr., chairman of GPI.

"Sussen, Inc. has contributed greatly to the success of the CARQUEST Corporation and has an outstanding record of customer service. Dan Sussen and his management team have provided their company with excellent leadership. We are pleased to have the opportunity to continue to grow together," said Temple Sloan, Jr.

Sloan also announced that Dan Sussen would join GPI's board of directors.

Dan Sussen added, "The merger with GPI will strengthen the position of our CARQUEST customers. We look forward to an exciting new chapter in the company's 75th year, working together with GPI, one of the most respected organizations in our industry."

The merger with Sussen, Inc. represented a major restructuring effort for GPI's team of associates. Sussen's Columbus distribution center was closed and merged into GPI's Cleveland Distribution Center, where storage capacity and conveyor systems were expanded. The accounting and purchasing functions were merged into existing GPI offices. Five new Joint Venture stores were added to the Sussen Group, which brought the JV stores count up to 20. Consolidated sales in Cleveland and Buffalo were up 9.3 percent for the year and further transactions were planned to increase market penetration in that region.

For more about Sussen's history, see chapter 12.

GPI Merges With Hatch Grinding Company

On April 1, 1996, GPI took a giant step forward by agreeing to merge with Pete and Annie Kornafel's company, Hatch Grinding. Pete Kornafel joined GPI's board of directors following the merger.

At the time, Hatch served 110 CARQUEST Auto Parts stores, seven of which were company owned. As a result, GPI saw an opportunity to establish a strong store group in the Denver and Albuquerque markets. During the nine months remaining in 1996, GPI consolidated two of Hatch's company-owned stores in Fort Collins, Colorado. It also acquired 15 additional stores in Colorado and three Joint Venture stores in New Mexico. GPI converted the Hatch computers to its own system and established a regional purchasing office in Denver.

GPI expected the new Denver Group would make a significant contribution in 1997. Its Albuquerque team worked hard to expand the base of both the Joint Venture stores and the independent CARQUEST Auto Parts stores. The Hatch/GPI team put forth a tremendous effort overall, and in particular, in the development of an outstanding Joint Venture management team.

For more about Hatch's history, see chapter 12.

A New President for CARQUEST

The Hatch merger's timing coincided nicely with the retirement of Dan Bock, CARQUEST's president since 1983. Bock had assumed this post after he and his brother sold their CARQUEST distribution company, Bobro, to the Stockel family. He was instrumental in developing CARQUEST's marketing effort and the CARQUEST brand (in 2006, a complete group of 32 separate product lines). After stepping down as president, Bock was appointed executive vice president of CARQUEST. In this role, he continued to provide guidance and assistance to the corporation. CARQUEST's board of directors then approved Pete Kornafel as CARQUEST's new president.

Kornafel was no stranger to the aftermarket or to CARQUEST. President of Hatch Grinding for 25 years, Kornafel held numerous leadership posts within various aftermarket trade groups. Previously, he had served two terms as CARQUEST's chairman, and also as chairman of the AWDA board. Kornafel discussed his appointment as CARQUEST president.

I'm excited to take over the leadership of the CARQUEST office. Under Dan Bock's fine guid-

GPI expanded its Buffalo Distribution Center in 1996.

ance, this organization has achieved something very special. Now, I'd like to continue to help CARQUEST evolve into the 21st century.

Since Kornafel was from Colorado, CARQUEST decided to move its national headquarters office to Lakewood in the Rocky Mountain state.

The Equipment Company Acquired

In 1994, GPI had acquired CARQUEST member DADI, located in Kansas City. In 1996, GPI acquired The Equipment Company, also located in Kansas City, a firm owned by Jim Green, and changed it to CARQUEST. The combined results exceeded expectations. For more about The Equipment Company's history, see chapter 12.

PSC Distribution in Phoenix Merged into GPI

GPI acquired PSC Distributing Inc. of Phoenix on November 1, 1996. PSC had joined the CARQUEST team in 1989. GPI quickly converted PSC's computer system to its own system and consolidated the accounting and purchasing offices. It also converted the Mesa and Tucson distribution centers into super stores. PSC's customer base underwent a significant reduction, and major efforts were made to expand with strong independent auto parts stores and Joint Venture stores. GPI consolidated four auto parts stores and acquired seven new Joint Venture stores. For more about PSC's history, see chapter 12.

On October 1, 1996, Apple Auto Parts and the CARQUEST Auto Parts stores in the Virginia cities of Newport News, Norfolk, and Virginia Beach joined forces and became part of the Raleigh, North Carolina, Joint Venture team.

Entry into this metropolitan area, comprised of an estimated 1.8 million people, proved to be a major step for

Pete Kornafel Jr., former owner of the Hatch Grinding Company, became CARQUEST president in 1996 after Dan Bock retired.

GPI/CARQUEST in Virginia. Before the move, GPI had 12 stores in the Tidewater, Virginia, area. Apple Auto Parts had 11 stores and CARQUEST had two stores. During the consolidation, one of the CARQUEST Auto Parts stores remained open while the second store was combined with two of the Apple Auto Parts stores. While CARQUEST had established an excellent name in its six years in the area, Apple was more established, having been in the area for 37 years.

Ernest "Apple" Lemonds had been a legend in the eastern Virginia and North Carolina markets for many years. When Lemonds finally retired from the business, he took pride in the knowledge that he had built an excellent team of executives and workers. Leading the team was Tyree Nickerson, Bobby Sears, Robert Layman, and Chris Lemonds, all original partners of Apple Auto Parts.

On February 15, 1996, GPI merged with Robertson Auto Parts Inc., of Daytona Beach, Florida, a company founded in 1924 by R.J. Robertson. In 1972, Eli Marley, a filter representative, bought the business, and 18 years later, he sold it to his son Thomas Marley. GPI was ecstatic about owning a store with 72 years of history in Daytona Beach, the "Capital City of Racing."

On November 29, 1996, GPI added five auto parts stores in Grand Rapids, Michigan, to its Central Division. The group, which had previously added 40 new associates to the GPI organization, was formerly known as Michigan Automotive. This company was founded in 1959. After the consolidation, Joe Wisdom remained as manager of the city stores. He had purchased the stores in 1982 from the original owner. Wisdom had been with the company for 28 years, working as a driver, a shop worker, and a salesman.

In 1996, several other important Joint Venture Auto Parts store acquisitions took place. One, West Bend Auto Supply, was a four-store group that was located in the Wisconsin cities of Bend, Slinger, and Grafton. After the acquisition, sales manager Jerry Sharpee joined the GPI JV store team. He later moved to Raleigh and took over management of the CARQUEST TECH-NET professional auto service program, an important program for the organization.

Also, the Joint Venture Store Group added Al Shackman's highly successful Eagle Auto Parts in

GPI STOCKHOLDER MEETINGS

GPI HAS ALWAYS DEDICATED ITSELF TO keeping its shareholders fully informed regarding the financial condition of the company. Since all shareholders are working associates of the company, the annual meeting is more like an employee meeting where all shareholders and their spouses are invited to a full and candid presentation regarding the current year's results.

The typical meeting normally runs about three hours. During the meeting, all shareholders are presented with personal statements of value that detail their particular investments in the company, along with a projection of their investments' values by the time they reach age 65. GPI factors all projections according to the previous three-year average return and on the current number of shares owned.

To be certain all shareholders could attend these meetings, GPI would hold several regional shareholders' meetings throughout the country. In earlier years, GPI's top management personally conducted the regional meetings. This became impractical as the company grew and the number of regional shareholder meetings increased.

GPI's Scott Ginsburg, aided by Tina Davis and her graphics arts staff, established a video studio to produce a 1996 shareholders' meeting presentation, with specific segments assigned to selected corporate staff members. These staff members were assigned to different GPI regional locations to videotape shareholder meetings and answer any questions. GPI's new video studio also developed training tapes for GPI/CARQUEST associates.

Chicago. Other Eagle stores were located in Wheeling and in the Illinois cities of Schaumburg, Addison, and Roselle.

Reorganization of Joint Venture Store Management Group

During the first quarter, GPI completely restructured the Joint Venture Stores' management group, a reorganization designed to focus on "direct authority and accountability." The new organizational structure provided a regional manager for approximately every 10 Joint Venture stores and five regional managers supervised by a general manager. Additionally, a divisional vice president was set up to supervise three general managers and approximately 150 Joint Venture stores.

On an annual basis, Joint Venture store sales in 1996 increased 21.5 percent, with same store sales up 4.8 percent, far greater than the industry average.

By the end of the year, the JV Group operated 681 stores, acquired or opened 139, consolidated 26, and closed 14 for a net gain of 99 for the past 12 months.

The JV sales force grew to 563 full- and part-time salespeople. During the year, GPI store associates held 511 customer appreciation events, 95 "Dealer-In-A-Box" sales presentations, conducted 53 market surveys, and hosted over 2,000 training clinics for customers.

Also during the year, GPI implemented and completed a counterman/machine shop training program in 73 stores. On December 31, 1996, GPI's Joint Venture Store Group was operating 123 machine shops, each employing at least one full-time manager. These shops recorded $8.3 million in labor sales and turned in a $1.3 million operating profit, an outstanding achievement.

Aftermarket Opportunities

By the end of 1996, 206,365,156 vehicles were registered in the United States and 15,823,004 in Canada. With the average new vehicle price approaching $20,000, GPI was confident that growth opportunities would continue to exist for the company within the aftermarket industry. The year 1996 marked the 16th year of increase—1.8 percent—in

A Funny Thing

It is a funny thing, but true,
That customers you don't like, don't like you;
I don't know why this should be so,
But just the same, I always know
If I am "sour," customers are few;
If I am friendly, they are too.

Sometimes, I get up in the morn
A-wishing I was never born;
I make of cross remarks a few
And then my customers wish this, too,
That I had gone some other place
Instead of showing them my face.

But let me change my little "tune"
And sing and smile, then pretty soon
The folks around me sing and smile
I guess 'twas catching all the while.
Yes, 'tis a funny thing, but true,
The customers you like
Will sure like you.

As with other maxims and sayings, GPI sent this inspirational "Funny Thing" poem to all associates and CARQUEST store owners to remind them that it always pays to be friendly.

miles driven, with the average annual miles driven per vehicle at 11,700.

Ward's Reports on U.S. New Vehicle Sales

According to *Ward's Reports*, from 1990 to 1996, U.S. sales of the top 12 new vehicle types shifted drastically from passenger cars to light trucks, which included mini-vans, SUVs, and pick up trucks. In 1990, only 15 percent of the top 12 new vehicle types sold in the United States were classified as light trucks. In 1992, this figure grew to 25 percent. In 1994, it jumped to 42 percent, and in 1996 reached 63 percent, due to increased sales of SUVs, pick up trucks, and mini-vans.

This consumer shift to light trucks proved to be a tremendous boost for the Big Three vehicle manufacturers. They had been regularly losing passenger car market share to Japanese manufacturers who were concentrating primarily on passenger car production. In 1990, Japanese manufacturers produced 35 percent of the top 12 vehicle types sold in the United States. In 1992, their share dropped to 28 percent. By 1996, the Japanese share of the top 12 vehicle types sold had dropped to 22 percent.

Of the top 12 vehicle types sold in the United States in 1996, 10 were manufactured by the U.S. Big Three. The other two were manufactured by Japanese firms and represented only 14.3 percent of unit sales in total. Toyota's Camry was No. 6 on the best-seller list and Honda's Civic was No. 9.

Bright Prospects for the Future

As 1996 drew to a close, GPI's future had never looked better. Sales in 1997 were projected to surpass the $1 billion threshold for the first time. This would represent a remarkable doubling of sales during the past four-year period. Just as important, a highly seasoned GPI management team was in place, efficiently organized and ably supported by the most up-to-date systems and procedures.

GPI had fully consolidated its purchasing and accounting offices. It had upgraded its computer systems with expanded capacity. The company understood that these operational moves were necessary to achieve the efficiencies and strengths needed to absorb and manage future growth.

During its rapid growth, GPI remained focused on its core strategic mission (CSM)—to be the No. 1 supplier to professional service technicians through CARQUEST Auto Parts stores. Indeed, GPI's regularly increasing market share was the best proof available regarding the dedication and commitment of its management team and associates in achieving their core strategic mission.

With each passing year, GPI's management team gained valuable experience through its numerous mergers and acquisitions. Their level of expertise and efficiency increased substantially with each new transaction. Every indication pointed to a future filled with additional opportunities to expand GPI through more such deals.

GPI's management team fully understood that the value of carefully planned mergers was not only the attraction of physical assets but also the expertise of the "people assets" gained. Since the early 1980s, reviewing the quality and experience of the people that would be joining GPI as a result of a merger or acquisition had long been preeminent on the company's due diligence list. It would remain so as GPI continued to move forward, expanding through adding more companies.

All in all, as the new year approached, GPI's expert management group and loyal team of associates were ready for new challenges and prepared to deal with the rapid changes taking place within the automotive aftermarket. They were determined to maintain GPI as one of the industry's top players.

1997

During 1997, GPI set another new record with sales up 16.3 percent, an increase of $133.3 million. The year also set another record for earnings, with operating income up 9.3 percent and net income up by 3.6 percent. The integration and startup costs associated with GPI's numerous mergers and acquisitions, along with the growth in interest costs resulting from additional investment in these transactions, impacted net income for the year.

Through its numerous acquisitions, GPI discovered that it wasn't usually until the third year after a company had been purchased that it was able to produce at GPI's expected high level of earnings objectives. This proved to be the case for GPI's 1996 acquisitions, whose operating results caused overall company income, as a percentage of sales, to drop slightly. However, operating income for all GPI businesses in existence prior to 1996 continued to show improvement. GPI's management was committed to bring the new companies to the expected earnings level of established units as quickly as possible.

During 1997, GPI absorbed five major acquisitions, all of which were accurately projected to have a notable impact on the company's future. As a result, more than 400 new associates joined the company in Nebraska, Maine, North Carolina, New York, and Canada. The Maine group marked

GPI's first venture into New England, and the Canadian group was the first venture outside the United States.

Millard's Inc.

On February 1, 1997, GPI finalized an agreement to merge with Millard's Inc. of Omaha, Nebraska. Ken Millard, owner and founder of Millard's Inc., was a good friend of Ken Rogers, an automotive aftermarket industry expert who had been helpful to GPI since the day it was founded. (*Editor's Note:* Rogers

GPI MISSION STATEMENT

IN 1997, GPI DEVELOPED A HIGHLY ambitious mission statement for the employee-owners of the company. We, the employee-owners of GPI, envision:

- Being the best at getting products to the point of installation quickly;
- Developing a company-wide culture that encourages teamwork among highly trained, highly motivated people who actively work to create and maintain an environment where customers want to do business and where GPI associates can achieve maximum personal growth;
- That our systems insure the maximum availability and highest quality of both products and services to our customers at the least possible cost;
- Remaining an employee-owned company maximizing equity growth while maintaining an investment grade credit rating; and
- Achieving a necessary annual sales growth, built upon the dual strategy of expanding sales of existing markets and developing new markets.

SLOAN HONORED

TEMPLE SLOAN JR., CHAIRMAN OF GPI and a member of the CARQUEST board of directors, received a 1997 Distinguished Service Citation from the Automotive Hall of Fame, awarded to leaders throughout the automotive industry for their contributions. He was one of six recipients of the award for the year. It was presented on February 2, 1997, at the Westin Peachtree Plaza during the annual convention of the National Automotive Dealers Association in Atlanta.

was also very helpful in the development of *The Legend of General Parts*.) He was instrumental in bringing GPI and Millard's together.

Ken Millard operated 15 Auto Parts stores and a distribution center, which also served several independent auto parts stores. After the merger, the Millard distribution center was consolidated into GPI's new Des Moines Distribution Center located in Ankeny, Iowa. Millard's son, Scott, remained in a key management position and Millard himself stayed on in an advisory position with GPI.

For more about Millard's Inc.'s history, see chapter 12.

Parts Wholesalers Inc. and Darling Auto Parts Join GPI

On February 28, 1997, Parts Wholesalers Inc., located in Bangor, Maine, and its 12 Darling Auto Parts stores merged with GPI. Parts Wholesalers had been a CARQUEST member since 1988, serving 32 CARQUEST Auto Parts stores.

The Darling companies had consolidated sales of $17 million in 1996. Earl "Yogi" Seymour stayed on with GPI as vice president and general manager, and John Darling continued on in an advisory capacity.

GPI retained an experienced management team while expanding its presence in Maine. For more about PWI's history, see chapter 12.

Steego

On May 31, 1997, GPI acquired 25 Steego Bumper-to-Bumper stores from Parts Depot Inc. in Maine. It also acquired the Parts Depot warehouse in Portland, Maine. GPI consolidated the warehouse into the GPI CARQUEST Distribution Center in Portland. These new stores added greatly to the current GPI customer base in Maine, further enhancing CARQUEST's presence in the state.

The negotiation with Parts Depot was a joint venture with BWP, GPI's CARQUEST partner in Armonk, New York. GPI also negotiated to acquire the Parts Depot warehouse in Foxboro, Massachusetts, with the opportunity to convert the stores it served to CARQUEST.

CJS Distribution and Motor Bearings & Parts Join GPI

On April 1, 1997, GPI completed the acquisition of CJS and Motor Bearings and Parts, headquartered in Raleigh, North Carolina. This acquisition resulted in the addition of eight new independent CARQUEST Auto Parts stores as well as five Motor Bearings stores. GPI consolidated these stores with independents and Joint Venture stores. GPI added nine stores to the Raleigh JV Group. Additionally, it consolidated the CJS Distribution Center into the GPI Raleigh Distribution Center.

The CJS/Motor Bearings and Parts team played a key role in the combined company, while the support of Monty and Bill White, the sons of S.M. White, the founder of CJS, was very helpful in making the difficult undertaking a successful one.

For more about CJS' history, see chapter 12.

GPI Merges With Molin Auto Parts Inc.

May 1997 marked a busy merger month for GPI. During that month, the company merged with Molin Auto Parts Inc., headquartered in Buffalo, New York.

After consolidations, CARQUEST added 15 new Joint Venture stores and 25 independent CARQUEST Auto Parts stores to its marketing area in western and upstate New York for a total of 84 stores. GPI consolidated Molin's distribution center in Buffalo into the GPI distribution center there. The Molin team, led by Kim Molin, Trey Molin, and Tom Brown Jr., worked closely with a dedicated GPI team to achieve a successful merger.

For more about Molin's history, see chapter 12.

CARQUEST Canada Ltd.

On May 1, 1997, GPI made its first move outside the United States to become a Joint Venture partner with Acktion Corporation. Through this arrangement, it acquired McKerlie-Millen Inc.'s automotive group. The new company, which was named CARQUEST Canada Ltd., operated distribution centers in Toronto, Ottawa, Quebec, and Montreal. They supplied 122 company-owned stores and 240 independent stores.

GPI's management and staff were excited about the new Canada association. It could not have become a reality without the active support of the tireless efforts of numerous GPI team members, along with that of the new Canadian associates.

The Canadian joint venture was a major step forward for GPI. The company made this move at a time when relationships between Canada and the United States had become far more investment-friendly because of the North America Free Trade Agreement (NAFTA).

For more about Acktion's history, see chapter 12.

In keeping with its important strategic move into Canada, GPI's 1997 management team's mid-year retreat was held at Sportsman's Lodge, located in Saskatchewan, Canada.

More Mergers and Acquisitions

In June 1997, GPI merged with Fade Auto Parts in Pensacola, Florida, a strategically important move for the company. Fade Auto Parts' owner, Bill Fade, had built a strong five-store auto parts company that dominated the Pensacola auto parts replacement market. Prior, Pensacola had been the only major market in Florida's panhandle where a strong presence was still needed by GPI to achieve the desired market share. Now, with the Fade Auto Parts acquisition, GPI was in a strong position for the Pensacola market.

Management team at the Sportsman's Lodge, Saskatchewan, Canada, where GPI sponsored a managers' retreat in 1997.

"We could not have made a better choice than to sell to General Parts," said Fade.

In November 1997, Jim Young's five CARQUEST Auto Parts stores joined the GPI team, increasing the company's presence in central Michigan. "My wife Joanne and I sold our stores to Temple Sloan," Young said. "We met with him for 30 minutes and had a handshake deal. Never once were any points discussed that ever became a problem. Temple made it fun and fair."

Also during the year, GPI made several other significant store acquisitions. Rick Stein's four-store grouping in Chicago was a major addition to GPI's Chicago Group. In November, GPI acquired Straus Frank's three stores in El Paso, Texas, and added seven independent auto parts stores, all serviced from the Albuquerque Distribution Center. Also, GPI added six stores in Denver, 11 in Phoenix, six in Cleveland, and seven in Chicago.

GPI assumed a great deal more work than normal to handle these acquisitions. This included closing seven distribution centers and liquidating their equipment and inventories. The closings included Omaha; Belle Plaine, Iowa; Portland, Maine; Foxboro, Massachusetts; Raleigh, North Carolina; Chicago; and Pensacola, Florida. GPI's distribution centers would now handle the auto parts stores that were formerly served by the closed distribution centers.

El Niño, Other Factors, Slow Sales

In December 1997, the impact of El Niño, a severe disruption of the ocean-atmosphere sys-

POSITIONING FOR THE FUTURE

AS 1997 CAME TO A CLOSE, O. TEMPLE Sloan Jr., chairman, C. Hamilton Sloan, vice chairman, and N. Joe Owen, president, collectively developed the following positioning paper for GPI.

During the two-year period for 1996 and 1997, we elected to seize the opportunity to build GPI into an influential player within the aftermarket. We also recognized the necessity of a major commitment by our people over a long period of time.

Acquisitions in our business are very sensitive due to the close relationships with our customers. Sustaining those relationships in an acquisition atmosphere requires a total commitment from the GPI team.

The risks were significant, but the transactions provide us with the opportunity for greater growth into the 21st century.

During these two years, we made 11 major acquisitions, added six distribution centers, expanded two distribution centers, added 225 joint venture stores, and converted 175 independent auto parts stores to the CARQUEST program.

We added 2,067 new full-time associates to the team, increasing our sales force by 185, installed 518 store J-CON systems, and increased our annualized sales by $400 million to exceed $1 billion in 1998 within the United States.

To accomplish this, we closed and consolidated nine distribution centers and 76 auto parts stores, and integrated all of the acquired purchasing and accounting offices into existing GPI operations. We also closed three existing GPI accounting offices.

During 1997, we entered the Canadian aftermarket through a joint venture with Acktion Corporation to acquire the third-largest aftermarket company in Canada. CARQUEST Canada Ltd. encompasses four distribution centers and 122 company stores and serves 240 associate stores. The company employs over 1,500 people, with annual sales of $200 million (U.S. dollars). The conversion of CARQUEST Canada Ltd. to our operating and marketing programs has required a major manpower commitment from the GPI team.

Now, our focus is to ensure, through audit and training, that our systems and procedures are functioning in the new operations and that our customer service levels and marketing programs are being implemented. With these moves, we will be better positioned for the future.

tem in the tropical Pacific, was felt in various parts of the country. This resulted in increased rainfall, destructive flooding, and the warmest winter on record. This all negatively impacted aftermarket sales. In addition, the continued improvement in vehicle quality, along with the leveling of the repair age vehicle population, slowed aftermarket sales growth.

In 1997, GPI's pure retail competitors—the large mass merchandisers—all faced a continuing decline in the DIY market. To offset this challenge, many tried to boost sales by capturing a share of the wholesale/professional installer market.

Parts proliferation was another problem affecting every company in the aftermarket business. It resulted, of course, from the continuing diversity of America's vehicle fleet. From 1987 through 1992, the number of aftermarket product applications grew 29 percent. From 1993 through 1997, the number of application parts grew another 38 percent. Many aftermarket players found it difficult to adequately stock so many new parts, but GPI sustained its high level of product availability sought by customers. It constantly made its inventory and management systems more efficient.

GPI's customer base continued to undergo major changes as 40 independent CARQUEST Auto Parts stores joined the Joint Venture Group during the year, mostly due to owner retirements. Eight new independent stores were added, and 99 new independents were converted to CARQUEST Auto Parts stores. The year 1997 ended with GPI serving 2,042 auto parts stores. Of these, 1,025 were independently owned.

Vehicle Statistics for 1997

At the end of 1997, *Ward's Reports* stated, "Once again in 1997 consumer infatuation with sport-utility vehicles (SUV) powered U.S. retail new truck deliveries to a record 7,230,000, up 4.2 percent from the 6,926,000 sold in 1996. Of the top 10 vehicle types sold in the United States in 1997, 56.4 percent were classified as 'light trucks,' all of which were manufactured by the Big Three U.S. vehicle manufacturers. The Big Three manufactured 73 percent of all the top 10 vehicle types sold in the United States in 1997."

A high level of new vehicle sales continued through 1997, and the vehicle population increased 2.5 percent to 203 million. The average age of domestic cars and light trucks remained over nine years, with foreign vehicles averaging 7.5 years.

Also, 1997 marked the 17th consecutive year of growth in miles driven, with an increase of 2 percent and average miles driven per vehicle of 11,900.

Below, left to right: In 1997, GPI completed a 109,000-square-foot distribution center in Columbia, South Carolina, and a Billings, Montana, distribution center expansion project.

Bottom, left to right: GPI's new distribution centers were completed in Southaven, Mississipi, and in Des Moines, Iowa. Each occupied 107,000 square feet.

Facilities and Systems Upgrading

GPI's Canada joint venture and the Sussen, Hatch, Equipment Company, and PSC mergers/acquisitions put the company's systems to a severe test, all coming together in only 12 months. During the last two months of 1997 and the first quarter of 1998, GPI's leadership focused on ensuring that efficiencies in customer service and cost controls would be fully in place throughout the greatly expanded corporation.

Busy With New Buildings

In 1997, GPI's operations team was busy building and occupying new distribution centers. The company moved from its old Memphis location into a new 107,000-square-foot location in Southaven, Mississippi, that served Tennessee, Arkansas, the boot of Missouri, and northern Mississippi. In February, a newly constructed 107,000-square-foot Des Moines, Iowa, distribution center became operational to serve Iowa and Nebraska. GPI opened a 109,000-square-foot distribution center in Columbia, South Carolina, in October. It occupied a newly constructed 30,000-square-foot Raleigh administration office building in September and completed construction of a 40,000-square-foot expansion of the Billings, Montana, Distribution Center and accompanying offices in November. Each new distribution center was equipped with state-of-the-art material-handling equipment.

GPI also planned to occupy a new 95,000-square-foot distribution center in Phoenix by the

summer of 1998. Additionally, future plans supported an expanded 88,000-square-foot distribution center in Bangor, Maine. When completed, this combined investment in brick, mortar, facility construction, and equipment would exceed $25 million.

Key Promotions

During the fourth quarter of 1997, GPI took a further step toward a new management organizational structure, with the promotion of Wayne D. Lavrack and O. Temple Sloan III to senior vice presidents. The company gave both men key operating responsibilities. It assigned Lavrack direct operating responsibility for the 817 Joint Venture stores, and Sloan III full operating responsibilities for all Independent Auto Parts stores, including sales, distribution center operations, and human resources activities.

TECH-NET Professional Auto Service Program

In 1997, GPI finalized the TECH-NET Professional Auto Service Program, one of the strongest marketing programs ever designed by CARQUEST. This comprehensive program assisted independent auto service shops with training in business management, advertising, and promotion. The CARQUEST professional markets committee developed the program. William Humber of CARQUEST's headquarters staff did an outstanding job finalizing all program details.

CARQUEST's headquarters office, which had been relocated to Denver from New York in 1996, was completely staffed by 1997. Kornafel, CARQUEST's president, organized a marketing task force from the CARQUEST member companies to meet monthly to assist his office in the development and implementation of all product selection and marketing activities.

In 1997, CARQUEST made an important decision to operate a dedicated sales force of 70 salespeople to represent major under-car product lines, brakes, chassis parts, and shock absorbers. The organization appointed Jim Ray, a veteran aftermarket sales manager, as manager for this new group, assisted by five regional managers: Rick Grady, Paul Farwick, Dale Lyon, Jim Ragone, and

Above: GPI's new under-car sales management team was formed in 1997. Shown, left to right, are Mike McInerney, Jim Ragone, Jim Ray, Rick Grady, Paul Farwick, and Dale Lyon. These regional managers were appointed to assist Jim Ray.

Below: The TECH-NET Professional Auto Service Program was finalized in 1997.

Mike McInerney. Due to this strategic move, CARQUEST was now positioned to more effectively meet marketplace challenges.

During 1997, GPI held 30 regional dealer council meetings with its best customers to discuss how to improve specific services. In addition, 600 customer appreciation events were held during the year.

In September 1997, GPI relocated the JV Store Inventory Management Group to Raleigh, North Carolina, under the direction of Braxton O'Neal, who had managed the Southeast Group since 1991. At this time, the group managed JV store inventories, store pricing, and gross profit. With the move to Raleigh, GPI consolidated the JV Store Product Management Group under O'Neal's leadership. Since then, the group has made continual improvements to the quality of JV store inventories.

Assisting O'Neal in the area of pricing and gross profit were Dan Seder, Chris Morgan, Mary Hebert, Dan Drahos, George Profit, Royce Bugg, Steve Michael, Janice Lamberth, Kenny Hinson, John Kubczak, Rich Schechter, Robert Rowton, Fernando Delicata, and Gerald Dourdages. O'Neal was assisted in the area of store product management by Scott Halford, Don Hensler, Frank Aukland, Andy Kennell, Penny Brisson, Glen Avery, Robin Sheppard, Wayne King, Randy Hicks, Mark Hounshell, Jerry Hard, and Line Desrosiers.

Along with these other management changes, GPI restructured the marketing committee in 1997 to enhance in-store price points, product selection, and end-cap promotions. GPI also purchased new Plan-O-Gram software, which greatly enhanced inventory merchandising at the individual store level and provided stronger management control over GPI's largest investment.

GPI—No. 1 in North Carolina

The October 1997 edition of *North Carolina Business* featured GPI and its founder, Temple Sloan Jr., on its cover and included a six-page article that discussed the company's rapid growth in becoming North Carolina's number one privately held company.

1998

During 1998, GPI produced record sales and earnings for the 37th year in a row. It passed new milestones, with sales growing to $1.1 billion, up 16.2 percent. Net earnings set a new all-time record with an increase of 37 percent over 1997. Operating income, as a percent to sales, returned to a more historic level but was still impacted by the newer acquisitions.

The performance accomplished during the spree of mergers, acquisitions, consolidations, systems upgrading, and software changes still was an incredible achievement.

GPI's First Full Year in Canada

During its first full year of operation, CARQUEST Canada concentrated on converting its store customer base. This involved changing all company auto parts stores and associates to the CARQUEST identity, products, and programs. The company was comprised of 307 stores identified as CARQUEST Auto Parts stores or CARQUEST Pieces D' Auto. It installed the J-CON computer system in all of its company stores and in 95 associate stores.

As acceptance by auto parts stores and installers continued to exceed all expectations, GPI converted 28 product lines to CARQUEST-branded products between April and December. The total product conversion would be completed during 1999.

Canadian sales for 1998 reached $218 million. Further, same store sales grew 4 percent over 1997, this in spite of the elimination of line-buying customers.

1998 CARQUEST Canada Store Statistics

- 19 company stores renovated
- 20 stores consolidated
- 2 stores closed
- 4 stores sold
- 7 stores acquired
- 116 company-controlled CARQUEST Auto Parts stores in operation by year's end

GPI adapted its store training programs for the Canadian marketplace and translated them into French for the Quebec market. Store managers participated in six different five-day training modules, while salesmen experienced two days of training.

Also, GPI set up a bilingual version of the TECH-NET Diagnostic HelpLine and launched a new GPI training center in Montreal.

The company broke ground for the new 127,300-square-foot Montreal Distribution Center

In 1997, GPI acquired Canadian-based McKerlie-Millen Inc.'s automotive group, which it renamed CARQUEST Canada Ltd.

in November 1998, with occupancy planned for July 1999. Both the older Quebec City and Montreal distribution centers would be consolidated into the new, modern facility. This would provide greater availability and service to all of GPI's Quebec associates and company-owned CARQUEST Auto Parts stores.

The Republic Automotive and APS Acquisitions— Rare Opportunities for GPI

The events leading to the Republic and APS acquisitions in late 1998 were interesting and inter-related. Both Republic Automotive and APS were highly respected competitors. Keith Thompson, Republic's CEO, and Fred Pisciotta, former APS CEO, were both good friends of Temple Sloan Jr. and Joe Owen.

APS

Charles Bluhdorn, CEO of Gulf and Western Inc., founded APS in 1958, just a few years before GPI itself was founded. At the same time, he developed a second aftermarket marketing program known as "Big A." For 30 years, APS was a growing and prosperous company. Fred Pisciotta, who spent 25 years at APS, with his last seven years as CEO, was responsible for much of the firm's success.

In 1985, after the death of Bluhdorn, Gulf and Western sold APS to an investment group. In early 1988, Pisciotta, then president, left APS and bought a group of auto parts stores, Beacon Auto Parts, in Pittsburgh. In late 1988, APS was again acquired by another investment group.

After Pisciotta left, the company initiated a new marketing plan to open a number of small auto parts warehouses that would buy direct from manufacturers and sell direct to installers. These units were called Installers Service Warehouses (ISW). The company later accelerated the ISW concept.

APS Holding Declares Bankruptcy

Dow Jones released the following news report concerning APS on January 13, 1998:

APS Holding Corporation's shares fell sharply Tuesday after the company said it will miss interest payments due January 15 on its 11 7/8 percent senior subordinated notes due in 2006.

APS Holding will continue to have access to its bank credit through Feb. 10. The company, which distributes automotive replacement parts and equipment, said failure to make the payment won't constitute default until Feb. 14.

For the nine months ended Oct. 25, the company reported a loss of $15.8 million, or $1.15 a share, compared with net income of $13.4 million, or 97 cents a share in the year-earlier period. Sales declined to $633.7 million from $669.5 million.

The company blamed its loss on weak performance at its Installers Service Warehouse and its company-owned Big A Stores—which are undergoing restructuring—and an increase in interest expense.

In February 1998, APS Holding declared bankruptcy.

Republic Automotive

In 1995, Pisciotta sold Beacon Auto Parts to Republic Automotive. The firm's CEO, Keith Thompson, was a good friend of Pisciotta. It was agreed that Pisciotta would remain at Beacon for a few years.

Under Thompson's leadership, Republic's revenues and earnings grew. The firm diversified with the acquisition of a company that specialized in automotive sheet metal "crash" parts such as body panels, fenders, and doors.

In 1998 Keystone Automotive, a firm specializing in auto body components, bought Republic for its auto body business. At the time, Thompson suggested that Keystone sell the Republic automotive replacement parts segment to GPI.

GPI considered Beacon Auto Parts to be Republic's most attractive subsidiary. Since Pisciotta was managing Beacon, a meeting with him was GPI's first order of business. Pisciotta recalls the 1998 meeting with Sloan and Owen.

Temple Sloan and Joe Owen came to Pittsburgh to discuss the possible acquisition of Republic's auto parts business from Keystone. I was pleased that they would pay me this courtesy. Knowing that Beacon was a family-owned business I had sold to Republic, Temple offered me the opportunity to buy it back from Keystone before the larger transaction took all of Republic into GPI.

But I had made a decision two and a half years earlier to sell the business to Republic, and it was for a sound reason. I felt that this reason had not really changed, so I explained to them that I was comfortable having our business go along with the total Republic auto parts package into GPI.

After spending dinner with Temple and Joe, and learning more about their employee ownership, I felt good for the employees of my former company, Beacon, becoming part of this bigger company, GPI.

The Chance of a Lifetime

With the APS bankruptcy and the planned Republic acquisition, a major one, overlapping within a period of just a few months, GPI was faced with one of its most serious decisions. With a full realization regarding the heavy work and due diligence that would be required, GPI's executive committee felt that the company could not walk away from this possible one-time chance to buy both APS and Republic, which was the opportunity of a lifetime.

Regarding APS, a quick study indicated that 10 of the firm's distribution centers would fit well into

CODE OF ETHICS

AS A CONSTANT REMINDER TO ALL that honesty and integrity are qualities expected of each GPI associate, this ethics code was posted in every JV store and distribution center:

Every GPI associate is a shareholder and is expected to follow a respectable code of conduct based on high standards. These standards are set forth as follows:

- We must expect complete honesty in day-to-day dealings with our customers, suppliers, and our fellow associates.
- We are expected to protect our own company assets from abuse by others.
- GPI associates, as shareholders, agree that their company must not be subjected to liability resulting from substance abuse by any GPI associate. Neither illegal drugs nor alcohol abuse will be allowed during working hours, at any company meeting, or at any time an associate is representing our company or operating company vehicles.
- We do not expect our company to accept anything from anyone or any other company that is not paid for or earned fairly. There will be no exceptions.
- Customers' employees must not be rewarded in any way that they personally benefit by buying from our company without the knowledge of top management.
- No GPI associate will engage in any fraudulent activity of falsifying documents, i.e., invoices, purchase orders, RGR claims, master installer claims, national account claims, or credit memos to create personal gain for any associate or any employee of a company that GPI sells to or buys from.

GPI's markets, creating only minimum conflicts with existing stores. Other CARQUEST members were polled to see if there was interest to acquire APS locations within their markets. BWP in the greater New York area and APW in California were interested and agreed to combine their individual offers with GPI's for APS so that one plan could be negotiated.

A Downside to the Two Acquisitions

GPI understood that one major downside to the APS and Republic acquisitions, both coming together around the same time, was that independent CARQUEST Auto Parts stores would not be

Right: Long-time industry veteran Fred Pisciotta owned and operated Pittsburgh-based Beacon Auto Parts, part of Republic Automotive when GPI decided to acquire Republic. GPI worked closely with Pisciotta during the acquisition. Afterwards, Pisciotta worked for GPI as a JV vice president.

Below: Keith Thompson, Republic Automotive's CEO at the time of the GPI acquisition. During his tenure, the company significantly increased its sales and profits.

able to see their distribution center sales representatives as often for several months. They would be busy with additional work resulting from the takeovers.

So, before GPI made a final decision to proceed with the APS and Republic acquisitions, Sloan and Owen called several of the company's largest independent CARQUEST customers and discussed this special opportunity facing GPI. They all responded by encouraging GPI to go forward with the acquisitions because the added companies would strengthen CARQUEST. GPI then sent a letter to all GPI CARQUEST independent store owners advising them of the company's decision to move ahead with the acquisitions and asking for their support. At the same time, GPI asked its distribution center and manufacturers' sales representatives to schedule daily and weekly agendas to minimize the loss of sales time spent with current customers.

Sloan announced the two acquisitions in a letter to GPI/CARQUEST associates and customers:

We feel very fortunate to merge these fine auto parts companies into GPI. Their reputation for excellent customer service has made them tough competitors and we are happy to have them on our team. We greatly appreciate the confidence of Charles Hogarty, Keith Thompson, and Fred Pisciotta. We also appre-

RON WEHRENBERG

THE YEAR 1997 SAW THE PASSING OF long-time associate Ron Wehrenberg, who died October 3, following complications from heart bypass surgery. He was 64 years old.

In 1980, Wehrenberg was president of General Trading Company (GTC) at the time of the GPI acquisition. GTC was GPI's first major acquisition and first expansion outside of the Carolinas. Wehrenberg set the example for GPI's new Minnesota associates through his focus, hard work, and most of all, his positive attitude during some difficult times.

Many times, Wehrenberg's sense of humor helped GPI get through some difficult times. He eventually became GPI's first Midwest Division president. With Wehrenberg's passing, GPI lost a real friend and a valued member of its management team.

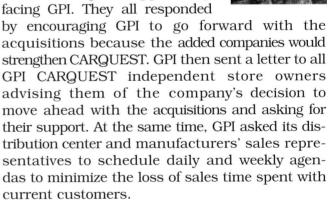

EVENTFUL YEARS THROUGH 1998

IN 1998, TEMPLE SLOAN JR. HIGHLIGHTED a number of key years that were significant in the development of GPI:

1973—The founding of the CARQUEST Marketing Program.

1976—The creation of the GPI Employee Stock Ownership Program (ESOP).

1980—The acquisition of General Trading Company in St. Paul, Minnesota, the first GPI expansion outside the Carolinas.

1983—The merger of Valley Motor Supply, in Montana, GPI's first step in auto parts store ownership. This acquisition marked the development of the joint venture store plan. Also in 1983, Joe Owen joined the GPI management team.

1987—The most important CARQUEST meeting in company history was held in 1987. During the meeting, it was unanimously agreed to sell CARQUEST branded products only through CARQUEST Auto Parts stores.

1997-1998—The time from mid-1997 through 1998 marked GPI's most intensive 18-month period ever with three large acquisitions, starting with Acktion in Canada in June 1997, Republic Automotive Parts, and APS Holdings in the fall of 1998. Handling these large acquisitions in an 18-month period would be a huge undertaking, but GPI's management team was unanimous in taking advantage of these special opportunities.

ciate the cooperation of APS Holding's creditors management group in making it happen.

So, in 1998, GPI made its dramatic move, acquiring eight Republic Automotive operating groups on September 1, and selective operations from APS Holding on October 10. These major transactions came during the same year that GPI was integrating the 11 major acquisitions made during 1996 and 1997.

After the Republic transaction was finalized, GPI's management was pleased that Pisciotta agreed to continue working with the company's Joint Venture Division as a JV vice president, responsible for western Pennsylvania, northern Maine, western New York, northern Virginia, and Washington, D.C.

The APS and Republic acquisitions presented GPI and CARQUEST with the opportunity to strengthen market share to a level that would have taken years to reach without the added companies. Along with APS and Republic, GPI/CARQUEST retained highly respected executives from the two firms. In addition to Fred Pisciotta and his son Randy,

seasoned industry veterans that would be joining GPI included Tom Belding, Mike Allen, Montie Loney, Doug Buscher, Tommy Salmon, Roy Hedges, Mike Tanji, Dan Conroy, Sandy Macomber, Jerry Repak, Bart Marshel, and Kevin Lair. They would make an immediate contribution to the integration of their companies into GPI.

For more about APS' and Republic Automotive's histories, see chapter 12.

$250 Million+ in Additional Annual Sales, Nearly 600 New Stores, and Major New Markets

Collectively, the APS and Republic acquisitions added in excess of $250 million in annual sales, four new markets (Alaska, Utah, Northern Virginia, and Pennsylvania), 145 company stores, and 438 new independent stores that soon converted to CARQUEST Auto Parts stores.

The major markets impacted by the APS acquisition were Arizona, Arkansas, Colorado, Illinois, Indiana, Iowa, Kansas, Maryland, Nebraska, New Mexico, Ohio, eastern Pennsylvania, Utah, Virginia,

West Virginia, and Wyoming. The Republic acquisition affected western Pennsylvania; Alaska; El Centro, California; Indianapolis; Davenport, Iowa; and the upper peninsula of Michigan.

The APS and Republic acquisitions involved a great deal of new work for GPI, which included converting 583 stores (representing Joint Venture, that is, GPI-owned, stores and independently owned stores) and four distribution centers to CARQUEST, consolidating 33 stores and 14 distribution centers, and installing more than 375 new computer systems. GPI and former APS and Republic managers and staffers worked hard to meet this major challenge. The acquisition was right on schedule, and, most important, was that the reception for GPI within the marketplace was very gratifying to its management team.

Not Ready to Rest on its Laurels

In 1998, GPI's important acquisitions included a three-store group in Wilmington, North Carolina, from Barnes Motor Parts; Lynn and Tom Kress' successful three CARQUEST stores in Oregon; and Ben Langford's three CARQUEST stores in North Carolina.

Wolf Supply Company

GPI purchased another firm in 1998, the Wolf Supply Company in Portland, Oregon, and Vancouver, Washington. Les Wolf and his team, led by Bruce Hershman, had built this second-generation, five-store company into a dominant position in the greater Portland market.

Wolf Supply Company was founded by Morris Wolf in 1919. Wolf emigrated from Poland at the age of 16—he came alone, did not speak English, and had no money. After completing his high school education, Wolf worked at various jobs until he joined the U.S. Army during World War I. After discharge, he bought a gas station in Vancouver, Washington with the money he earned playing poker while in the army.

Wolf's son, Leslie R. Wolf, began working in the company store at age 12. He purchased it from his father in 1963. At that time, the company was a redistributing jobber. In the late 1970s, Wolf redirected his company's sales efforts almost exclusively toward installer accounts.

At the time of the acquisition, Wolf's owned a distribution center in Vancouver, Washington, and branch warehouses in Beaverton, Oregon, and Milwaukee, Oregon, for a total of five stores. In 1998, Wolf Supply was celebrating its 79th year providing auto parts to the auto service industry. It was one of the oldest automotive parts suppliers in the nation that was still owned by the founding family. The company employed 70 people and operated 30 delivery vehicles.

For GPI, the Wolf Supply transaction was a critical move for the company in terms of its growth in the greater Portland, Oregon, market. Indeed, the Wolf acquisition became the catalyst for GPI's current—and outstanding—Portland CARQUEST store group. Wolf and Hershman worked hand-in-hand with GPI's team to ensure a successful changeover. Hershman joined the GPI JV team and was named a vice president for market development.

A Move to Southwest Wisconsin

In 1998, GPI entered the greater Milwaukee market by acquiring Bill Mabry's 10-store Wisconsin Auto Supply Company. This third-generation company, with a proud history of well over 50 years, held a significant share in an excellent market.

Wisconsin Auto Supply Company grew from a one-store auto parts company that opened in the mid-1940s in Milwaukee by Bob Biegert, a former salesman for McQuay-Norris. Bob Biegert was Bill Mabry's father-in-law. The original store was named Automotive and Aircraft Supply. With hard work and aggressive selling, Biegert's small company prospered and opened a second store in Milwaukee and in 1960, started expanding into the

Les Wolf, top, bought Wolf Supply Company from his father in 1963. Bruce Hershman, bottom, was in charge of Wolf Supply Company, when GPI purchased the firm in 1998.

Top left to right: In 1998, GPI completed an expansion of the Bangor, Maine, distribution center, and a new 95,000-square-foot distribution center in Phoenix.

suburbs with a store located in Cedarburg. In the mid-1960s, as auto parts manufacturers began to recognize warehouse distribution as a needed step in serving auto parts stores, Biegert rented a vacant building across the street from the Cedarburg store and established Automobile Parts Warehousing to serve his own stores as well as independently owned auto parts stores.

Bill Mabry joined the company in 1968 and played an important role in its growth and development. That year the company stores were incorporated as Wisconsin Auto Parts and grew to become a 13-store chain with several locations in Milwaukee, along with stores in Sheboygen, Whitewater, Watertown, and Cedarburg. Wisconsin Auto Supply Company gave GPI an immediate presence in this important part of Wisconsin.

All in all, during 1998, the JV store group acquired or opened 228 stores. It consolidated, sold, or closed 61 stores, for a net gain of 167 stores. The Wolf Supply, Wisconsin Auto, APS, and Republic transactions created most of this activity. GPI ended 1998 with 984 joint venture stores, including the new stores in Canada.

Facilities and Systems

Following the occupancy of three new facilities and the major expansion in 1997, GPI completed and occupied the new 95,000-square-foot Phoenix Distribution Center in June 1998.

The long-awaited new Kansas City Distribution Center building was scheduled to be operational in November 1999.

Additionally, GPI purchased land in Winchester, Virginia, and in Denver for new distribution centers, with anticipated completion dates in late 1999 and early 2000, respectively. Both were fully occupied in 2000. Plus, a major expansion of the APS facility in Albuquerque was scheduled to be completed in October 1999.

GPI completed two material-handling system expansions for the Chicago and Indianapolis distribution centers in 1998. These expansions helped to accommodate growth in these two important markets. Also in 1998, GPI consolidated the Syracuse Distribution Center into the Buffalo Distribution Center.

Restructuring Accounting

In 1998, GPI decided to restructure its accounting offices to maximize efficiencies gained from the implementation of newly purchased Oracle financial software. This involved centralizing all distribution center and corporate accounting in Raleigh. GPI moved supplier payables to the Lexington, Kentucky, office. All Canadian accounting functions were consolidated in one central office in London, Ontario. Six joint venture accounting offices were maintained in Raleigh, North Carolina; Montgomery, Alabama; Bay City, Michigan; Billings, Montana; Lexington, Kentucky; and Lakeville, Minnesota. GPI centralized all independent customer accounting offices in Bay City.

New Facilities Management

A very important key to GPI's success has been the realization that sales will grow only if customer service is maintained consistently at a high level. Maintaining this level of service depends on staying ahead of the curve with adequate facilities. This job had really been a challenge for GPI during the 1980s and 1990s when acquisitions and mergers were at a peak. With almost every merger and acquisition, facility upgrade, new facility construction, and relocation

INDUSTRY STATISTICS FOR 1998

IN 1998, PART NUMBERS PROLIFERATION continued to impact the aftermarket significantly. The increasing diversity of vehicles and the aging of the vehicle population prompted this heavy part numbers growth. Lang Marketing estimated that the stock-keeping units (SKUs) required to service the aftermarket had more than doubled in the previous 10 years. This trend did not favor companies intent on maintaining inventories of only popular application parts.

Lang also reported that independent auto service centers continued to capture the largest share of the automotive service market in 1998, with a 32.6 percent share. New car dealers were second with a 25.1 percent share, followed by specialty shops at 20.5 percent, and tire shops at 8.6 percent. Over the previous 10 years, the number of cars and light trucks per service bay increased by 27 percent.

Under significant pricing pressure, the aftermarket enjoyed practically no price increases in 1998. On the other hand, the North American market featured more low-priced products originating from countries in South America and the Pacific Rim. Competitors compounded those pressures with a strong retail mentality that used low prices as the only way to generate sales.

Growth in vehicle miles continued for the 18th consecutive year but at the lowest rate of growth of any year during the 1990s.

World Vehicle Production

According to *Ward's Reports*, in 1998, the Big Three U.S. vehicle manufacturers produced 32.95 percent of all cars and trucks in the world, followed by European vehicle manufacturers with 30.98 percent, Japanese manufacturers at 27.60 percent, Korean manufacturers at 4.02 percent, and others at 4.45 percent.

By the end of 1998, 211,616,553 cars, trucks and buses were registered in the United States and 16,535,877 in Canada. This represented an increase from the previous year of 1.9 percent in the United States and 2.9 percent in Canada.

SUVs Continue to Dominate U.S. Vehicle Sales

In 1998, *Ward's Reports* stated, "Once again, sports/utility vehicles posted the largest increase in the red-hot light-truck market as SUV deliveries rose 14.8 percent over 1997. Ford Explorer remained the top-selling SUV with sales of 431,488 units in 1998 as compared with 383,852 the year before."

Below left: A typical CARQUEST professional service shop offering technologically advanced services.
Below right: CARQUEST store on Millbrook Road in Raleigh, North Carolina.

from an old to a new facility were necessary. These responsibilities, along with day-to-day internal operations, fell on the shoulders of Ham Sloan, who was ably assisted by Mac Graham, R.D. Carson, and Charles Shaw.

Distribution Center Sales

In 1998, fully 80 percent of GPI's distribution center sales continued to be products with specific automotive applications, and 94 percent of those application products were sold under the CARQUEST, Proven Value, and Bravo brand labels.

The CARQUEST TECH-NET
Professional Auto Service Program

In 1998, GPI implemented the first full year for CARQUEST TECH-NET. The company set up this professional auto service program for independent auto service repair centers. Nearly 1,500 of America's finest auto service shops identified with the new CARQUEST TECH-NET program.

CARQUEST
Headquarters Office

In 1998, CARQUEST staffers completed their first full year at the organization's headquarters office

Ham Sloan (right) and Charles Shaw (left), along with Mac Graham and R.D. Carson, were responsible for ensuring GPI's new distribution center buildings and facility upgrades were handled efficiently.

in Denver. Kornafel and his staff of 15 professionals, working with the marketing task force committee, continued to develop product lines and marketing programs to keep CARQUEST Auto Parts stores competitive. The CARQUEST office staff included Bob Barron, Matt Davis, Mike DeSorbo, Mary Folker, Todd Hack, William Humber, Jim Kendrick, Linda Ortiz, Lisa Patterson, Dan Rader, Jim Ray, Sandra Ray, Steve Switzer, Louise Yeasman, and Jennifer Zezza.

Market Changes

The rapid change and consolidation of the automotive aftermarket may have reached a peak in 1998. Manufacturer, re-manufacturer, distributor, auto parts store, and installer mergers and consolidations reached record numbers. The Advance/Western Auto and the AutoZone/Chief combinations represented the key mergers in the retail segment. The Dana/Echlin merger, along with Federal Mogul's acquisition of Cooper Automotive and Fel Pro represented the most notable mergers and acquisitions among manufacturers.

In 1998, NEAPCO became the new supplier of CARQUEST universal joints. This enabled the organization to provide better agriculture coverage.

Bankruptcy Claims Arrow Automotive

In 1998, bankruptcy claimed one of GPI's major suppliers, Arrow Automotive. For years, Arrow had been one of the industry's premier suppliers of re-manufactured products. It supplied a number of GPI distribution centers located in the Southeast with remanufactured electrical products, clutches, water pumps, and crankshaft kits. With help from other current suppliers of these products elsewhere in the country, and the formation of a special sales force of former Arrow salesmen, GPI was able to weather the Arrow bankruptcy with practically no disruption or loss of sales.

GENQUEST

With the help of Neal Williams, owner of the N. A. Williams Company, a reputable Atlanta-based sales agency, GPI was able to retain the

TRANSITIONS

1995—After 22 years as a corporate secretary, **Harriet Camak** retired. Her loyalty and efficiency were greatly missed by Joe Owen, Ham Sloan, and the entire GPI family. **Garland Reynolds** also retired in 1995.

1995—New additions: **Tom Hines** as real estate manager, **Bill Mann** as director of security, Raleigh corporate, and **Bobby Tyson** as JV regional manager, Raleigh, Mid-Atlantic Division. Promotions: **Allen Dedman** to division vice president, **Norm Ferguson** to regional vice president, distribution center sales, **Randy Haneckow** to JV general manager, Belle Plaine, Minnesota, **Ward Haugen** to JV Stores J-CON systems manager, corporate, **Chuck Henline** to regional vice president, distribution centers, **Wayne Lavrack** to group vice president, JV Stores, corporate, **Jeff Lundh** to regional vice president, Chicago, **John Martens** to division vice president, Chicago JV stores, **Don Robinson** to sales manager, Albany and Montgomery distribution centers, **Hoke Smith** to vice president, JV Stores South Central Division, and **Chris Winters** to regional vice president, Northwest Division.

1996—In October, **Temple Sloan Jr.** accepted an invitation to join the board of directors of Nations Bank, later to become Bank of America. That same year, **John Martens** won the JV general manager of the year award.

1996—New additions: **Donna Bellew** as assistant purchasing manager, corporate, and **Bud McQuillan** as vice president, purchasing, corporate. Promotions: **Jerry Berryhill** to operations manager, Lansing, **Dave Ellison** to JV Stores general manager, Nashville, **Jay Everage** to JV general manager, Baton Rouge, **Dan Fochtman** to vice president,

Above: Harriet Camak and John Martens (right).

Arrow Automotive southeast sales team. They were organized as a new division of N. A. Williams to work exclusively for GPI-CARQUEST stores in the southeast. The new division, named GENQUEST, was supervised by Sales Manager Keyma Harris who had been selling for Arrow for 20 years. He and six other former Arrow sales representatives had a cumulative 140 years of sales experience. The salesmen were Marvin Stephens, Ron Crunk, Randy Childers, Lee Lusk, Bob Drumm, T. J. Karkheck, Mike Murzi, Robert Hendrick, and Mark Carnesi. This new GENQUEST sales team was responsible for a number of re-manufactured product lines.

GPI's Joint Venture Stores Sales Team

By the late 1990s, GPI's Joint Venture Auto Parts stores fielded one of the industry's largest sales forces, with 825 full- or part-time salesmen. In addition, there were 20 Joint

Left: Neal Williams, owner of the N. A. Williams Company, helped GPI retain the entire Arrow Automotive Southeast sales team with the formation of GENQUEST.

Opposite: GPI chose long-time Arrow Automotive sales executive Keyma Harris to manage its new GENQUEST division.

Left: Mac Graham and John Sronce (right).

Northeast Store Division, **Annie Kornafel** to vice president, operations, **Mike Najdowski** to finance director, Michigan, **Kevin Sharp** to finance director, Albuquerque and Denver, **Ashton Wells** to finance director, Albany and Montgomery, and **Al Wheeler** to vice president of JV Store Sales, corporate.

1996—Retirements: December 31st marked the retirement from full-time responsibilities of **M.C. (Mac) Graham**. Graham was the second-longest serving associate of GPI, having joined the company in its infancy 35 years earlier, in 1961. His contributions were many and varied. GPI would not be where it is today without his dedication and commitment. After his retirement, Graham would continue to be active at GPI in an advisory capacity. **Herman Markell,** who had served as chairman of the Memphis Distribution Center since the 1986 merger, elected to slow down to a semi-retirement and spend time training GPI's sales and management associates and customers. Other retirees in 1996: **Evan Butterbrodt** (33), **Clarence Davis** (38),

Fred Farmer (41), **Willie Cameron** (22), **Ernest "Apple" Lemonds** (37), **Dave Lockwood** (27), **Vernon Moss** (35), **Rodney Pinkston** (45), **Don Spriggs** (45), **Freddie Stinson** (24), **Dee Stoll** (20), **Ralph Studinski** (38), **Charlie Walker** (44), **Sarah Weigel** (27), and **Wayne Wetherelt** (20).

1996—In Memoriam: GPI lost **John Sronce,** a valued friend, associate, and family member to a sudden heart attack. Sronce was manager for five CARQUEST stores in Asheville, North Carolina. He joined GPI in December 1989 when his family's business merged into GPI. Sronce was a strong-willed person who stood up for what he believed in. No one understood the words "customer service" better than he did. His honesty, integrity, and character will always be a testimony to his life. Another loss for the GPI family: In August 1996, **Neale Browning** a long-time salesman with the Lexington, Kentucky, CARQUEST Distribution Center died. "Neale made many contributions to our Lexington group by epitomizing the meaning of service to our customers," said Temple Sloan.

Venture sales managers. This team managed more than 2,000 technical training clinics, 625 customer appreciation events, and 110 technician appreciation nights. GPI also hosted numerous technician advisory council meetings designed to help understand the needs of its prime customers.

In 1998, in response to retirements, market consolidations, and estate planning considerations, 28 independent CARQUEST Auto Parts stores became a part of the Joint Venture Store Group. Including the Big A Stores, GPI added more than 475 new independent customers during the year for a total of 1,605 independently owned CAR-QUEST customers.

Heavy-Duty Products

Back in 1994, GPI had introduced a heavy-duty truck brake program. As a result, enough interest was generated among CARQUEST stores to expand coverage to other heavy-duty product categories. So, in 1998, Lee Williamson, with many years of heavy-duty experience, joined GPI and completed the necessary coverage to put CARQUEST stores in a strong position in this important market.

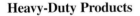

By the end of 1998, GPI was serving 2,896 CARQUEST stores in 43 states in the United States and Canada, including 984 joint venture stores.

1997—**Kim Patch** won the JV general manager of the year award.

1997—New additions: **Bill Kuykendall** as vice president of finance, **Kim Molin** to board of directors, **Mike DeSorbo** as national training director, and **William Humber** as professional markets manager. Promotions: **Steve Blanton** to sales manager, Chicago Distribution Center, **Charles Garrison** to director of corporate tax, JV Stores, **Rich Merchant** to operations manager, Phoenix, **Al Minnis** to regional vice president, distribution center sales, Central Region, **Allen Till** to director of distribution center and cost center accounting, corporate, **Bobby Tyson** to vice president, JV Division.

1997—Retirements: After 36 years of service, **Bill Norris** decided to officially retire but continued to assist on a part-time basis. Norris was the first associate to be hired in 1961 when the original GPI warehouse was moved from Sanford, North Carolina, to Raleigh, North Carolina. He was expert in stockroom management. **Mike Zeltinger,** salesman for the Missoula, Montana, stores, retired on December 31. Zeltinger completed 40 years of service. During his career, he was an outstanding salesman, winning the top sales producer award for the Northwest Division for many years. Zeltinger always commanded the deepest respect from his customers and his associates. Throughout the years, Zeltinger's leadership along with his commitment to GPI never wavered. Other retirees: **Don Annala** (35), **Lenora Carrington** (21), **Dale Cutsinger** (20), **Frank Howard** (24), **Clarence Kamerman** (35), **Robert Klus** (35), **Vern Meyers** (32), **Marv Muchlbauer** (30), **Dick Pagel** (20),

Clockwise from left: Kim Patch, Mike Zeltinger, Harry Evans, Bill Gruenthal and Bill Norris.

During the period 1995–1998, GPI's sales increased 81 percent and earnings increased 61 percent. This map shows the extent of GPI's marketing reach at the end of 1998.

GPI entered the last year of the 20th century with a renewed commitment to the future of the company, its people, customers, and suppliers. Strategic acquisitions, strong customer relations, focused marketing programs, and the investment and implementation of new Oracle financial software positioned the company for an even brighter future.

Most of all, GPI was ready to continue earning strong

Heavy-duty parts veteran Lee Williamson joined GPI in 1998 to help build its heavy-duty parts business.

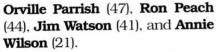

Orville Parrish (47), Ron Peach (44), Jim Watson (41), and Annie Wilson (21).

1997—In memoriam: On December 3, Harry Evans passed away in his sleep. Evans joined Hayes & Hopson Auto Supply Warehouse Distribution Company (WNC Parts Distributors) when it was founded in 1968. He joined GPI when WNC Parts Distributors was acquired. For the next 20 years, on both a full-time and a part-time basis, Evans served GPI in a sales capacity. His work contributed greatly to the growth of the Asheville Distribution Center.

1998—Bill Gruenthal won the JV general manager of the year award.

1998—Promotions: Mike Allen to regional vice president, David Bartelt to JV general manager, Minneapolis, Doug Buscher to regional vice president, Bob Conley to eastern sales manager,

JV Stores, Danny Durham to vice president, regional operations, Bruce Hershman to western sales manager, JV Stores, Montie Loney to regional vice president, distribution center sales, David McCartney to vice president, regional operations, Rich Merchant to operations manager, Baton Rouge, Kim Patch to regional vice president, JV Stores, Tommy Salmon to regional vice president, JV Stores, Mike Tanji to regional vice president, operations, David Wehrenberg to operations manager, Memphis, and John Weinmann Sr. to operations manager, Cleveland.

1998—Retirees: Ivan Feurlinger (42), Jan Gardner (29), James Gies (37), Leo Hice (29), Annie Kornafel (27), Ed McIntosh (25), Marvin Sumner (43), and Gerard Vititoe (21).

In loving memory of the following additional associates who passed away during this period: Dana Robinson and Nathaniel Stokes.

> Retiree information shows years of employment after names. This may include time spent at acquired companies.

sales and profits during the upcoming century, just as it had every year that it had been in business. Joe Hughes, the former owner of Indian Parts Warehouse and one of the first three members of CARQUEST, had a favorite saying that he routinely shared with those around him: "The one who wins is the one who prepares to win." This time-tested maxim represented an almost perfect metaphor for GPI—it definitely was prepared to win—and win big—in the years to come.

In 1999, GPI/CARQUEST made the largest charitable donation in its history in support of the 1999 Special Olympics World Games, held in Raleigh, North Carolina, from June 26 through July 4.

CHAPTER NINE

CONTINUING TO EXPAND

1999–2001

Every GPI associate has earned the right to be proud. If we were a football team, we would have just won the Super Bowl with a record-breaking performance against record-breaking odds.

—Temple Sloan Jr., Joe Owen, and Ham Sloan,
in a message to employees in the December 1999 *General Idea.*

A S GPI PREPARED TO enter the new millennium, its new business activities remained robust. In 1999, new business for the firm showed a substantial increase of 20 percent. And profits were strong as well, despite $17 million in associated costs with the APS and Republic acquisitions. Indeed, with all of this expense absorbed, GPI's net profits still were up 6 percent in 1999, and operating profits improved 10.1 percent.

By the end of the year, 2,345 GPI associates held equity positions in the firm. Net income as a percent of beginning investor's equity was 12.8 percent. The debt-to-equity ratio was 1.42, improved from 1.47 in 1998. Continued improvement was expected with the completion of the APS consolidations and the remaining inventory liquidations.

The 16-month period ending December 31, 1999, was a time of great challenge and opportunity for GPI. The company made industry history when it switched 605 Big A and Republic stores to CARQUEST Auto Parts stores.

In the Pittsburgh, Pennsylvania, market, GPI added 25 Joint Venture stores and nine independent CARQUEST Auto Parts stores. In Alaska, GPI converted 13 Republic Joint Venture stores and 10 independent stores to the CARQUEST program, plus four Republic Joint Venture stores in California, three

independent and seven Joint Venture stores in Iowa, and five Joint Venture stores in the upper peninsula of Michigan.

Another 1999 challenge was the duplication of distribution center facilities and off-site storage in several markets. This prompted some distribution center consolidations. Phoenix, Arizona, was the first completed market, with Indianapolis following soon after. In Albuquerque, New Mexico, GPI constructed a 30,000-square-foot addition to the APS Distribution Center to accommodate the newly expanded business.

In Denver, Colorado; Great Bend, Kansas; Kansas City, Missouri; Omaha, Nebraska; Salt Lake City, Utah; and Winchester, Virginia, crews of GPI associates and dedicated factory representatives traveled on two- or three-week assignments to complete store changeovers. Stores served by Salt Lake City and Omaha were completed during October. The majority of the Omaha changeovers were reassigned to the Des Moines Distribution Center.

The newly constructed, 125,000-square-foot Kansas City Distribution Center was occupied on

This map shows the extent of GPI's sales and marketing reach during 1999.

TEMPLE SLOAN JR. RECEIVES OUTSTANDING BUSINESS LEADER AWARD

IN 1999, DR. DAVID E. FRY, PRESIDENT OF Northwood University, a special purposes college with campuses in Florida, Michigan, and Texas, awarded its Outstanding Business Leader Award to O. Temple Sloan, Jr. at The Breakers in Palm Beach, Florida. His commentary concerning Sloan:

This etching of O. Temple Sloan Jr. was mounted on a plaque.

Temple Sloan is the chairman of General Parts Inc., of Raleigh, North Carolina, one of the nation's largest wholesale distributors of auto parts. Mr. Sloan founded the company in 1961 at the age of 21 while still a student at Duke University. Today, General Parts is a $1.5 billion organization with more than 11,000 associates and more than 1,150 stores and is a supplier of an additional 1,800 operator-owned stores, which do business across the United States and Canada under the brand name CARQUEST.

Mr. Sloan has been active in many professional, civic, education, religious, and other charitable organizations, both local and national, and is the recipient of numerous awards for his achievements and contributions. He serves as chairman of the board of Highwoods Properties Inc. and is a member of Bank of America's board of directors. Mr. Sloan is a trustee of St. Andrews College and Peace College, Presbyterian Homes Inc., and Boys and Girls Homes, all in his home state. He is a member of the Who's Who in America and has received the distinguished service citation from the Automotive Hall of Fame. He has been recognized for his contributions to the Boy Scouts and is active in his church. He and his wife Carol are the proud parents of three children who have provided them with 10 grandchildren.

GPI's new Kansas City Distribution Center opened in 1999.

November 4, 1999. The new facility served Big A stores that were previously served by APS' Great Bend, Kansas, distribution center, and some stores from APS Omaha.

APS changeovers in Denver were completed in November. The APS facility located in Denver soon would be consolidated into the existing GPI Denver Distribution Center. At the same time, a new state-of-the-art Denver Distribution Center was under construction. Operating two distribution centers each in Denver, Albuquerque, and Phoenix during the APS changeovers represented a large but necessary expense to maintain service levels in the individual stores.

In total, as a result of the acquisitions, more than 20,000 individual product line changes were planned, controlled, and quickly executed by GPI associates, the CARQUEST undercar sales force, the underhood associates, and manufacturer representatives. Additionally, the GPI team installed 384 new J-CON Systems and also handled the training associated with each installation.

The automotive aftermarket had never seen a project of such magnitude. The Herculean task could not have occurred without the total support of GPI's suppliers, whose commitment was outstanding. Through those combined efforts,

GPI/CARQUEST gained a large number of outstanding CARQUEST customers, as well as many new GPI associates who would make valuable contributions to the future growth of the company.

Parts Source (DBA Ace Auto Parts) in Florida

In 1966, the Cox family, which included Robert A. Cox Sr., Robert A. Cox Jr., and Thomas D. Cox, moved to Florida from Ohio and purchased a 50 percent share in an outdoor advertising company in Bradenton. In 1971, the family decided to diversify, and its company, Florida Outdoor, purchased Ace Auto Parts from Bill Hayden in St. Petersburg. At the time, Ace consisted of two small stores. By 1977, Ace had grown to 11 stores and was generating $4 million in annual sales. During 1977, the family sold the outdoor advertising company and joined the management team of Ace Auto Parts.

Ace began an aggressive store expansion program and by 1988 had grown to 29 store locations and a warehouse with a consolidated annual sales volume of $20 million. At this time, Robert A. Cox Sr. decided that it was time to retire and began to search for a buyer. In late 1988, Frank McPeak purchased the assets of Ace Auto Parts and planned to expand the volume to $50 million and then take the company public. Thomas Cox and Robert Cox Sr., left Ace around 1990. By this time, the business was not doing well. McPeak continued to manage the company but was unable to expand its operations as originally planned. Indeed, in October 1992, he was forced to file for company bankruptcy. Once Thomas Cox and Robert Cox, Sr., learned of this upcoming action, they purchased Ace's assets, along with their partner, APS Corporation.

During 1997, Ace opened seven new stores, acquired three stores, and consolidated four stores into existing operations. These moves gave the company a total of 44 stores at year's end. In February 1998, APS Holding declared bankruptcy and in October of that year, GPI acquired selective operations of APS Holding.

In February 1999, GPI purchased all of the outstanding shares of stock of The Parts Source (DBA Ace Auto Parts).

"We believe that our customers, employees, and our shareholders will be pleased with this

PROUD TO BE PROUD

THE FOLLOWING WAS TAKEN FROM A message to all GPI associates titled "Proud To Be Proud." The message appeared in the December 1999 "General Idea" and was signed by Temple Sloan Jr., Joe Owen, and Ham Sloan.

Every GPI associate has earned the right to be proud. If we were a football team, we would have just won the Super Bowl with a record-breaking performance against record-breaking odds. And every player on the GPI team got a chance to not only play but to contribute in victory.

The automotive aftermarket is a tough conference with lots of big, mean, and talented players. But the challenge that faced the GPI team in 1999 was enormous and, in our opinion, only the GPI team could have won.

While our competition sat on their benches and waited for us to stumble, fumble, and fall, our team rolled up their shirtsleeves, flexed their muscles, and showed the whole automotive aftermarket what they are made of.

The challenge was that of acquiring nine American Parts distribution centers which served well over 500 Big A Auto Parts stores. And that couldn't begin until we completed the Republic acquisition that started at the last half of 1998. With these two acquisitions, 11 distribution centers and 600 stores were changed to CARQUEST by the GPI team.

There just couldn't be a better way to start the year 2000 than serving 25 percent more CARQUEST Auto Parts stores. GPI will be ready for the next millennium and whether it starts with the year 2000 or 2001, our team is experienced, battle tough, and prepared to face any problem ahead.

So, no matter what day-to-day responsibilities you may have as a GPI associate, you have been instrumental in this successful venture. You should enjoy the thrill of victory and the pride of success.

And most important, a huge "thanks" to each and every one of you. May you and your family have a Happy Holiday Season.

---

decision," said Thomas Cox, president of The Parts Source. Sloan responded, "Our sincere thanks to Tom and Bob Cox for this opportunity to expand our presence in central Florida."

The merger was finalized in May 1999. At that time The Parts Source was serving 41 company stores and 15 former Big A independent stores. Construction of a new distribution center in Ocala started immediately and was completed in March 2001. With The Parts Source acquisition, GPI received an extra bonus—Jerry Repak, a real go-getter who was the company's operations manager. By the end of 2004, Repak had become vice president of distributor center operations for the Western Division of GPI.

In January, GPI acquired an additional nine APS stores in Ohio that became available through bankruptcy court. In February, GPI acquired eight stores headquartered in Fort Myers, Florida, from Ed Hendrick.

In addition to the Ohio, Ace, and Kirby acquisitions, GPI acquired several other strategic store groups during 1999. They included a number of excellent stores picked up from retiring owners of CARQUEST independent customers. Included in the group were James Avera's five stores in eastern North Carolina; Nick Bouchard's two stores in Michigan; Stan Ray's store in Greenville, Ohio; Kurt Carlson and Larry Lutz's store in Rochester, Minnesota; four of Merle Bauman's stores in Arizona; George's in Green Bay, Wisconsin; and Gordon Harley's store in Springfield, Oregon.

JV Program

In 1999, introduction of the Joint Venture program to the wholly owned Canadian store management team began, with 14 stores implementing the plan by the end of the year. GPI store associates enthusiastically accepted the program. In 2000, the goal would be to accelerate the conversion of additional wholly owned stores.

Sales of the Joint Venture Store Group grew to $900 million, and annualized store sales in the United States were approaching $1 billion. Investment continued in the expansion of the JV Store sales force, with 875 full- or part-time salesmen. These salesmen were supervised by two national sales managers and 24 regional sales managers.

CARQUEST Canada

Also in 1999, CARQUEST Canada completed the 30-month transition of GPI's customers, marketing, products, and systems to the CARQUEST program. CARQUEST Canada ended the year serving 301 CARQUEST Auto Parts stores. It was comprised of 192 associates and 109 company-owned stores, with sales in excess of $203 million (Canadian dollars).

Machine Shop Sales

In 1999, machine shop sales grew $1.7 million to $13.6 million, up 14.3 percent over 1998, while operating profit reached $2.7 million, an increase of 20 percent over the prior year. Also during 1999, 19 GPI shop associates earned President's Club status by producing outstanding sales and profit results.

Products

In 1999, CARQUEST focused its marketing efforts on brakes. This product line represented a two-year project that began in 1997. It involved changing the supplier to Raybestos, a division of Dana. The plan was finalized and launched with great success in June 1999. Also that year, GPI greatly improved its heavy-duty truck product offerings with various product lines: brake drums, expanded brake shoe coverage, clutches, water pumps, and brake hardware. In addition, GPI added axle oil bath seals and exhaust stacks to the product offering.

In 1999, an important decision was made to integrate the CARQUEST-dedicated sales force from engine controls and temperature controls into the CARQUEST undercar sales force, forming a new underhood sales force. Under Jim Ray's guidance, the new sales group totaled 175 experienced sales technicians working exclusively with CARQUEST Auto Parts stores. Ray challenged each member to achieve at least one ASE certification, a measure of technical expertise and a step toward achieving the ASE Blue Seal of Excellence. This combined undercar/underhood sales team represented a major step toward sales efficiency.

National GPI/CARQUEST Business Conference

September 1999 marked the first GPI/CARQUEST National Business Conference, held at the Mirage Hotel in Las Vegas and attended by more than 1,000 people. Because of the success of the program, a national conference was held every two years thereafter.

Aftermarket Trends

Although 1999 recorded the industry's third-lowest sales growth during the 1990s at just 1.5 percent, there were strong indicators that the replacement parts business would continue to be a good business for established firms like GPI. At the same time, DIY-ers attempting auto repairs found it increasingly difficult to install replacement parts. According to the *Lang Report*, in 1990, 49 percent of sales to DIY customers were replacement parts; in 1999, that percentage had dropped to 39 percent.

Also, according to the *Lang Report*, the impact of retail-chain growth over the past decade had created a slight decline in the traditional auto parts stores' share of the DIY volume. In 1989, traditional auto parts stores' DIY business represented 24.1 percent of the total. Ten years later, the share had dropped to only 20.9 percent. At the same time, vehicle manufacturers, through their dealerships, were increasing their penetration

ASE certification acknowledges technical experience.

of the aftermarket service business, but the independent auto service shops were still receiving the top share with 29.8 percent.

Ward's Report: "Car of the Century"

In February 1997, 118 automotive journalists from 32 countries, members of the "Car of the Century" (COTC) committee, gathered in Amsterdam, The Netherlands, to cut in half a list of 400 award nominees. Voting was then opened to the public as well ... Ford's Model T [was named] the "Car of the Century." Trailing it, in order of their scores were: Rover Mini, Citroen DS 19, VW Beetle, and Porsche 911.

In 1999, *Ward's Report* stated, "With trucks accounting for half the market, U.S. new vehicle sales in calendar year 1999 surpassed the 1986 record of 16.3 million by 6.7 percent to an all-time-high of 17.4 million units."

GPI registered substantial growth during the 1990s. In 10 short years, GPI grew from a company with sales of $238 million to $1.324 billion, not including sales of its new Canadian company. Net earnings increased more than six times, and equity grew almost seven-fold. The number of CARQUEST stores served increased from 844 to 2,785. Joint Venture stores increased from 179 to 1,019.

HAM SLOAN–A STORIED CAREER

WHEN HAM SLOAN JOINED GPI in 1970, sales the previous year were $4.2 million. When he retired as vice chairman 29 years later, sales for the United States and Canada had grown to $1.3 billion, placing GPI near the top of the largest privately owned companies in the United States.

After attending Duke University, spending a few years in the department store business, and serving four years in the United States Coast Guard, Sloan became a key member of the GPI team. From his first day, he was instrumental in the growth of the company. At a time when GPI was focused on building sales and the customer base, Sloan turned his attention to GPI's employees and the efficiency of GPI's only distribution center, in Raleigh, North Carolina.

Although Sloan's contributions are too numerous to mention, his primary areas of responsibility were distribution center operations, human resources, purchasing, and facility site acquisitions, design, and development. As a result of his planning and direction, GPI became the aftermarket leader for modern automated distribution cen-

ters. His latest projects were the "total paperless warehouse systems" in Des Moines and Kansas City.

During GPI's aggressive expansionary period of the 1980s and 1990s, Sloan's steady hand enabled GPI to retain numerous talented associates, many of whom went on to become members of the management team.

Sloan served for 10 years on the board of AWDA and was chairman in 1988. He was a leader in the development of the AWDA educational program, which subsequently became known as the "University of the Aftermarket." For more than 20 years, he played a role in the development of the warehouse management curriculum, and he lectured in this area as well. In 1989, Sloan was recognized as AWDA's Automotive Man of the Year, the organization's highest award. After retiring, Sloan remained a member of GPI's board of directors and continued to share his vast experience and knowledge to keep the company strong.

Portrait courtesy of Sam Gray at SamGrayPortraits.com.

2000

In 2000, GPI registered its 11th consecutive year of record earnings and its 39th consecutive year of sales growth. GPI's sales registered an increase of 10.3 percent over 1999. Net income increased 9.5 percent, while operating profits grew 12.4 percent over the prior year. This performance came at a time when the industry was flat, and many companies were struggling to maintain sales and profit levels.

CARQUEST Canada

On January 4, 2000, GPI completed the acquisition of the remaining stock of CARQUEST Canada Ltd. from Acktion Corporation, making the Canadian operation a wholly owned GPI subsidiary. K. (Rai) Sahi, chairman and chief executive officer commented on the transaction:

These transactions are in accord with our previously announced intention to divest ourselves of interests which are non-core to our principal real estate investments. We wish GPI and CARQUEST all the best in their future endeavors and feel confident that CARQUEST, its customers, and employees will prosper under the focused, professional ownership of GPI.

GPI was appreciative of the important contributions Jack Moritz made in the development of a subsidiary to a CARQUEST and GPI company. As president of CARQUEST Canada, Moritz provided confidence, calm leadership, and a new vision. As initially planned, Moritz retired as president at the end of 1999.

Robert Blair, the new president of CARQUEST Canada Ltd., was surrounded by a highly talented management team. The new partnership provided the programs and tools required to increase sales and earnings in the years ahead.

CARQUEST CANADA's first year as a full member of the GPI family was highlighted by a 68 percent increase in operating income. At the same time, the Canadian aftermarket was experiencing the same softness as the U.S. aftermarket.

During 2000, the Ottawa Distribution Center was closed, and its customers began being served

Right: Jack Moritz provided expert, seasoned leadership as CARQUEST Canada's president.

Below: GPI's Toronto headquarters. One out of three Canadians live within 100 miles of Toronto.

from the Montreal and Toronto distribution centers. Both distribution centers experienced substantial improvement in customer service and operating efficiencies as the year progressed.

Toronto is home to one of the GPI/CARQUEST distribution centers. The Toronto Distribution Center encompasses more than 170,000 square feet, including 20,000 square feet of mezzanine space. The distribution center was originally built in 1962 as a warehouse for Atlas Tire. A major remodeling of the stocking, receiving, and shipping area was recently completed along with an upgrading of the conveyor system.

One-third of Canada's population is located within a 100-mile radius of Toronto, while one half of the population of the United States is within a one-day's drive. Known as "Silicon Valley North," Toronto is home to seven of the top 10 information technology companies in Canada. It has a population of more than 2.4 million. More than 80 languages are spoken in Toronto, and one-third of its residents speak a language other than English in their homes.

SUPPORTING THE SPECIAL OLYMPICS

ON MARCH 20, 1999, THE ANNOUNCEment was made that GPI/CARQUEST would make the largest charitable donation in company history. The donation would help support the 1999 Special Olympics World Games, held in Raleigh, North Carolina, June 26 through July 4, 1999.

Annually, this is the largest assembly of Special Olympic athletes in the world, with more than 7,000 participants from 150 countries, accompanied by 2,000 coaches and 15,000 family members. More than 45,000 volunteers help make the Games a yearly success. For 1999, this included a large contingent of GPI associates and customers.

For the Games, GPI/CARQUEST initially committed to raise a minimum contribution of $500,000. This amount quickly snowballed and by July 1999, GPI/CARQUEST had raised $1.1 million for the event.

Temple Sloan Jr. listed the following reasons for the company's involvement:

- The Special Olympics movement is an extremely effective way to give dignity, confidence, and achievement to physically and mentally challenged people, by allowing them to earn recognition for athletic excellence.
- We can have a positive impact on thousands of people much less fortunate than ourselves.
- There is a Special Olympics presence in almost every one of our communities that needs volunteers daily, and each one of us can make a difference.
- Our involvement gives CARQUEST and GPI an opportunity to focus the attention and efforts of the finest body of associates and owners toward one worthy cause.

Sloan appointed Herman P. Markell, Memphis Distributor Center chairman and Ed Whitehurst, retired GPI board member, to head CARQUEST's involvement in the Special Olympics on a nationwide basis. He commented on the efforts of GPI personnel who assisted with the Special Olympics Games activities, or other aspects of GPI/CARQUEST's sponsorship.

This is a tremendously proud moment for all of us at GPI. It is our way of saying thank you for all the good fortune that has grown our company in the past, allowing us to help folks much less fortunate. We have a dynamite committee. They are: Donna Bellew, Deborah Bowers, Bill Carter, Tina Davis, Scott Ginsburg, Mike Hollingsworth, Randal Long, Paul May, Bud McQuillan, and Carolyn Peebles. Ed Whitehurst and Herman Markell will serve as Co-Chairmen of the Games Operating Committee.

At the conclusion of the 1999 Special Olympics World Summer Games, Sloan had this to say:

Now that the excitement and thrill of the Special Olympics World Games have passed, it is only fitting that we pause to remember the joy that so many of us saw in the smiling, exhausted faces of the 7,000 Special Olympic Athletes during the Games. From the torch run to the opening ceremonies, the Olympic Festival Village and the Games themselves, climaxed by the closing ceremony, the pace never slowed.

Over a two-year period, GPI/CARQUEST people have labored in every imaginable way to raise funds for the Games' sponsorship. Fund-raising events were held in thousands of locations from Alaska, Canada, New Mexico, Maine, Texas, and every state in between. We raised over $1.1 million, making CARQUEST a Gold Sponsor of the Games. Over 300 of our people gave three or more

days of their time as volunteers. In excess of 70 GPI people, chosen by their associates and representing every market, came to Raleigh for three days to serve as volunteers. CARQUEST jobbers from as far away as upper Michigan attended the Games.

The CARQUEST Team was second to no one in their dedication, effort, excitement and commitment during the long week. Our people put in days that ranged from 6:30 A.M. to midnight in their volunteer efforts. Each of them will tell you it was a privilege and an experience they will never forget.

I have never been prouder to be a member of the CARQUEST Team. Our people came together with a spirit and commitment that was contagious to everyone who met them. There were so many who went above and beyond the call, that it would be impossible to mention their names without missing someone. They know who they are, and the personal satisfaction and fulfillment they received is all the recognition they expect.

Throughout the year 2000, GPI and CARQUEST associates across North America continued their outstanding fundraising efforts, this time as a platinum-level sponsor, on behalf of the Special Olympics World Winter Games in Anchorage.

Company efforts were led by the CARQUEST Games Operating Committee: Bill Carter, Randal Long, Scott Ginsburg, Tina Davis, Mike Hollingsworth, Bill King, Fred Kotcher, Herm Markell, Paul May, Ed Whitehurst, Tom Belding, Natalie Elliott, Ron Jones, and Jeanette and Gary Mohar.

The 1999 World Games commends the CGOC and the CARQUEST family for their dedication to the World Games and the Special Olympics movement.

Late in 2000, CARQUEST agreed to a new two-year commitment to become the premier international partner of the Law Enforcement Torch Run for Special Olympics. Joining with more than 75,000 members of the law enforcement community, GPI lent its support to raise money and awareness for Special Olympics. GPI extended its commitment to the Law Enforcement Torch Run as their premier international partner for 2002 through 2004. For this three-year period more than $2.5 million was raised by CARQUEST for Special Olympics. The Law Enforcement Torch Run enabled GPI/CARQUEST to connect with the Special Olympics at the local level. Sloan thanked those involved.

To each of you who participated in this incredible effort, thank you for making us all proud. Thank you for offering a friendly hand to those who are less fortunate. It reminded us so often of how God has blessed us, and yet how those less fortunate, when given an opportunity, will produce positive things with their lives. It is a privilege to be your partner on Team CARQUEST.

Since its initial involvement in 1999, CARQUEST has raised more than $5 million for the Special Olympics through 2005.

Top left and right: Late in 2000, CARQUEST became a premier international partner of the Law Enforcement Torch Run for the Special Olympics.

Center: By July 1999, GPI/CARQUEST had raised $1.1 million for the event.

CARQUEST Auto Parts Stores

In the United States, GPI ended 2000 serving 1,417 independently owned CARQUEST Auto Parts stores. The company added 68 new stores and enjoyed sales increases with 65 percent of its larger customers and 1,158 Joint Venture stores, compared to the 1999 total store count of 1,128. Sales for the Joint Venture Store Group increased to $1 billion for 2000.

In 2000, GPI acquired 75 auto parts stores, sold two stores and consolidated 12 stores for a net gain of 61 new auto parts stores with an estimated volume of $67.5 million. This included the merger of six Ohio-based stores owned by Bill Herring Jr. Others included Stinson Adam's Marietta, Georgia, store, and the Palmer Brothers' store group based in Great Falls, Montana. This store group would greatly strengthen GPI's local paint business. The four-store chain of Varney Auto Supply in Bangor, Maine, also added market share to the Bangor market.

In October, GPI acquired Jim Yates' 13-store group, which was located in the northern Virginia and District of Columbia markets. Yates' store group had been a strong player in this huge market and GPI was fortunate to have an immediate presence there. GPI ended 2000 with the acquisition of two Harbert stores in Kenosha, Wisconsin, and Racine, Wisconsin, and three parts stores in Lebanon, Tennessee.

GPI merged with a number of outstanding CARQUEST Auto Parts stores in 2000: Pat Hilliard at Speed's Automotive in Cadillac, Michigan; Ronnie Leet in Selma, Alabama; John and Dave Sobeck in Woodland, Colorado; Gary Wise in Molalla, Oregon; Koji Howland in Green River and Price, Utah; Sig Friedman in Winnemucca, Nevada; and Ron Webber's store in Watertown, South Dakota.

Facilities and Operations

In February 2000, GPI completed its move to an enlarged 75,500-square-foot distribution center in Albuquerque. The next month, GPI moved into a new 118,900-square-foot facility in Winchester, Virginia, and in August it occupied the new 121,000-square-foot facility in Denver. Each of these investments provided significantly improved operating efficiencies. GPI developed plans to move into a new 124,000-square-foot Cleveland Distribution Center in January 2001 and into the new 123,000-square-foot Ocala, Florida, Distribution Center in March. The Montreal Distribution Center, located in St. Laurent, Quebec, was relocated into a new facility in Boucherville on the south shore of Montreal in mid-October.

Below left: GPI moved into an enlarged 75,500-square-distribution center in Albuquerque in 2000.

Below right: Boucherville Distribution Center serves both corporate and associate CARQUEST stores.

The new facility faced the heavily traveled Highway 20, which connects Montreal with Quebec City. On a property of nearly 500,000 square feet, the 110,000-square-foot warehouse floor is topped with a 40,000-square-foot mezzanine. Double conveyors serve both the mezzanine and main floor. A unique elevator system leads to a collector conveyor then back down to the barcode reading shipping lanes. Offices for the 25 Quebec division administration staffers and a 4,000-square-foot store complete the facility. The new Boucherville Distribution Center serves a network of 44 corporate and 70 associate CARQUEST stores throughout the province of Quebec.

TECH-NET Professional Auto Service

During 2000, the 2,750th independent auto service center joined the TECH-NET Professional Auto Service and the Canadian program, AutoPLACE. This represented an increase of more than 750 auto service centers. The TECH-NET and AutoPLACE Professional Auto Service Programs are powerful marketing plans that emphasize improving CARQUEST Auto Parts store sales to professional auto service centers.

Above right: GPI moved into its 121,000-square-foot building in Denver in August 2000.

Above left: The Winchester Distribution Center features 118,900 feet of warehouse space.

Below left: The TECH-NET Professional Auto Service program focuses on improving store sales to professional auto service centers.

London Leasing Company

During 2000, GPI introduced London Leasing, a new leasing operation. As of December 31, 2000, the company had registered $1.2 million in outstanding leases. The new venture enhanced the sale of equipment and strengthened the relationship with professional auto service technicians. London Leasing in Canada is managed by Doug Gilbert and in the United States by Paul Becton.

Status of the Industry at the Millennium

Even though the population of light trucks and passenger cars continued to grow and age (9.2 years), the mix of America's overall vehicle population shifted dramatically in the latter half of the 1990s. According to *Ward's Report*, vehicle registration in the United States reached 221.3 million by the end of 2000 and 16.8 million in Canada, both countries showing increases over the 1999 calendar year. The average miles driven grew 2 percent in 2000, resulting in more than 10 years of consecutive increases. The light truck market, which includes vans and SUVs and is of great importance in the United States, grew 53 percent, or 25 million trucks, during the past 10 years. Off-shore vehicle manufacturers responded to the U.S. consumers' love for SUVs by adding SUVs to their own product lines, thus slowing the Big Three's dominance. Of course, American society continued to be fully dependent on motor vehicles. The continued growth of the U.S. economy depended on the daily movement of people and goods, the majority being handled by cars and trucks.

As with the rest of the industry, GPI's sales results for 2000 slowed during the second half of the year. To produce an earnings increase with little sales growth was a tribute to the efforts of the GPI management team. Slower sales in no way reflected the many actions GPI's management took to strengthen the company.

2001
New Corporate Management Structure

On January 1, 2001, GPI announced some important changes in the corporate management structure:

Wayne Lavrack, who has managed the GPI JV stores since 1990, was appointed president of the JV store group. Lavrack, a 24-year veteran with GPI, has been instrumental in forming and growing our Joint Venture Store program. Joe Owen, who has served the past 17 years as president of GPI, has been appointed to the position of vice chairman. With more than 48 years in the automotive aftermarket Owen has been a driving force for GPI and holds the respect of the entire industry. He will continue to oversee our marketing initiatives and manufacturer relations. O. Temple Sloan III has been appointed to the position of president of GPI, where he will direct our distribution center operations, independent sales, market development, human resources, and purchasing. Most recently a senior vice president of the DC Group, "TIII" brings a wealth of experience from his positions at GPI over the years, including division president, sales manager, district sales manager, and purchasing manager.

When Temple Sloan III graduated from the University of Wyoming in 1983, he was fully aware that a career with GPI was not guaranteed. He knew that his father would be pleased to see him achieve a key position in management, but he also understood that his father would require him to earn every promotion by starting out at entry level and performing professionally and with complete responsibility during each new assignment. During this period, TIII took the time to marry and with his wife, Joy, raise a family of three daughters and two sons. He and his family have lived in nine different cities from Bozeman, Montana, to Andalusia, Alabama.

TIII truly earned the respect of all within the company as a leader—not because he is the son of the founder and CEO of GPI—but because of the way he routinely conducted himself in producing superior results at every management assignment while learning the business. He is well prepared through "hands on" experience to lead GPI to its next level.

A newly created position, senior vice president, market development–North America, will be filled by Dennis Fox. He will act as our focal point for continuing aggressive market development initiatives in the United States and Canada.

Mike Allen has been named group vice president. A seasoned veteran of the aftermarket, Allen will direct our independent store sales operations. Filling his former position as vice president, sales, Southern Region, is Shipman Northcutt, a long-time GPI associate who will relocate to Raleigh, North Carolina, from Memphis.

These appointments would position GPI well into the future for growth and achievement of its business goals. In 2001, its 40th year, GPI achieved record sales and earnings—also its 40th consecutive year of sales growth and profitability. Sales increased 7 percent over 2000. Net income grew 21 percent. Operating income was up 17.6 percent. All of GPI's operating groups, including Canada, increased their operating income as a percent of sales over the year 2000. The company achieved this level of record performance during a recession, the tragic terrorist attacks on September 11, and the subsequent war in Afghanistan. Additional 2001 highlights:

• Merger of the A.E. Lottes Company, St. Louis

- Significant reduction in debt and debt ratios
- The consolidation of the Cleveland and Pittsburgh distribution centers into a new facility in Brunswick, Ohio
- The occupancy of a new distribution center in Ocala, Florida
- Moving the CARQUEST marketing office from Denver to Raleigh, North Carolina

Another major highlight was a significant improvement in gross margins, improved productivity, reduction in operating expenses, and new efficiencies gained from consolidations. Performance for 2001 achieved a 13.5 percent return on beginning equity, meeting the objective of a 13 percent plus annual return on investors' equity. Also, GPI associates purchased $9.5 million of common stock. The debt-to-equity ratio improved to 1.11 from 1.37 the previous year and the debt-to-EBITDA ratio dropped to 3.21 from 3.93 at the end of the previous year. This represented a major step in de-leveraging GPI's balance sheet from the acquisitions during the previous two years.

'T's Corner

THE DECEMBER 2000 EDITION OF the "General Idea" included, a new feature, "T"'s Corner, prepared by O. Temple Sloan III. Here is the first column.

Welcome to the first installment of 'T's Corner. Through this regular column, we will share information with you about our company and important matters concerning our business. As owners of the company, we all must have the information necessary to insure that GPI continues to grow and prosper.

The first topic we want to discuss is, by far, the most important one to all of us and to GPI: customer satisfaction. As consumers, we have all experienced situations where we receive unsatisfactory service from a department store, grocery store, or restaurant. In today's economy, we all expect more and more from the businesses that we deal with. Our customers expect this of us as well. In order to continue the growth of our company, we must continue to bring more and more focus to our customer. After all, they are the reason we are here.

One of the initiatives we are undertaking is to increase our attention to our distribution center customers through the Customer Service program. This will involve a number of important changes as we create a Customer Service Department in each distribution center. The key to the program is in providing all the distribution center customer service department representatives with the increased knowledge and training that will empower them to greatly enhance our customer satisfaction levels. To insure that we keep this focus over time, we are also initiating an annual customer satisfaction survey of our distribution center customers. In this survey, we will ask customers to tell us how well we are meeting their needs. We will then use this information to continually "raise the bar" of service.

While this program is focused on our distribution centers, the need to increase the satisfaction of our customers is something we must all take to heart. Whether the customer is a store, a garage, or the person who works on his own car, our objective is very simple—to have them see us as the best auto parts provider in North America. Each and every one of us holds the key to accomplishing this objective. We must all be driven to satisfy the customer.

9-11-2001

THE ENTIRE NATION WAS STUNNED by the events of September 11, 2001. GPI's customers and associates quickly answered the call to aid the victims of these horrible attacks. GPI quickly committed $50,000 to the 911 Fund. CARQUEST associates and stores raised another $160,000.

Independent Sales

GPI ended 2001 servicing 1,583 independently owned CARQUEST Auto Parts stores—1,401 in the United States and 182 in eastern Canada. It added a total of 54 new independents to the CARQUEST program during the year—48 in the United States and six in Canada. Included in these are six Economy Automotive stores based in Lockhaven, Pennsylvania, and served by the Buffalo Distribution Center, three Kearney stores based in south central Arizona and served by the Phoenix Distribution Center, and two Summerside Automotive stores in St. John's, Newfoundland, served by the Saint John, New Brunswick, Distribution Center.

A new 123,750-square-foot Cleveland Distribution Center, located in Brunswick, Ohio, was occupied in January 2001, and the Pittsburgh Distribution Center was consolidated into this new facility in May. In March, the new 123,500-square-foot distribution center in Ocala, Florida, was occupied. The existing Albany, Georgia, Distribution Center would be relocated into this facility. This move allowed the Montgomery, Alabama,

The reason people pass one door
   to patronize another store
is not because the busier place
   has better silks or gloves or lace
or cheaper prices; but it lies
   in pleasant words and smiling eyes.
The greater difference, I believe,
   is the treatment folks receive.

Distribution Center to expand its southern market. Also, it provided GPI with a deeper market penetration into Florida.

Canada

The CARQUEST Canada team continued to improve its contribution to GPI's overall profitability. Sales grew 4 percent and Canada's operating profit was up 21 percent, a solid performance on top of a 68 percent earnings growth in 2000. Most notably, improvements were made in sales, gross margin, expense control, and productivity. Sixty-five of the 114 stores were joint-ventured. The outstanding benefits of the GPI ownership program quickly began to accrue to the new partners.

The Canadian marketing effort utilized the GPI/CARQUEST programs that best fit the Canadian market, plus Canadian-specific CARQUEST programs to meet local market needs. The Canadian team was poised to build on its solid 2001 performance.

A. E. Lottes Company Joins GPI

In 2001, GPI was pleased with a rare opportunity to strengthen and grow through a merger with a longtime member of the CARQUEST family, A. E. Lottes Company St. Louis, Missouri.

A. E. Lottes Company joined CARQUEST in 1979 and was a major contributor to the growth and development of the CARQUEST program. Lottes served 92 CARQUEST stores, consisting of 52 independently owned and 40 Joint Venture stores. Founded in 1919, the A.

Right: O. Temple Sloan III GPI's new president as of January 1, 2001.

Left: A poem circulated to encourage customer service.

E. Lottes Company was owned and operated by three generations of the Lottes Family.

On February 13, 2001, an announcement concerning the merger was made jointly by O. Temple Sloan, Jr. and Art Lottes III, president of A. E. Lottes Company. "The merger with GPI combines the solid team of associates and jobbers with one of the aftermarket's leading companies. This will make us a stronger competitor and give our people new opportunities for growth," said Art Lottes III. "This is truly a unique pleasure to have the entire A. E. Lottes team join GPI," said Sloan. "The A. E. Lottes Company is, without doubt, a premier company. We have spent many years working closely with Art Lottes Jr. and Art Lottes III in building a strong CARQUEST marketing program. Bringing these two companies together is a natural. Art III will continue to serve GPI as president of CARQUEST, president of product management, and as a member of GPI's board of directors. His talents will be needed as GPI and CARQUEST continue to grow."

For more about Lottes' history, see chapter 12.

CARQUEST's Leadership

Over the years, seamless leadership transitions at CARQUEST Corporation have provided the membership with seasoned and steady management. This experienced leadership at the helm always allowed CARQUEST to maintain an uninterrupted high level of service. In 1981, Dan Bock and his brother Jay decided to sell their CARQUEST distribution company in New York to the Stockel family, and Bock became president of CARQUEST. He wanted to remain in New York, so the CARQUEST office

Above left: The Ocala, Florida, Distribution Center was occupied in March 2001. The facility was 123,500 square feet.

Above right: In January 2001, the Cleveland Distribution Center was occupied in Brunswick, Ohio.

was moved from Memphis to Tarrytown, New York, where it remained until Bock retired in 1996. Around this time, Pete Kornafel was considering merging his company with GPI. The timing was perfect for Kornafel to finalize the merger of his Denver and Albuquerque CARQUEST distribution centers with GPI and accept the board of directors' offer to assume the presidency of CARQUEST. When he did, the CARQUEST office was moved from Tarrytown to Lakewood, Colorado. Besides his vast aftermarket experience, Kornafel was also highly knowledgeable regarding computers and the Internet. He wore two hats at CARQUEST—as president and as chief advisor on computer, Internet, and Web-based issues.

Timing again played an important role when Art Lottes III and his family were considering merging their 80-year-old company with GPI. When he did, Lottes became the third president of CARQUEST. Lottes had served as secretary/treasurer of CARQUEST and also had served on CARQUEST's marketing task force and strategic planning committee. He also served as CARQUEST chairman in 1989-90, had served as chairman of various CARQUEST committees, and helped direct CARQUEST Products Inc. In addition to his new duties as CARQUEST president, Lottes would also serve as a director on the GPI

These CARQUEST presidents were instrumental to the success of the company. From top to bottom: Dan Bock, Pete Kornafel, and Art Lottes III.

Board and assume responsibility for product management.

Lottes' appointment allowed Kornafel to spend most of his time on developing Internet and computer initiatives for CARQUEST. He would continue to serve as secretary/treasurer of CARQUEST and as a director of GPI.

With Lottes' appointment, CARQUEST's marketing office was moved, this time to Raleigh, North Carolina. For the first time, this vital office would be located in the heart of GPI/CARQUEST's operations, and adjacent to a fully functional CARQUEST distribution center. Transitioning to the new CARQUEST headquarters in Raleigh were Todd Hack, executive vice president; Mike DeSorbo, training; Dan Rader and Steve Switzer, product managers; Jim Ray, Sandra Ray, and Jim Kendrick, sales; Bob Barron, marketing; Matt Davis, communications; and Mary Folker and Linda Ortiz, accounting.

CAR Parts Inc., Milwaukee

CAR Parts Inc., also known as Monark Auto Parts, possessed a rich and colorful history. In 1920, two innovative individuals, Al Reichardt and August Reichardt, opened the Reichardt Automotive Supply Company in Milwaukee. The company was known at the time as "the most complete detailed stocks in the Northwest." In 1932, during the height of the Great Depression, the company changed its name to Monark Auto Parts. It was purchased in 1949 by an investor group. Then, in 1989, Guy Theune and Phil Wisniewski, two former executives of a Milwaukee oil distributor, decided that they wanted to operate their own company, so they bought Monark. This worked out well and they soon tripled the business. GPI then acquired the firm. Combined with the recent Mabry acquisition, the purchase of CAR Parts Inc., gave GPI a strong presence in the Milwaukee marketplace. After the GPI acquisition, Wisniewski joined the GPI JV store management team, first as sales manager of the Marshfield group and later as vice president of GPI's major account development.

Rodefeld Co. Inc. in Indiana and Ohio

On November 5, 2001, GPI merged with Rodefeld Inc. of Richmond, Indiana, a company with a history spanning more than 100 years. The company was founded in 1900 by August H. Rodefeld Sr., a pioneer in automotive transportation. Hard-working, adventuresome, and inventive, he worked as a designer, engineer, blacksmith, and master mechanic. Rodefeld's original building was located at 96 W. Main St. in Richmond, Indiana. Originally, the business was known as Rodefeld Machine & Blacksmith Shop.

After he started the business, Rodefeld designed and built a one-cylinder motorcycle. The success of this design spurred him to build a Rodefeld automobile. In 1916, nine of the 1,026 cars registered in Wayne County, Indiana, were Rodefelds. Although building automobiles never proved financially lucrative for Rodefeld, this activity earned him a place of honor in the early history of the automotive industry.

Four generations later, under the leadership of Gary Rodefeld, a great-grandson of the founder, Rodefeld included an automotive distribution center and 18 auto parts stores in Indiana and Ohio. GPI then bought the firm. "It is a pleasure to have the Rodefeld team join GPI. We have admired and respected them as a competitor," said Sloan. "We are confident that the merger with GPI is in the best interest of our stockholders," said Rodefeld.

Other auto parts stores merging with GPI in 2001 included Douglas and Sharon Davel's Tomah, Wisconsin, location; Phil Bauer's Joliet and Plainfield, Illinois, stores; Doug Updenkelder's Newport, Oregon, location; Craig and Lindy Stonecypher's store in Covington, Louisiana; Mike

Left: GPI merged with Rodefeld Inc., in 2001, a company that began in 1900, as a machine and blacksmith shop.

Below: The Global Solutions Marketing concept was launched in 2001.

Colvin's Prior Lake, Minnesota, store; and Jacques Normandin's three Montreal locations.

Marketing

In 2001, CARQUEST launched a new product line—and a new marketing concept—which it called "Global Solution." The first introduction was CARQUEST brakes. The new "Global Solution" packaging was designed to emphasize the import offering and to indicate that the product was equal to the original part in form, fit, and function. After brakes, the goal was to expand the "Global Solution" packaging and product concept to other CARQUEST lines. The import specialist was a growing segment of the market and CARQUEST would continue to work on expanding its import replacement parts market share.

Industry

In 2001, according to *Ward's Report*, 8,637,889 people were employed in the United States in motor vehicle and related industries, representing 7.5 percent of all people employed in the United States. Although new vehicle sales declined in 2001 from the previous year, it was the second-best year on record as sales topped 17 million for a third consecutive year.

The GPI management team improved nearly every operating unit within the company in a tough business environment. This performance gave optimism for 2002 and beyond.

By the end of 2001, GPI was serving 2,809 CARQUEST Auto Parts stores in 43 states and eastern Canada. Of these, 1,226 were Joint Venture stores.

TRANSITIONS

1999—**Ed Whirty** joined GPI as corporate vice president of human resources. Promotions: **Deborah Bowers Tyson** to vice president, human relations; **Tony Bridges** to tax compliance coordinator-corporate; **Chandler Ellis** to vice president, information technology-corporate; **Don Eure** to vice president, human resources; **Ken Karber** to vice president, store operations-corporate; **Harry Moulton** to vice president, human resources; **Kevin Nelson** to national sales manager, PBE; **Steve Redfern** to JV general manager, Kansas City; **Robert Saxby** to finance director, Phoenix; **Celeste Smittyklas** to vice president, human resources; and **Brian Wiggs** to electronic catalog auditor. Also in 1999, **Randal Long** was elected vice president of marketing. Long joined GPI in 1976 after graduation from North Carolina University. He had been involved in sales, marketing, and product development for 24 years and also had participated in GPI's Special Olympics activities. The GPI board of directors was strengthened by the addition of **Wayne Lavrack,** GPI senior vice president, JV Stores Division, and also by the addition of **Fred Pisciotta.**

1999—Awards: **Don Kohlbeck,** JV general manager of the year.

1999—**Russell Huffman** retired after 45 years of service between Womwell's Auto Supply and General Parts. He served as president of Womwell for many years and continued his position of leadership for several years after the GPI merger. Russell's contributions to both Womwell and GPI have been numerous. Other retirees: **Joann Bunn** (26), **John Carlson** (38), **Jenks Cleveland** (46), **Johnny Crider** (26), **Jack Crumrine** (26), **Paula Crumrine** (26), **Maurice Gillispie** (20), **Reid Hamlin** (39), **Allen Herbert** (20), **Raymond Hicks** (35), **Ed Johnson** (20), **Rose King** (20), **Dwayne Loney** (29), **Louie Miller** (38), **Chuck Nau** (47), **Joe Olinde** (35),

Clockwise from top left: Randal Long, Fred Pisciotta, and Wayne Lavrack.

Ruth Sawyer (20), **Rachel Stroud** (20), **Sylvia Warrell** (22), **Bob Wusterbarth** (20), and **Ed Johnson** (20).

2000—GPI appointed two new board members: **Larry McCurdy,** former CEO of Echlin and president of the Automotive Marketing Group of Dana Corporation, and **Glenn Orr,** former CEO of Southern National Bank and president of Orr Management Company. Promotions: **Mike Allen** to group vice president, independent CARQUEST business; **Tom Belding** to sales manager, Seattle and Anchorage distribution center; **Donna Bellew** to director of purchasing, corporate headquarters; **Gary Brown** to operations manager, Salt Lake City; **Bob Conley** to vice president, JV Sales, East; **Don Davis** to operations manager, Billings, Montana; **Dennis Fox** to senior vice president, market development–corporate; **Randy Gerringa** to sales manager, Billings Distribution Center; **Bob Greathouse** to sales manager, Albany, Georgia, Montgomery, Alabama, and Ocala, Florida distribution centers; **Hersey Hall** to operations manager, Asheville, North Carolina; **Jim Hergenroder** to operations manager, Buffalo; **Bruce Hershman** to vice president, JV Sales, West; **Rick Lease** to general

manager, Alaska JV Stores; **Jeanette Leftwich** to operations manager, Anchorage; **Gary Ljunggren** to operations manager, Winchester; **Guy Martin** to Operations Manager, Baton Rouge; **Rich Merchant** to operations manager, Seattle; **Kirk Miller** to JV General Manager, Louisiana; **Mike Mills** to operations manager, Ocala, Florida; **Mike Mizelle** to database manager–corporate; **Kim Molin** to director, corporate administration; **Dave Murley** to operations manager, Indianapolis; **Kevin Nelson** to national PBE sales manager, JV stores; **Jerry Repak** to operations manager, Toronto; **Mike Rice** to JV general manager, Bangor, Maine; **Barbara Stephens** to corporate manager, human resources; **Dennis Weiland** to general manager, JV Stores, Winchester, Virginia; and **Kevin Wilson** to sales manager, Indianapolis and Chicago.

2000—Awards: **Dave Bartelt,** JV general manager of the year, **Shipman Northcutt,** distribution center sales manager of the year, and **John Kahut,** distribution center operations

Clockwise from top left: Don Kohlbeck, Dave Bartelt, Shipman Northcutt, and Russell Huffman.

manager of the year. The Bangor, Maine, Distribution Center received the distribution center of the year award for 2000.

2000—Two years after merging his Pittsburgh-based store group with GPI and serving as a JV Stores vice president, **Fred Pisciotta** decided to retire. GPI would forever be grateful to Pisciotta for the tremendous contributions he made not only in successfully merging his Beacon Auto Parts stores, but also for his valuable assistance regarding the APS Big A changeovers. Pisciotta would continue to serve as a director on the GPI board. On March 31, **Bill Ball** retired in Billings, Montana, after 35 years of service. Ball served as a salesman, store manager, and ended his career as a JV regional manager with responsibility for JV stores in Montana and Wyoming. Ball's contributions to the success of GPI were numerous and outstanding. On May 18, **Bill King** retired as director of human resources, a position he held for almost 20 years. King joined GPI when it owned only four distribution centers, no auto parts stores, and there were about 300 associates. His contributions to the company's success will never be forgotten. Other retirees in 2000: **Dick Bujok** (38),

Robert Cassidy (46), **Howard Davis** (23), **Baxter Gilliam** (30), **Frank Guarino** (45), **Mike Hollingsworth** (20), **Russell Kelly** (22), **Hershell Murphy** (44), **Bryce Nimtz** (41), **Edward Pross** (37), **Gene Rabon** (39), **Edward Reevey** (31), **Johnny Richards** (50), **Dave Rickell** (20), **Emma Slaughter** (21), **Larry Stanley** (32), and **Frederic Ulrich** (28).

2001—**Hugh McColl** and **Art Lottes III** joined GPI's board of directors. McColl had recently retired as the chairman and CEO of Bank of America Corporation. Lottes joined the board following the merger with A. E. Lottes Company. Both would make significant contributions to the future of GPI. Promotions: **Terri Ballard** to manager of financial systems–corporate; **Jerry Berryhill** to operations manager, Cleveland; **John Gardner** to vice president, finance–corporate; **Rick Hazelton** to sales manager, Memphis Distribution Center; **Roy Hedges** to distribution center national sales manager–corporate; **Tom Hines** to vice president, real estate, corporate; **William Humber** to sales manager, Raleigh, North Carolina; **John James** to operations manager, Memphis; **John Kahut** to vice president, operations, Eastern Region; **Don**

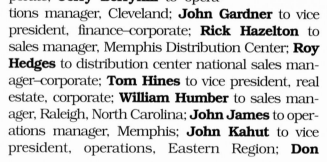

Clockwise from top left: John Kahut, Bill King, and Bill Ball.

This map shows the extent of GPI's marketing reach at the end of 2001. From 1999 through 2001, GPI sales increased 41% and earnings increased 40%.

Kohlbeck to JV vice president, Southeast Region; **Phil Luepke** to operations manager, Lansing, Michigan; **Kirk Miller** to JV general manager, Baton Rouge; **Dave Murley** to operations manager, St. Louis; **Danny Rains** to manager, CARQUEST Links; **Mike Riess** to operations manager, Raleigh, North Carolina; **Hamilton Sloan Jr.** to sales manager, Marshfield, Wisconsin and Chicago distribution centers; and **John Weinmann Sr.** to operations manager, Bangor, Maine.

2001—Awards: **Dave Bartelt,** JV general manager of the year, **Sandy Macomber,** distribution center sales manager of the year, and **Jerry Berryhill,** distribution center operations manager of the year. The Des Moines, Iowa, Distribution Center received the Distribution Center of the Year award for 2001. Also in 2001, **Chris Isted** of the CARQUEST store in Bloomington, Illinois, was named *Counterman Magazine's* 2001 Counterperson-of-the-Year. Isted was chosen for this honor because of her exemplary career within the automotive aftermarket parts distribution industry. **Carl Andrews,** manager of the CARQUEST store where Chris works said, "There's no doubt in my mind that Chris truly is the pre-

mier counterperson in the country. She's a very valuable asset to the team."

2001—After 29 years of service, **Darwin Pippin** announced his retirement. Pippin built a strong reputation in Alabama and Florida's panhandle section. His retirement was well deserved and his service to GPI will be long appreciated. Other retirees: **Bill Armstrong** (41), **Duane Cromwell** (18), **Jim Dise** (39), **Joe Domino** (44), **Ben Gibbs** (37), **David King** (39), **Noel McCoy** (28), **Ken Palmer** (27), **Earl Seymour** (42), **Merlin Townsend** (30), and **Bonner Mills** (20).

In loving memory of the following additional associates who passed away during this time period: **Richard Bitner, Tony Fields, Clif Hughs, Gary Lenhardt,** and **Larry Pfeifer.**

Clockwise from top left: Jerry Berryhill, Darwin Pippin, and Sandy Macomber.

Retiree information shows years of employment after names. This may include time spent at acquired companies.

SOME OF THE MANY WHO HELPED

Brian Taylor Dave Bartelt Jim Hergenroder Chris Torres Rene Primeau George Wallace Francisco Garcia Grant Taylor

Rob Saxby Gary Brown Bob Markus Rich Merchant John Jackson Mark Peterson Mike Wescott Don Beam

Roger White Danny Wusterbath Marc Howard Jim McMurtrey David Jordan Don Sauls David Layher Jean Ferland

Gary Whiteis Jeanette Leftwich Tim Tolosa Dave Jordan Ed Shields Daryl Holmes David Harman John Mehalovich

Charlotte Morgan Jerry Starling Pat Winters Rudy Cervantes Adam Dawson Dave Thorman Dave McMurtrey John James

Rob Scott | Phil Ward | Tom Henderson | David Schnoebelen | George Wills | Bill Luckhardt | Gene Ford | Roger Payne

Frank Luna | Terry Jasinksi | Faithe Hart | Ken Shupp | Tom Kenney | Randy Onorato | Steve Duran | Chris Chesney

Warren Hayes | Rick Lease | Tim McNutt | Scott Ellern | Brian Spalding | Jim Ray | Bob Barron | Jim Kendrick

Kevin Stuart | Jim Watson | Mike McInerney | Jim Ragone | Rick Grady | Pat Klootwyk | Greg Rouble | Matt Davis

Dean Lewis | Will South | John Williams | Adam Rice | Jason Hughes | Gary Chelgren | Sylvia Brown | Jerry Starling

Dan Ure | Nikki DeLuca | Mark Carney | Gilles Dubreuil | ReJean Lortie | Bradley West | Michael Rondeau | Paul Becton

To address the need to expand the foreign car parts coverage, the addition of WORLDPAC will help define the CARQUEST store as a major supplier of both foreign as well as domestic parts to the professional automotive service technician.

CHAPTER TEN

MOVING AHEAD

2002–2005

To continue to succeed will require teamwork, dedication, sacrifice, and hard work. Each of us must carry our share of the responsibility. The future holds great things for us …

—Temple Sloan Jr.

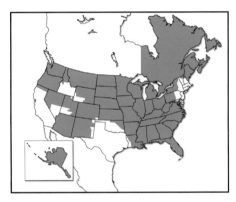

OVER THE PAST FOUR decades, GPI has built a company based on honesty, integrity, strong sales growth, and excellent service to its customers. The company's recent focus has been to sustain its strong success and expand in the years to come into an elite company with a dominant presence throughout North America. According to the GPI definition, an elite company is one that fosters a single, consistent culture reflective of an absolute and unwavering commitment to the preservation and championing of a set of core values and beliefs. At GPI, employees and associates have proved they are fully dedicated to such core values and beliefs. Indeed, for more than 40 years, this dedication has made the company not just a good but a great place to work.

In 2002, GPI reported record sales and earnings. Net income increased 20.2 percent on sales growth of 5.7 percent. Return on equity improved to 14.2 percent. Operating income was up 8.8 percent and EBITDA increased 6.8 percent. The year ended with the strongest balance sheet in 15 years, and with a debt-to-equity ratio of .94 to 1. The last time the debt-to-equity was below 1 to 1 was 1985; the last time the debt to EBITDA was below 3 to 1 was 1984. The debt to EBITDA ratio at the end of the year was 2.89 to 1.

Since 1984, GPI's sales grew 18.7-fold to $1.65 billion, net income grew 17-fold, and equity increased 19.4-fold. Clearly, GPI achieved many key milestones during this 18-year period.

Bragg Auto Parts Merger

On February 1, 2002, GPI merged with one of the premier regional auto parts suppliers in the country, the Bragg Auto Parts Stores in central and northern Maine. N.H. Bragg Inc. had operated nine auto parts stores in Maine, and also was the premier supplier of industrial, welding, and janitorial supplies throughout the state. After considering the many changes taking place in auto parts distribution, John Bragg, the president of the company and representative of the fifth generation of family management, decided to merge his auto parts business with GPI.

N.H. Bragg Inc. was founded in 1854 when Norris Hubbard Bragg left his home and blacksmith shop in Dixmont, Maine, and opened a store on Broad Street in downtown Bangor, Maine. It sold bar iron, anvils, forges, horseshoes, bolts, wagonwheel rims and spokes, and the era's various tools of the trades. Most

This map shows the extent of GPI's sales and marketing reach in 2002.

customers were blacksmiths or carriage and wagon builders, but also included local foundries, saw mills, and job shops. After the turn of the century, as the blacksmith shops morphed into automotive garages, welding shops, or machine shops, N.H. Bragg's customers needed different products. The inventory of blacksmiths' supplies evolved into one of industrial and welding supplies. Additionally, the company added carriage parts for the newfangled "horseless carriage" that was becoming increasingly popular.

For more than 100 years, the company grew and prospered on Broad Street. In 1967, as a result of an urban renewal project in downtown Bangor, the company moved to a new 50,000-square-foot building on Perry Road. "Mr. N.H. Bragg would be proud of his company and pleased that its officers are his great-great grandsons and that its employees are over 150 good Maine folks," said John Bragg.

Auto Parts Express Merger

In 2002, GPI and BWP Distributors of Armonk, New York, a CARQUEST member, announced an agreement to purchase the assets of Auto Parts Express. The agreement was finalized on June 7.

The acquisition of Auto Parts Express involved distribution centers in Augusta, Maine, and Moline, Illinois. BWP Distributors added 34 company-owned stores and eight independent locations, all serviced from the Augusta location. GPI acquired five new independent and one company-owned location from the Augusta distribution center and 26 company-owned and 12 independent locations from the APX Moline distribution center. "We are delighted with the rare opportunity to expand our company with the acquisition of a quality organization, and we thank Mike Preston for his trust and assistance," said GPI's CEO, Temple Sloan Jr. With this acquisition, GPI gained the valuable experience of Gary Whiteis and Jerry Coiner, who moved into key management positions with the firm.

Other Acquisitions

GPI also acquired Mark Roazen's three-store Standard Auto Supply in the Portland, Maine, market. Once the transaction was concluded, Roazen joined GPI's JV management team in Bangor, Maine. GPI also acquired Knox Auto Parts Stores, which had three different stores in operation. In April 2002, GPI

IN MEMORIAM: A.C. BURKHEAD

A.C. BURKHEAD, 85, PASSED AWAY on September 12, 2002. A.C. or "Mr. B" as many called him, was GPI's first employee. Although he spent the first 15 years of his career with Brown's Auto Supply, his last 20 were with GPI. Temple Sloan Jr. had this to say about Burkhead.

He taught me how to spell "auto parts" when I was 19 years old, keeping me out of trouble. A.C. knew Mac Graham and helped me convince him to join GPI. He served as our only purchasing agent for many years and headed the

purchasing group until his retirement. Most of those years he ordered from cards since it was prior to the days of computers. To put it simply, A.C. was one of us and his contributions to GPI stand tall in our history. He was the first of a few who got GPI through the early years of our history. A.C.'s passing closes another great chapter in the history of GPI; but more important, those of us who worked with him all those years have lost a true friend and colleague.

acquired Al Barlow's Motor Parts & Supply, a seven-store chain headquartered in Opelousas, Louisiana. Troy Matherne, the company's general manager, joined the JV management team as a regional manager. Also, GPI acquired 10 stores in the Seattle, Washington, and Portland, Oregon, markets, with the goal to strengthen the company's market presence in the Pacific Northwest.

In November 2002, GPI acquired eight stores from Lowell Zitzloff, known as Lowell's Auto Parts Stores, a highly successful auto parts company in the Minneapolis/St. Paul market. When coupled with GPI's 16 existing stores, this acquisition greatly strengthened the company's market position in the Minneapolis/St. Paul area. In Alabama, GPI acquired Brannon Auto Parts, a three-store operation. And in Nashville, Tennessee, GPI acquired the two-store Thornton Auto Parts organization.

That same year, GPI consolidated its Albany, Georgia, Distribution Center into its Ocala, Florida, and Montgomery, Alabama, operations. This move allowed the company to achieve operating efficiencies without sacrificing customer service.

Canada

CARQUEST Canada Ltd. performed strongly in 2002. Operating profit increased by 43 percent, following a 21 percent increase in 2001. The com-

pany's focus was on achieving better execution, and reducing bad debts and expenses.

In 2002, Canadian JV Stores adjusted sales increased 8.4 percent, and sales to Canadian independent stores grew 4.3 percent. Eight new JV stores were acquired, three were opened and four new, independently owned CARQUEST stores joined the CARQUEST team.

Also that year, construction was started on a new 100,000-square-foot distribution center in Saint John, New Brunswick. This state-of-the-art distribution center would provide the capacity to support additional stores in this fast-growing region.

Products

Professional automotive technicians continued enthusiastically to select the CARQUEST brand. They trusted the brand and understood the quality commitment associated with placing the CARQUEST name on any product.

Above: In April 2003, construction was completed on a new distribution center in Saint John, New Brunswick.

Right: From left to right: Wayne Johnston, Robert Blair, and Magella Boutin.

GPI's heavy-duty product line was expanded in 2002.

CARQUEST Global Solutions was a new concept introduced in 2001 with CARQUEST brakes. It was enhanced in 2002 with the addition of oxygen sensors and ignition wire sets. Global Solutions products retain the original equipment fit, function, and form with packaging designed to emphasize the import-parts offering. The import specialist was a growing segment of the aftermarket, and CARQUEST continued to work on expanding and growing this share of the market.

In 2002, GPI's heavy-duty truck and trailer product offerings were expanded to 11 distribution centers. This additional coverage, along with six sales professionals focused on training people to sell the heavy-duty product line, was responsible for an increase of 18 percent in company-wide heavy-duty product sales.

CARQUEST National Business Conference

CARQUEST's National Business Conference for independent customers was originally scheduled for September 20–23, 2001. After the events of September 11th, however, management rescheduled the event for spring 2002. The conference was held April 18–21 at the Hyatt Regency Hotel in New Orleans, and about 1,000 independent customers, vendors, and GPI/CARQUEST staff members attended.

Highlights included a vendor booth show, seminars, a luncheon riverboat cruise on the Mississippi River, and a group dinner at Decatur Hall in the French Quarter. The General Session included presentations by Temple Sloan III, Joe Owen, Temple Sloan Jr., Scott Ginsburg, Randal Long, and Roy Hedges of GPI, as well as by John Washbish of Dana Corporation. The grand finale was a group dinner featuring a private concert by the Oak Ridge Boys.

Supporting the Journey

While values and beliefs were the foundation of the GPI journey, great strides were made to honor the commitment to being an elite company by establishing several supporting initiatives in 2002. These were CARQUEST University, the CARQUEST Charitable Foundation, and the Founder's Scholarship Program.

CARQUEST Charitable Foundation

For many years, GPI had been an enthusiastic supporter of the United Way. The 2002 campaign once again reflected GPI associates' generosity and commitment to the communities in which they do business.

In 2002, GPI committed to the development of the CARQUEST Charitable Foundation. Through the Foundation, GPI associates will be capable of making a significantly greater contribution to charitable organizations than ever before. The mission of the Foundation is to support non-profit charitable projects and programs that promote family values, educational development, and quality of life in communities throughout the United States and Canada where its associates live and work. From donations made by the company and its association, the CARQUEST Charitable Foundation would make grants available to organizations that best reflect CARQUEST'S values and beliefs. Input from associates has helped guide the Foundation in the distribution of funds.

Founder's Scholarship Fund

Another exciting addition in 2002 was the establishment of the Founder's Scholarship Program. The Scholarship Program will be endowed with initial funding from GPI and with future annual contributions from the CARQUEST Charitable Foundation. This program was established to support the educational pursuits of the children of associates in the United States and Canada. It further demonstrates GPI's commitment to the future as it invests in the development not only of its associates, but also of their families.

Favorable Industry Trends

In 2002, GPI/CARQUEST was encouraged that a large number of sport utility vehicles (SUVs) were now exiting their warranty period and entering the most favorable age group of vehicles to be served in the non-original equipment aftermarket. Other favorable trends included the decline in leased vehicles; improved technical training for independent professional automotive technicians; improved public awareness regarding the illegal withholding of diagnostic information by vehicle manufacturers; reintroduction of U.S. House Bill 2735, "Motor Vehicle Owner's Right to Repair Act"; an increasing population of potential vehicle owners (according to *Lang Reports*, the number of people 16 years old and older would increase by nearly 25 million between 2000 and 2010); and the continued aging of the cars and light trucks on the nation's roads (average age 9.3 years).

2002 represented another year of progress for GPI and its associates. The company successfully completed several strategic acquisitions, improved the performance of the operating units, grew sales at a faster rate than the industry, strengthened the balance sheets, and achieved a significant improvement in net income. These results could not have been achieved without the hard work and dedication of GPI associates throughout North America. Temple Sloan Jr. commented on successes achieved during 2002:

Our country continues to face challenges that create uncertainty in the lives of the American people. This uncertainty has had an impact on our slower economic growth. We must manage our company through these difficult times of slower growth. We operate within a large, fragmented industry. Our market share has steadily increased during the last 15 years, and we are confident that we can continue this trend.

AWDA Names Joe Owen as 2002 Automotive Leader of the Year

In 2002, Joe Owen, vice chairman of GPI, was named by the Automotive Warehouse Distributor Association (AWDA) as its Automotive Leader of the Year. Michael Cardone, president of Cardone Industries, Philadelphia, Pennsylvania, and the 2001 AWDA award winner, presented the award during AWDA's 55th Annual Business/Education Conference at The Venetian in Las Vegas. "Joe has been a role model for many and, I am proud to say, one of my informal mentors over the years," said Cardone. The inscription on Owen's 2002 Automotive Leader of the Year trophy reads: "The Jobber's Champion."

2003—the 42nd Year

In 2003, GPI's sales increased 10.2 percent and net income grew 18.2 percent over the previous year. Operating income increased 11.4 percent and EBITDA scored a 10.6 percent increase over 2002. Return on stockholders' equity improved to 14.4 percent. In December, the board of directors declared the first dividend for common shareholders. A dividend of $0.40 per share was paid.

2003 was very active for distribution center operations. GPI's partnership with HighJump software resulted in a new paperless warehouse management system first implemented in the Raleigh Distribution Center.

CARQUEST Canada Ltd.

CARQUEST Canada Ltd. achieved an outstanding operating performance in 2003. Consolidated sales increased 5.8 percent, and operating income reached a record high. During 2003, seven stores were acquired, two new locations were opened, and two independent stores were changed over to CARQUEST. GPI ended the year with 131 JV stores and 164 independent stores in Canada. Independent stores purchasing more than $500,000 represented 26 percent of the stores served. Profit objectives were exceeded for the fourth consecutive year—the result of sales growth, expense control, and improved asset management.

In April 2003, construction was completed on a new distribution center in Saint John, New Brunswick. The 104,000-square-foot facility more than doubled the size of the previous location.

GPI's Canadian team reached a number of key milestones in 2003. TECH-NET Professional Auto Service was launched, finishing the year with more than 600 locations. The cornerstone of GPI's

O. TEMPLE SLOAN JR.
AFTERMARKET MANAGEMENT PROGRAM AT NORTHWOOD UNIVERSITY

NORTHWOOD UNIVERSITY PRESIDENT Dr. David Fry announced a $2 million gift from GPI. The gift will provide funding toward the university's planned 25,000-square-foot automotive aftermarket facility on its Midland, Michigan, campus. The gift was announced on behalf of the company by O. Temple Sloan III, president of GPI, during a gathering of 1,100 GPI suppliers, associates, and the extended Sloan family in Raleigh, North Carolina. The building will be named The Sloan Family Building for Aftermarket Studies.

Fry simultaneously announced the naming of Northwood's automotive aftermarket program in honor of O. Temple Sloan Jr.

The program from this point forward will be the O. Temple Sloan Jr. Aftermarket Management

Program. This unique four-year undergraduate dual major enables students to enroll in core industry courses in aftermarket manufacturing, heavy duty marketing, aftermarket retail/wholesale management, supply chain management, lean distribution, logistics, and current issues affecting the industry, as well as general education and strategic management courses. Additionally, students will complete an industry internship and create an operational business plan.

Canadian marketing effort, TECH-NET was enthusiastically received by the company's best customers. Other important advancements were made in the Canadian PBE Business. The Journey to the Elite, a comprehensive program addressing the improvement of all major aspects of the business, was introduced in two languages and Canadian associates embraced this program with enthusiasm and commitment.

Auto Parts Wholesale Merger

On February 10, 2003, GPI announced a merger with Auto Parts Wholesale (APW), headquartered in Bakersfield, California, with a strong presence in California—the largest automotive market in the United States with more than 30 million vehicles—and in Mexico. Owned by Don and Jon McMurtrey, APW had been a CARQUEST member since 1993. APW's sales were $124 million in 2002. At the time of the acquisition, the company's three distribution centers in Bakersfield, Sacramento, and San Diego were serving 58 company-owned

stores and 185 independently owned CARQUEST stores. The firm's presence in Mexico would enhance the opportunity to grow GPI sales through CARQUEST stores in that country. Temple Sloan Jr. commented on the merger.

Our sincere thanks to Jon McMurtrey, Don McMurtrey, and the entire McMurtrey family for this unusual opportunity to expand our presence in California. We have followed the progress of APW for years and have respected their aggressive growth, management team, and outstanding customer service.

During 2003, GPI acquired an additional 38 stores in California. A new 143,000-square-foot distribution center in Riverside was built, with occupancy planned for July 2004. This facility would consolidate the San Diego Distribution Center and would serve Los Angeles, San Diego, and Mexico's Baja peninsula. Also, GPI established a new store accounting office in Bakersfield,

Above: The Bakersfield Distribution Center was owned by Auto Parts Wholesale before the company merged with GPI in 2003.

Right: Joe Owen received the Outstanding Business Leader Award from Northwood University in 2003.

California, headed by Paul Neal who transferred from Raleigh, North Carolina.

GPI viewed the California market as one of its major growth opportunities—it represented one of the largest populations of motor vehicles worldwide. The new Riverside Distribution Center and the conversion of the computer systems in the JV and independent stores were major projects for the future. For more about APW's history, see chapter 12.

Additional Acquisitions

In August 2003, GPI purchased the assets of ROX Automotive from Pro Parts Express Inc. The addition of the 16 ROX stores significantly strengthened the company in northern California. As part of the transaction with Pro Parts, GPI and fellow CARQUEST member CAP Warehouse in Las Vegas jointly acquired the eight locations of Midwest Undercar from Pro Parts, providing strengthened marketing positions in Omaha, Denver, Kansas City, and Las Vegas. Additionally, in October, the California division merged with Ron Hanson's United SYATT of America Corporation. United SYATT's 14 locations served several key markets within the Los Angeles metropolitan area, and enabled the development of the new Riverside Distribution Center.

In March, Burnham Uhler and Frank Mathis decided to merge their firm, Spartan Automotive,

Spartanburg, South Carolina, with GPI. Spartan Automotive had served the Spartanburg market since 1940 and would be a significant addition to the CARQUEST family.

In September, GPI acquired the operating assets of Hutchins Automotive Supply Company in western New York. The 15 Hutchins stores expanded GPI's ability to service the greater Buffalo, New York, and Erie, Pennsylvania, markets.

Joe Owen Receives Northwood University's Outstanding Business Leader Award

In January 2003, Dr. David E. Fry, president of Northwood University, awarded the school's Outstanding Business Leader Award to Joe Owen at the Breaker's Hotel in Palm Beach, Florida. In a letter to Owen, Dr. Fry wrote:

I am delighted to confirm that you have been selected and have accepted to receive Northwood's Outstanding Business Leader Award on Friday, January 24, 2003, at the Breaker's in Palm Beach,

JOE OWEN: A TRIBUTE FROM GPI'S 2002 ANNUAL REPORT

JOE OWEN JOINED GPI IN THE FALL OF 1983. During his 20 years, GPI experienced many mergers and acquisitions. His experience and guidance were invaluable to its success.

For more than 15 years, Owen chaired the professional markets committee of CARQUEST. He led the development of the TECH-NET Professional Auto Service Program and the establishment of the Technician's Advisory Council. It was through Owen's insistence that CARQUEST Products Inc. was created in 1993. He was determined and successful in convincing CARQUEST's board of directors in his third attempt.

He served our industry as a director of AWDA and in 2002 was recognized by AWDA as its 2002 Automotive Leader of the Year. Michael Cardone, president of Cardone Industries, had this to say about Owen when he presented him with the award:

He represents what is good about the automotive aftermarket. Those who have been associated

with him have been influenced by his unwavering integrity and honesty.

In 2003, Owen was recognized by Northwood University, which presented him with its Outstanding Business Leader Award.

It is important to realize that Joe is only "semi-retired." He will continue as vice chairman of our board of directors and on the operating committee. As a result, GPI will continue to benefit from his experience and knowledge of the business.

From the day he joined GPI until today, there is no one who is more the epitome of what CARQUEST and GPI have become.

—Temple Sloan Jr.

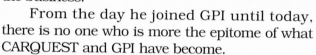

Portrait courtesy of Sam Gray at SamGrayPortraits.com.

Florida. In case you are unaware, the primary nomination from Temple Sloan was augmented by individual and powerful nominations, many of them handwritten, from Michael Cardone, Larry McCurdy, Robert Egan, Bill Grote, Dick Morgan, Ken Rogers, Ken Mullen, Bill Steele, Dimitri Monge, Neil Williams, Wilton Looney, Joe Magliochetti, and probably a few others that have yet to flood our mailbox. Extraordinary!

Industry Trends

The American car buyer's enthusiasm for SUVs kept the U.S.' Big Three dominant in market share during the mid-1990s. This trend was duti-

fully noted by the Japanese vehicle manufacturers who immediately added more fuel-efficient SUVs to their branded menus. By the late 1990s, sales of their brands had slowed market growth in the United States of the Big Three. While the Big Three were focused on trucks, vans, and SUVs, Japanese vehicle manufacturers focused on passenger car sales in the United States. Combined with SUVs, by the end of the 20th century, foreign vehicle manufacturers started gaining market share in the United States.

An increasing concern of GPI in recent years had been suppliers' inability to provide adequate coverage of replacement parts for non-domestic vehicles. As the import vehicle population increased, this concern became a serious issue not only for GPI but for the entire traditional automotive aftermarket in the United States.

Temple Sloan Jr. spoke at the close of the 2003 stockholders' meeting:

2003 was a busy and challenging year for GPI and our associates. The mergers in California give us a significant presence in our country's fastest-growing market. With California, Florida, and our recently announced merger in Texas, we now have a solid market presence in the three largest, fastest-growing markets in the United States. This gives us the unique opportunity to develop our market share in these states, which can provide the springboard for our growth during the next five years.

During 2004, we will develop a number of new initiatives to assist us in growing sales, but they must be coupled with a renewed focus and dedication by each GPI associate to strengthen our customer service and aggressively pursue every possible sale. Our economy is once again growing, which will help our growth opportunities.

We enter 2004 with great expectations. Our execution and growth in California will begin to yield greater rewards. The opportunity to pass $2 billion in sales is very humbling to those of us who have been around for a long time. Our future is exciting as we strive to meet our customers' needs better than anyone in the market in which we operate.

We have a unique company owned by the people in this audience. It is a huge partnership that is built on trust and respect for each other. GPI is not a social club … it is a large business in a very competitive industry. We are leaders in our industry, and we have enjoyed great success to date. But, it is important to remind ourselves that we control our own destiny. To continue to succeed will require teamwork, dedication, sacrifice, and hard work. Each of us must carry our share of the responsibility. The future holds great things for us if we have what it takes to make it happen. I have total confidence in your ability and desire to make this happen.

GPI continued its emphasis on integrity by creating motivational messages for its associates.

2004—the 43rd Year … Another Milestone

In 2004, both sales and earnings for GPI set new records. Sales grew 17 percent and net income increased 19.3 percent. Return on stockholders' equity was 14.5 percent. The second annual dividend was paid, totaling $0.41 per share, a 3 percent growth over 2003.

In 2004, *Forbes* magazine listed GPI Inc. as the 145th-largest private corporation in the United States. Also, in the October 2004 edition of the *Business North Carolina* magazine, GPI Inc. was listed as the largest private company in North Carolina.

In January 2004, GPI announced the acquisition of Auto Parts Unlimited (APU) in Van Nuys, California. With the APU merger, GPI also acquired AutoComLink (ACL) in southern California. John Christie built ACL into a leader in providing online Internet applications and computer management services for automotive technicians. GPI's management was pleased to have Christie and his staff join the company and looked forward to his expanding ACL's customer base through CARQUEST stores.

THERE IS NO RIGHT WAY TO DO THE WRONG THING

Straus-Frank Company

On February 19, 2004, GPI announced a merger with Strafco Inc., also known as Straus-Frank Company, of San Antonio, Texas. Straus-Frank Company was established in 1864 and had been a member of the CARQUEST Distribution Group for more than 30 years. The merger was finalized May 1. Straus-Frank Company operated distribution centers in San Antonio, Dallas, Houston, and Amarillo, Texas, serving 113 company-owned stores in Texas, Louisiana, and Oklahoma. David Straus then joined the GPI board of directors where he continues to contribute to the future of CARQUEST.

Over the years, David Straus, his family, Jack Trawick, Roger Pritt, and Bob Mangold made numerous important contributions to the development of CARQUEST. Their company enjoyed a proud history and GPI was excited with the opportunities presented by the merger. For more about Straus-Frank's history, see chapter 12.

Left: The CARQUEST San Antonio Distribution Center.

Bottom: WORLDPAC joined The International Group in November 2004.

The International Group Inc.

To offer more clarity in the marketplace, a new holding/parent company named The International Group Inc. (TIG) was formed. GPI shareholders' interest were transferred to this new holding company. TIG was created to own 100 percent of the stock of GPI Inc., CARQUEST Canada Ltd., World Wide Parts and Accessories Corporation (WORLDPAC), Valley Welders Supply, Inc., and Northern Welding and Supply Inc.

WORLDPAC Joins The International Group (TIG)

In September, the joint announcement was made by Tom O'Hare, CEO at WORLDPAC, and Temple Sloan Jr., chairman of TIG, that WORLDPAC would join TIG, effective November 1, 2004. Temple Sloan discussed the new arrangement:

WORLDPAC has a strong team of professionals and a supply chain system second to none. We are fortunate to have Tom O'Hare, John Mosunic, and their team as part of our family of companies. The strength of WORLDPAC in the supply of import parts and CARQUEST's experience in serving the domestic market will create a team capable of serving the needs of all our professional customers. Both organizations will be able to leverage technology, customer intimacy, training, and quality of parts in order to continue to foster and support their respective customer bases.

Tom O'Hare had this to say of the merger.

We are excited to join The International Group family of companies. Aligning our companies will provide unequaled availability for our customers and opportunities for our associates. Our mutual dedication to the professional technicians and continued private ownership will

WORLDPAC
World Wide Parts and Accessories Corporation

TEMPLE SLOAN JR. RECEIVES PRESTIGIOUS TRIANGLE AWARD

TEMPLE SLOAN JR., THE CHAIRMAN and CEO of The International Group Inc., was honored in 2005 with the Motor & Equipment Manufacturers' Association's (MEMA) highest honor, the Triangle Award. He was recognized November 1 at the Automotive Aftermarket Products Expo (AAPEX) in Las Vegas, organized by the Automotive Aftermarket Suppliers Association (AASA).

"Today, after more than 40 years, Temple Sloan is still enthusiastic about our business," noted MEMA Chairman Michael Cardone Jr. "He is truly an accomplished leader and has contributed greatly to the growth of our industry."

"Temple Sloan has been a visionary leader in the aftermarket," said Bob McKenna, president and CEO of MEMA.

Motor & Equipment Manufacturers' Association (MEMA) Chairman Michael Cardone and MEMA President and CEO Bob McKenna present Temple Sloan Jr. with the prestigious Triangle Award.

keep us focused on our customers' needs. The acquisition gives WORLDPAC continued financial strength and organizational synergies from a premier organization that truly understands the automotive aftermarket.

WORLDPAC has 42 locations served by distribution centers in Newark, California, and Edison, New Jersey. For more about WORLDPAC's history, see chapter 12.

Hurricane Disaster Relief

In 2004, many of GPI's associates provided hurricane disaster relief to Americans displaced as a result of a particularly severe hurricane season (four major hurricanes devastated parts of the country). Florida and Alabama were hit the hardest, but locales as far north as Pittsburgh suffered significant damage from wind and/or flooding. Additionally, on May 20, a tornado struck GPI's Lexington Distribution Center, causing extensive damage. GPI associates responded immediately, however, and the distribution center missed only one day of shipping product to CARQUEST stores.

2004 National Business Conference

In April 2004, more than 900 independent CARQUEST Auto Parts store owners and guests enjoyed some genuine Texas hospitality at GPI's 2004 Business Conference in San Antonio, Texas. The Marriott Rivercenter, located along the picturesque San Antonio RiverWalk, was the host hotel. The three-day conference featured informative business training and entertainment from six-time Grammy award-winning artist Ronnie Milsap.

GPI continued to strengthen the independent CARQUEST Auto Parts store customer base. Same store sales were up 4.2 percent in 2004 and average store purchases increased 9.8 percent over 2003.

Paul Farwick (inset) led CARQUEST's North American Undercar/Underhood sales force to achieve the ASE Blue Seal of Excellence.

Distribution Centers

In 2004, new distribution centers were built in Baton Rouge, Louisiana, and Riverside, California. The company consolidated the Jackson, Mississippi, Distribution Center, and the Baton Rouge, Louisiana, Distribution Center into a new 124,600-square-foot facility. This consolidation improved service capability to the CARQUEST stores in the lower Mississippi river region. The new Riverside, California, Distribution Center replaced the San Diego facility. It enables GPI to increase growth in the Southern California and Mexico markets.

Safety Culture

In 2004, GPI's risk management department developed a set of safety culture principles for all associates to follow. The goal? A reduction of vehicle accidents and associate injuries, protecting company resources and creating an environment to insure the safety and well-being of associates and members of the communities in which they operate.

In 2004, CARQUEST's North American Undercar/Underhood Sales Force, under the direction of Paul Farwick, achieved the ASE Blue Seal of Excellence for the third consecutive year. Members of the Undercar/Underhood sales team have earned 688 ASE certifications and 20 members are ASE master technicians. This team made well over 100,000 sales calls to auto service centers in 2004.

'Right to Repair' Legislation

The motor vehicle owner's "Right To Repair" Act, HR-2735, introduced in 2003 in the U.S. House of Representatives by Joe Barton (R-Texas), and Edolphus Towns (D-New York), gained strength in 2004, along with the Senate version, S-2138, introduced by Lindsay Graham (R-South Carolina). There were 118 house members along with 10 senators who signed up in support of the act—but the proposal never made it out of committee. In 2005, Barton and Towns, along with help from Darrel Issa (R-California), reintroduced the "Right To Repair" concept with House bill HR-2048 in the 109th congress.

HR-2048 requires that vehicle manufacturers make the same service information and tools available to independent service centers and vehicle owners that they provide to new car dealers. This "Right To Repair" legislation is important, not only to the thousands of small businesses that comprise the automotive service industry, but also to vehicle owners who depend on local independent auto service centers to keep their vehicles operating safely at reasonable expense.

By 2004, with the introduction of water pumps, sensors, and modules CARQUEST Global Solution brand now featured nine categories. The Global Solution brand provides GPI's stores with an exclusive brand of import vehicle products guaranteed to fit and perform like the original equipment part.

New Stores

By the end of 2004, the Joint Venture store group had grown to 1,525 stores, including 105 added with the Straus-Frank merger. The group acquired 41 stores and opened 13 new stores. Included in the store count are 216 locations operating as super stores, 35 more than the previous year. Several store groups were acquired, starting with John Christie's three APU stores in California; Michael Capozzi's three stores in Washington; Terrell Shelley's three stores in Hayward, California; Doug Brown's warehouse and eight stores; the Jocko store group in Iowa; Bill Parker's three Halco Express stores in the Atlanta area; Mark Novick's three paint stores in Virginia; Tom Cianthette's three stores in Maine; and Roger Hunley's CARQUEST store in Hermitage, Tennessee. By the end of 2004, GPI was serving 3,156 CARQUEST Auto Parts stores in 43 states in the United States, eastern Canada, Mexico, Samoa, Saipan, and The Virgin Islands. Of these, 1,524 were joint venture stores.

O. Temple Sloan Jr. closed the 2004 shareholders' meeting with these thoughts:

Our future will be controlled by our efforts and focus to be the best at what we do and our unwillingness to accept anything less.

Three major initiatives for 2005 will have a major impact on the future: an expanded new store management training program, a new salesman training program, a new in-store computer system, and the establishment of a separate marketing department. In addition, there will be initiatives to create sales synergies between the CARQUEST programs and WORLDPAC.

SHAREHOLDER GROWTH

ANY ASSOCIATE IN A SUPERVISORY position is offered the option to purchase shares in GPI. Key supervisory associates in joint venture stores have the option to buy GPI shares as well as shares in the store or stores where they work. The number of shareholders has grown consistently since the Valley Motor Supply merger in 1983.

1983 – 23	1988 – 293	1993 – 922	1998 – 1,933	2003 – 3,250
1984 – 69	1989 – 372	1994 – 1,093	1999 – 2,345	2004 – 3,450
1985 – 189	1990 – 420	1995 – 1,282	2000 – 2,664	2005 – 3,725
1986 – 216	1991 – 519	1996 – 1,590	2001 – 2,798	
1987 – 230	1992 – 647	1997 – 1,781	2002 – 3,100	

In addition, by the end of 2005, 12,700 associates were shareholders through the GPI ESOP.

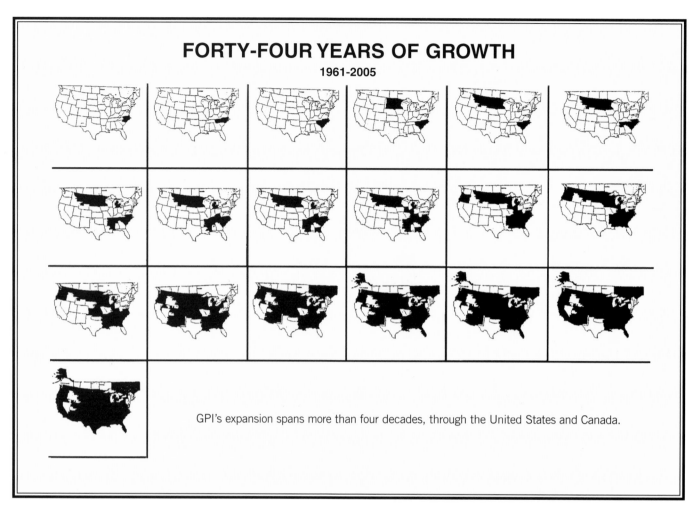

FORTY-FOUR YEARS OF GROWTH
1961-2005

GPI's expansion spans more than four decades, through the United States and Canada.

The following appeared in the 2004 GPI Annual Report:

A Special Message

After 43 years of leading this company, it gives me great comfort to turn the leadership reins to Temple, III. He has worked in every department of our company during his 21-year career. Your board and I have great confidence in him and our senior management team to lead us to a great future. I will continue to serve as chairman of The International Group board of directors and contribute to our long-term strategic plans. It has been an honor to work with each of you in building this great company. I have total confidence and great expectations for our future growth and success, and I am proud to be your partner.

—Temple Sloan Jr.

2005

Consolidated sales for The International Group Inc. represented the largest growth in the company's history. The sales increase over 2004 was 22 percent. Return on investors' equity was 14.9 percent, the 42nd consecutive year of double-digit returns, a defining characteristic for GPI throughout its history. The return on investment for ESOP members was 14 percent. Since its beginning and through 2005, the plan had paid more than $100 million to GPI associates in retirement benefits.

Temporary Fuel Disruption

In 2005, a disruption of the fuel supply caused a dramatic jump in gasoline and diesel prices. This created more than $9 million in added expenses for TIG. However, various cost-saving innovations

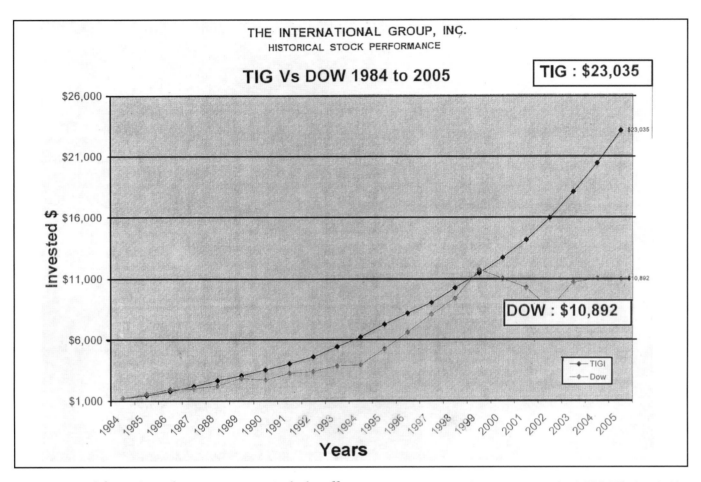

THE INTERNATIONAL GROUP, INC.
HISTORICAL STOCK PERFORMANCE

TIG Vs DOW 1984 to 2005

TIG : $23,035

DOW : $10,892

were created for TIG and its customers to help off-set the rising fuel costs.

Despite natural disasters, soaring energy costs and a few unstable aftermarket suppliers, the TIG team worked to provide the company's customers with the best possible service and product coverage in the industry. As in 2004, many TIG associates again helped fellow associates, customers, and others who suffered the brunt of three powerful hurricanes, Katrina, Rita, and Wilma in the Gulf Coast region and Florida. In the weeks following, thousands of TIG associates donated food, clothing, shelter, and more than $125,000 in contributions to those in need.

An unusual number of issues were addressed on the supply side in 2005. Because of inadequate performance by certain suppliers and the financial failure of a few others, it became necessary to make changes in sourcing several major product lines. CARQUEST's product managers worked diligently in researching and selecting new suppliers on several product lines, including

Above: This is a favorite chart among the 3,725 TIG shareholders who have responsible management positions and the additional 12,700 associates with ESOP interests. It shows the results of an equal $1,000 investment in 1984 in TIG and in DOW from 1984 through 2005.

Below: The WORLDPAC Distribution Center in South Brunswick, New Jersey.

electronic sensors, remanufactured brake calipers, remanufactured axle shafts, air-conditioning parts, shock absorbers/struts, and hand tools. Although some of these changes were not implemented in the field until early 2006, research and preparation was done in 2005.

CARQUEST Auto Parts—United States

Although 2005 was a rare year that had no major mergers or acquisitions, attention was directed to several projects. One of the highest priorities was the installation of the new Exploris point-of-sale computer systems. In the Joint Venture store group, 1,266 stores were running on Exploris by year's end.

Another priority was to improve business in the CARQUEST stores by using eServices to serve professional auto service centers and national accounts. eService offers WEBLINK, which helps customers manage their businesses and provides electronic access to CARQUEST stores' products, promotions, and information.

National account business from independent CARQUEST stores grew 7.8% in 2005 and TECH-NET accounts sales increased 9.7%. Average annual purchases from independent CARQUEST Auto Parts stores in the United States increased 7%. This was the fifth consecutive year of increased average store volume.

At the end of 2005, the U.S. JV store group had grown to 1,356 locations. There were more than 180 locations operating as Super Stores. These stores maintain sizable inventories, which are critical in supplying the needs of metropolitan markets.

WORLDPAC

2005 marked the first full year for WORLDPAC as a division of TIG. The integration was a huge success as WORLDPAC continued its dedication of satisfying the vital needs of the professional auto service technician. The focus was to provide an in-

Clockwise from top left: Ron Cannon, CAP Warehouse; Neil Stockel, BWP Distributors, Inc.; Eugene Kaminaka, Automotive Warehouse, Inc.; and John Albano, Muffler Warehouse, Inc.

Art Lottes III served as president of CARQUEST and as GPI board member before he retired in 2005.

depth catalog of O.E. replacement parts for import vehicles, a high rate of product availability, and a comprehensive roster of customer support programs. The WORLD-PAC unique "best-in-class" online catalog (SpeedDial) and order fulfillment system kept them ahead of competition.

WORLDPAC continued its geographic expansion strategy in 2005 by adding new locations in Miami, Florida; Baltimore, Maryland; Houston, Texas; and Ottawa, St. Hubert, and Edmonton, Canada.

In November, WORLDPAC and GPI collaborated and the first WORLDPAC location began operating within a GPI distribution center. Housed within the Kansas City Distribution Center, this new distribution model will increase the overall market share of TIG.

Also in 2005, WORLDPAC completed a major step in furthering its growth strategy with the relocation of its Edison, New Jersey, Distribution Center to South Brunswick, New Jersey. This new state-of-the-art warehouse increased WORLDPAC's

ROBERT J. BLAIR, CARQUEST CANADA LTD.'S PRESIDENT, HONORED

ROBERT J. BLAIR, PRESIDENT OF CAR-QUEST Canada Ltd., was named the recipient of the prestigious Automotive Industries Association (AIA) of Canada's Distinguished Service Award for 2003-04. The award recognizes the distinguished service and outstanding leadership recipients provide to encourage the growth and development of Canada's automotive aftermarket industry. It is the highest award presented by the AIA of Canada to outstanding individuals within the association.

From left, AIA Chairman Ken Coulter presents CARQUEST Canada, Ltd. President Robert J. Blair with the prestigious Automotive Industries Association of Canada's Distinguished Service Award.

distribution center capacity by more than 100,000 square feet.

Welding Group

The combined welding companies in Montana and the upper Midwest achieved record sales in 2005 and set all-time records in profits as well. The Northern Welding operation, headquartered in Wausau, Wisconsin, had a sales increase of 16.5% in 2005. The Valley Welders operation, headquartered in Montana, ended 2005 with a sales increase of 19.4%.

During 2005, the Valley Welders' gas plant, known as Industrial Gas Distributors, completed its remodeling plan, which resulted in a more efficient process in converting cryogenic liquids of oxygen, nitrogen, and argon into high-pressure gas cylinders and mixing ingredients to meet customers' orders.

The welding companies continue to evaluate opportunities for expansion of welding and gas distribution. Valley had acquired bulk tankers to haul liquid oxygen, nitrogen, argon, and carbon dioxide to serve a segment of the market that had previously been beyond their reach. This bulk distribution opened new doors for this group.

William Vandiver joined the board of directors of The International Group Inc. in 2005.

TRANSITIONS

2002—New additions: **Dean Lewis** joined GPI as corporate manager of benefits. Promotions: **Hersey Hall** to operations manager, Columbia, South Carolina; **David Harman** to operations manager, Marshfield, Wisconsin; **Jim Hazlett** to JV Stores general manager, Denver; **Gary Knewtson** to sales manager, Lakeville, Minnesota, Distribution Center; **David McCartney** to corporate vice president, operations; **Doug McIntosh** to distribution center finance director, Ontario and Atlantic Divisions; **Randy Onorato** to operations manager, Albuquerque; **Mike Riess** to western region vice president, operations; **David Sharer** to vice president, credit–corporate, **Jeff Swanson** to JV general manager, Alaska; and **Grant Taylor** to operations manager, Asheville, North Carolina.

2002—Awards: For the second year in a row, a GPI associate was honored by *Counterman Magazine*.

Jerry Ives, manager of the CARQUEST store in East Syracuse, New York, was recognized for his dedication, talent, and customer focus.

Ives said, "I'm fortunate to work with such a great bunch of associates. We all work as a team and I have to give much of the credit to them."

Randy Onorato, distribution center operations manager of the year; **Brian Dobson,** JV general manager of the year; **Tom Belding,** distribution center sales manager of the year, and Albuquerque Distribution Center, distribution center of the year.

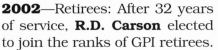

2002—Retirees: After 32 years of service, **R.D. Carson** elected to join the ranks of GPI retirees. After college, Carson became a school teacher and coach. In 1970, he was looking for a summer job when Temple Sloan Jr. asked him to join GPI. This summer job developed into a 32-

Clockwise from top left: R.D. Carson, Mike Riess, and Brian Dobson.

CARQUEST Canada Ltd.

In 2005, CARQUEST Canada Ltd. achieved sales and record earnings for the seventh consecutive year.

The net number of CARQUEST Auto Parts and Auto Paint stores in Canada in 2005 increased to 303 and included nine new JV stores. New "Greenfield" stores were opened in New Glasgow, Nova Scotia; and Dolbeau, Quebec. Four independent stores also converted to the JV program. Conversions of competitors' stores to the CARQUEST

Independent jobber program reached record levels in 2005.

William Vandiver joined the board of directors of The International Group Inc. in June. Vandiver retired from the Bank of America in 2002 where he served most recently as vice chairman of Bank of America NA and as the executive of corporate risk management.

Hugh L. McColl Jr. retired from the TIG board. Temple Sloan Jr. had this to say about McColl:

For five years, his tremendous experience, focus, and advice has greatly enhanced the growth and

year career at GPI. Working closely with Ham Sloan, Carson spent his entire career in distribution center operations. His strong operating experience proved to be a key to GPI's success in the company's first two acquisitions, Asheville, North Carolina, and Lakeville, Minnesota, where Carson resided and was in charge of operations. In 1985, he returned to Raleigh where he continued in operations management. For the past few years, Carson was corporate group vice president of operations. His contributions have been instrumental to GPI's success. **Fred Kotcher** retired in 2002 after more than 30 years in the industry. Kotcher joined GPI in 1986 as a result of its merger with Parts Warehouse Company in Michigan. He became division vice president of the upper Midwest group. In 1992, Kotcher moved to Raleigh, North Carolina, as corporate vice president, administration, member of GPI's board of directors, and member of GPI's management team. He retired from these posts, including his position on the board of directors, in 2002. Kotcher had long been active in the industry, serving on AWDA's board of directors and as a

Top left, Fred Kotcher; bottom left, Chris Winters.

recipient of AWDA's Memorial Scholarship Award. In addition, Kotcher received Northwood University's Automotive Replacement Education Award. Like many other members of GPI's management team, Kotcher would continue to serve the company in a part-time capacity after he retired. After 40 years in the automotive aftermarket, **Chris Winters** retired in 2002. In 1992, Winters and his partner merged their company, Pacific Wholesalers Inc., into GPI. As president, Winters was responsible for the day-to-day operation of the business. He hired and developed a management team that helped him build the firm into one of the premier warehouse distributors in the Pacific Northwest. After the GPI/Pacific Wholesalers Inc. merger, Winters remained in Portland, Oregon, and assumed the responsibilities of division president for GPI. Shortly after GPI purchased the operating assets of APS, Winters and his wife, Meade, were relocated to GPI's corporate headquarters in Raleigh, where he served as the vice president of credit management until his retirement. Also in 2002, **Dan Sussen** retired from GPI's board of directors. Other retirees: **Judith Brim** (24), **Joseph Camack** (24), **Walter Ellerson** (26), **Don Frankfather** (20), **Glenn Hobbs**

success of our company. We are thankful to have had Hugh on our team.

Art Lottes III Retires

After 26 years in the automotive aftermarket, Art Lottes III retired. Before the merger of GPI and the A.E. Lottes Company—where Lottes III served as president and CEO—he was active in AWDA, served as chairman of AWDA in 1992, when he was named AWDA's Man of The Year. Since 1979, when the A.E. Lottes Company joined

CARQUEST, Lottes III served as CARQUEST chairman and board member, as well as an active leader in all CARQUEST activity. After the GPI/Lottes merger, Lottes III served as president of CARQUEST and as a GPI board member.

CARQUEST Corporation

At the end of 2005, in addition to General Parts, Inc., there were four member companies. They were: BWP Distributors, Inc., Armonk, New York, Neil Stockel, CEO; Automotive Warehouse,

(36), **Lyndele Matot** (35), **Walter Moore** (31), **Frank Niemiec** (46), and **Richard Wehrenberg** (21), **Roy Schoessler** (28), and **Maxie Thompson** (45).

2003—Following the merger with Auto Parts Wholesale (APW), **Jon McMurtrey,** the former president of the firm, joined GPI's board. He was a principal owner of APW and was actively involved in the transition and conversion of the California company to GPI. Promotions: **Don Beam** to sales manager, Albuquerque Distribution Center; **Bob Conley** to JV vice president, Mid-Atlantic Region; **Jim Hergenroder** to market development manager, Buffalo; **Bruce Hershman** to vice president, market development, Western Region; **Marc Howard** to operations manager, Buffalo; **William Humber** to vice president, Southeast Region JV Stores; **Don Kohlbeck** to vice president, Great Lakes Region, JV Stores; **Robert Layman** to general manager, JV Stores, California; **Hamilton Sloan Jr.** to sales manager, St. Louis Distribution Center; **Bobby Tyson** to vice president, major account development; **Al Wheeler** to senior vice president, store sales and market development, corporate; and

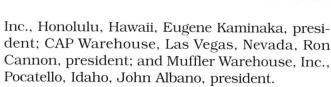

Phil Wisniewski to vice president, major account development.

2003—Awards: **Wayne Johnston,** JV general manager of the year, **Jerry Repak,** distribution center operations manager of the year, **Tom Belding,** distribution center sales manager of the year, and the Columbia Distribution Center, distribution center of the year.

2003—Retirees: **Jack Boyle** (20), **Darold Cutsinger** (23), **John Hamilton** (20), **Jacqueline Lynch** (31), and **Gerald Smith** (21).

2003—In memoriam: GPI associates mourned the passing of **Lee Meriweather, Jr.,** who was very courageous in fighting a degenerative lung disease. Meriweather was highly respected throughout the automotive industry in Alabama, Georgia, Florida, and Mississippi. In 1971, Meriweather founded Automotive Central Inc. in Montgomery, Alabama, and in 1981 merged it with Taylor Parts Inc. in Andalusia, Alabama. Meriweather was a great friend of GPI and will long be remembered for his tireless efforts in making the GPI-Taylor merger a success.

2004—**Rick Young,** who had served as J-CON general manager since the program was originated, was promoted to director of IT sales and marketing. **John Chachere** replaced Young as director of store computer

Inc., Honolulu, Hawaii, Eugene Kaminaka, president; CAP Warehouse, Las Vegas, Nevada, Ron Cannon, president; and Muffler Warehouse, Inc., Pocatello, Idaho, John Albano, president.

TIG consisted of General Parts, Inc., CARQUEST Canada Ltd., WORLDPAC, Valley Welders Supply, Inc. and Northern Welding and Supply, Inc., and finished 2005 with 1,750 operating locations. GPI operated 40 distribution center locations, serving 1,495 joint venture CARQUEST store locations and 1,550 independent CARQUEST store locations. CARQUEST Canada Ltd. operated three CARQUEST distribution center

locations, serving 140 joint venture CARQUEST locations and 163 independent CARQUEST store locations. Valley and Northern Welding combined had 12 locations and WORLDPAC operated from 60 locations.

Temple Sloan Jr. commented on the opportunities that lay ahead for TIG at the 2005 shareholders' meeting:

What a unique opportunity we have. 2006 stands to be an exciting year for The International Group, Inc. For the year, our sales will approach $2.8 billion, and we are privately owned by

At left, Todd Hack; bottom right, Ron Anderson.

Opposite: Lee Meriweather.

systems. Other promotions: **Tom Belding** to vice president, sales, Northern Division; **Gerry Bennett** to regional vice president, JV Stores, North Central; **Jerry Berryhill** to operations manager, Lansing, Michigan; **Robert Blair** to executive vice president, marketing, corporate; **Mike Buss** to sales manager, Salt Lake Distribution Center; **John Chachere** to director of store computer systems, corporate; **Bob Conley** to vice president, JV Stores, eastern division; **Norman Delisle** to director of operations, information technology; **Ed Dobbs** to vice president, JV Stores, Texas Region; **Paul Farwick** to vice president, undercar/underhood sales; **Jean Ferland** to distributor center operations, Montreal; **Bill Gruenthal** to vice president, JV Stores, Midwest; **Dan Guilfoil** to director of corporate industrial engineering; **Steve Gushie** to regional vice president and general manager, Ontario Division; **Todd Hack** to general manager, CARQUEST Products Inc.; **Jim Hazlett** to vice president, JV Stores, Southwest Region; **Chuck Henline** to vice

president, shared services, corporate; **Marie Hubbs** to vice president, human resources, Northern Region; **John James** to operations coordinator, San Antonio; **Dave Jordan** to operations manager, Sacramento; **Don Kohlbeck** to vice president, JV Stores, Western Division; **Robert Layman** to regional vice president, JV Stores, California; **John Maholvich** to operations manager, Kansas City; **Bart Marshel** to regional vice president, JV Stores, Pacific West; **Mark McDonald** to operations manager JV Stores, Canada; **Trey Molin** to JV operations manager, Phoenix Store Group; **John Mosunic** to chief financial officer, corporate; **Dave Murley** to operations manager, Montgomery, Alabama; **John Nummela** to finance director, Salt Lake and Phoenix distribution centers; **Dan Owczarzak** to operations manager, Ocala, Florida; **Michael Patterson** to operations manager, Baton Rouge, Louisiana; **Roger Payne** to operations manager, Winchester, Virginia; **Randy Pisciotta** to operations manager, Nashville; **Dan Rader** to director of product management, CARQUEST; **Jerry Repak** to vice president, operations, Western Division; **Mike Riess** to president of CARQUEST Canada Ltd.; **Ken Shupp** to JV operations man-

This map shows the extent of GPI's marketing reach at the end of 2005. For the four-year period, 2002 through 2005, GPI sales increased 67%, and earnings increased 101%.

more than 3,700 TIG associates. It might surprise you to know that we are the largest privately owned automotive aftermarket company in the world. The U.S. and Canadian economies are growing and should provide a solid environment for our continued success.

Our future will be controlled by our efforts and focus to be the best at what we do and our unwillingness to accept anything less. We have a great leadership team with fresh ideas and new objectives that will continue to direct our course and we have a great team of associates who are dedicated to our success.

John Martens.

ager, St. Louis Store Group; **Dave Thorman** to JV operations manager, Buffalo; **Fred Wood** to regional vice president, JV Stores, Northeast; **Rick Young** to director of IT sales and marketing, corporate; and **Mark Zuanich** to regional vice president, JV Stores, Carolinas.

2004—Awards: **Kevin Wilson,** distribution center operations manager of the year; **Frankie Underwood,** distribution center sales manager of the year; **Rick Lease,** JV general manager of the year; **Randy Onorato** and **Chandler Ellis,** spirit of CARQUEST award; and the Des Moines, Iowa, Distribution Center, distribution center of the year. The 2004 journey spirit award was given to **Robert Blair, Ed Dobbs, Charles Garrison,** and **John Kahut.**

2004—Retirees: After 40 years of service, **Ron Anderson** elected to retire on December 31, 2004. As the sales manager for the Lakeville, Minnesota, Distribution Center for 20 years, Anderson's diligent and caring efforts proved to be a driving force in mak-

ing Lakeville GPI's third-largest operating unit. Also, after 14 years of building a strong CARQUEST store presence from the ground floor up in the greater Chicago metropolitan market, **John Martens** (50) elected to retire. His contributions to the JV store division played a key role in GPI's success. Other retirees: **Clarence Beck** (45), **Allison Brown** (39), **Jean-Yves Brunell** (45), **Leon Curtis** (37), **Maurice Gosselin** (38), **William Jadot** (40), **Harry Johnson** (42), **Real Mercure** (20), **Ron Miller** (40), **Charles Pickell** (20), **Dennis Radawitz** (25), **James Spencer** (20), and **Michael Trommlitz** (21).

2004—On July 25, 2004, GPI's very first joint venture partner, **Duane Cromwell,** passed away in Pierre, South Dakota. In his last years, Cromwell suffered failing health and retired from GPI in 2002. He was an outstanding store operator for GPI and a great friend and partner of the firm.

2005—**Joe Zucchero** joined The International Group as president of information technology. Zucchero has 25 years of experience in IT. **Scott Derrow** joined GPI as corporate vice president, human resources operations. **Jim Felman** joined GPI as corporate director of tax. **Robert Blair,** who served as executive vice president of marketing and product management, was chosen to replace

Art Lottes III as president of CARQUEST, while also maintaining his product management responsibility. **Ray Birden** was promoted to senior vice president of marketing, a position previously held by Robert Blair. With Blair accepting the responsibility of leading the new marketing group, **Mike Riess** was promoted to president of CARQUEST Canada Ltd. **Cecil "Bubba" McDonald** was promoted to Gulf States regional JV vice president. McDonald has more than 23 years of experience within that market. In June, **John Mosunic** was elevated to chief financial officer (CFO) of The International Group. Mosunic previously held the position of president and chief operating officer (COO) of WORLDPAC. **Chuck Henline** was promoted to vice president of shared services. He was also elected to the board of directors of The International Group, Inc. Other promotions: **Janet Higgins** to director of corporate payables; **William Humber** to vice president distribution center sales, Eastern Division; **Bryan Johnson** as JV operations manager for the Pacific West Region; **Jim Madson** to director of distribution center accounting; **Jerry Sharpee** as professional markets business development manager;

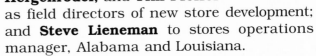

Clockwise from left: Troy Matherne, Mark Miller, and Jim McWilliams.

Roger Smith as director of professional markets; **Louis Salazar** as JV operations manager for the Southwest Region; **Keith Swainey** to vice president of technical services; **John Taylor**, **Jim Hergenroder**, and **Tim Pfeifer** as field directors of new store development; and **Steve Lieneman** to stores operations manager, Alabama and Louisiana.

2005—Awards: **David Harman**, distribution center operations manager of the year; **Dan Conroy**, distribution center sales manager of the year; **Brian Dobson**, JV Stores regional vice president of the year; **Mark Miller**, JV Stores operations manager of the year; **Troy Matherne**, JV Stores sales manager of the year; **Al Adams**, JV stores district manager of the year; and Salt Lake City, Utah, Distribution Center, distribution center of the year. Also, the 2005 spirit of CARQUEST award was awarded to the Baton Rouge, Louisiana,

At left, Jimmy Taylor; bottom right, Walter Ray Fowler.

erson, **Bubba McDonald**, **Troy Matherne**, **Randy Gray**, **Rodney Morales**, **Aubrey Weil**, **Jimmy Sumerall**, **Chris Peak**, **Ron Schexnayder**, **Shane Lynch**, and **Israel Styrain**.

2005—After launching and growing CARQUEST Products (CPI) since 1993, **Jim McWilliams** announced his retirement from the company in early 2005. CARQUEST members are deeply indebted to McWilliams for his hard work, ability to get the details right, and his unwavering commitment to excellence. McWilliams and his team built a great business with a solid foundation for the future. Upon McWilliams' retirement, **Todd Hack** agreed to lead CPI. McWilliams continued working with Hack and the company's product managers on a part-time basis. In early 2005, **Bill Waltman** announced his retirement after 37 years of service in store management in Laurel, Mississippi. Waltman's dedication to customer service resulted in outstanding sales and profit performance year-in and year-out. He was known throughout GPI as one of the company's funniest managers, a

reputation that was well deserved. Other retirees for 2005: **Zdenka Aster** (23), **Larry Bleau** (35), **Mary Blomme** (26), **William Cagle** (35), **Edmond Casida** (45), **Willie Dabney** (36), **John Erhardt** (24), **Jay Everage** (27), **Ronald Fletcher** (20), **Jerry Gainsworth** (46), **James Gillan** (28), **Bruce Hershman** (20), **James Hooper** (42), **Norman Horning** (26), **John Huebner** (35), **Mark Ihlan** (27), **Russell Johns** (20), **Ronald Jonov** (38), **Joe Kappel** (38), **Edward Keck** (30), **James Koziol** (24), **John Kremers** (37), **Deborah Lange** (30), **Serge Lessard** (22), **Laurent Levesque** (27), **Dianne Lindvall** (20), **Ron Maich** (21), **Garther McGhee** (47), **Roy McKinney** (20), **Karl Michels** (35), **Gary Moldenhauer** (31), **Ronald Moose** (48), **Charles Nau** (53), **Gary Plank** (34), **Ronald Plantz** (29), **Edward Richard Jr.** (22), **Kenneth Smith** (53), **Ronald Sprink** (45), **William Stepp** (36), **Clinton Tanner Jr.** (20), **Real Thomas** (44), **Gerry VanHorn** (25), **Joseph White** (38), **Johnny Wiggins** (40), **Henry Wilde** (26), **Raymond Williams** (50), and **Bobby Windham** (29).

2005—In memoriam: On August 11, 2005, GPI lost a close friend when **Jimmy Taylor** succumbed to a long battle with cancer.

Taylor and his brother Riley, along with Lee Meriweather, were managing partners in Taylor Parts Inc., which was merged into GPI in 1992. Taylor was a highly respected business and civic leader in Andalusia, Alabama, and the southern portion of the state. In October, GPI associates and customers were saddened by the dealth of **Walter Ray Fowler.** In 1961, he became the general manager of Taylor Parts Inc. After the GPI-Taylor merger in 1992, Fowler managed the Cleaner and Equipment Division that he pioneered. He was recognized and respected throughout the industry as the most knowledgeable equipment person in America. Also in 2005, GPI was saddened by the news of **Reed Roberts'** sudden death. For more than 30 years, Roberts managed the GPI joint venture store in Hazard, Kentucky, and was a consistent leader in generating sales and profit. He also was heavily involved in the community. He was presented with the "Honorary Citizen of Hazard" award and the "Key To The City" Award. The news of the death of **Guy Martin** who courageously fought a battle with cancer, was sadly received by the many GPI associates who knew and respected him. Martin had spent his entire career in the automo-

At right, Guy Martin; bottom left, Reed Roberts.

tive aftermarket in both sales and operations management positions in the Montgomery, Alabama, and Baton Rouge, Louisiana, distribution centers.

In loving memory of the following associates who also passed away during this period: **Larry Abke, Ray Breedlove, Nat Cannady, Don Castle, John Duffy, Hyrom Fisher, George Houston, Robert Johnson, Philip Kniss, Mac McCullough, Michael Moore, Bud Myhre, Darrel Oats, Richard Pagel, William Rogers,** and **Pete Zimmerman.**

> **Retiree information shows years of employment after names. This may include time spent at acquired companies.**

CORPORATE CAMPUS

Corporate Headquarters Building

N. Joe Owen Building

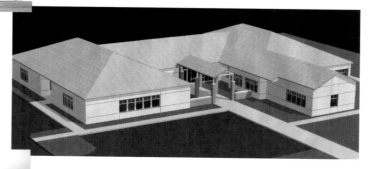

Hamilton Sloan Building

Malcolm C. Graham Building

Edward J. Whitehurst Building

The GPI campus has expanded over the years, honoring those who have significantly contributed to the company's success.

CHAPTER ELEVEN

MEETING MARKET NEEDS: TECHNOLOGY, ADVERTISING, AND EDUCATION

Leadership is a privilege, not a right.

—GPI tenet

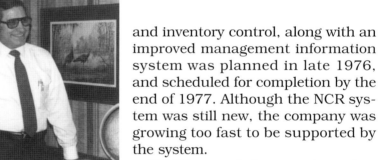

BEFORE COMPUTERS, GPI maintained its inventory through a complex network of index cards. At first, these index cards were stored on four custom-built tables located in the distribution center. The cards were painstakingly updated and filed by hand. To a distributor with thousands of parts, inventory control was an essential skill. Thus, it made sense to computerize as early as possible. In 1970, the company purchased a NCR Century 100 Disc System, replacing its first IBM "wash-tub punch card" system.

"We decided we needed a more powerful computer system, one with disc drives and things of that nature," said Mac Graham, who was in charge of GPI's computer operations at the time. "We were still in the batch-processing mode. Not many companies were real-time and online at that time. I hired a systems analyst named Gene Pitts who worked for NCR to help us program the machine."

With the new NCR computer, development of an order-entry system had begun. This would provide GPI distribution centers direct access to the computer, creating improved inventory control and efficiencies. By 1975, inventories for all three GPI distribution centers were stored off a single system, and the company was beginning to develop an automated order-entry system that would markedly improve efficiency.

A major upgrade of the computer system, which provided capabilities in order processing and inventory control, along with an improved management information system was planned in late 1976, and scheduled for completion by the end of 1977. Although the NCR system was still new, the company was growing too fast to be supported by the system.

"We felt we needed a computer system that was capable of doing more. We heard about a gentleman named Glenn Staats in Columbia, Missouri," said Graham. He explained.

[Staats] had designed and implemented a computerized distribution system. So along with our data processing manager, Temple and I visited Glenn and looked at his system. We talked at length with him, but the decision was that Glenn did not have the system that we required. However, we thought he was capable of writing the software for what we really needed. So we signed on with his company, Cooperative Computing Incorporated (CCI).

We were CCI's first big customer. The CCI team set up CRTs in a conference room upstairs and that's where the programming was developed. Temple and I were there day and night working with them.

Mac Graham was in charge of GPI's early computer system.

GPI ACCEPTS CCI AWARD

IN DECEMBER 1989, CCI PRESENTED GPI with an award in recognition of more than 500 CARQUEST Auto Parts Stores then using the J-CON computer system.

In receiving the award, Rick Young, director of J-CON Operations, and Mac Graham, corporate secretary, thanked the J-CON managers for their contributions to the program. This thanks was given to Doug Adams, Mary Ann Bellor, Milton Craft, Leroy Glowiak, Joe Kappel, Ken Karber, Andy Kennell, Joe Kneer, Rob Korn, Roman Kube, Dave Matejko, Sandy Michel, David McCollum, Shipman Northcutt, Braxton O'Neal, Tom Peymann, Rich Reather, Kevin Sharp, Jeff Sykes, John Styers, Mark Walley, Jon Wehling, and Al Wheeler.

The relationship with CCI would yield benefits to GPI. CCI eventually designed a proprietary system called ADIS (Automotive Distributors Information System), for the company's warehouse distribution network that set the industry standard.

GPI Computer Evolution: Jobber System

Until the mid-1970s, inventory management in auto parts jobbing stores was done by manually posting daily invoice activity on file cards numerically kept by product category in a card desk.

Through GPIs relationship with CCI, the first computer system for auto parts stores was introduced in the late 1970s and called J-CON 1 (J-CON was an acronym for Jobber Connection). This primary system used the finest electronic technology available to handle inventory management, eliminating costly man-hours in card desk maintenance. As computer technology progressed so did the J-CON systems and the CCI computer system for distribution centers inventory and accounting management.

In 1983, the next generation of J-CON was introduced called the J-CON 10 Point-of-Sale system. This new system provided a dynamic view of inventory and daily review of gross profit margins and accounts receivable. It also eliminated the need for handwritten point-of-sale invoices as well as pricing. There was no longer a need to physically check availability of inventory as J-CON 10 maintained live inventory records ("live" A/R information was also maintained). Now CARQUEST store owners printed their own management reports and statements. Communications between the store and its CARQUEST distribution center included automatic polling for the daily stock order.

A huge advantage for J-CON 10 Point-of-Sale systems was ADM (Advanced Data Management). Through ADM, the CARQUEST store's inventory was updated daily with part number description, actual cost, and suggested selling prices.

In 1987 the next generation, known as the 5000 system, was introduced. It offered increased

Opposite: The J-CON Point-of-Sale system allowed store owners to check the availability of parts at any time.

Below: A CARQUEST associate uses GPI's integrated up-to-date computer network.

speed and data storage capacity, as well as a tape "back-up" system, a vast improvement over the diskettes used by J-CON 10. The next major upgrade of J-CON hardware was in 1994 with the release of the J-CON Polaris, which offered a faster processor and increased storage capacity. A year later the Polaris LX was introduced and designed for smaller-volume stores.

Electronic cataloging was introduced to J-CON users in 1988. The system was called Partfinder and was a significant step forward in computerization at the store level. It allowed store personnel to serve customers faster by finding the parts electronically rather than by using paper catalogs. In 1999, this system was upgraded to higher levels of functionality and called PartExpert.

In 1987, GPI established a toll-free J-CON HelpLine, which provided post-implementation assistance to J-CON customers. The first technician on the HelpLine was Joe Kappel, who moved to Raleigh from Billings, Montana. As the number of customers using J-CON increased, so did the number of HelpLine technicians. By the end of 2004 the J-CON HelpLine was managed by John Chachere, who came from the 688 merger in Baton Rouge, Louisiana, and was staffed by 22 technicians who provided customer assistance six days a week, from 7:30 AM to 10:30 PM.

J-CON Managers

GPI offered the CARQUEST customer a significant advantage as GPI J-CON managers were responsible for implementation of the J-CON system. These managers were experienced in automotive parts and had a genuine interest in helping customers.

The role of a J-CON manager was a varied one. Not only were the J-CON managers responsible for implementing the system, they also were teachers. J-CON managers conducted post-implementation group training sessions for more advanced J-CON operators. At the end of 2004, Chachere supervised 35 full-time J-CON managers and 43 contract technicians.

In 1989, GPI, through CCI, introduced the first J-CON integrated automotive technician connection called ICON (Installer Connection). ICON allowed the service technician to access the serving CARQUEST store's J-CON system for sourcing parts and placing the order. Later features included a labor guide and even a full-shop management system called Service Expert EZ. Many service deal-

DATA WAREHOUSE AND PAPERLESS WAREHOUSE MANAGEMENT

THE INITIAL DEVELOPMENT OF A COMpany-wide data warehouse was undertaken in 1998. Mark Walley was instrumental in its development. The first phase was completed to process national account sales for rebating purchases. Additional phases included timely marketing data and daily product movement from Joint Venture stores and access to information, which would improve inventory management.

The High Jump Paperless Warehouse Management System (WMS) gives distribution centers improved efficiencies and metrics. WMS helps better serve customers and gives CARQUEST a competitive edge in the marketplace. It represents a very large capital investment that will have a significant return on investment. Daily, WMS will enhance the ability of the distribution center teams to produce consistent experience to the customer base. As of year's end 2005, GPI WMS distribution centers included Raleigh, Kansas City, Des Moines, Riverside, and Ocala. Nine additional sites were planned for 2006.

ers found electronic access a major advantage as it eliminated trips or phone calls to the CARQUEST store. Because the J-CON system ran 24 hours per day, the service dealer had unlimited access to the catalog and order placement.

Probably the biggest advantage provided by J-CON 1 was the store owner's ability to check the distribution center inventory immediately for availability of part numbers not stocked by the store.

By the end of 2004, more than 2,700 CARQUEST Auto Parts stores were using J-CON Point-of-Sale systems. J-CON has played an important part in improving efficiency, profitability, and level of service for the CARQUEST Auto Parts stores. Yet in 2005, after months of consideration, GPI decided to develop and implement a new store point-of-sale system, Exploris, using Windows-based software from icarz, a software solutions provider. When combined with Automotive Communications Link, Inc. (AutoCom-Link), a complete technology solution for all CARQUEST Auto Parts stores and its professional auto service customers would be offered.

The year 2005 ended with 1,266 JV stores and three independent stores running Exploris. By April 2006, installation should have been completed in all JV stores. Orders have been received for more than 700 store systems from CARQUEST independent jobbers and conversions will start in late 2006 with the balance of independent customers being converted in 2007.

Information Technology Strategy

During 1998, GPI implemented an information technology strategy designed to position the company for the future. The goal was to build a network infrastructure that would support quick and easy access to the information necessary to run the company. Local area networks (LAN) were installed in 30 GPI distribution centers. The distribution centers were connected to the Raleigh corporate headquarters creating a wide side area network (WSAN). The network provided GPI associates with nationwide access to centralized data, e-mail, Oracle financial systems, and Oracle human resources applications. The software and hardware were key elements in making the Year 2000 Initiative a reality. All PC hardware and software were standardized to enhance the sharing of information and minimize support requirements.

In 1998, installation of Oracle financial systems and Oracle human resources applications to improve financial reporting and cash disbursements were implemented in all six accounting offices. Before the end of 1998, the decision was made to implement the Oracle payroll application, full accounts receivable, and collection software.

Professional Auto Service Centers

The Service Expert EZ, Standalone Dealer System was introduced in 1995, providing the CARQUEST Auto Service Professional customer a business management system and a simple, reliable computer connection to the local CARQUEST Auto Parts store. Service Expert EZ later evolved to CARQUEST TechLink.

In January 2004, GPI announced the acquisition of AutoComLink, a California-based company owned by John Christie, which offered technology solutions for automotive repair shops. After the acquisition, Christie continued with GPI as vice president of electronic services. Within CARQUEST, Christie's AutoComLink was renamed FastLink. The combination of AutoComLink with CARQUEST TechLink and CARQUEST FastLink

Prior to computers, auto parts inventories were controlled manually with index cards similar to the E/Z-Way Stock Control System.

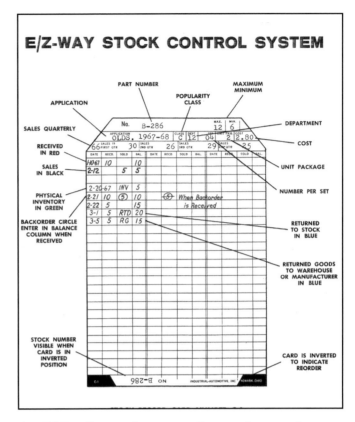

strengthened the CARQUEST value as a supplier to the professional auto service center. The offering included a suite of products, such as ESTIMATOR and myCARQUEST HOMEPAGE. These features improved efficiencies and increased customer service for both the CARQUEST store and the professional service centers. Christie would play an important role for the CARQUEST team in technology development for this important customer base.

Streamlining Communication

CARQUEST Link was developed to streamline communications throughout the company by providing CARQUEST associates instant access to current information. CARQUEST Link support included programs such as confidential payroll deposit notification and benefits reporting, as well as training registration. In addition to communicating with associates, CARQUEST Link also was directed to CARQUEST stores and vendors. The system is available in English, French, and Spanish.

CARQUEST Vision is another recent development that provides fast access and full visibility of GPI's supplier's inventory to CARQUEST distribution centers and auto parts stores. This allows CARQUEST stores to give customers instant answers regarding availability of products not stocked by the store or the store's serving distribution center.

Instant Access was another major initiative in 2005. The product provides CARQUEST independent jobbers with all day/everyday electronic access to account information and payment options. At the end of 2005, there were 456 stores active on the system. The deployment of this initiative was completed in the first quarter of 2006.

Frame Relay

TIG is embarking on a project to move all stores and distribution centers to a reliable high-speed network. This network will support Exploris and future technologies that CAR-

QUEST will introduce over the next several years. The Next Generation Network is built around a network technology called "Frame Relay." Frame relay is the standard communications network for large companies that support technologies such as voice, streaming media, video conferencing, and e-mail.

Information Technology—Going Forward

GPI continues with new technology initiatives to strengthen the CARQUEST brand and its service model. CARQUEST Link continues to be a driving force to distribute and collect information via the Internet. GPI continues expanding CARQUEST Link functionality to include online access to expanded management reporting and offer multilingual capability. Systems to support electronic invoices, online accounts receivable statements, and electronic warehouse returns enable customers to access information conveniently. Other initiatives include centralized processing and electronic reporting of telecommunications, fuel and vehicle management, consolidated freight payments, energy management, and property taxes.

In 1999, upon Mac Graham's retirement, Chandler Ellis was elected vice president of information technology and served in that capacity until mid-2005 when she left the company to pursue other interests. Joe Zucchero joined GPI at that time as vice president of all company information technology.

CARQUEST Advertising Evolution

From the beginning of CARQUEST in 1973 until the mid-1980s, the Pitluk Group, an advertising agency in San Antonio, Texas, was responsible for CARQUEST advertising activity. During this period Martha Merrill was GPI's advertising and promotions manager. She was assisted by Phil Corbin and Rachel Stroud and directed by Ed Whitehurst. Tina Davis, a graphic artist, joined GPI in 1984 and eventually supervised the printing department, the graphic arts production, and promotions.

In the early 1980s, with three of the four GPI locations in the Carolinas, the advertising budget targeted ACC College Basketball with television and radio ads. With the fourth location in Minnesota, college hockey was the target. There was some national CARQUEST expo-

sure in *Hot Rod*, *Car Craft*, and *Mechanics Illustrated* magazines. Outdoor billboards were also used in all locations.

Advertising at this time within CARQUEST was directed primarily to retail sales promotions, and the CARQUEST retail committee coordinated major sales events such as Christmas sales, spring sales, Father's Day sales, and fall sales. The Pitluk Group, taking direction from the retail committee, was helpful in offering professional retail advertising advice.

In the early 1980s, with the advent of fuel-efficient vehicles with onboard electronics controlling fuel/air ratios, cars became more complex with each model year. CARQUEST membership recognized the need to concentrate more on the professional automotive service technician as the prime customer rather than the retail do-it-yourself customer. In 1987, the membership unanimously agreed to support professional auto service technicians and market its own CARQUEST brand name on the products they sold. These decisions dictated a change in advertising direction. Two messages needed to be delivered to the public. Motorists were advised to take hi-tech vehicles to professionals for repairs and also reminded that current automotive technicians were highly trained with both electronic and mechanical skills.

Also, there were two messages to be delivered to auto service technicians: CARQUEST was dedicated to supporting the profession, and CARQUEST-branded products would always be high quality. CARQUEST advertising would deliver these messages to motorists and automotive service technicians.

Among the many talented people employed by Parts Warehouse Co. (CARQUEST member), Bay City, Michigan, was Scott Ginsburg who also served on the CARQUEST

From the mid-1980s through 2004, CARQUEST placed advertisements in trade magazines to reach its target customers.

NOT ALL SUPERHEROES WEAR A CAPE.

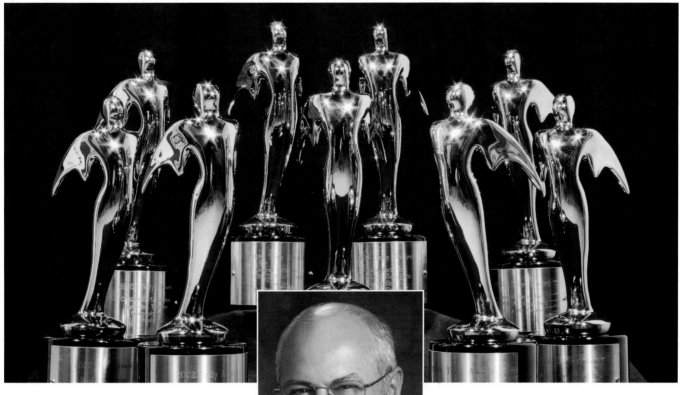

CARQUEST has won nine International Telly Awards for its video productions. Scott Ginsburg, left, has managed GPI's advertising and audiovisual production for more than 20 years.

retail committee. Shortly after the merger of Parts Warehouse Co. into GPI in 1986, Scott was asked to relocate to Raleigh and manage a new advertising direction for GPI. Scott accepted the challenge and 20 years later continues to manage all of GPI's advertising activity and audiovisual production. Additionally, Scott has assumed other responsibilities including marketing meeting planning and various training, public relations, and communications activities.

The redirection of advertising expenditures to the professional auto service was gradual and not intended to ignore the retail market or the need to create public awareness of the CARQUEST brand. In 1976, the first spokesman for CARQUEST was racecar driver Johnny Rutherford, three-time winner of the Indianapolis 500 and CART national champion in 1980. Singer Roger Miller was hired in 1988 for radio and television ads and in 1989 country-western singer and actor Roy Clark was hired to do the same. Print ads and promotions for the farm and ranch market were produced twice a year. Similar promotions were directed to tool and equipment, used car lot, paint and body, and marine

and fleet markets. In 1991, West & Vaughan became GPI's advertising agency. It later became French-West-Vaughan and secured the CARQUEST Corporation account. In January 2006, the account was moved to The Stone Agency in Raleigh, North Carolina.

To help meet the training and communications needs of a rapidly growing company, GPI established its first Audio-Visual studio in 1989. Through this facility and the many upgrades since, each distribution center had its own video training library—more than 250 titles were available for stores and technicians. In-house training videos, marketing conference videos, and company communication pieces were also produced.

The GPI-CARQUEST Studio has been honored as the winner of nine International Telly Awards for its various video productions. The Telly Awards honor outstanding local, regional, and cable televi-

SPONSORSHIPS

IN THE MID-1990S, WITH A GROWING budget and the cost efficiencies of television, a gradual move was made away from radio advertising to television.

Football

The CARQUEST brand and the importance of professional auto service was aired on NFL football, regional professional sports, auto racing, and CARQUEST'S own college football bowl. The first CARQUEST bowl was broadcast on CBS on New Year's Day 1994. The sponsorship continued for four more years moving to TBS through 1998.

1999 saw the beginning of a six-year association with CBS and the NFL. In addition to placing commercials in regular season broadcasts, CARQUEST became the name-in-title sponsor of the "CARQUEST Chalk Talk" segment during the *NFL Today*.

Motorsports

Beginning in 1996, CARQUEST advertising moved to motorsports with CARQUEST vehicle sponsorship, including the Sarver-Kinney NHRA (National Hot Rod Association) Top Fueler, the Nathan Butke CARQUEST Monte Carlo in the Grand National series, Ray Brothers Racing in the IHRA (International Hot Rod Association), and Harold Fair's ASA car. Reaching a huge national television audience, the CARQUEST 420K NASCAR Supertruck

season finale was broadcast on CBS from Las Vegas Motor Speedway.

In December 1996, CARQUEST announced a five-year agreement with Charlotte Motor Speedway (now known as Lowes Motor Speedway), Concord, North Carolina, for sponsorship of the CARQUEST Auto Parts 300, a NASCAR Busch series race to be held for the first time on May 24, 1997, and broadcast live on TBS. The contract for this event runs through 2010 and is the longest-running sponsorship in the Busch series.

In 1997, CARQUEST began a successful seven-year sponsorship of Paul Romine and his Top Fuel dragster. Together, they won the IHRA

Left: The first CARQUEST Bowl was broadcast in 1994.

Below: CARQUEST became involved with sponsoring motorsport events in 1996.

Opposite, clockwise from top left: CARQUEST became the associate sponsor of the TEAM ASE NASCAR truck driven by Scott Riggs in 2001.

In 2004 and 2005, CARQUEST sponsored Kyle Busch. A 2005 television commercial featuring Busch debuted in February.

In 2002, CARQUEST was the associate sponsor of Ricky Hendrick, pictured with his father Rick, in the NASCAR Busch series and the "Official Auto Parts Supplier to Hendrick Motorsports."

Top Fuel World Championship in 1997, 1998, and 2000, and went on to compete in the NHRA Drag Racing series with CARQUEST sponsorship through the 2003 season.

After sponsoring IHRA series events starting in 1997 through the 2002 season, CARQUEST moved the NHRA drag racing in 2003 with sponsorship of the CARQUEST Auto Parts Nationals from Pacific Raceways in Seattle. In 2004 a second NHRA event in Chicago was added. In 2005 CARQUEST signed a multi-year agreement to sponsor the legendary NHRA Winternationals from Pomona, California.

Involvement in motorsports broadened in late 2000 with the addition of NASCAR driver John Andretti as a CARQUEST spokesman. Andretti and the legendary Petty Enterprises #43 car appeared in a new television commercial that debuted in the 2001 Daytona 500 on FOX.

Further enhancing a close alliance with the professional automotive technician, CARQUEST agreed to become the associate sponsor of the TEAM ASE NASCAR truck driven by Scott Riggs for the 2001 season. Sponsorship of the team continued through the 2004 season with Jason Leffler, Jimmy Spencer, and Andy Houston driving.

For 2002, CARQUEST became the associate sponsor of Ricky Hendrick in the NASCAR Busch series and became the "Official Auto Parts Supplier to Hendrick Motorsports." After an injury at the Las Vegas race, Ricky retired to become a team owner. Ricky and nine others died in an October 2004 plane crash in Virginia. Three family members of Rick Hendricks also died, including his brother John; four other victims were Hendricks' employees. Also among the victims was Joe Jackson, director of Motorsports for Dupont and a good friend of GPI.

For the 2003 racing season, CARQUEST, GMAC, and Hendrick Motorsports teamed up to put Brian Vickers behind the wheel of a Busch series car. He eventually won the championship. Two new television commercials were produced that year highlighting CARQUEST's relationship with the Hendrick team and the dedication of CARQUEST to get the right parts in the hands of professional automotive service technicians.

During the 2004 season, CARQUEST moved to Nextel Cup racing with Hendrick Motorsports. GPI became the primary sponsor of Kyle Busch in the #84 CARQUEST Chevrolet for six races and the associate sponsor of Brian Vickers for the entire season. New television commercials were produced stressing the quality and dependability of CARQUEST Auto Parts, both on and off the track.

In 2005, CARQUEST co-sponsored the #5 Nextel Cup car driven by Kyle Busch. A television commercial showing Kyle at the counter of a CARQUEST store made its debut in February.

CARQUEST continued to support one of its own associates, Rex Gardner, in Kansas, in the annual Great Race. In addition to back-to-back wins in 1998 and 1999, Rex and his teammate Gary Kuck have four 2nd place finishes, three 3rd place finishes, and two 4th place finishes in 16 starts.

sion commercials and programs, as well as the finest video and film productions. Since 1978, its mission has been to strengthen the visual arts community by inspiring, promoting, and supporting creativity. Telly Awards encourage a diverse field of entries. In 2004, Telly received more than 10,000 entries from all 50 states and five continents.

In April 1991, the first CARQUEST Driving Force audiotape was produced and monthly editions have followed for more than 15 years. Through the tapes (and later CDs) GPI transformed a salesman's "windshield time" into training and selling information.

Supporting the Professional Technicians

In 1992, to further strengthen the position as the leading supplier to the professional automotive technician, CARQUEST produced "Welcome to the Pros," followed in 1993 by "Daddy Works." Both television commercials were designed to highlight the CARQUEST commitment to the professional.

In 2002, CARQUEST debuted television commercials in Professional Bull Rider Association events carried on NBC and CBS and supported this effort with its ASE co-sponsorship of World Champion Bullfighter, Rob Smets.

From the mid-1980s through 2004 CARQUEST budgeted heavily for ads in trade magazines to reach its target customer. Its first trade magazine advertising in 1985, produced by the Pitluk Group, won the National Advertising Agency Network's Award of Excellence for the CARQUEST service technician ad, "It's 3:30, Do You Know Where Your Parts Are?"

GPI/CARQUEST continued a leadership role in the area of automotive trade journal advertising within the automotive aftermarket. Making its debut was the highly successful "To Be the Best, You Gotta Use the Best" advertising slogan along with a series of ads acknowledging the professionalism and skills of the automotive service technician. GPI/CARQUEST won two Readers Choice awards from *Underhood* and *Import Service* magazines.

From a budget of $1 million in 1976 to $21 million in 2005, CARQUEST advertising has evolved to meet the needs of a highly competitive marketplace.

QUALITY ADVERTISING

This sampling of trade advertisements acknowledges the professionalism of automotive service technicians and highlights the quality of CARQUEST auto parts.

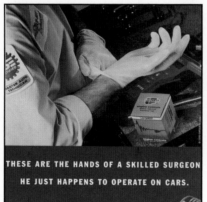

Training and Education

Since its beginning, GPI has focused on education through training for associates and customers at all levels, including technical training for CARQUEST store customers. In early years, training was available through videotapes in video libraries at each distribution center; seminars at annual business and owner's conferences; scheduled courses conducted by Herm Markell, Tom Easton and others; CARQUEST Cornerstones and Sales Tips bulletins; Driving Force audiotapes and CDs; product seminars by manufacturers and CARQUEST undercar/underhood salesmen; J-CON HelpLine and full-time J-CON field-training managers; CARQUEST scholarship awards; and AWDA and Northwood University's University of the Aftermarket.

But as the company grew so did the need for more organized, better-targeted training. This plan started with the GPI Management Institute in 1996, followed by the CARQUEST Training Institute in 1999, and the CARQUEST University in 2002.

CARQUEST UNIVERSITY

CREATED IN 2002, CAR-QUEST University brought together major elements of education to ensure that GPI company values and culture were pervasive elements in everything the company would do. It was designated as the center for all learning and development in GPI.

The University was represented by four centers, and each focused on a different aspect of learning. These were Management Enrichment, Developing Tomorrow's Leaders, the Knowledge Institute (when CARQUEST University was developed, the GPI Management Institute became part of the University and was renamed the GPI Knowledge Institute), and Sustaining the Culture.

The College of Management Enrichment was designed to uphold the GPI tenet: "Leadership is a privilege, not a right." All supervisors and managers at GPI are required to participate in annual development to improve their leadership acumen.

Developing Tomorrow's Leaders is a separate college oriented to high potential development and includes the Leadership Development Program. GPI recognizes that a bench strength of talent is required to sustain the organization for the future.

GPI recognized the importance of quality processes to support customer service. The Knowledge Institute provides just-in-time training on procedures and processes that support its marketing environment. The Institute's trainers travel throughout North America teaching more than a dozen core components of store operations.

The International Quality and Productivity Center recognized CARQUEST University in 2003 as one of the best new corporate universities in the United States. Other colleges were added to ensure that the necessary skills were being taught and emphasized. The College of Sales Excellence, launched in 2005, ensures that GPI's sales professionals are skilled at customer relationship management. The sales training combines assessments, classroom time, and coaching to elevate performance and increase organic sales growth.

Technology is a new venture for CARQUEST University. In 2005, the University developed learning processes to support Exploris, the new point-of-sales system, as well as for Instant Access, the online accounts receivable tool for customers. The College of Technology will also develop learning to support WMS (the paperless warehouse system) and Vision (procurement). Technology is not just a college for the University; it also supports the organization. In 2005, the University partnered with www.learn.com to launch the new Learning Management System (LMS).

In 2006, the University will be housed in the new Hamilton C. Sloan Learning Center on the corporate campus of GPI in Raleigh. This state-of-the-art facility will be a showcase for learning and an example of the level of commitment that GPI has for learning and development.

GPI Management Institute

In 1996, GPI developed the GPI Management Institute, which represented an upfront investment of more than $500,000, to create a new level of training for all JV store associates. The curriculum consists of six modules, requiring 14 days of classroom training. The six modules include sales, marketing, and customer service; computer operations; financial and store procedures; inventory and gross profit management; personnel practice; and management responsibilities. Associates are tested at the beginning and end of each module and required to achieve a score of at least 90% to graduate.

George Couch, who had management responsibility for JV stores in Raleigh and Columbia and was a seasoned veteran in store operations, developed the curriculum for the GPI Management Institute. He began developing training material in late 1995. In 1996, he selected six experienced JV store associates to assist him as instructors. They were Arnold Jenkins, Mickey White, Mike Hedge, Craig Porter, Mark McDonald, and Gerard Bourdages. An annual budget of $450,000 was established for the Management Institute.

Vice presidents, general managers, and regional managers were required to complete the course in 1996, and all store managers completed the course in February 1997. Every assistant manager and counter salesperson completed initial training in 1997. Also in 1997, a two-day training program was developed for all JV store outside salespeople.

CARQUEST Technical Institute

CARQUEST Technical Institute (CTI), developed in 1999, became the industry leader in quality technical and business management training for the professional repair facility owner, manager, and technician. CTI offered 36 technical and six business management courses taught

Right: Mike DeSorbo was instrumental in the success of CARQUEST Technical Institute.

Below left: George Couch developed the curriculum for the Management Institute.

by 38 world-class instructors. Through mid-2005, almost one-and-a-half million technician training hours, or continuing education units (CEUs), had been conducted by CTI—more than 20,000 technicians had participated from 4,000 automotive service centers throughout North America. CTI had earned the Automotive Society of Engineers (ASE) Blue Seal of Excellence recognition and ASE certification as a provider of Continuing Automotive Service Education (CASE).

Under the direction of Mike DeSorbo, director of market segments, and Chris Chesney, director of technical training, CTI is recognized by professional auto technicians throughout North America for quality technical training. Norm Nall, technical training instructor, was also helpful in the success of CTI.

CTI received the 2003 Automotive Training Managers Council (ATMC) National Training Excellence Award for Traditional Leader Led Training. The award is given annually to providers of automotive technical training.

In 2005, its seventh year of being one of the industry's premier training organizations, CTI has become one of GPI's "crown jewels." 2005 saw more stand-alone courses held, allowing more customers to attend training than ever before. CTI was recognized for the sixth consecutive year as an ASE Blue Seal of Excellence training provider and remains CASE certified since 2003. The year 2006 will see 25% of the courses offered via Internet, more nameplate specific courses, and more courses translated into Spanish.

LEADERSHIP GOING FORWARD

From left: Fred J. Pisciotta, David J. Straus, F. William Vandiver Jr., Hugh L. McColl Jr., Clifford H. Henline Jr., O. Temple Sloan III, C. Hamilton Sloan, O. Temple Sloan Jr., N. Joe Owen, Peter R. Kornafel, Larry W. McCurdy, L. Glenn Orr Jr., and Jon E. McMurtrey.

From left: Richard B. Guirlinger, John W. Gardner, and John Mosunic.   From left: O. Temple Sloan III and O. Temple Sloan Jr.

From left: Steve Sharp, Tom O'Hare, and Robert Cushing.

From left: Magella Boutin, Douglas R. Gilbert,
Wayne F. Johnston, and Steven P. Gushie.

From left: Joe Zucchero, Chuck Henline, Ed Whirty,
Ray Birden, and Robert Blair.

From left: Paul R. Farwick, David L. McCartney, Micheal G. Allen,
and J. Michael Riess.

LEADERSHIP GOING FORWARD

Ron Adkins

Normand Allard

Terri Ballard

Tom Belding

Gerry Bennett

Paul Chamberlain

John Christie

Bob Conley

Bryan Copeland

George Couch

Donna Cuomo

John Cuomo

Laura Davis

Tina Davis

Mike Deal

Allen Dedman

Normand Delisle

Scott Derrow

Mike Desorbo

Dale Dockter

Ed Dobbs

Brian Dobson

James Felman

Dan Fochtman

Ignagio Fortuna

Dennis Fox

Doug Freeman

Scott Ginsburg

Susan Grass

Bill Gruenthal

Danny Haag

Todd Hack

Peter Hafford

Ward Haugen

Jim Hazlett

Patrick Healy

Roy Hedges

Mike Hellweg

Janet Higgins

Tom Hines

Steve Hoeven

Claude Hould

William
Humber

Paul
Isenbarger

Hines
Johnson

Matt Johnson

John Kahut

Ken Karber

Doug Kemp

Peter Klotz

Don Kohlbeck

Wayne
Lavrack

Robert
Layman

Stephany
Lerer

Montie Loney

Randal Long

Jeff Lundh

Dale Lyon

Jeanne Lyons

James
Madson

Bart Marshel

Bubba
McDonald

Mark
McDonald

John
McMurtrey

Peter McNally

Bud
McQuillan

Al Minnis

Kim Molin

Trey Molin

Paul Neal

Kevin Nelson

Braxton O'Neal

Kim Patch

Jonathan Pease

Tom Petruccione

Paul Pierce

Dan Rader

Todd Rasmussen

Mario Recchia

Jerry Repak

Tom Roscrow

Jeff Seiter

David Sharer

Hamilton Sloan Jr.

Hoke Smith

Shane Smith

Keith Swainey

Lenore Swenson

Mike Tanji

John Taylor

Allen Till

Judy Tobia

Cindy Toon

John Turcotte

Bobby Tyson

Deborah Tyson

John Weinmann, Jr.

Al Wheeler

Brian Wiggs

Phil Wisnieski

Fred Wood

Hans Wulff

Rick Young

Mark Zuanich

Larry Zucker

Regardless of the companies acquired or merged with General Parts, Inc., the best asset will always be the people who join GPI.

CHAPTER TWELVE

ACQUISITIONS AND MERGERS

We've done a lot of acquisitions, and you would like to think in every acquisition that there's some pearl that you can bring back and spread throughout the whole company.

—John Gardner

A PRIME OBJECTIVE IN PUBlishing a book about General Parts, Inc. is to preserve the history of each of the companies acquired by or merged into GPI. Each of these companies has interesting beginnings and it is important to see that it is recorded.

Much of GPI's growth has been through successful acquisitions and mergers and much could be written about the reasons for this success. First on the GPI due diligence checklist is the word...PEOPLE. Every successful company has one or more key people responsible for its success. To GPI, these people represent the most valuable assets of the company and must be retained. This must be determined upfront before the transaction proceeds. GPI has maintained a great record in assuring these particular people that they will have a bright future.

From the first, Asheville in 1971, to WORLD-PAC in 2004, every addition has played an important role in GPI's success.

W. N. C. PARTS DISTRIBUTORS, INC.
March 1972
Asheville, North Carolina

Hayes & Hopson, one of the best-known automotive firms in Western North Carolina, was started in 1924, about two blocks north of the building shown on the following page. The original building

was much smaller and it had gasoline pumps outside. The company had only five employees.

The founders were Max A. Hayes (O.L. "Pete" Garner's father-in-law) and John S. Hopson, who died in 1943. Pete Garner left a good government job to join Hayes.

The firm grew and prospered, and when Hayes died in 1960, he left the company ownership to his daughter, Ruth Garner. Ruth's husband Pete took over the operation. The company continued to expand and five branch stores were added.

In 1966, W.N.C. was formed to function as a warehouse distributor, selling to other independent jobbers. The warehouse was operated as a separate business and operated from the entire lower level of the Hayes & Hopson Building. William A. West was the CEO of W.N.C. Parts Distributors, Inc.

In 1971, O. Temple Sloan Jr., met Pete Garner through a mutual friend, Arthur Page. Following several visits, in 1972 Pete informed Temple that he was ready to sell his company and the very first GPI acquisition was finalized on March 30, 1972.

General Parts, Inc., expanded with well-planned acquisitions and mergers with reputable companies that ultimately strengthened its core.

At the time of the acquisition, GPI did not own any parts stores and the Hayes & Hopson stores were sold to independent CARQUEST store owners, a practice that was later reversed with the advent of the GPI Joint Venture Store Program in the early 1980s.

"The W.N.C. acquisition took several years to develop, but the Asheville Distribution Center has been a very successful operation for GPI," said Temple Sloan.

In the Hayes & Hopson acquisition, GPI found some key people who would contribute greatly to the company's operations in later years. For example, Dennis Fox, who eventually became senior vice president of market development for GPI, was a part-time college student working on the loading dock at the time of the acquisition. Harry Evans was another important addition.

Harry Evans was a salesman, but he was really, for lack of a better word, the glue with the customers. He had the relationships, and they were good ones. He maintained them for years, and he was a quality partner for many years. One of the most effective ways we found good people was through acquisitions, and we worked hard to retain them. Indeed, the vast majority of our current senior management first joined us through acquisitions.

—Temple Sloan Jr.

GENERAL TRADING COMPANY
July 1980
Minneapolis/St. Paul, Minnesota

General Trading Company, St. Paul, Minnesota, was an automotive replacement parts company that could trace its roots back to 1855. It began as a retail iron store founded by John Nicols and Captain Peter Berkey when they purchased a company known as Sligo and Tyrone Iron, which manufactured and sold heavy iron used in the manufacturing of sled castings, plow shares, chairs, nails, and other related products, from William R. Marshall.

New products included wagon-makers, supplies, blacksmith and lumbering items, and carriage and sleigh stock. Salespeople traveled from Minnesota by train and dusty trails as far west as the state of Washington to market those products.

In 1901, the directors of those companies introduced the first complete line of automobile accessories to be sold to dealers and garages in the northwest. By 1905, there were 78,000 horseless carriages. Nicols, W. J. Dean, and Jesse Gregg planned skillfully to protect and expand their businesses and purchased the Grant Dadey Company of Fargo, North Dakota. A similar acquisition was made in 1926 with the Minot Supply Company.

Above: Dennis Fox, senior vice president of market development for GPI, worked on the loading docks of Hayes & Hopson at one time.

Left: Hayes & Hopson, pictured in the 1920s, was GPI's first acquisition. It was completed in 1972.

Even in the Depression, the companies went about the tasks of business expansion wherever they could expect to serve customers more adequately. With the death of Gregg in 1935 and Dean in 1941, an era was coming to an end. However, after a decade of expansion during the 1920s and another decade of holding the line during the Depression, General Trading Company emerged in 1941 better equipped for service.

In 1954, after a final consolidation between Nicols, Dean, and Gregg and the Minneapolis Iron Store, General Trading became one operating unit with complete integration of all activities including buying, selling, and distributing the company goods.

Principals of the General Trading Company in 1956 were Sidney and Winter Dean, both quite elderly. They brought Arnold Main in as president. Having primarily automotive interests, Main sold the steel warehouse business to concentrate on auto parts. In 1958, Main left, and General Trading was acquired by H. B. American.

Mr. J. Weaver was hired as president, and in 1962, the company was sold again, this time to Gould

Above: General Trading Company, acquired by GPI in 1980, began in 1855 as Nicols & Dean, a retail iron store, in St. Paul, Minnesota.

Below: The GTC building on Prior St. in 1955.

National Battery Company which created G.N.F. Finance for the express purpose of selling company-owned stores. A concerted effort was made to sell those stores to their managers or employees at the time, thus creating opportunities for many to become independent businessmen. In slightly less than one year, all 47 company stores were sold to managers and employees.

During 1962, Gould National and Gulf & Western Industries, operators of the American Parts

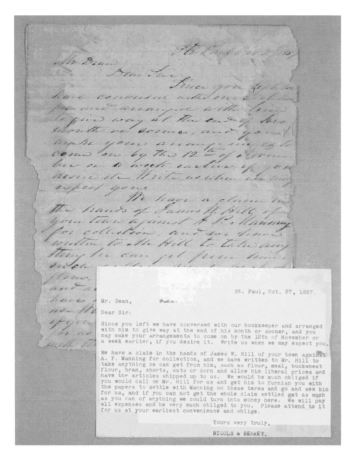

Above: Murf Handmaker, left, and Carl Pohlad sold General Trading Company to GPI in 1980.

Left: This collection letter shows the collection process of General Trading Company in 1857.

System (APS), attempted a merger, which was not consummated.

In 1963, Joe Davis became president of General Trading Company. In 1967, Maremont Corporation of Chicago, Illinois, acquired General Trading Company under its C & L Distribution Group.

In 1973, Maremont Corporation was ordered by the Federal Trade Commission (FTC) to divest the entire C & L Distribution Group, including General Trading. As a result, General Trading was sold to the Bellfonte Co., of Minneapolis, Minnesota, which was headed by Carl Pohlad, Murf Handmaker, and Paul Christen.

Through all of those sales and changes of ownership over a 30-year period, General Trading continued to grow and prosper. The original 47 stores expanded to more than 100 and eventually to 126 independents, operating under the "Little General" identification.

In 1977, as the industry began to change and the era of programmed distribution began, the principals of General Trading Company dropped their own identity program to join the CARQUEST program. On January 2, 1980, Ron Wehrenberg

became the president of General Trading Company and, shortly thereafter, it was purchased by General Parts, Inc.

The merger with General Trading Company was a significant event in the history of GPI. It was the first major merger, the first merger with a CARQUEST member, and the first outside the Carolinas.

This merger included the three key ingredients for success—a strong customer base, significant room for market development, and the quality of people in key management positions. GTC was particularly blessed with people like Wehrenberg, Don Annala, Ron Anderson, and Judy Miller, who all provided excellent leadership for a dedicated group driven to be winners.

Also, the history and success of the GTC merger cannot be complete without a mention of Dennis Fox. He was promoted to president of the GPI Midwest division in late 1992 when Wehrenberg's health began failing. Dennis spent four years providing outstanding leadership for the upper midwest.

In October 1979, I was a speaker at The General Trading Company/CARQUEST's convention in Ashland, Wisconsin. No one, including Carl Pohlad, Murf Handmaker, or Ron Wehrenberg would have predicted what was to happen in the next few months. Following Murf Handmaker's heart attack that fall, Murf and Carl decided they should sell General Trading. During the CARQUEST meeting in January 1980, Murf invited me to the bar for a drink and convinced me that

From left to right: Instrumental to the success of General Trading Company were Ron Wehrenberg, Don Annala, Ron Anderson, and Terry Langhorst.

Below right: Dennis Fox and Judy Miller.

GPI should acquire General Trading. While we were ready for the challenge, one must remember interest rates were 21 to 23 percent and the economy was in decline and unemployment was 14%. After a hard sell, Ham Sloan and Ed Whitehurst agreed to GPI taking a giant step. Originally, Joe Hughes was to be our partner, but later decided against it.

Working closely with several key suppliers, we were able to structure the financing to shield us from the incredible interest rates. Without that support, it would not have been possible. Byron Pond of Maremont, Bill Herring of Dana, and Larry Sills of Standard were leaders. The rest is history.

—*Temple Sloan, Jr.*

VALLEY MOTOR SUPPLY COMPANY, INC.
1983
Motor Parts Warehouse
Valley Welders Supply
A Montana Success Story

In 1927, in Havre, one of Montana's smaller cities midway on the highline and a few miles south of the Canadian border, Valley Motor Supply began as a dealership to handle Oakland and Pontiac cars.

A man who would figure prominently in the development of the new company was Walter C. Olson, who was hired by the parts department in 1928. Olson was a native of Wisconsin and looking for an opportunity to share in business ownership. He became a small stockholder in the Valley Motor Company.

With the onset of the Great Depression, new car sales dropped, and Olson encouraged the stockholders to shift directions and enter the field of wholesale replacement parts. By 1931 a wholesale automotive parts store was operating in what had been the car dealership's showroom. The firm's name was changed to Valley Motor Supply Company and started as a NAPA jobber.

In late 1933, the first branch store in Glasgow opened. J. B. Wilford and Muryl W. Myhre, who would figure prominently in Valley's future, got their start at the Glasgow branch in 1934. George B. Hall joined the firm and would become a major contributor to Valley's success. Hall was in the service station business when his good friend, Walter Olson, persuaded him to come to Valley Motor Supply. In 1936, Olson became president of the company and Hall secretary-treasurer.

Because of World War II plans for further growth were postponed, but by 1944, Hall and Olson were surveying the state for other locations. They turned to Miles City, rented a building, and opened a store.

Meanwhile, J. H. Clark's Billings parts business was purchased in September 1944. There were now four Valley branches.

Following World War II, expansion came quickly as Americans resumed their love affair with the automobile. Valley stores were established in Sidney and Whitefish and, in 1948, Valley Motor Supply crossed state boundaries with a store in Cody, Wyoming. A branch was established at Lovell the following year. The construction of a dam near Lemmon, South Dakota, suggested a likely location, so the company reached into a third state in 1949. Meanwhile, an opportunity arose for a store in Great Falls and by the end of the decade, Valley Motor Supply had stores in 11 cities in a three-state region.

Above: Valley Motor Supply expansion enabled the company to grow to 36 stores strong by the early 1980s.

Left: James Hall was part of the management team for Valley Motor Supply during the 1940s.

Valley's growing success and vitality was credited to its commitment to provide quick and reliable service. When the company did not have an item in its inventory, managers were authorized to order it from a competitive warehouse. Customer satisfaction was a key consideration.

Equally important was the company's policy encouraging its employees to become stockholders, fostering healthy participation and interest in the firm's success. Each new store was organized as a subsidiary corporation with the manager and other key personnel holding stock along with the officers of the parent corporation. Along with this went a practice of promoting from within—all of the branch managers started as countermen or machine shop employees.

Valley was fortunate to have strong management leadership over the years. Along with Walter C. Olson and George W. Hall, there were men like Art Chapman and Muryl Myhre to help guide the firm's solid growth. Other key management people joining Valley Motor Supply during the 1940s included Doug Dolven, Chuck Keene, Chuck Romee, and James Hall.

During the first half of the new decade, Valley Motor Supply added branches in Kalispell, Bozeman, Cut Bank, Glendive, Missoula, Malta, and Wolf Point. But the most significant development of the mid-1950s was the opening of the Motor Parts Distribution Centers in Havre and Billings in 1956.

Continued store expansion located branches in Dillon, Helena, Harlem, Chinook, Baker, Roundup, Missoula, and Libby. It expanded into Wyoming at Gillette, Sheridan, Powell, Worland, and Riverton. By the early 1980s, Valley Motor Supply stores numbered 36.

With the advent of the 1980s, the company faced retirements of several long-time and high-level management personnel and saw the need to find a company interested in taking over operations, with the guarantee that the principles and policies would be preserved. That was accomplished in 1983 when the Valley shareholders selected General Parts, Inc., of Raleigh, North Carolina, as the best company to continue moving Valley Motor Supply Company in the direction that provided store growth by using key store management in ownership positions. On October 31, 1983, GPI finalized an agreement to acquire a majority ownership position in Valley Motor Supply Company which, at that time, operated distribution centers in Billings and Havre, Montana; and 36 parts stores, and two industrial welding supply companies located throughout Montana, northern Wyoming, and South Dakota.

The merger was complex. Several major parts distribution companies, namely Genuine Parts Company, GKN, and Gulf & Western's American Parts, were interested in acquiring Valley, but each of them wanted 100 percent of the stock. Adding to the complexities were 86 shareholders who had to agree on the buyer. Temple Sloan Jr., John Gardner, Chuck Romee, and Jim Hall spent two weeks in one-on-one meetings throughout Montana and Wyoming with shareholders, convincing them that GPI was the right choice.

The Valley acquisition had a major impact on GPI and its future as it immediately put the company in the business of owning and operating auto parts stores with a plan that allowed the store's key management the opportunity of partial ownership. An important part of this plan was retiring managers' desire to see existing stockholders given the same opportunity to become store managers that they had. This philosophy was the basis for GPI's joint venture store plan, which became vital to future growth.

Valley Motor Supply was rich in talent. In addition to those already mentioned were Jim

Russell, Mike Hedge, Allen Dedman, Bill Ball, John Turcotte, Kim Patch, Brian Dobson, Dan Smith, Jon Cockerham, Ron Girard, Searle Stroup, Dennis Peterson, Tony Dyba, Roger Trotman, Joe Kappel, Clif Franklin, Roger Hastings, Mike Zeltinger, Dave Rickell, Ron Adkins, Bill McMullen, and a multitude of the very best parts store managers, machine shop personnel, and outside salesmen who sustained Valley's growth and dominant position in Montana and northern Wyoming.

Valley Welders Supply Before GPI

Another key in the Valley merger was the introduction of GPI to the welding supply business, which has been a vital part of GPI's growth. It was always the belief at Valley Motor Supply that the welding supply business fits the auto parts business like a glove fits a hand. This was recognized before World War II when many of the auto parts stores in Montana started selling packaged gases such as oxygen and acetylene.

Valley Motor Supply Company in Havre started hauling cylinders from Butte, Montana, in 1941. They delivered cylinders on U.S. Highway 2 from Glacier Park to the North Dakota border. A gas and oxygen refilling center in Butte was the only one in Montana until the late 1940s. In 1949,

Valley Motor Supply started Valley Welders Supply with a store in Billings. Sourcing product was a problem. Trucks were bought by Valley and driven by Valley employees to save freight charges. A diesel tractor and a 40-foot trailer were used, and different Valley employees would take turns driving and sleeping while traveling to places like Chicago, Milwaukee, Seattle, Los Angeles, San Francisco, and Denver. They would leave

Thursday night and return by Sunday so that the diesel tractor could be ready to go out with the cylinder trailer Monday morning. They would have boxcars of welding rods shipped to Beach, North Dakota, and parked, then take trucks to Beach, unload the welding rod and drive back to Billings.

In the late 1970s a welding supply store was opened in Sheridan, Wyoming.

The Industrial Gas Plant was built in 1948-49 by the Linde Air Products Company, a division of Union Carbide Company. The plant filled oxygen and acetylene cylinders for Valley Welders Supply, Northwestern Auto, Deaconess Hospital, and the U.S. Air Force in Great Falls. In 1987, after the GPI merger, this plant was purchased from Union Carbide Company by Valley Welders.

Valley Welders was managed by the top management of Valley Motor Supply until 1960 when Chuck Romee was made general manager. Chuck had joined Valley Motor Supply in 1948 in Billings where he worked in various positions. In the early 1950s he was selected to manage the Valley Motor Supply store in

Miles City. Romee managed Valley Welders from 1960 to 1980. During that time, Valley Welding Supply added machine tools to its industrial offering.

Art Chapman, one of the pioneers of Valley Motor Supply, died in 1980 and Chuck Romee was appointed sales manager at Valley Motor Supply. He turned Valley Welders Supply over to Roger Trotman who retired in 1988 and at that time Jim Downs became manager and Ron Adkins served as sales manager.

At right, from top to bottom: Chuck Romee, Roger Trotman, and Ron Adkins. At left, from top to bottom: Allen Dedman, Bill Ball, and Jim Russell.

Above left: Valley Welders brought GPI into the welding supply business.

Above right: Valley Welders would haul products to Chicago, Milwaukee, Seattle, Los Angeles, San Francisco, and Denver.

In 1993, Ron Adkins became president of Valley Welding Supply and later sold the machine tool division to Jim Downs and Doug Neill.

Valley Welders' annual sales in 1960, when Chuck Romee became manager, was less than $200,000. In 2004, sales had reached $14.9 million with record profit.

In the fall of 1982, I called Jim Hall, president of VMS, concerning a rumor that the company might be for sale; a rumor Hall denied. In February 1983, Hall called me, asking if GPI was still interested. John Gardner and I traveled to Great Falls, meeting with the senior management, Muryl Myhre, Jim Hall, Chuck Romee, Chuck Keene and the company's accountants. The company had a very complex structure with multiple corporations, different year-ends and cross ownership with 85 stockholders. This was all governed by a very complicated shareholder agreement.

The nine senior shareholders wanted to retire and felt the company could not financially redeem them all at once. They were emphatic about the younger stockholders having the same opportunity they had to build equity. This was good for GPI, for Valley's assets exceeded those of GPI. By April, an agreement had been reached, but the transaction was held up for several months by a stockholder lawsuit.

With the advice of Carl Pohlad of Minneapolis, GPI proceeded with the merger. The lawsuit was

settled within 90 days. Following one-on-one meetings with each shareholder by John Gardner and myself, the transaction was consummated in October 1983.

The General Trading Company and Valley Motor Supply transactions changed the direction of GPI and gave us the foundation for the major growth of the 1980s, 1990s, and 2000s, and most important, the confidence to turn GPI into a privately owned company. From Valley, came the basis of our Joint Venture Store Ownership Program.

—*Temple Sloan Jr.*

S & S DISTRIBUTORS WAREHOUSE, INC.
1985
Nashville, Tennessee

The history of S & S Distributors Warehouse, Inc., Nashville, intertwines Parts Distributors Warehouse, Memphis with the William Loewenberg family.

In 1943, two families, Ira J. Lichterman and William A. Loewenberg of Memphis bought Auto Bearings in Nashville, Tennessee. Auto Bearings was a large automotive jobbing operation and did a considerable volume in automotive-related equipment.

The Lichterman-Loewenberg Group, known as L & L, decided to transition from the retail auto parts business into the wholesale warehouse distribution business.

L & L sold Auto Bearings to S & S Sales Co., a small warehouse distributor, in 1961. The name was changed to S & S Parts Distributors Warehouse, Inc. E. R. (Mac) McCarter was vice president and general manager of the new company and remained so until his retirement in 1980.

Under the guidance of William Loewenberg, S & S developed a close and loyal relationship with its customers and employees, which resulted in a steady growth of the customer base. Market conditions dictated a change in S & S's sales philosophy and the company changed from a line-selling distributor to a program-selling distributor. L & L, which also owned Parts Distributor Warehouse (PDW) in Memphis, Tennessee, had developed a marketing program known as Gold Star. The program was also implemented by both S & S and PDW.

Bert Berry, who was credit manager at PDW in Memphis, moved to S & S in Nashville and was promoted to vice president and sales manager. Under the direction of Bert Berry and Mac McCarter, sales continued to grow. In 1971, S & S moved into a new, 40,000-square-foot, air-conditioned facility on Fairfield Avenue. The company continued to expand, and S & S, along with PDW, made the decision to join CARQUEST in 1976. In the 1970s, the Loewenberg family bought the Lichterman stock and became sole owner of S & S.

In 1981, the Loewenberg family sold its interest in S & S to Bert Berry and Richard Murchison, who was PDW's controller. Berry became president and Murchison, a CPA who joined PDW in 1968, became executive vice president.

In the fall of 1984, Berry began to experience serious health problems and was advised to retire. Berry and Murchison made a decision to sell the company and General Parts, Inc. was the number one prospect. GPI purchased the stock on September 1, 1985. In February 1986 Berry passed away.

Berry had been the key in sales and customer relations and with this particular acquisition GPI inherited a customer base of strong and loyal independent CARQUEST Auto Parts store operators led by Ed Florida, Bert Knight, Ralph Lee, Roger Hunley, and Steve Kress.

Under the leadership of John Anthony and Al Wheeler, Nashville became a consistent performer.

Bert Berry and Richard Murchison built a successful, but unique, partnership. When Bert was diagnosed with cancer, Richard did not want to purchase Bert's interest. Following a phone call from Bert, we had a short negotiation in Nashville. Bert's special relationship with his customers became evident as Joe Owen and I traveled with Bert and

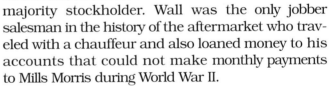

From top to bottom: John Anthony, Al Wheeler, and Bert Berry, from S & S Distributors Warehouse.

Richard to visit each customer, and we traveled to Italy on their annual customer trip. We lost a good friend when Bert died in 1986.
—*Temple Sloan Jr.*

PARTS DISTRIBUTOR'S WAREHOUSE, INC.
1986
Memphis, Tennessee

In 1919, W. B. Mills, Mr. Morris, and Whit Wall founded an automotive parts company in Memphis, Tennessee, and named it The Mills Morris Company. As with most firms started in those days, they had difficulty but grew throughout the 1920s and 1930s. Prior to World War II, they had a number of branch stores including Greenville, Mississippi; Jonesboro, Arkansas; and Union City and Milan, Tennessee. Mills was the majority stockholder. Wall was the only jobber salesman in the history of the aftermarket who traveled with a chauffeur and also loaned money to his accounts that could not make monthly payments to Mills Morris during World War II.

In 1943, Ira Lichterman and William A. Loewenberg purchased the Mills Morris Company and proceeded to expand it. After World War II, branches were added in Bowling Green, Kentucky; Columbus, Ohio; and Tupelo, Mississippi, to name only a few. In 1949, the largest branch was opened combining two existing businesses in Jackson, Mississippi: Jackson Road Equipment and Capital City Welding.

Mills Morris was a major factor in equipment of all kinds, including shop equipment, steam cleaners, jacks, and wreckers. They also handled new tires and placed recapping plants in Memphis and Jackson. Motorola Radios were sold prior to World War II and afterward they expanded to a full appliance division. They were also a major distributor of steel shelving and office furniture.

In 1956, there were 47 outside salesmen doing business from 18 branches throughout six states.

In 1957, C. T. Turner, general manager of Mills Morris, decided to concentrate on serving the growing auto parts jobber business by creating a separate division. The name chosen for the division was Parts Distributor's Warehouse. The sales volume for the PDW Division in 1957 was $1.2 million. There were two salesmen who handled the PDW accounts; Grover Kerr was responsible for all accounts west of the Mississippi River and Bobby Webb handled all those east of the Mississippi.

The growth in the remainder of Mills Morris peaked in the 1950s and branches began to be sold; many became PDW customers. Eventually Mills Morris was sold to a local car dealer and faded away.

The growth at PDW was explosive and Loewenberg, known to the entire community as "Uncle Willie," built a new 100,000-square-feet warehouse facility on Phelan Avenue, occupied Labor Day 1960.

Under the leadership of Uncle Willie as president, Herm P. Markell as general manager and Bobby Webb as sales manager, sales reached $5 million in 1960.

In 1963, Markell met with a group of young warehouse distributors in the South to talk about an umbrella organization to assist in marketing their auto parts through jobbers. The group, which included Jack Alexander from Atlanta, Georgia; Dick Downey from Birmingham, Alabama; Joe Agnew from Jackson, Mississippi; Temple Sloan from

Herman Markell (middle) and Bobby Webb (bottom) purchased Parts Distributor's Warehouse from William Loewenberg (top) in 1981. Five years later, a majority of the interest in the company was sold to GPI after Webb retired.

Raleigh, North Carolina; "Rock" Rockafellow from Columbia, South Carolina; and others met in Atlanta on a couple of occasions, but nothing ever came of the discussions.

In the mid-1960s, PDW developed and introduced its Gold Star Franchise Marketing Program. The program contained an emphasis on retail selling, designed to complement the jobbers' wholesale business. While the program was used by most PDW jobbers, in 1976 it was decided to join the relatively new CARQUEST Program believing there were more benefits being part of a larger group.

In 1981, Webb and Markell purchased the company from the Loewenberg family. In 1986, a majority of their interest was sold to General Parts, Inc. when Webb decided to retire.

A strong base of independent CARQUEST auto parts storeowners were served by PDW represented by Ralph Taylor, J. C. Wright, Bobby Davis, Carlton Ashley, Terry Simmons, Keith Faulkner, Donnie Majors, Pat Hamlin, and others.

Giving to Local Charities

Even before the merger with GPI, PDW in Memphis started sending small year-end gifts to its jobber customers in appreciation of their business. In 1968, PDW management and a representative group of jobber customers suggested that the money spent on these gifts combined with donations from individual jobbers be directed to various charities that focused on catastrophic children's diseases. These annual gifts are made in honor of CARQUEST Auto Parts stores. At the end of 2004, more than 100 mid-southern agencies had received close to $100,000. Markell, who has spearheaded this program since its beginning, said, "We feel that this type of giving is much more appropriate to the spirit of the Christmas season, more so than the small gift we would give directly to the customers. It was safe to say that thousands of children and adults of all races and religions have benefited from this tradition and we hope to continue it for many years."

Following our purchase of S&S Parts Distributors in Nashville, I received a call from Herm Markell and Bobby Webb expressing their desire to discuss a sale

or merger. During the discussions, Herm Markell decided to remain with the company and swapped his stock for GPI stock, and we purchased Bobby Webb's interest.

Few people know that I met with Mr. Loewenberg in 1981 about GPI acquiring Nashville and Memphis. Having just purchased General Trading in Minnesota, we had to pass due to our capacity to deal with both transactions. Mr. Loewenberg then sold Nashville and Memphis to his key management. When you are patient and maintain good relationships, things have a way of working out for all concerned. Bobby Webb said his motivation was he was afraid GPI would run out of money before he could sell.

—Temple Sloan Jr.

PARTS WAREHOUSE COMPANY
1986
Michigan

In July 1986, General Parts took another giant step in growth with the merger of Parts Warehouse Company headquartered in Bay City, Michigan. The history of the Parts Warehouse Company centers around the Rogers family—Al, Sam, and Al's son Bob—but reflects their talent to surround themselves with capable associates.

After World War II Sam Rogers returned to Bay City to resume work at City Auto Parts Company. He had joined his brother Al's fledgling business

Above: Parts Distributor's Warehouse's holiday donations benefitted a number of causes, including St. Jude's Research Hospital.

Right: In 1977, Temple Sloan welcomes Parts Warehouse Company's Samuel L. Rogers, president, and Robert G. Rogers, executive vice president, to CARQUEST.

shortly before the war and as partners they had built a reputation as the place with all auto parts needed to repair "Depression Era" cars. Both customers and employees remember Sam as the man who would never say no to a customer.

By the mid-1950s, City Auto Parts Company had achieved a leadership position in the mid-Michigan aftermarket; however, by the late 1950s it became apparent that automotive parts warehouses were necessary for parts jobbers to properly serve their customers.

In 1959, Sam and Al incorporated Parts Warehouse Co. (PWC). Sam, along with a handful of City Auto Parts employees, built a 19,800-square-foot warehouse in the south end of town. After four major expansions and the addition of conveyors and a mezzanine, PWC represented one of the largest and most modern distribution centers in Michigan with more than 207,000 square feet.

In 1963, the company built a new warehouse in Lansing, Michigan, to serve the South, Central, and Western Michigan markets. Originally 40,000 square feet, it was expanded three times to its present size. Al Rogers' son, Robert Rogers joined the company in 1967. Working with Sam, it quickly became apparent that the two would provide the company with dynamic leadership to meet the changes ahead. In 1977, the company joined CARQUEST.

In the early 1980s, PWC made a decision to invest in a number of auto parts stores. The number peaked at 27 by 1985.

An unfortunate accident left Al Rogers paralyzed in 1984 and by late 1985, Bob and Sam decided to sell PWC. It was fortunate for GPI that the Rogers selected it as their first choice.

The PWC customer base was among the strongest of any company merged into General Parts, Inc. They included the Seehase family, Dewey, Dick and Dave; Wayne Foote; Mark and David Peterson; Donald Landon; Carl Staat; Randy Wabeke; Jim Young; and Kalvin Klotz.

A Funny Thing Happened
on the Way to the (Forum) Pick-up Warehouse
(According to Joe Owen)

One of the most humorous events occurred during the merger with Parts Warehouse in Michigan in 1986. Temple, Sam, Dick Egan, and I were traveling together visiting PWC's CARQUEST Auto Parts stores, as was our custom. On our way back to Bay City we decided to stop by PWC's pick-up warehouse in Flint, Michigan. Dick Egan, PWC's sales manager was driving and Sam was sitting on the passenger side in the front seat. Temple and I were in the back catching up on our reading.

As we approached Flint, there were several choices of exits from the interstate 75 to downtown Flint. Although preoccupied with our reading, we couldn't help noticing that Dick and Sam were not sure which exit to take. Knowing the embarrassment facing them not knowing how to find their own warehouse location, they were hopeful that they could find it without Temple or me knowing of their disorientation. However, after missing the last exit opportunity it was obvious that neither Dick nor Sam had a clue on how to find their pick-up warehouse.

Temple remarked, "You know Joe, I'm not sure we should buy a company when the owner can't find one of his three warehouses."

We have never let Sam Rogers forget that day and we enjoyed sharing the story with Sam's many friends. —Joe Owen

I got to know Bobby Rogers through our CAR-QUEST affiliation, and I got to know Sam Rogers, when, with our wives, we were guests of Hub Moog and Jim Busseyhead of Moog Automotive at Hilton Head for the Heritage Golf Tournament

for several years. Following Al's tragic accident, we were fortunate to have the opportunity to acquire such a great company. The incredible talent that Rogers had attracted has played a major role in the growth of GPI. The best included Fred Kotcher, Rick Guirlinger, Wayne Lavrack, Ken Karber, J.R. Roth, and others.

No former owner has remained more loyal to our company than Sam Rogers. At a young 86 years, he still visits, golfs, and dines with our key customers. PDW has been a great contributor to GPI's success.
—Temple Sloan Jr.

THE FOCHTMAN COMPANY
1987
Northwest Michigan

It all began in 1928 with the Fochtman Motor Co., located in Petoskey, Michigan. The dealership sold Essex and Graham Paige automobiles, as well as Hi-Speed Gas from pumps in front of the dealership building.

L. W. (Lou) Fochtman founded the company and was joined by his brother Eugene Fochtman in the late 1930s. In 1937, auto parts were added to the dealership. Edward Fochtman, Eugene's son, played a key role in auto parts development in the early days. David Fochtman, Lou's son, joined in 1942 and Vincent A. Fochtman started in the Traverse City store in 1950.

The Fochtmans were business pioneers and in the early years were also involved in the department store business. In later years, the company evolved into four divisions: automotive, industrial, welding, and janitorial/paper.

The Fochtman family, especially Vince who served as president of Michigan Automotive Wholesalers and president of the Automotive Service Industry Association, were active in industry activities.

The automotive division consisted of auto parts stores located in the following cities in Michigan: Petoskey, Traverse City, Alpena, Gaylord, Charlevoix, Cheboygan, Boyne City, Grayling, Kalkaska, Sault St. Marie, and Hillman.

Over the years, Sam Rogers had maintained a close relationship with Dave and Vince Fochtman. In mid-1986 Sam opened a discussion about the future of their company and an exit strategy for the two of them. These discussions were picked-up by key GPI management people in Bay City and Raleigh. A workable plan was carefully implemented allowing the current Fochtman store managers to either buy an interest in the stores they managed and become a joint venture partner with GPI or to buy the store outright, with GPI financial assistance, after it was changed to CARQUEST. The plan also allowed both Vince and David to retire completely.

All 11 stores were changed to CARQUEST; all were bought by Fochtman managers except those in Alpena and Grayling. GPI bought Alpena and became JV partner with Ken Tenniswood who had managed the store for years. GPI also bought Grayling and became JV partner with Dan Fochtman who likewise had managed the store. Dan Fochtman eventually became a regional vice president for 113 joint venture stores for GPI.

As independent CARQUEST stores, this group ranks among the most successful served by GPI. Mark and Dave Peterson acquired the Petoskey store, which they had managed for Fochtman, and now they own four CARQUEST stores. Equally successful was Don Landon who bought the Fochtman store he managed in Cheboygan and today also owns a CARQUEST store in Indian River. Jim Fochtman bought the store he managed in Kalkaska, worked hard, retired, and sold the store to GPI. Scott Fochtman did likewise with the Traverse City store and is a joint venture partner with GPI in that city.

Dale Holzchu in Gaylord and Mike Fochtman in Hillman both bought the Fochtman stores they managed and both were successful independent CARQUEST Auto Parts store owners. Dale Holzchu sold his Gaylord store to GPI in 2004 and became a JV partner managing the store.

Fred Kotcher was vice president of sales of the GPI Michigan division. Fred quarterbacked the Fochtman/CARQUEST conversion and every facet was implemented with perfection. The transaction was an incredible success, not only for GPI but for the Fochtman team who purchased the stores.

From that July day in 1987 at the Traverse City Country Club, when Joe Owen, Fred Kotcher, and I met with Dave Fochtman, Vince Fochtman, and Vic Cilke to finalize the merger talks Sam Rogers had begun a year earlier, and bring the 11 Fochtman Motor Parts stores into the CARQUEST organization, until December 10 of that year when the Petoskey warehouse and store, as the last of the group to unfurl the CARQUEST signs and banners, completed the changeover task, the Michigan CARQUEST team had committed every possible resource to an amazing project that no one in the GPI organization had ever attempted. The Michigan organization had just become part of GPI in July 1986. Two field teams, one headed by Dick Egan, sales manager of the Bay City DC, and one headed by Frank Howard, sales manager of the Lansing DC, each tackled a complete store changeover every three weeks. The schedule called for them to completely swap every bit of merchandise in the store, convert the computer system, merchandise the display area, change the building signs, introduce the store employees to CARQUEST and train them on the new product lines and computer, meet with all the store's customers to introduce the CARQUEST program, while keeping the store open for business and not missing a sale in a two-week period. The following week each team member would return to their respective sales territories and other duties to attend to the rest of our customer base, and then

From left to right: Edward Fochtman, L.W. Fochtman, Eugene Fochtman, Vince Fochtman, and David Fochtman, all took part in the family business, the Fochtman Company.

it was off to the next two Fochtman stores. From late September to early December, every GPI Michigan Division DC salesman, JCON manager, and DC and administrative support associate stayed focused on the huge task, foregoing vacations, birthdays, high school football games, and the like. But when it was over, GPI had announced its presence to the state of Michigan like no one could have ever imagined. This would rank at the top of successful transactions in which we have participated.

—Temple Sloan Jr.

KENTUCKY JOBBERS SUPPLY
1988
Lexington, Kentucky

Negotiations for the purchase of Kentucky Jobbers Supply based in Lexington, Kentucky, were completed March 28, 1988, which brought to 12 the number of distribution centers within the General Parts family. Jack Creamer, at Distribution Marketing Service, was tremendous in facilitating the negotiations with the owners, the Alghanim family in Kuwait.

While stationed in Fort Zachary in Louisville, Kentucky, after World War I, Joe Wombwell received a letter from his family in Bonham, Texas, telling him that the cotton crop had failed and that he would have to stay in Kentucky to make his living, as there was nothing in Texas for him.

After being discharged from the Army, he remained in Louisville where he found employment with a company that sold auto and truck parts. In

1923, with $500 in his pocket Joe bought Saylor Auto Parts in Lexington, Kentucky. He immediately changed the name to Wombwell Automotive Parts.

In 1927, Barkley Storey had come to Lexington from Alabama to start the first "Ford U-Drive It" rental car business. The rental business did not live up to his expectations so he sold the business and became a partner with Joe in Wombwell Automotive Parts.

Joe Wombwell died in 1931 and Stanley Rees, who had been one of Wombwell's customers in Cynthiana, Kentucky, joined Storey as part owner.

Before Rees died in 1937 he had opened 10 branch stores in Central and Eastern Kentucky. After Rees' death, Storey purchased all outstanding stock in the company, reorganized it and changed the name to Womwell Automotive Parts Co., Inc.

In 1960, Storey sold the company to five long-time employees—Paul Shaw, Roy Adams, W. P. Smith, W. B. Warren, and Russell Huffman who started with the company in 1943. Smith became president; Adams, vice president of marketing and sales; Shaw, vice president of purchasing; Warren, vice president of finance; and Huffman, manager of company store operations.

Shaw retired in 1967 and the four stockholders had a strong desire to sell their stock. The company was sold to Curtis Noll Corp. In 1974, a warehouse company, the Kentucky Jobbers Supply, was formed.

Curtis Noll named Adams as president and he ran the company until his retirement in December 1976. Huffman assumed the title of president in December 1977.

Ownership changed to Congoleum Corporation in 1978 and again to AI Automotive in 1982. The AI Corporation consisted of the Alghanim family from Kuwait. AI also purchased Autowise Warehouse located in Kentucky.

The strength of Kentucky Jobber's Supply was its 34 company-owned auto parts stores. Without question, some of the finest store managers within the GPI JV store group became a part of GPI with this merger. Some of the top performers were

Russell Huffman was one of the owners of Womwell Automotive Parts, which later became Kentucky Jobbers Supply.

Reed Roberts, Lacky Peavy, L. J. Hampton, Bobby Combs, William "Dub" Hedrick, and Pat McIntyre. On the distribution center side, Kyle Bugg and Neale Browning deserve mention. Huffman was a tremendous help in implementing GPI systems with the KJS distribution center and with the store group.

When it became apparent that the AI Corporation was not performing up to the Alghanim family's expectations, I called our friend, Jack Creamer, to ask his help in meeting the New York representatives of the family to see if we could acquire their Kentucky operation. While I did not know Russell Huffman, we had a number of mutual friends who spoke highly of him and his former company. There was no CARQUEST presence in Kentucky, except the Southern area of the state, through our Nashville operation. With Jack Creamer's help, we were successful. When I met Russell Huffman, his opening comment was, "Why did you buy this company as it has not made money in years?" With Russell's help

Joe Wombwell established Wombwell Automotive Parts in 1923 in Lexington, Kentucky. Ownership changed a number of times before GPI purchased the company, then called the Kentucky Jobbers Supply, in 1988.

and a core of great store managers, Kentucky has made a strong contribution to GPI.

—Temple Sloan Jr.

SERVICE PARTS WAREHOUSE & KEENAN AUTO PARTS
1990
Albany, Georgia

The Keenan saga began in 1914 when P.A. Keenan, a young man, came to Georgia from New York to work in the development of pecan orchards for the United and Empire-Georgia Peach companies, companion Yankee-financed ventures. His

job played out after a few years but instead of returning north, Keenan opened a blacksmith business, the Empire Smithing Company in Albany, Georgia, in 1914, and shortly moved the business into the Old Bridge Hall Building at 112 N. Front St. The main business was shoeing mules and horses, putting spokes and felloes, setting tires on wheels, sharpening plows, laying picks, welding in a coal fire axel subs on wagons and buggy axels, building log carts and wheels, repairing wagons, including circus wagons and on automobiles, welding springs, and straightening axles. Blacksmithing was a good business and at one time, 16 men were employed.

Then Henry Ford put the Model T out in quantity—roadsters or touring cars could be delivered for $395. After the purchase, various accessories were available to make it a complete car, such as a modern windshield assembly, horn, windshield wiper, foot accelerator, or a muffler cut-out. These types of purchases added a new line of work to the blacksmithing business as repairs were made to Fords and other cars. Additionally, old cars were bought for rebuilding and resale. The blacksmithing business still thrived but the day was beginning to belong to the automobile.

In the post-World War I period, steel mills were hungry for scrap and Keenan bought old cars, tractors, and saw mills, took off the resalable parts and

Above: P.A. Keenan, on left, running down a ramp out of Bridge Hall, circa 1919. Below: A managers' meeting was held in the Keenan Building in 1964.

sold the scrap. The proceeds from these sales allowed him to enter the auto parts business. He was prepared when parts manufacturers and automobile manufacturers were looking for distribution.

Wanting to serve their customers better, in 1934 branch stores were opened by Keenan in Moultrie, Bainbridge, Fitzgerald, and Americus, Georgia. And in early 1946, stores were opened in Cuthbert, Blakely, Caino, Hawkinsville, and Montezuma.

Paul Keenan, above left, and his father, P.A. Keenan, above right, built Service Parts Warehouse & Keenan Auto Parts.

Years earlier, Keenan Auto Parts Co., had become the first NAPA jobber in Georgia, outside of Genuine Parts Company, the NAPA distributor in Atlanta. Carlyle Fraser, owner of Genuine Parts Company, and P.A. Keenan were good friends and worked closely together until a dispute occurred between their companies in 1954, which resulted in Keenan opening up his own parts warehouse.

During the 1950s growth in the number of auto parts jobbing stores grew rapidly. Keenan recognized the need to boost sales by redistributing parts to the independent jobbers and, in 1959, established Service Parts Warehouse.

The following management changes were made in 1961: C. Howard Hunt moved up to president of the Keenan Stores while G. C. "Preacher" McRainie became president of Service Parts Warehouse Corp., Jim Jarrett became sales manager.

When P. A. Keenan died September 4, 1978, his son Paul A. Keenan assumed the responsibility of CEO. Paul left his profession as a lawyer to manage Service Parts Warehouse and Keenan Auto Parts Stores.

Service Parts Warehouse was located on Greenvale Avenue in Albany. Executive offices for the company were headquartered in an addition to the historic Bridge Hall Building, a two-story pre-Civil War structure built beside the Flint River by Nelson Tift. The Bridge Hall Building was designed so it could collect tolls and control traffic on the bridge in the early days of Albany's economic growth.

The merger with General Parts, Inc. was finalized on June 1, 1990. At that time, Frank Ahouse was president and general manager. John Weinmann Sr. was in charge of operations, Vernon Norris was independent stores sales manager, Olen Baucom was inventory manager, and Orville Parrish was controller. With assistance of these and a strong group of Keenan store managers, the merger went smoothly.

Paul Keenan became good friends with Joe Owen and myself after joining CARQUEST. Paul's strong family pride made the sale of his company very difficult for him. Once he made the decision, he was fully supportive during the integration process. Our friendship has continued to this day.
—Temple Sloan Jr.

INDIANA PARTS WAREHOUSE
1991
Indianapolis, Indiana

In 1945, Marty Larner returned to New York from World War II. He wanted to start a business and saw in the *Wall Street Journal* that an auto parts company, Motive Parts of America, was for sale in Indianapolis, Indiana. He told his wife, Clara, who was raised in Indianapolis, that he was going to look at the business. Two days later, he called Clara from Indianapolis and said, "Start packing, we are moving to Indianapolis." The purchase was completed and Larner started a very successful career building a dynamic auto parts business.

In 1958, Larner saw the need for what he called "a new breed of cat," known as a warehouse distributor. He and Gene Campbell, his assistant and executive vice president, named their new "cat" Indiana Parts Warehouse (IPW) and located it at 840 North Senate Avenue. In 1964, IPW was moved into a six-story building at 225 W. South Street in downtown Indianapolis. Later, a separate warehouse called Indy Specialists was established in Southwest Indianapolis, specializing in high-performance products.

Joe Hughes arrived in Indianapolis during 1960, working for Goodyear Tire & Rubber Company. After beating Larner in a game of handball, Hughes was offered a job with IPW. Hughes started at the bottom, putting up stock and maintaining stock records and purchasing. He was soon positioned

in sales where he earned a reputation as IPW's best salesman.

In 1965, Michiana Parts located in South Bend, Indiana, was purchased. George Stein and Larry Palmer were retained to operate the business.

In 1970, Hughes was appointed president of IPW and subsidiaries, and he also became a stockholder.

Hughes and Temple Sloan Jr. along with Dan Bock of Bobro in New York had developed a close friendship through AWDA activities and in 1973, Joe and Dan joined Temple to form the CARQUEST marketing program.

The Hoosier Dome was built across the street from IPW's main warehouse on South Street. Hughes seized the opportunity and painted a 30-foot CAR-QUEST logo on the six-story, white IPW building. On Sundays when the Indianapolis Colts were playing at the Dome, more than 40,000 fans could view the CARQUEST logo.

Larner was a "people need people" believer. In a speech to IPW auto parts store owners he said, "Here at Indiana Parts Warehouse, we are 'People'

The Indiana Parts Warehouse building on South St. sported the CARQUEST logo, visible from the Hoosier Dome.

Below, from left to right: Joe Hughes, Gene Campbell, and Marty Larner of Indiana Parts Warehouse.

Temple Sloan Jr., left, and Joe Hughes witnessed the "shortest negotiation" in GPI's history when it merged with IPW.

dedicated to provide the most efficient warehousing service of quality automotive parts at the best price. Our future depends on you. We must help you grow and we must grow with you.

"You are the most important 'People' in this chain of distribution. You serve the dealers, independent garages and service repair shops who are battling to keep the vast fleet of public transportation moving. A steady flow of parts must move smoothly from your shelf to these repair outlets. Our job is to make your job easier and more profitable."

Larner died in 1977, and Hughes was faced with trying to purchase the company from the Larner family. Temple Sloan, Jr. assisted Joe in forming an ESOP, which enabled him to buy the Larner family's interest in IPW.

Many key people contributed to the success of IPW and CARQUEST: Marty Larner, Joe Hughes,

Gene Campbell, Carleen Snyder, Karl Allen, Ken Freeman, Willie Cameron, Ron Cooper, Mark Roth, John Hill, Kevin Wilson, Dan McGuire, and Jimmy Keene.

The merger was finalized in April 1991.

My association with IPW goes back to the 1960s when I kept Marty Larner up to all hours of the night learning what was required to be successful in our industry. Through Marty, I met Joe Hughes, who became the epitome of a "good friend." When Joe decided it was time for him to retire, he wanted to merge and not sell. Following the shortest negotiation in our history, Joe has been an incredible advisor, critic, supporter, and friend.

—Temple Sloan Jr.

WORLD SUPPLY CORPORATION
1991
Chicago, Illinois

In May 1939, World Auto Supply Company was established by Andrew Ballum and Basil Hicks on Collins Street in Joliet, Illinois, an industrial town located about 50 miles southwest of Chicago. Ballum and Hicks, who also owned the local gasoline station and grocery store, saw the need for improvement in auto parts distribution. In those days, auto parts stores sold mostly at wholesale prices to repair garages and gasoline stations.

The new business grew as the owners firmly believed in adequate inventories and supreme customer service. In March 1948, World Supply Corporation was incorporated and strictly operated as a wholesale distributor of automotive parts.

By 1952, the company had outgrown its facilities and constructed a new warehouse across the street. In the years that followed, they purchased a building across the alley and another building later behind that building. Those buildings remained the home of World Supply until 1983.

On April 1, 1973, Ballum and Hicks retired and sold the business to Henry Banks and Benjamin Roscrow and the next 18 years were growth years as the company expanded product lines and customer service, and in 1983, moved into a state-of-the-art distribution center in Lemont, Illinois. Roscrow and Banks previously were partners in a tombstone business.

In the late 1980s, Banks retired and sold his share of the business to Roscrow. In 1985, World Supply Corporation joined the CARQUEST Program and continued to experience substantial growth.

In a tongue-in-cheek announcement to the CARQUEST Board about the World Supply merger with GPI, Temple Sloan, Jr. had this to say about Ben Roscrow.

It is very appropriate this morning to recognize a CARQUEST partner who is retiring. Following a successful and outstanding business career and after the sale of his tombstone business, Ben and his former partner purchased World Supply in 1973. I'm told Ben had a real adjustment from the tombstone business, learning to deal with thousands of part numbers, returns, obsolescence, back orders, and all those things that make our business so exciting.

Those of you who know Ben well know how reckless he is with a dollar. After several visits during which we discussed the feasibility of putting World Supply and General Parts together, Ben suggested we go downtown to meet his new attorneys. Now we have had the privilege of merging with some successful people but none with a law firm with 250 partners, occupying the 80th to 85th floors of the Sears Tower. Even a country boy knows when he is in over his head. Well, if you want to reach Ben in the future, he has a corner office on the 85th floor in the Sears Tower.

He's the new financial partner with Keck, Mahin, and Cate.

But seriously, Ben Roscrow is an excellent businessman, totally honest in his dealings with his people, his customers, and his suppliers. The best testimony to Ben is the outstanding group of people he surrounded himself with in building World Supply into a successful company. Just to mention a few, Jeff Lundh, Tom Rafferty, Tom Cantwell, Jeff Fletcher, Don Frankfather, Pam Brinkman, Peggy Hampton, Rodney Pinkston, Paul Zimmerman, and Steve Blanton.

The merger of World Supply was a huge step in developing market share in a gigantic metropolitan market. Much of the success in this venture was because John Martens was convinced to join GPI at the time of the merger. John owned a successful parts store in Libertyville, a Chicago suburb. John was looking for a bigger challenge and John's son Craig and Craig's brother-in-law, Mike Ralston were capable and highly motivated to buy John's Libertyville store and change it to CARQUEST. Today it ranks in the top 10 independent CARQUEST stores served by GPI.

Martens teamed with Jeff Lundh, and they wasted no time

Above from left to right: John Martens and Jeff Lundh helped build World Supply Corporation into a successful company.

Left: Temple Sloan Jr., left, with Ben Roscrow of World Supply Corporation.

putting CARQUEST "on the map" in one of the largest metropolitan markets in the United States.
—Temple Sloan Jr.

TAYLOR PARTS, INC.
1992
South Alabama

In 1908, in the Southern Alabama town of Andalusia, a cotton gin operator named J. M. Taylor saw a better future in automobiles than cotton. To devote his full time to repairing automobiles and gasoline engines, a side line he had practiced several years in the off season, he resigned from the Southern Cotton Oil Company and established the J. M. Taylor Auto Co.

In 1928, four years of poor health prompted Taylor to sell controlling interests to his sons and the business was converted into a fulltime wholesale operation. With Marion D. (Buck) Taylor in charge of sales and Robert Perkins Taylor operating the machine shop, the J. M. Taylor Auto Co. became one of the south's leading automotive wholesale houses.

In 1939, a branch store opened in Panama, Florida, but further expansion plans were curtailed by World War II. The company aided the war effort by conducting a government-sponsored night school for machinists, which operated 24 hours a day to keep vital automobiles, trucks, and tractors rolling.

In 1952, the expansion program got moving. In rapid succession, branches were opened in Fort Walton Beach and Funiak Springs, Florida, and Dothan, Alabama, with others following.

Buck Taylor died in 1961 and was succeeded as president by his son, James M. Taylor II, who had been vice president of sales since 1950. Walter Ray Fowler was made general manager.

In 1968, a new firm, TPS, was organized to serve automotive wholesalers exclusively. James' brother, Riley Taylor, vice president since 1961, became president of TPS. Other officers included Dan Studstill, vice president; and W. M. Till, secretary-treasurer.

In 1972, two key sales people were hired for TPS, Ralph Wells and Darwin Pippin. A few years later, Darwin was promoted to sales manager; he retired in 2001 with 29 years of service. Ralph

From top to bottom: Ralph Wells, Riley Taylor Sr., James Taylor III, and John Taylor of Taylor Parts Inc. The company was sold to GPI in 1992.

Wells achieved the sales manager's position shortly after the merger with GPI.

Meanwhile, in Montgomery, Alabama, Lee Meriwether Jr. who had joined his father Lee Meriwether Sr. in 1950, began to open auto parts branch stores. Lee Sr., like Buck Taylor, was one of Alabama's real pioneers in the parts business having started his business, Genuine Auto Parts in 1929. By 1956, when Lee Sr. retired, Genuine had 10 parts stores in and around Montgomery. In 1971, Lee Jr. opened Automotive Central, Inc., a full-line warehouse to serve his stores and independent auto parts stores.

Taylor Parts needed better market share in Montgomery and in 1979 acquired Auto Parts & Tool Company and P & T Warehouse, both located in Montgomery. Two years later, Lee Jr. merged Automotive Central into the Taylor Company and began to operate as TPS Central. Prior to the merger all of the Genuine stores had been sold, and TPS Central was serving only the independent market in Central and North Alabama. Lee Jr. retired shortly after the GPI merger and died in 2003 after spending several years in the real estate business with his son, Lee Meriwether, III.

In the early 1980s the fourth generation of Taylors entered the firm, James M. Taylor's son, John, and Riley Taylor's son,

From top down: Walter Ray Fowler, Lee Meriweather Jr., and Darwin Pippin, of Taylor Auto Parts.

Bottom: Chris Winters of Pacific Wholesalers Inc., which was merged with GPI in 1992.

Riley, Jr. It was also about this time that marketing programs were surfacing throughout the country and TPS was the founding member of the ALL PRO program, which later became a part of the Alliance Group along with Auto Value and Bumper-To-Bumper.

Since the main thrust of the Taylor Company was toward controlled distribution, Taylor continued to open branches and look for possible store acquisitions. In 1983, East Alabama Auto Parts with seven stores and Parts Distributor's Warehouse were brought into the Taylor Company by merger. Those two companies had been founded by D. B. Jones in 1946 and they controlled a good share of the market in East Alabama. One year later, Taylor Parts acquired Motor Parts & Supply Company located in Mobile, Alabama, and in March 1998, a satellite warehouse was opened in Tallahassee, Florida.

A wealth of auto parts talent came into GPI with the Taylor merger. In addition to those already mentioned, these include Guy Martin, Chandler Ellis, Ashton Wells, Allen Till, Hines Johnson, Hoke Smith, Bubba McDonald, Jay Everage, Walter Scott, Jerry Reynolds, Grant Taylor, and a great group of professional store managers, machine shop per-

sonnel, and store salesmen. John Taylor's leadership ensured the success of this merger.

Following Riley Taylor's untimely death and Jimmy Taylor and Lee Meriwether reaching retirement age, the family decided to pursue the sale of their company. For a number of years, prior to his merger with Taylor Parts, Meriwether's company had been a CARQUEST member.

With Lee's recommendation to the family and Jack Creamer's friendship with Jimmy Taylor, we were given the opportunity to negotiate a successful transaction. It was not easy, as the sons were not fully supportive of the family's decision. Taylor Parts and TPS were successful companies and have been great contributors to GPI. Jimmy Taylor and Lee Meriwether, until their deaths, were strong, loyal supporters and advisors.

—Temple Sloan Jr.

PACIFIC WHOLESALERS, INC.
1992
Portland, Oregon

The history of Pacific Wholesalers began in 1949 with a retail store named Pacific Auto Supply, located in Springfield, Oregon owned by Louis Southworth Sr. In 1952, Southworth opened a second store across the Willamette River in Eugene, and opened a third store the following year in Salem, Oregon. Bud Lawson was hired to call on the independent auto parts store customers.

The three stores continued to grow and in 1956, Pacific Wholesalers, Inc. was formed in Eugene, Oregon, by Louis Sr. and his son, Louis Jr. to warehouse and supply their three stores plus independent parts stores. Louis Jr. and Bud Lawson began calling on independent stores in Southern Oregon and supplied primarily automotive accessory products and certain hard parts lines only to auto parts stores.

It had been said that Louis Jr. had a vision for the aftermarket. He was active in the Oregon Auto Parts Association, AWDA, Distributors Institute, and ASIA. He loved the business.

Pacific Wholesalers continued to grow and in 1960 expanded into a 27,000-square-foot facility. At that time Southworth Sr., decided to retire and Southworth Jr. became president.

In 1962, Chris Winters was hired as a third salesman. The market territory was expanded and in 1964 Southworth Jr. purchased the company from his father. Lawson became the company's first sales manager. The company experienced large sales growth as many manufacturers were closing warehouses in the northwest, and more auto parts stores began purchasing from local warehouses.

The Pacific Wholesalers, Inc., market consisted of Southern Oregon until 1975 when Southworth purchased the Chancelor and Lyon warehouse in Portland, Oregon. Neil Imes, former chancelor and Lyon general manager, was hired to manage the Portland operation. Lawson was appointed vice president and Winters became sales manager. In 1975, Pacific Wholesalers, Inc. joined the Bumper-To-Bumper marketing program.

In the late 1970s, Lawson left Pacific Wholesalers, Inc., and Winters was appointed vice president. In 1976, Troutman and Winters purchased an auto parts store in Eugene, Oregon, and two more stores were added in the next two years.

In 1981, Lou Jr. retired, and Winters became president and appointed Troutman to sales manager. In 1982, Winters acquired Pacific Auto Supply in Eugene from Gordon Harley and combined it with the store presently owned by Pacific Wholesalers, Inc., in Eugene. In January 1983, Troutman and Winters purchased PWI from Louis Jr. The headquarters were moved to Portland and the Eugene warehouse was closed.

In 1989, because of temporary turmoil in the Bumper-To-Bumper program, Pacific Wholesalers, Inc., changed its marketing direction and joined the CARQUEST program. In June 1992, Winters purchased Troutman's interest and became the sole owner of Pacific Wholesalers, Inc. Shortly thereafter Winters merged Pacific Wholesalers, Inc., into General Parts, Inc.

Winters continued with General Parts, Inc., as president of Pacific Wholesalers, Inc., along with his key management team of Dale Morris, John James, Dick Harrington, and Larry Morris.

After joining CARQUEST in 1989, Chris Winters became a good personal friend. That friendship, and his association with our people, gave Chris the comfort of merging his company into GPI.

With GPI, Chris Winters served as division president in two markets and completed his career in Raleigh, managing our company-wide credit exposure.

Chris has been a tremendous team member and has made GPI a better company by his presence.

—Temple Sloan Jr.

NORTHERN INDUSTRIES, INC.
NORTHERN WELDING & SUPPLY COMPANY
1992
Marshfield, Wisconsin

The Northern Auto Supply Company was organized on April 18, 1918, in Marshfield, Wisconsin, with E. M. Lee as one of the stockholders. At the first organizational meeting, Lee was elected secretary, while he continued on with his employment with another firm located in Wausau. In the early years, Northern Auto Supply handled side curtains for touring cars, bumpers (before they became original equipment), visors, sunshields, starting cranks, and luggage carriers.

On February 15, 1919, Lee was asked to take charge of the company. He resigned from the Wausau firm, moved to Marshfield, and was elected president of the corporation.

Lee's capable and aggressive leadership included the 1931 opening of the first branch store in Stevens Point, the 1933 opening of a branch in Rhinelander, and the 1934 purchase of Wausau Auto Equipment Co. In 1935, a store was opened in Wisconsin Rapids, in 1940 another was opened in Merril, in 1943 a Medford store was established, and in 1946 the Neillsville store was founded. The year 1948 brought the opening of the Welding Division at Wausau, a company incorporated as Northern Welding & Supply Co., on March 1, 1951. In 1948, a store opened in Antigo, and in 1953 a branch store was established in Stanley.

The firm was in the process of starting a store in Park Falls when tragedy struck and Lee was killed in an automobile accident near Milwaukee on July 10, 1955.

Lee's son Lawrence M. "Lorrie" Lee became chief executive and president. At that time, another son, Francis J. Lee was elected vice president.

Under their direction, stores were added and in 1964, there were 18. The business consisted

Left: Northern Industries Inc.'s distribution center in Marshfield, Wisconsin.

Bottom, from left to right: Don Komis began his career with Northern Industries working in the warehouse in 1959. Charles Harwick started as a delivery driver in 1955.

of wholesaling parts, accessories, and equipment in about a 150-mile radius of Marshfield.

Recognizing the need for the service and marketing by parts stores, Distributors Warehouse, Incorporated (DWI), was founded in 1958. Francis was elected president and served DWI until he died in 1973.

Don L. Komis began employment with Northern Industries, Inc. on December 18, 1959. He started in the warehouse, moved to inventory control, and then the general office before moving to Wisconsin Rapids as a counterman. After that, he was a jobber salesman and later returned to Marshfield to become store coordinator and office manager for all of the companies.

At the time of Francis's death in 1973, Komis was named general manager and served in that capacity until Lorrie's retirement in 1982. At that time he became chief operating officer and general manager for all the companies and held those responsibilities and titles until the merger with General Parts.

Charles Harwick started as a delivery driver for the Northern store in Rhinelander in 1955. In 1959, he worked as a store salesman. Shortly after the formation of DWI in 1961, Harwick joined Leroy Gosh to make up the DWI sales force. From his first assignment as district sales manager headquartered in Iron Mountain in the upper peninsula of Michigan, Harwick earned his next promotion with hard work, passion for the business, and respect for the customer. After Gosh left the company in 1971, Harwick became DWI sales manager. Later he assumed full responsibility for all DWI marketing and developed a store marketing program, called "Red Car."

With the GPI merger, a Wisconsin division was formed with Komis as president and Harwick as vice president of sales. Also, Dale Dockter became general manager of the Welding and Carbonics Company.

The northern merger was not only timely, it presented GPI with the strongest team possible in obtaining immediate market share through independent auto parts stores and company-owned stores. The organizational strength throughout the company was remarkable.

This history of strong leadership resulted in Northern Industries becoming one of the most successful and strongest regional companies in the automotive aftermarket.

Northern Welding and Supply Company

Northern Welding and Supply was a division of Northern Industries and was included by GPI in the August 1992 transaction. Its growth had been stagnant in recent years. Ron Adkins was acquainted with Dockter through various welding industry events and recommended that he manage Northern Welding. Dockter accepted the offer and immediately embarked on a plan for growth.

One of the plans was to be more aggressive in selling carbon dioxide. Kevin Budnik was hired as a fulltime outside salesman calling on hospitals

and laser cutting companies. Sales of carbon dioxide took off and have never slowed. At the end of 1992, annual sales at Northern Welding were $3.1 million and at the end of 2004, annual sales were $8.1 million. Seven hospitals have long-term contracts with Northern for oxygen and other gases.

Northern Welding sells argon, argon mixes, nitrogen, oxygen, acetylene, and carbon dioxide. They also sell welding and cutting equipment, dry ice, and fire extinguishers. There are four stores and 41 employees serving most of Wisconsin and the upper peninsula of Michigan.

According to Dockter, "The bottom line is good people, good product, and good service."

Ron Wehrenberg and I recognized, for many years, the quality and strength of Northern Automotive in Wisconsin. It would be a natural fit with our Minneapolis operation.

For 10 consecutive years, sometimes at the AWDA meeting in Las Vegas or a hotel in Minneapolis, we met with Don Komis, discussing the future and the quality of our companies and how we would be stronger as one company. As with all good family-owned companies, family circumstances determine the timing of any exit strategy. Don Komis and his team delivered a great group of people to GPI, who have continued to make the Wisconsin group number one, or number two in GPI year after year.

Dale Dockter became general manager of the Welding and Carbonics Company after the merger with GPI.

A highlight of the merger talks was John Gardner's advice to Father Henry Lee on creating a trust to serve his wishes to benefit retiring Catholic nuns and avoiding taxes on his part of the sale.

The Northern transaction is an excellent example of persistence and patience.

—Temple Sloan Jr.

MOTOR SUPPLY WAREHOUSE COMPANY
1993
Belle Plaine, Iowa

The growth of Motor Supply Company was the result of continuous determined adherence to sound principles established when Edwin and Lyman Blanchard moved from Waterloo, Iowa, to Belle Plaine to start a machine shop. In 1946, they expanded from buying parts for the machine shop to a full jobbing store called Belle Plaine Motor Supply. The principles of service and merchandising were implanted early in the history of Motor Supply Company.

In 1952, they purchased a jobber store in Vinton. Two additional stores were incorporated to form Belle Plaine and Vinton Motor Supply Company in 1960. In 1962, a store opened in Toledo, Iowa, followed one month later by the purchase of a store in Osage.

Beryle Blanchard, Ed's son, transferred from outside sales to start a warehouse operation supplying its four stores in 1966. The operation grew to become a full-line warehouse distributor. In 1969, the warehouse was incorporated as Motor Supply Warehouse (MSW) Company. MSW operated as an independent warehouse. In 1980, MSW joined the Bumper-To-Bumper program group.

Ed retired in 1979 and Beryle began serving as president of the MSW organization. Lyman retired in 1984 and his son, Dan, became executive vice president. Dan's primary responsibility was the implementation of the computer system.

Between 1980 and 1988 eight additional stores were acquired. In 1991, Gene & Chris, Inc., in Waverly, Iowa, owned by Gene and Chris Ford, entered into a joint venture that was profitable for both corporations.

Beryle had this to say in a memo to the MSW employees: "For sometime we've watched the growth of General Parts and CARQUEST. Recently, we've spent a lot of time analyzing their business philosophies and marketing direction. We believe this merger will be compatible in every respect and gives us the opportunity to provide the products and service so necessary for success today."

Temple Sloan, Jr. was quoted in the GPI "General Idea": "It would have been difficult, if not near impossible, to have found an organization with business philosophies closer to General Parts, Inc., than Motor Supply Warehouse Company of Belle Plaine, Iowa."

Beryle Blanchard was introduced to me by Jack Creamer. Motor Parts became the foundation of our growth in Iowa and our new distribution center in Des Moines. Beryle's untimely death prevented him from witnessing the growth and success of his company. His son, Doug, and his good customer, now partner, Gene Ford have contributed greatly to GPI.

—Temple Sloan Jr.

FREMONT ELECTRIC COMPANY
December 1993
Seattle, Washington

Fremont Electric had been a leader in the distribution business since it was established in 1915 as the first battery charging station. It was located at the present site of its corporate headquarters in Seattle, Washington's Fremont District.

From left to right: Ed Blanchard, Beryle Blanchard, and Doug Blanchard of Motor Supply Warehouse Company.

As Fremont developed, it became an auto electric repair shop and expanded into a parts business. It was one of the original Automotive Electric Association (AEA), which eventually became the AEA Service Division of ASIA (Automotive Service Industry Association). The company operated as a service distributor for many years, becoming well-known in the Northwest.

In 1946, Fremont became an Onan Generator Distributor in Washington, Northern Idaho, and Alaska. It was the oldest Onan distributor in the United States.

In 1985, the Fremont warehouses were located at the Seattle Headquarters in the Fremont District; at Lay & Nord in Yakima and Pasco, Washington; and an industrial branch in Anchorage, Alaska. Other facilities include Bailey Service, a parts store in Aberdeen; Lake Stevens Auto Parts in Everett, Washington; and Lay & Nord purchased in 1966.

At the time of acquisition by General Parts, Fremont operated a distribution center and 10 company-owned CARQUEST Auto Parts stores. They employed more than 170 people and supplied 65 CARQUEST independently owned auto parts stores.

Together with Moore M. McKinley, Jr., members of the management team, Buz McKinley, Gary Pratt, and Jim Bigelow had served on various CARQUEST Committees and contributed greatly in developing CARQUEST Programs.

McKinley continued with GPI in an advisory capacity and was instrumental in the GPI acquisition of Skaggs Automotive, which provided significant presence in the Spokane market. He served as chairman of the newly formed Pacific Division until his death in 1996. His guidance and his friendship will forever be remembered.

If one would make a list of the truly outstanding human beings who we have been privileged to know, Moore McKinley would definitely be on this list. His courageous battle with cancer was an inspiration to us all. While his son, Buz, and son-in-law, Gary Pratt, helped us through the transaction, we were disappointed when they chose to leave the industry. Moore would be proud of our new DC in Kent and the growth of our Seattle group.

—Temple Sloan Jr.

SERVICE PARTS WAREHOUSE
& 688 PARTS SERVICE, INC.
January 1994
Baton Rouge, Louisiana

With the merger of 688 Parts Service, Inc./Service Parts Warehouse of Baton Rouge, Louisiana, nineteen 688 Stores and 18 independent jobbers were converted to the CARQUEST marketing program. Aubrey Weil, with his store management and sales team, led the successful conversion of the 688 Store Group.

688 Parts Service was established in 1926 by L. E. Simoneaux, a bulk oil jobber who repackaged bulk oil in five gallon cans and sold them to gasoline stations. In 1927, 688 Parts Service added the standard motor service ignition product line and started in the automotive parts replacement business. Since the phone number was "688," his only employee Wallace Voorhies answered the telephone as "688 Parts"—that was how the company name was born.

In February 1951, the business was sold to George E. Tricou Sr. The business operated as a sole proprietorship until 1954 when he added his son, Mark, and Roy K. Rogillio as partners.

The partnership was incorporated into 688 Parts Service, Inc., in 1955. Shortly after they opened the first branch store on Plank Road, the focus was directed toward building company-owned jobber stores and independent jobbers.

The redistribution business started in 1959 and they began servicing jobbers within a 150-mile radius of Baton Rouge. Their jobber business continued to grow and a warehouse was established January 1, 1979, to serve jobber stores exclusively.

From 1955 to 1985, the growth rate was about 20 percent per year; it later leveled off because of the collapse of the oil industry in South Louisiana.

General Parts was deeply indebted to George Tricou for his support and guidance during the transaction.

Through the efforts of Dennis Fox, we were able to get to know George Tricou. Following a number of meetings, George and his partners made the decision to pursue the sale of their successful company to us. George, his son Mark, and Aubrey Weil were key to our good transaction.

Our old friend, Rudy Flashner, of the former CARQUEST member in New Orleans (Borden-Aicklen), introduced us to several acquisitions and key people during this time. One was Vic Hymel, who was a great partner and controller in several GPI accounting offices.

Following several acquisitions and the consolidation of our Jackson, Mississippi, distribution center into a new facility in Baton Rouge. Baton Rouge, has become a large successful group within GPI.
—Temple Sloan Jr.

Above, left to right: Moore McKinley and Buz McKinley, of Fremont Electric Company, contributed greatly to the CARQUEST program.

Left: George Tricou and Aubrey Weil ensured the sale of Service Parts Warehouse & 688 Parts Service to GPI.

DIVERSIFIED AUTOMOTIVE DISTRIBUTORS, INC.
October 1994
Kansas City, Missouri

The Myers Tire Service Co. was established in Joplin, Missouri, in 1917 by W. D. Myers Sr. In 1927, the company expanded into Kansas and Oklahoma as Myers Tri-State Supply Co., and then in 1931 into Kansas City with the purchase of Motor Supply Co., to become a new entity called Myers Motor Supply Co. Myers Sr. died in 1938 and his son W. D. Myers Jr. (Bill) became president. By 1956, Myers Motor Supply had established 36 company jobber stores throughout Missouri, Kansas, Oklahoma, and Arkansas.

A central warehouse facility was established in Kansas City in 1956. In 1962, the jobber stores were sold and a new company that would be a 100 percent warehouse distributor operation, called Automotive Distributors, Inc. (ADI), was formed. It was located at 3155 Terrace Street in Kansas City, Missouri.

In 1979, W. D. Myers, III (Dan) was elevated from sales manager to president. His father, Bill, became chairman of the board. During 1985, Dan became CEO and purchased his father's equity.

Martin G. Brown acquired the assets of ADI through Martin G. Brown Associates, Inc., on January 3, 1989. At the same time the name was changed to Diversified Automotive Distributors, Inc. (DADI). DADI operated two divisions—ADA Warehouse Division and CARQUEST Auto Parts stores (Kansas City). The store group concentrated on store operations in the Kansas City–metro area. Between 1989 and 1994, the customer list was reduced to 110 customers with 98 CARQUEST Auto Parts stores purchasing 99 plus percent of the sales volume.

Among the fine group of DADI associates, Al Minnis and Sue Weland were exceptional performers and continued to contribute greatly to GPI's success while holding responsible management positions. Brown continued with GPI in a consulting position.

For many years, Marty Brown had been both a friend and a fierce competitor. As the founder of the Bumper-To-Bumper marketing group and Keystone Automotive in Kansas City, Chairman of AWDA,

From top to bottom: Al Minnis, Martin Brown, and Sue Weland of Diversified Automotive Distributors, Inc.

Photo courtesy of Olan Mills.

Marty was a leader in our industry. Prior to his forming Bumper-To-Bumper, we had tried to convince Marty to join CARQUEST after acquiring DADI in 1989.

Marty and his team did an incredible job of turning the company around. With the subsequent acquisition of The Equipment Company in 1996, our Kansas City group has been a consistent performer in GPI. Marty has continued to be a good friend and advisor since our transaction.

—Temple Sloan Jr.

SUSSEN, INC.
January 1996
Cleveland, Ohio / Buffalo, New York

Joseph J. Sussen began his business career on February 13, 1919, at the age of 19. His first company, a sole proprietorship, was Standard Automotive Machine Company. He borrowed $2,000 and began manufacturing an automotive stoplight that was sold to supply stores and repair shops. In January 1921, he started the Sussen Rubber Company. The new operation and the addition of automotive equipment, body shop supplies, and refinishing paints and materials marked the beginning of the company's growth.

Many small businesses of the late 1930s to the mid-1950s saw a recovery from the Great Depression and the post-war boom. Those years firmly established Sussen Incorporated as a leader in the automotive aftermarket in the greater Cleveland area.

After graduating from John Carroll University and serving as an officer in the United States Marine Corps., Dan Sussen joined his father in the family business. By the early 1960s, Dan had inherited day-to-day control and saw the company grow rapidly into one of the largest distributors of automotive parts in Ohio.

Left: In the early 1960s, Dan Sussen inherited day-to-day control of Sussen, Inc.

Bottom: Alice and Pete Kornafel Sr. took over Hatch Grinding Company in 1951.

In 1982, Dan purchased the Jobber Supply Distribution Center in Columbus, Ohio, together with the PJ Group of parts stores. In 1986, the company acquired Avro Auto Warehouse in Buffalo, New York, the CARQUEST member, along with its company-owned stores, which completed the plan to cover the northern two-thirds of Ohio, western Pennsylvania, western New York, and western West Virginia. Avro Auto Warehouse was owned by Seymour Hesch and his brother Morrie.

There were many people who had an impact on the growth of Sussen Incorporated. Besides Joe Sussen there were Jean Tacaks, Mary Buzak, John Pippin, Bernard Lindway, Frank Guarino, Bill Ostrum, and Bill Fording.

Dan brought the company into the CARQUEST marketing group in 1976 and was active in the organization. In 1996, the Sussen family merged the company into GPI and Dan continued in an advisory capacity serving on the General Parts, Inc., board of directors through 2003.

When Dan Sussen and his family made the decision to merge their 75-year-old company with GPI, it opened a great opportunity for growth in Ohio. Our new 123,750-square-foot distribution center was built in Brunswick, Ohio, and also serves as the backup site for our computer centers. From 1996 through 2003, Dan Sussen served as a director of GPI and his insight and advice helped GPI to continue its growth.
—Temple Sloan Jr.

HATCH GRINDING COMPANY
April 1996
Denver, Colorado

Hatch Grinding Company began as a machine shop in the 1930s by Charlie Hatch. In addition to automotive work, Hatch did a lot of general machine work and was equipped with a large lathe and a milling machine. He sharpened the belt slitter blades for Gates Rubber Company and made fire hose nozzles for the Denver Fire Department.

Pete Kornafel Sr., a salesman for American Hammered Piston Ring Company, was assigned to the Hatch Grinding account. Kornafel eventually was promoted to western regional manager for American Hammered, and in 1950 was offered the position of national sales manager, which would require relocating to Baltimore, Maryland. Just before Kornafel Sr. accepted the promotion, Hatch called, and said he was ready to retire and wanted to sell his shop. Kornafel Sr. purchased the shop in 1951, and by year-end 1952, the store had annual sales of $141,000. Kornafel Sr.'s real love was parts and he enthusiastically began building a parts inventory.

Kornafel Sr.'s wife Alice kept books for Hatch Grinding at home and his son, Pete Kornafel Jr. started working in the shop at age seven.

The company's first big break came in the early 1950s when Federal-Mogul and Victor Gaskets signed Hatch directly to distribute their products.

By the mid-1950s Hatch was handling 15 product lines, including Columbus Shock Absorbers, AP Exhaust, Airtex, Republic Gear, Perfect Circle, Victor Gaskets, Federal-Mogul, Toledo, American Hammered, Sterling Pistons, Zollner Pistons, Neihoff Ignition and Eis Brake Parts. The company also carried DuPont paint.

Pete Jr. and Annie Lindsey were married in 1967, and he initially worked in Detroit, Michigan, for Ford Product Planning. Pete Sr. died in 1968 at the age of 56 and Alice ran the company from 1968 to 1970. Pete Jr. and Annie moved to Denver in June 1970, and he became president of Hatch Grinding Company at age 26. Annie began full-time work at Hatch in November 1971.

During 1971, when the last machinist retired, the machine shop was closed. In 1972 Hatch introduced one of the first Engine Kit Programs east of California, which was extremely successful. Hatch moved to

Above right: Charlie Hatch, founder of Hatch Grinding Company. This photo was taken outside the Hatch Grinding Company, circa 1940.

Above left: Annie and Pete Kornafel Jr. broached the subject of merging Hatch Grinding Company with GPI with Temple Sloan Jr.

become a full-line distributor and upgraded several product lines.

Hatch moved into a new 75,000-square-foot distribution center in January 1975, which was equipped with state-of-the-art material-handling equipment.

In 1979 Hatch joined CARQUEST and became the group's 16th member. This marked a shift from an engine parts specialists/warehouse distributor to a program-selling/warehouse distributor.

In January 1982, Hatch purchased the Tepee Parts Warehouse located in Albuquerque, New Mexico, from Waukesha Pearce Industries.

Alice Kornafel died unexpectedly in 1987.

Pete Jr. and Annie both were involved in aftermarket activity and served separate terms as chairman of AWDA, and in 1988 Peter was honored as AWDA's "Man of the Year."

During the Kornafel family ownership, Hatch Grinding grew from four employees and $141,000 in sales to 200 employees and $35 million in sales, and it became the largest locally owned warehouse distributor in the Rocky Mountain states.

The Hatch merger was a major transaction for GPI. Pete and Annie Kornafel had built a quality company and surrounded themselves with good people. To mention a few there was Jack Moritz, Jim Hazlett, Mike Everett, Mike Riess, Ed Wortman, Frank

Lindsey, Joe Pollack, Robert Rhyne, Louise Veasman, and Dede Geary. Following the merger with GPI, Annie became vice president of operations for the GPI western division and Pete became president of the CARQUEST Corporation serving until 2001. He continues to serve on the board of the CARQUEST Corporation and the International Group, Inc.

Over Labor Day weekend in 1995, Pete and Annie Kornafel were our guests in Montana. Sitting on the porch, they broached the subject of merging Hatch Grinding and GPI. Their comments came as a total surprise. With their age, I felt such a decision was a number of years off.

The impact of this decision had far-reaching impacts on GPI's direction: i.e., (a) the number of Hatch's customers ready to retire resulted in a total change in Hatch's business mix, from more than 95% independent volume to a major joint venture store group; (b) opened the door for Pete to become president of CARQUEST for six years as a result of

Jim Green sold The Equipment Company to General Parts in 1996 when he retired.

Dan Bock's retirement; (c) introduced us to Jack Moritz who became president of CARQUEST Canada, LTD for two years, converting our Canadian company to CARQUEST and bringing a diverse group together as one company; (d) paved the way for our acquisition of Big A Auto Parts in Denver, which would more than double our Denver company; (e) opened the same opportunity with Big A Auto Parts in Albuquerque; (f) Annie became vice president of operations for several critical years during the Big A transitions; (g) Pete became and continues as a director of GPI (now TIG) and has us given invaluable advice in the transition of our IT world in light of the rapid growth of our company.

Needless to say, sitting on our porch in Montana, drinking a Coors Light, not even Pete could have envisioned all that would follow.

—Temple Sloan Jr.

THE EQUIPMENT COMPANY
April 1996
Kansas, Missouri

The Equipment Company was established in 1911 and consisted initially of two companies; Equipment Company and The Faeth Company. At this time there were six owners. Jim Green bought the company in 1961 from his mother. Jim's father became involved in the ownership after working for Cummings Diesel. Later he left Cummings and bought the L. D. Fox Company, a wagon jobber being supplied by the Equipment Company.

At the time Jim bought the company, annual sales were $180,000. The business was located in a two-story building on Walnut Street in Kansas City and consisted of a total of 5,000 square feet. The inventory consisted of one-half auto parts and one-half equipment. Jim sold off the equipment and directed his energy to the distribution of parts.

Jim had extreme difficulty in purchasing product lines direct from manufacturers. Delco agreed to sell him but when the order was due to arrive he was advised by Delco that they would not sell to him. In the late 1970s there

was a trend among parts distributors to join marketing program groups. After research, Jim elected to start his own. In 1980, he started APA (Auto Parts Association) and hired an advertising man, Robert Luna, to run the APA Group. Luna eventually left and Joe Buehler was hired to run APA.

Jim continued to build a highly successful company and in 1996 decided to retire. GPI was deeply appreciative that Jim picked it when selling The Equipment Company in 1996. Along with the merger with Marty Brown's DADI in 1994, GPI has enjoyed a significant presence in the Kansas City market.

In early 1996, Jim Green called Raleigh when I was out of town and talked to John Gardner. He told John to tell me that we needed to buy his company and that I would disagree, but to tell me that he knew the KC market better than I did. John and I traveled to Kansas City and met Jim in Howard Hughes' old TWA office at the downtown Kansas City airport. It goes without saying that Jim was right and the combination of our Kansas City company and The Equipment Company would not only make a large company but a very successful one. No one has ever worked harder or lived up to his commitments during the transition more than Jim Green did with GPI.

—Temple Sloan Jr.

PSC DISTRIBUTION, INC.
October 1996
Phoenix, Arizona

In 1964, Jim and Penny Eaton started PSC as a small rebuilding business, and they were joined by Jim's brother, Tom. The business was moved to the Van Buren location. They began distributing several product lines along with their rebuilt lines, and the first year's sales volume was $12,000.

In 1970, the company moved to a larger building on Grand Ave., and continued to add product lines. In 1975, it discontinued rebuilding completely, added more product lines, and grew to 10 employees. Gross sales exceeded the $1 million mark.

By 1977 the company grew to 21 employees, relocated to a larger building on Black Canyon and topped the $3 million mark in sales.

In 1982, PSC opened a branch warehouse in Mesa, Arizona, which was totally destroyed by fire. The following year, the company located to another building and was completely operational in 17 days. The business continued to grow and in 1985 relocated to 21st Ave., with 30 employees, and recorded sales that exceeded $5 million. One year later PSC joined Road Pro Automotive Group.

In 1990, Jim and Tom joined CARQUEST and opened a branch warehouse in Tucson, Arizona, to service southern Arizona.

Between 1992 and 1996 PSC acquired 17 auto parts stores. These stores, combined with 32 independently owned stores, were served by three PSC warehouses. There were 204 employees and gross sales topped $24 million.

The PSC merger was an important addition to GPI, providing opportunities for developing the entire state of Arizona, and Jim and Tom were very supportive, ensuring the success of the transaction. Little did either of them know that the APS transaction would create a tremendous expansion opportunity in the Arizona marketplace.

Our friendship with Jim and Tom Eaton, through CARQUEST, led to our opportunity to acquire their company in 1996. Jim, especially, worked very hard with us during the transition. This, like Denver, opened the opportunity to acquire Big A Auto Parts in Phoenix to create a major company and

the development of a new 95,000-square-foot distribution center in Phoenix.

—Temple Sloan Jr.

MILLARD'S INC.
February 1997
Omaha, Nebraska

Ken Millard graduated from the University of Nebraska and went to work for the B. F. Goodrich Tire Company. After six years he started his own tire company, which was called Hook-Millard Tire Co., with locations in Omaha and Boone, Iowa.

In 1963, the Carl Anderson Company, an old time AEA (Automotive Electric Association) distributor, asked Ken to sell his interest in the tire business and join its automotive division as general manager. Ken strongly assisted in building the company into a two-warehouse business, one located in Omaha, Nebraska, and the other in Des Moines, Iowa.

In 1978, after Carl Anderson's death, Ken purchased Acts Auto Parts, an Omaha parts store with two stores. In 1979, he opened his own warehouse and called it Millard's, Inc. and business grew rapidly. A number of the old-line warehouse distributors went out of business and Millard's, Inc., began buying up some of their customers, as the ownerships grew older.

In the early 1990s Millard's had grown to 15 stores and a warehouse. Ken and his wife Shirley had worked very hard and were pleased to have their son Scott join them in the business. They built an addition to the warehouse and continued to grow, rising to become one of the premier independent warehouse distributors in the Midwest.

Ken was thinking of retirement around 1995, and shared his thoughts with Ken Rogers. He asked if it was okay to talk to Temple Sloan and explore the possibility of an acquisition. In 1996, a contract was concluded with GPI and a "handshake deal" was made with an early 1997 transaction plan. With the APS transaction in 1998, Omaha has become an important market for GPI.

The Millard's distribution center was consolidated with the new GPI Des Moines, Iowa, CARQUEST distribution center. Ken continued with GPI in an advisory capacity for several years.

I had met Ken Millard in the mid-1970s when he was managing the Carl Anderson Company.

Our acquisition of Ken's company and our subsequent acquisition of Big A Auto Parts in Omaha created the opportunity to build a major distribution center in Des Moines. Omaha has continued to be a strong part of our company. Scott, his son, continued with us for several years before entering the real estate business in Omaha.

—Temple Sloan Jr.

PARTS WHOLESALERS, INC. & DARLING'S AUTO PARTS
February 1997
Bangor, Maine

The name Darling had been associated with the automotive business since 1901 when V. S. Darling opened the Darling Automobile Co. in Auburn, Maine. Darling originally sold and repaired bicycles; in 1903 he branched into selling Reos and Maxwells, two automotive names long vanished. By the 1920s Darling employed a nephew, Clarence "Hubby" Darling who eventually purchased the Bangor store from his uncle.

Clarence eventually left the automotive business, but in 1937 his son Owen parlayed a $2,500 investment into a new business called the Darling's. The company sold DeSotos and Plymouths, and by the mid-1940s, Owen established Darling's Auto Parts.

Until November 1968, NAPA supplied Darling's Auto Parts from a warehouse in Cambridge, Massachusetts. Owen ventured that a Maine-based warehouse could better supply not only the Darling's Auto Parts but independent jobbers as well. Owen opened Parts Wholesalers, Inc.

Owen guided Darling's and related businesses until his retirement in 1976, when John Darling, his son, became company president. Owen remained actively involved in company operations until his death in 1984.

Ken Millard secured the sale of Millard's Inc. with Temple Sloan Jr. through a "handshake deal."

From left to right: Owen Darling, Earl Seymor, and John Darling of Parts Wholesalers, Inc. and Darling's Auto Parts.

Following the death of his father, John selected Earl "Yogi" Seymour to be vice president and general manager of Parts Wholesalers, Inc., and president of Darling Auto Parts. Yogi had joined the company in 1950 and was a seasoned veteran of the Maine auto parts aftermarket. John and Yogi joined CARQUEST in 1988 and Yogi represented PWI and DAP well within CARQUEST.

With the Darling Auto Parts business under the leadership of Yogi Seymour, John was able to devote his time to his first love, the new car dealership business. John has built a dynasty of new car dealerships in Bangor and Ellsworth with franchises with Ford, GMC, Pontiac, Buick, Chrysler, Dodge, Honda, Nissan, Volvo, Volkswagen, and Audi. He has also developed used car companies in Manchester, Lewiston, and Waterville.

Under John's leadership, Darling car dealerships have prospered as a family business and have become a major employer in the area.

With the merger of Parts Wholesalers and Darling Auto Parts as a foundation, GPI was blessed with opportunities to expand its presence ever further in the state of Maine. Almost immediately was the chance to acquire 25 Steego Stores from Parts Depot. This was finalized in May 1997.

In February 2002, Bragg Auto Parts, a premier company with a proud 113-year history in central and northern Maine was acquired. In June of the same year, the Auto Parts Express acquisition was finalized. Also in 2002, Mark Roazen's three Standard Auto Supply stores in Portland were acquired followed by three Knox Auto Parts Stores.

GPI and CARQUEST are proud to be well represented in the state of Maine and grateful for the opportunities to grow with timely acquisitions of well-respected companies.

—Temple Sloan Jr.

CJS & MOTOR BEARINGS AND PARTS CO.
April 1997
Raleigh, North Carolina

In 1920, Motor Bearings and Parts Co., was started in Raleigh, North Carolina, by L. T. White. There was an initial inventory of $1,000 of automotive bearings. Within a few years other locations were established in eastern North Carolina including Rocky Mount, Fayetteville, and Goldsboro. As the automotive aftermarket grew, Motor Bearings evolved into a redistributing jobber, with locations from Greensboro to Elizabeth City.

After World War II, both of L. T. White's sons joined him in the business. L. T. White was responsible for purchasing, while S. M. White looked after day-to-day operations.

In 1954, the company moved its main office to a new 30,000-square-foot location in downtown Raleigh, which included a machine shop. Additional large stores with machine shops were built in Durham and Greensboro, which served smaller branches.

In the 1960s, when the practice of offering warehouse discounts became more common, Motor Bearings purchased many products from WDI, Inc., Atlanta, Georgia, on a drop-ship basis. The company also purchased several product lines, including Victor gaskets from a new Raleigh warehouse named General Parts, Inc. In 1968 Motor Bearings decided to start its own warehouse company and CJS (Carolina Jobbers Supply) was formed.

In the 1970s, the third generation of the White family entered the business. S. M. (Monty) White Jr. joined the company in 1970 and Bill White in 1976. Monty became president of CJS and Bill became president of Motor Bearings and Parts Co.

In the 1970s the company saw the need to affiliate with a program group. S. M. White Sr. had been friends for many years with Frank Norfleet, with Parts, Inc., in Memphis and the two had discussions about the possibility of joining the newly formed Parts Plus Group. In the 1970s CJS, Inc. built a new warehouse, joined the

From top to bottom: Monty White, Bee White, Bill White, and Brad Carter of CJS Motor Bearings and Parts Co.

Parts Plus Group and began to solicit independent jobber business actively.

CJS was an active member of the Parts Plus marketing group and used the program to continue building a great business through excellent service and strong customer relationships. Making it happen were a number of dedicated, hard working people led by Brad Carter, Paul Becton, Jim Coffey, David Henderson, Tommy McGhee, Don Henseler, and Don Garner.

The CJS merger added eight new independent stores, five stores were consolidated with existing JV and independent stores, and nine stores were added to the Raleigh JV store group. The CJS distribution center was consolidated into the GPI Raleigh CARQUEST distribution center.

The automotive aftermarket and the city of Raleigh were saddened by the news of Bee White's death in 1995.

I had a unique friendship with S. M. "Bee" White. Never has there been a finer gentleman and I often wondered why he created the opportunity of our friendship, but I will be forever grateful. He became my sponsor into several Raleigh civic activities, including the Rotary Club and Peace College Board of Trustees. Motor Bearings dominated the auto parts business in Raleigh for decades and on more than one occasion, we talked about putting our companies together. Unfortunately, in some ways, our merger with Bill and Monty came after Bee's death. But, somehow, I feel he would have been pleased. The merger created the opportunity for us to become the number one distributor in Raleigh, and our CARQUEST independent, Sloan Auto Parts, to become number one in Durham. Monty and Bill were great supporters and continued as major stockholders for a number of years.

—Temple Sloan Jr.

MOLIN AUTO PARTS, INC.
May 1997
Buffalo, New York

Molin Auto Parts was founded by Carl Molin in 1922 as a retail home and auto supply store. Incorporated as Molin's Service, Inc., in 1932, the name was changed to Molin Auto Parts, Inc., in 1958. At that time a new warehouse called Auto Parts Warehouse, Inc. was started and Art Vigneron was named president.

Carl Molin Jr. opened the first Molin Branch in Hamburg in 1959 and a second branch the following year in Kenmore. In 1961, Tom Brown Sr., treasurer, ran Don Urban Auto Supply in North Tonawanda.

Carl Molin retired as president in December 1966 and was succeeded by Carl Molin Jr. During this time, the company's accelerated growth was from acquisitions of premier auto parts stores and distribution centers. Starting in 1962 with the purchase of the automotive division of H. D. Taylor, the company was renamed Molin-Taylor, Inc.

Other well-known acquisitions were the automotive division of the Joseph Strauss Company. Then, in 1972, the Federal Trade Commission ordered Maremont, an exhaust manufacturer, to divest its auto parts distribution companies. The Molin Group acquired its C & L Syracuse warehouse and nine auto parts stores doing business as Parts Supply Co. At the same time the Molin Auto Parts Warehouse division in Buffalo was renamed C & L Buffalo, Inc. Several smaller but high-quality stores were added during the 1970s and 1980s.

Molin Auto Parts was started in 1922 by Carl Molin as a retail home and auto supply store. It was acquired by GPI in 1997. Front: Carl Molin Jr. Back from left to right: Tom Brown Jr., Tom Brown Sr., Trey Molin, and Kim Molin.

During the mid-1970s the third generation began to work for the company when Tom Brown Jr. and Kim Molin joined Molin Auto Parts, Inc., followed by Trey Molin in 1981.

Molin Auto Parts joined the Association of Automotive Aftermarket Distributors (AAAD-Parts Plus) in 1976. In 1980, the Parts Supply Auto Stores were merged into Molin-Taylor, Inc., all owned by Molin Auto Parts, Inc. Art Vigneron retired in 1981.

In 1986, C & L Parts Corp. and Molin-Taylor, Inc. were merged into Molin Auto Parts, Inc. Carl Molin Jr. was elected CEO and chairman of the board, and Tom Brown was elected president. The company purchased a building at 3896 Union Road and moved its Buffalo distribution center and general office into the building.

In 1990, Tom Brown Sr. retired as president and was succeeded by Kim Molin. Tom Brown Jr. became secretary and Trey Molin became treasurer. Carl Molin Jr. retired as CEO and chairman of the board.

The Molin merger played an important role in GPI's growth in Western New York and Pennsylvania.

Shortly after our merger with Dan Sussen, he told us of the conversations he'd had over the years with Carl Molin about putting their companies together. It was clear that a combination of Avro sales, which Dan had acquired, and Molin would create a significant player in the Buffalo market.

Following several meetings with Carl Molin and his brother-in-law, Tom Brown Sr., they agreed to merge their company with GPI. Tom Brown Jr. continues to serve as sales manager in Buffalo. Trey Molin is vice president of our northeast store group and Kim Molin is in Raleigh, heading up our corporate services group. In 2003, we were successful in adding the Hutchens stores to our Buffalo group.

—*Temple Sloan Jr.*

ACKTION CORPORATION
Canadian Entry
March 1997

K. (Rai) Sahi, chairman and CEO of Acklands, and O. Temple Sloan, Jr., chairman of GPI, signed an agreement in principle that will result in an equal investment by GPI and Acktion in a new company that would take over all the operations of McKerlie-Millen, Inc.

The new company, which was renamed from McKerlie-Millen, Inc., to CARQUEST CANADA, LTD., operated distribution centers in Toronto, Ottawa, Montreal, and Quebec City supplying 122 company-owned stores and 240 associate stores under the McKerlie-Millen name.

McKerlie-Millen was a significant marketing force in Eastern Canada for more than 100 years with consolidated sales near $200 million (Canadian dollars), and employing more than 1,700 associates.

Jack Moritz, a GPI associate from Denver, Colorado, and a former senior management member of American Parts Systems was selected to serve as president and CEO. Together with a strong management team, he directed the conversion of the marketing program to CARQUEST. He also led the successful conversion to one computer system, to one purchasing system, and to one accounting system. The integration of three separate companies into one unified company was well done under Jack Moritz's direction.

The management team selected to operate the company were Robert Blair, vice president/marketing; Steve Mara, vice president and general manager, Ontario division; Magella Boutin, vice president and general manager, Quebec division; and Ted Reevey, vice president and general manager, Atlantic division.

McKerlie-Millen had a long, illustrious history. Since the early 1900s when John Millen and Sons entered the automotive aftermarket in Quebec to the 1997 change to CARQUEST, the company had grown through strategic acquisitions and aggressive sales programs.

John Millen II opened his first store with $458, at the corner of Plessis and Ste-Catherine in Montreal on April 24, 1869. John Millen III started working for his father and opened a bicycle department. The company supplied motors, wheels, and lamps to Mr. H. E. Bourassa, for the first car built in Canada in 1899. In 1948, Lou McKerlie started McKerlie Automotive Ltd. in London, Ontario. The business grew quickly through acquisition and opening new stores to become one of the largest distributors in Canada. Automotive Warehousing Ltd. was formed in 1960 to serve independent jobbers. A year later, Automotive Warehousing Limited established a presence in Toronto with distribution facilities located at 79 Wingold Ave.

In 1970, the operations of McKerlie Automotive and John Millen & Sons were merged and the new company was named McKerlie-Millen, Inc. and included all branches except Garage Supply Ltd. The first McKerlie Associate Program for independent jobbers was introduced in 1972. In 1974, G. L. Stone became president and the A. W. L. Ottawa Distribution Centre opened. In 1976, Magella Boutin and Robert Chevrier formed Autopoint Limited providing automotive replacement parts in Quebec. Autopoint expanded rapidly, eventually being sold to Auto Stock Ltd. in 1990 and to Acklands in 1995, when it was merged with the Quebec-based operation of McKerlie-Millen.

In 1980, Automotive Warehousing Limited changed to A. W. L. Steego, following the name change of U.S. Sterling Precision, Inc., to Steego Corp. Industrial Equity (Pacific) Ltd. acquired McKerlie-Millen from Steego Corp. in 1987. In 1993, Acklands purchased the assets of Atlas Supply Company of Canada Limited. Acklands purchased Autotec in the Maritimes, owned by Ted Reevey, Auto Paint Supply of Toronto, and Automotive Finishes Supply of Toronto in 1994. In 1995, McKerlie-Millen and Atlas operations were merged.

In 1997, CARQUEST CANADA LTD. was formed with Acklands retaining 50% ownership and General Parts, Inc., holding 50%. The Canadian Joint Venture was a major step forward for GPI and was taken at a time when the economic borders between Canada and the United States had become much more conducive to that type of investment under the North American Free Trade Agreement (NAFTA). Purchase of these assets was a difficult step for the company in light of all the other activities running concurrently, but such opportunities present themselves infrequently and the decision was made to press on and establish a presence in Canada.

I was attending the Global Symposium in Chicago when I heard that Rai Sahi had sold his western Canada parts operation and industrial supply business to W. W. Grainger. Rai had visited us in Raleigh several times and I knew him reasonably well. No one ever fit the word "entre-

preneur" better than Rai Sahi, and his successful track record continues to this day in Canada. Picking up the phone in Chicago, I asked Rai what he was going to do with his Eastern Canada companies. Having known Greg Stone, who had managed the original company for a number of years, I felt the foundation of a good, solid opportunity should be in place. Before leaving Chicago and after Rai agreed to meet, I asked Greg Stone to be a part of our team, and for reasons I still do not understand, he refused.

The subsequent meeting with Rai led to our unique partnership with our agreement to purchase his interest at the end of five years. This was driven by his desire to focus on his highly successful real estate company, known today as Morguard Corporation. I enjoyed the privilege of serving on his Board for six years. In December 2000, Rai asked us to accelerate the purchase of his interest, due primarily to his investment in the auto parts business being a conflict in a publicly traded real estate company.

The success of CARQUEST CANADA, LTD., is well documented in this book, but we should never lose sight of the opportunity, direction, guidance, and introductions Rai Sahi afforded us, by agreeing to a partnership. Rai exceeded every commitment he made with me personally or with GPI.

—*Temple Sloan Jr.*

REPUBLIC AUTOMOTIVE PARTS
September 1998

Republic was founded in 1923 as the Republic Gear Company. In the early years, Republic Gear's business was principally the manufacturer of parts for the automotive manufacturers with some of its products going to the automotive aftermarket. There were three product lines consisting of gears, universal joints, and axle shafts.

Wayne Johnston, top, and Magella Boutin, bottom, of CARQUEST CANADA.

In 1955, Republic Gear began directing its activity to the rapidly growing automotive aftermarket. Additional product lines were added and in 1950 Republic divested itself of all of its manufacturing facilities and concentrated exclusively on serving the aftermarket as a service line company. The company distributed eight product lines—transmission parts, oil pumps, motor mounts, power steering hose, timing gears, chains and sprockets, universal joints, and the all'n one general service line. The product lines were sold under the Republic name and were purchased from about 160 different manufacturers.

In the mid-1960s, the parent company, Republic Automotive Parts, Inc., entered the warehouse distribution sector of the aftermarket. To support its entry, Republic introduced jobbers and warehouses to its "Car Care Man program."

Republic became a public company in 1970. Steve S. Gordon was president until 1980. He was followed by Kenneth L. Rogers in 1980 and Keith Thompson in 1985. Fred Kotcher served as president of the Aftermarket Distribution Group.

Republic rapidly began acquiring warehouse distributors and jobber stores. Some of the more notable warehouse distributors acquired were: Beacon Auto Parts, Pittsburgh, Pennsylvania; Crumm & Lynn, Inc., Los Angeles, California; Tri-Co Automotive Warehouse, Bakersville, California; Best Distributing Company, Portland, Oregon; Western Automotive Warehouse, Denver, Colorado; Arrow Warehouse Distributors, LaVerne, California; Evergreen Warehouse Distributors, Seattle and Spokane, Washington; Major Parts Warehouse, Green Bay, Wisconsin; Parts Warehouse Company, Anchorage, Alaska; B & C Supply Corporation, Arkansas; Harbor Hill Auto Parts Distributors, Long Beach, California; Pomona Motor Parts, Pomona, California; Valley Auto Supply, El Centro, California; National Automotive Warehouse, Tacoma, Washington;

CARQUEST CANADA's management included Robert Blair, top, and Jack Moritz, bottom.

Carroll Motor Supply, Inc., Marquette, Michigan; Columbia Warehouse Distributors, Longview, Washington; Great Lakes Jobbers, Green Bay, Wisconsin; Boggs & McBurney, Southern California; Holt Distributing Company, Denver, Colorado; three warehouses purchased from Standard Motor Products, located in Lathum, New York, and Hartford and Stratford, Connecticut (had been part of the Parts Post Program); R. A. Industries, Inc. & Rupp Auto, Chillicothe, Missouri; Specialized Service Company, Klamath Falls, Oregon; Superior Automotive Parts, Duluth, Minnesota; O. K. Auto Parts, Ironwood, Michigan; Thrifty Auto Supply, Spokane, Washington; and Arizona Jobbers Supply, Phoenix and Tucson, Arizona.

Under Thompson's leadership, Republic entered the automotive collision segment of the aftermarket and established a separate division, Fenders and More. This division grew rapidly and not only provided diversification for Republic but also enhanced profitability.

In June 1998 Thompson, with directors' approval, finalized negotiations to sell Republic to Keystone, a West Coast company specializing in auto collision parts and supplies. Keystone's attraction was Republic's Fenders and More division. Charles Hogarty, Keystone's CEO, solicited Thompson's assistance in finding a buyer for the traditional auto parts distribution segment of Republic. Thompson recommended General Parts, Inc. and he called Joe Owen to see if GPI would have an interest. Thompson arranged a meeting in Nashville for him and Charles to meet with Temple, Joe, and John Gardner. The transaction was finalized on September 1, 1998.

We feel very fortunate to merge these fine auto parts companies into GPI. Their reputation for excellent customer service has made them tough competitors and we are relieved and happy to have them on our team. We greatly appreciate the confidence of Charles Hogarty and Keith Thompson in making it possible.

—Temple Sloan Jr.

APS HOLDING, INC.
1998

APS was founded in 1958 by Charles Bludorn, the chairman of Gulf & Western Industries, and

John Duncan, its president. The company has a long history in the parts business.

Having recognized the success of Genuine Parts (NAPA), Bludorn and Duncan conceived and began developing a national automotive replacement parts distribution system headquartered in Houston, Texas.

During the early years, growth was slow as APS management and operational strategies were being developed. The real architects of the Big A concept were Frank V. Rogers, recruited from Genuine Parts in Boston, Massachusetts; and Everett Kelly who came to G & W through the acquisition of the B. K. Sweeney Co., Denver, Colorado. In the early 1960s, growth began with the acquisition of established automotive warehouse distributors from private owners. By 1970 there were 28 distribution centers of which only six were started internally. During the 1970s APS' strategy changed from rapid growth through acquisitions to the expansion of the Big A system through customer additions and the construction of four new distribution centers.

Following the death of Bludorn in 1980, APS lost its "favorite son" status as Gulf & Western focused on the entertainment, financial, and communications industries.

There were several illustrious persons involved with APS in the early days. Thomas S. Perry, who was president of AWDA in 1959 and 1960, was one of the leading distributors in the south. Perry had three companies—The Thomas S. Perry Company, Jobbers Service Co., and Jobber Gasket Supply. He sold his businesses to Gulf & Western as part of the development of the American Parts System (APS). Thomas Plant left United Motors Service Division of General Motors Corporation as general sales manager, to become an early president of APS. Other early president and industry leaders associated with APS were Robert V. Daly (who also left United Motors Service as director of sales), Frank Rogers, and Everett Kelly. Fred J. Pisciotta presided as president during seven of APS' most productive years.

APS, a separate division of Gulf & Western, moved to the building products division and then to the manufacturing division in the early 1980s. During late 1984, APS' growth focus was revitalized with the acquisition of four dis-tribution centers. Then in September 1985, APS was sold to Wickes Companies, Inc., as a part of the G & W Manufacturing division. APS was the most profitable of the aftermarket companies purchased by Wickes, which included Guaranteed Parts and Sorenson (ignition manufacturers) and Vera (import/foreign car specialist).

Shortly after the acquisition by Wickes, management began rationalizing APS' operating units to reduce investment and generate cash to aid in meeting Wickes' loan obligations. Until late 1988, much of APS' management time was spent analyzing and rationalizing the business rather than focusing on growth. APS did, however, continue to operate profitably and maintain market share.

In November 1988, Wickes Companies, Inc., was bought by Blackstone Partners, L. P., and Wasserstein Perella Partners, L. P. At that point, all growth activity was placed on hold.

Clayton & Dubilier, flush from a $690 million sale of Uniroyal-Goodrich Tire to French-owned Michelin Group, organized APS Acquisition Corp., to acquire the company from Wickes Companies, Inc., a subsidiary of WCI Holdings Corp., paid $200 million for APS. At that time, APS operated 30 distribution centers serving 1,400 independent jobbers and 109 company-owned jobbers in 48 states.

The aforementioned history led up to the bankruptcy proceedings when General Parts acquired selected locations.

Following APS going into bankruptcy, the court approved the Blackstone Group to reorganize or sell APS. Once they decided to sell APS, they circulated an offering memorandum book to a select list of potential buyers. It became apparent to us, that unless a venture capital group stepped forward, there was not a likely buyer for the whole company.

Our strategy was to see if we could convince Blackstone to sell us a significant, but selected, group of the operations. In the process, we were able to interest BWP in New York, APW in California, Straus-Frank in Texas, and Muffler Warehouse in Idaho, our CARQUEST members, to join our bid, greatly enhancing our chances of success. We were successful in convincing Blackstone, who got approval from the bank-

ruptcy court in Wilmington, Delaware, for us to proceed.

Following extensive due diligence, including meetings with APS management, followed by complex negotiations with Blackstone and their attorneys (all complicated by the bankruptcy procedure), we were successful in completing the transaction.

The efforts of Blackstone, led by Bettina Whyte and her team, our bankruptcy attorney, Robert Rosenberg, with Latham-Watkins, out of New York, made a complex transaction possible. Mike Preston, Dave Barbeaux, and Gene Lawer purchased the remaining operations of the company, forming Auto Parts Express (APX), which was ultimately acquired by GPI in 2002.

With this transaction, we retained an outstanding group of management who hold key positions throughout GPI today. To mention a few are Vice Presidents Mike Allen, Roy Hedges, Montie Loney, Mike Tanji, and Jerry Repak, and most importantly, a tremendous group of outstanding independent jobbers.

—*Temple Sloan Jr.*

A.E. LOTTES COMPANY
2001
St. Louis, Missouri

In 1911 in St. Louis, Missouri, Arthur E. Lottes Sr., at the age of 20, became a salesman for Simmons Hardware Co., the country's largest hardware distributor. His sales included hardware stores and the fast-growing automotive industry. In 1919, Lottes Sr. left Simmons Hardware to go into business serving the automotive market.

He founded the A. E. Lottes, Co., and became a distributor of tires, inner tubes, and related items from his warehouse located at 820 North 1st Street, on the northwest corner of what is now known as Laclede's Landing.

The company survived the Depression and the worldwide instabilities of the rubber market. In 1935, Arthur E. Lottes Jr. joined the company, and in 1941 the warehouse facility was moved to a larger facility at 2902 Olive Street.

In December 1941, the Lottes family was faced with an important decision. Rubber became a critical commodity in the World War II effort, and the government froze all tire inventories. The company had two options: It could sell tires only if it followed strict guidelines enforced by the government, or it could voluntarily return the tires to the manufacturers. The company returned the tires and focused on expanding the auto parts business.

Paul Lottes Sr. joined the company in 1946. Arthur Lottes Jr. was in the U.S. Air Force, stationed in Europe for three years. At the conclusion of the war, the company experienced a slow but steady growth with 12 employees.

In 1959, after several building expansions, growth dictated a move to a larger facility of 13,000 square feet, located at 2735 Olive Street.

In 1966, Arthur Lottes Sr. passed away unexpectedly and Arthur Lottes Jr. became president. Richard Lottes Sr. became secretary/treasurer and Paul Lottes Sr. assumed the position of vice president. The company

Above: Art Lottes III, top, and Art Lottes Sr., bottom.

Left, from left to right: Paul Lottes, Dick Lottes, and Art Lottes Jr. *(Photo courtesy of Josephine.)*

Above: A.E. Lottes distribution center located at 800 North 17th Street.

acquired its first computer in 1969, an IBM 1130 with 4K memory and also built a new warehouse at 2600 Olive Street and Jefferson Street.

In May 1975, Arthur E. Lottes III, joined the company. The company continued to grow and add new customers but the market was slowly beginning to change. Customers wanted suppliers to provide marketing support, which was being offered by some competitors. Most auto parts distributors were joining forces with program groups. After considerable research, A. E. Lottes Company joined CARQUEST in 1979. The CARQUEST board members were delighted to have A. E. Lottes as its reputation of being a premier auto parts distributor was well-known.

In 1986, Arthur Lottes III, assumed the presidency and Arthur Lottes Jr. became chairman. Arthur Lottes III became a vital and active member of CARQUEST as well, serving on many committees as well as the CARQUEST board of directors. Rounding out the third Lottes generation, Richard Lottes Jr. served as secretary/treasurer and Paul Lottes as vice president–stores. As the business continued to grow construction of an expanded distribution center at 800 N. 17th Street was begun in February 1986 and was occupied in February 1987.

The company formed its first joint venture auto parts store in 1985, in Kirksville, Missouri, and that led to a total of 40 joint venture stores at the time of the merger with GPI.

The A. E. Lottes Company had survived and prospered for 81 years under the ownership of the Lottes family.

We were surprised when Art and Paul Lottes approached us about merging our companies. A. E. Lottes was one of the best-managed companies we have had the privilege to join with. Having Art join the GPI management team and to lead CARQUEST was a great addition to both organizations. Art has also been a real asset to our board.

—*Temple Sloan Jr.*

AUTO PARTS WHOLESALE – CALIFORNIA
2003
California

The McMurtrey family entered the automotive industry because of N. C. "Mac" McMurtrey. Mac was born in Stella, Missouri, in 1919. His mother gave him a big hug, $5, and told him to see the world. By age 18, he made it to the West Coast. Mac settled in Bakersfield and started his career at Pioneer Mercantile. He stayed with Pioneer until 1956, working his way up the ladder until he became the number one outside salesman.

After 18 years in the parts business working for someone else, Mac decided to work for himself. He was married and had three sons, Jon, Don, and Gene. A small parts store in downtown Bakersfield, called Southern Auto Supply, became available. The store was started in 1928 by C. Bob Porter, who wanted to retire. The deal was made and Mac took over in March 1956.

Mac's oldest two sons, Jon, 16, and Don, 14, started working in the business. Gene helped but continued with his schooling and became a lawyer. Jon and Don stayed in the family business and became full partners in 1966. By then Southern Auto Supply had 16 employees and annual sales of almost $1 million.

In 1972, the family purchased a small automotive warehouse with three retail parts stores in Bakersfield. The name of this company was Auto Parts Wholesale. The family now had nine retail stores and its own warehouse. Jon managed the warehouse business and Don managed the retail store business. Mac became CEO and continued in that role until he retired in 1993.

In 1973, APW purchased another warehouse in Bakersfield from Republic Gear Company. In 1978, they built a 40,000-square-foot warehouse in Bakersfield and expanded in the San Joaquin Valley.

In 1981, APW opened a branch distribution center in Santa Maria, a coastal city about two hours west of Bakersfield. Jon's son, Mike, who started working in the business when he was 10 years old, moved to Santa Maria to help run the new distribution center.

In 1987, APW purchased a warehouse distributor with one retail store in Fresno. The warehouse business was making more than $15 million from three locations. Southern Auto Supply now had more than 12 retail stores making $10 million in sales.

In 1988, APW purchased two additional warehouses and four retail stores in Sacramento and Stockton from the Henderson family. This was the first entry in Northern California and Nevada. In 1989, APW purchased a warehouse in Ventura from the Diedrich family, and in 1992 they purchased a warehouse in San Jose from the Arthur family.

The biggest purchase of APW's history occurred in 1993 with the assets purchase of the Cardis Corporation. Cardis was the sole CARQUEST distributor in California. With the purchase, APW joined the CARQUEST family and for the next 10 years worked hard to make CARQUEST a household name in California. By 2002, APW's sales had reached $124 million.

A great deal of credit for APW's success was the family's teamwork. Jon's oldest two sons, Mike and Jim, and Don's oldest son, David, worked side-by-side, and two other sons, John and Steve, joined the team when they finished school.

On March 31, 2003, the McMurtrey family merged with General Parts, Inc.

Jon and Don McMurtrey had grown their company with major acquisitions in the late 1990s. The willingness to merge APW into GPI opened the largest market in the United States to GPI. While Don and Jon were ready for retirement, three of their sons have filled key management roles within GPI, and Jon has been a strong addition to our board.

—Temple Sloan Jr.

STRAUS FRANK COMPANY
2004
Texas

The Straus Company was started by two brothers, Joseph and Jacob, in Jefferson City and St. Louis, Missouri, in 1864. The company started as a wholesale saddle and harness distributor and later became a very successful manufacturing business. A key employee was Lazarus Frank, Jacob Straus' brother-in-law. In 1870, Lazarus moved to San Antonio for health reasons and established one of the city's first saddleries and harness manufacturing businesses, L. Frank Saddlery. Although he suffered from poor health, his insight and shrewdness helped him build a prosperous business.

In 1887, Lazarus persuaded Jacob to be his partner, and the two worked together until Lazarus' death in 1895. With the loss of Lazarus Frank, Jacob asked his nephew, David J. Straus, to move

At left, from left: Jon McMurtrey, Mac McMurtrey, and Don McMurtrey of Auto Parts Wholesale.
At right: Tony Staus, top, and David Straus III, bottom, of the Straus-Frank Company.

to San Antonio to help manage the business. David was Joseph's son.

Two years later Jacob was elected president of the Straus Company of St. Louis, Missouri. Before he left San Antonio, Jacob arranged for David, who was 26 at the time, to purchase the interests of Mrs. Lazarus Frank for $30,000—Joseph loaned him the money.

Shortly after Jacob's death in 1910, David was elected president of the L. Frank Saddlery.

Under David's leadership, the company prospered. A huge amount of business was obtained with contracts to military units not only in the United States but throughout the world. By the end of World War I, L. Frank Saddlery had become one of the largest saddlery manufacturers in the world, with more than 500 craftsmen. David was respected as one of the most able and honest businessmen in the leather industry.

Although saddles and harnesses were in great demand, David realized that the business would eventually decline. Mechanical improvements had made the automobile an increasingly important factor in the transportation market. Realizing this, David attended the 1917 automobile show in New York City and soon, L. Frank Saddlery was in the automotive business. In 1923, the name of the company was changed to Straus-Frank Company.

Starting with sporting goods in 1927, the company rapidly expanded their products to include refrigerators, tires and radios with top-of-the-line brand names like Remington, Frigidaire, U.S. Royal, Atwater-Kent, and RCA Victor.

David died in 1932 at age 60. He and his wife, Ida Oppenheimer Straus had three sons—Joseph, Fred (Fritz), and Robert. In January 1933, Joe, David's oldest son who was head of automotive, became president. Fritz was vice president, and Robert, the youngest, was appointed vice president and assistant treasurer.

In 1964, Joe Straus Sr., who had served as president since 1932, became chairman of the board.

Above: The L. Frank Saddlery Co. Wholesale was one of the largest saddlery manufacturers in the world.

At left, from top to bottom: Joe R. Straus Sr., Jack Trawick, Joe R. Straus Jr., and David J. Straus III.

Joe's oldest son, David J. Straus II, was appointed president. Joe Straus Jr. was appointed vice president. Joe Straus Sr. died in 1985.

At the time of the merger with GPI, David J. Straus, II, was chairman and CEO, Joe Straus, Jr. was vice chairman, Jack Trawick was president, Roger Pritt was vice president and general manager of the company store group, and Bob Mangold was vice president and general manager of the independent store group.

A few other names deserve mention for their contributions: Simon Wallach; J. B. Andrews; Morris Strum; Joe Schmidt; Ed Buckley; B. E. Waggoner; Elmer Miller; John Reynolds; Arlie Hibits; Phil Costello; Ray Arnold; E. A. Wenderoth; Bill Bratten; Casey Golightley; members of the Rose family, including Albert Sr., Albert Jr., and John; Kenny Faulkner; George Wallace; David J. Straus, III; and Fredric (Tony) Straus.

David J. Straus II
Military Biography

Enlisted in USMC in April 1943, Boot Camp San Diego. Rose to rank of Staff Sergeant and went to OCS 1944. Commissioned as 2nd Lieutenant went to Pacific and assigned to E Company, 5th Marines, 1st Marine Division as rifle platoon leader—participated in Okinawa Campaign. Went with the Division to China in October 1945. Stationed in Peking (Beijing). Came home 1946 and discharged as Staff Sergeant (had temporary commission). Sworn back into USMCR as 2nd Lieutenant.

Recalled to active duty in 1951 as 1st Lieutenant. Attended Junior School (now Amphibious Warfare School) at Quantico. Then went to Korea and assigned as Exec. Officer, F Company, 5th Marines, 1st Marine Division. Awarded Bronze Medal with Combat V. Became F Company Commander then transferred to Kimpo Provisional regiment staff as S-3. Returned to U.S. in 1953. Discharged in 1954 as Captain.

Awards include Bronze Star Medal with Combat V, Presidential Citation with 2 stars, Asiatic-Pacific Campaign medal with star, National Defense medal, American Campaign medal, China Service medal, with 2 stars, United Nations service medal, Marine Corps Good Conduct medal, Combat Action ribbon with star.

Our relationship with Straus-Frank and David and Joe Straus goes back nearly 35 years. The sharing of ideas between the Straus and GPI managements had become a tradition. During the last 10 years, there had been numerous discussions about putting our companies together. It came close in 1996, and reached conclusion in 2004. The merger was supported by the Straus management, with Jack Trawick and Roger Pritt being

David J. Straus II was chairman and CEO of the Straus-Frank Company at the time of the merger with GPI.

OFFICE OF

Jacob Straus Saddlery Co.,

MANUFACTURERS OF

Harness, Collars and Whips

Jefferson City, Mo., January 26th 1898

Whereas I, the undersigned did furnish to Dave J. Straus the sum of $30,000.00 for the purchase of interest of Mrs Sarah Frank of the firm of L. Frank & Co of San Antonio Texas. I hereby acknowledge that of said amount $10,000.00 was the property of said D. J. Straus, and $20,000.00 of said amount is a loan made by me to said D.J. Straus and payment of same is not to be exacted by me as per agreement with said D. J. Straus for a period of not less than five years from date

Joseph Straus.

The Straus company evolved from a wholesale saddle and harness distributor into a successful manufacturing company.

---

critical to the successful integration. We were pleased to have David join our board.

—Temple Sloan Jr.

WORLDPAC
2004

WORLDPAC was founded in 1993 by the Friedkin family of Houston, Texas, as an importer, distributor, and deliverer of OEM-quality replacement parts to the import repair specialist. It was created through strategic acquisitions and opportunistic organic expansion.

The initial acquisition in 1993 was World Wide Trading in Northern California, a leading European importer/distributor with six western United States locations.

In 1994, WORLDPAC acquired Impac, headquartered in Southern California, a leading Asian and Swedish importer/distributor with 11 locations in the western states, including Texas.

Also in 1994, Pacific Automotive was acquired. Pacific was headquartered in Portland, Oregon, its only location.

In 1995, WORLDPAC established both short-term and long-term goals that would position the company for growth. These were to establish a hard-driving and goal-oriented management team, establish technology as a high priority, adopt a best practice, no down time, a "nothing for granted" philosophy, establish uniform credit practices, establish an integrated part numbering system, and grow sales more than 10 percent annually.

It also established a business goal: "To win with class and style, to be the number one importer/distributor in all markets served."

A specific strategy was outlined as follows:
* Provide superior customer service through operational excellence.
* Motivate associates by providing opportunity for all.
* Widen same-day distribution through acquired market representation.

Objectives were defined as:
* Achieve overwhelming share of installer's parts business.
* Provide total solutions to issues confronting our customers, thereby helping to ensure their success.

The key members of the management team at WORLDPAC at the time of merger with The International Group, Inc., were Tom O'Hare, CEO; John Mosunic, president and COO; Jeanne Lyons, vice president of strategy and business development; Ray Birden, vice president of strategic development; Bob Cushing, vice president of sales and operations–East; Steven Sharp, vice president of sales and operations–West; Paul Isenbarger, vice president, distribution center–West; Patrick Healy, vice president, distribution center–East; Hans Wulff, vice president of supply and product strategy; Matt Johnson, vice president of credit; Mike Hellweg, vice president of information technology; and Mario Recchia, vice president of marketing and business development.

WORLDPAC's management at the time of the merger with the International Group included John Mosunic, president and COO, left, and Tom O'Hare, CEO, right.

In 2002, J. P. Morgan visited with John Gardner to discuss opportunities in the import car aftermarket. Among those opportunities was WORLDPAC, owned by the Friedkin family of Houston, Texas. WORLDPAC would provide CARQUEST the opportunity to enhance its product coverage and to establish a needed business link to the import specialty installers. Following visits to the company and WORLDPAC's management, we were not able to meet the family's objective.

Our team agreed that we liked the business and needed to explore other opportunities within the industry. In the summer of 2004, we learned that the family was going to get J. P. Morgan to sell WORLDPAC. Following a visit with the Friedkin management team, we met with our board and financial advisors. All agreed that WORLDPAC was a strategic move for GPI.

With our board's support, we returned to Houston, meeting with Jerry Pyle, president of Friedkin's Automotive Group and Frank Gruen, CFO of the Friedkin companies and representatives of J. P. Morgan.

—Temple Sloan Jr.

Evolution of CARQUEST Membership

Year Founded	Company		1973	1974	1975	1976	1977	1978	1979	1980	1981	1982	1983	1984	1985	1986	1987	1988	1989	1990	1991	1992	1993	1994	1995	1996	1997	1998	1999	2000	2001	2002	2003	2004	2005
1929	*Automotive Central Inc. - Montgomery, AL	ACI								X	Withdrew																								
1917	Automotive Distributors Inc. - Kan City	ADI												⊗	X	X	X	X	X	Acquired by DAD															
1956	Auto Parts Wholesale - Bakersfield	APW																					⊗	X	X	X	X	X	X	X	X	X	Merged into GPI '03		
1925	Avro Warehouse Sales - Buffalo, NY	AVRO			⊗	X	X	X	X	X	X	X	X	X	X	X	X	X	X	X	X	X	X	X	X	X	X	X	X	X	X	X	X	X	X
1963	Automotive Warehouse, Inc. - Honolulu	AWI													X	⊗	X	X	X	Acquired by Sussin	X	X	X	X	X	X	X	X	X	X	X	X	X	X	X
1918	Border-Aicklen Auto Supply Inc. - New Orleans	BAASCO		X	⊗	X	X	X	X	X	X	X	X	Withdrew																					
1939	Bobro - Bronx, NY	BOBRO	⊗	X	X	X	X	X	X	X	X	X	Acquired by BWP																						
1962	BWP Distributors Inc. - Bronx, NY	BWP										X	Acquired by Bobro	X	X	X	X	X	X	X	X	X	X	X	X	X	X	X	X	X	X	X	X	X	X
1958	CAP Warehouse - Las Vegas, NV	CAP										X	X	X	X	X	X	X	X	X	X	Acquired by APW	X	X	X	X	X	X	X	X	X	X	X	X	X
1985	Cardis	CARDIS													X	Acq. C&L	X	X	X	X	X	X													
1904	Chansler & Lyons	C&L					X	X	X	X	X	X	X	X	X	X	X	Acquired by CARDIS																	
1989	Diversified Automotive Distributors	DAD																			⊗	X	X	Merged into GPI '94											
1915	Fremont Electric Co. - Seattle, WA	Fremont											⊗	X	X	X	X	X	X	X	X	X	Merged into GPI '93												
1961	General Parts, Inc. - Raleigh, NC	GPI	⊗	X	X	X	X	X	X	X	X	X	X	X	X	X	X	X	X	X	X	X	X	X	X	X	X	X	X	X	X	X	X	X	X
1855	General Trading Co. - St. Paul, MN	GTC							⊗	Merged into GPI '80																									
1940	Hatch Grinding Co. - Denver, CO	Hatch				⊗	X	X	X	X	X	X	X	X	X	X	X	X	X	X	X	X	X	X	Merged into GPI '96										
1915	Illinois Auto Electric - Elmhurst, IL	IAE		X	⊗	X	X	X	X	X	X	X	X	X	X	Withdrew																			
1959	Indiana Parts Whse. Inc. - Indianapolis	IPW				⊗	X	X	X	X	X	X	X	X	X	X	X	X	X	Merged into GPI '91															
1946	Kay Automotive Whse. Inc. - Philadelphia	KAY							⊗	X	X	X	X	X	X	X	X	Withdrew																	
1919	A.E. Lottes Co. - St. Louis, MO	Lottes					X	X	X	X	X	X	X	X	X	X	X	X	X	X	X	X	X	X	X	X	X	X	X	X	Merged into GPI '01				
1930	Muffler Warehouse, Inc. - Pocatello, ID	Muffler										X	X	X	X	X	X	X	X	X	X	X	X	X	X	X	X	X	X	X	X	X	X	X	X
1956	Pacific Wholesalers, Inc. - Portland, OR	Pacific													X	X	X	Withdrew		⊗	Merged into GPI '92														
1924	Parts Distributors, Inc. - Waltham Ma.	PDI					X	X	X	X	X	X	X	X	X																				
1915	Parts Distributors Whse - Memphis - S&S Nashville	** PDW & S&S					X	X	X	X	X	X	X	X	**S&S Merged into GPI '85	PDW Merged into GPI '86																			
1965	PSC Distributing Inc. - Phoenix, AZ	PSC													X				X	X	X	X	X	X	X	Merged into GPI '96									
1945	Parts Wholesalers, Inc. - Bangor, ME	PWI													X				X	X	X	X	X	X	X	Merged into GPI '96									
1958	Parts Warehouse Inc. - Little Rock	PWI									X	Withdrew																							
1937	Parts Warehouse Co. - Bay City, MI	PWC					X	X	X	X	X	X	X	X	Merged into GPI '86																				
1870	Strauss Frank Co. - San Antonio, TX	Stratco			X	⊗	X	X	X	X	X	X	X	X	X	⊗	X	X	X	X	X	X	X	X	X	X	X	X	X	X	X	X	X	Merged into GPI '04	
1950	Service Parts Whse. Corp. - Albany, GA	SPW				⊗	X	X	X	X	X	X	X	X	X	X	X	X	Merged into GPI '90																
1921	Sussen, Inc. - Cleveland, OH	Sussen			⊗	X	X	X	X	X	X	X	X	X	⊗	X	X	X	X	Merged into GPI '91															
1935	World Supply Corp. - Lemont, IL	World Supply					X	X							X	X	X	X	X	Merged into GPI '91															

*Note: In 1980 Automotive Central, Inc. of Montgomery, Alabama joined CARQUEST and withdrew less than a year later and was merged into Taylor Parts, Inc. Andalusia, AL which was merged into GPI in 1992.

**Note: PDW Memphis / Nashville until 1981 operated as one company. In 1981 these companies were seperately sold to the management teams of each company and continued as CQ members.

The CARQUEST marketing program, from its first year in 1973 with three members serving 181 stores, reached a high in membership with 20 in 1986, serving 417 stores. At the end of 2005, through mergers and acquisitions, there were only five members serving 3,346 stores.

GPI AND CARQUEST GROWTH

	# CQ Members	# CQ Stores	GPI-CQ Stores	GPI-JV Stores	% of GPI Total DC Sales going to CARQUEST Stores
1974	3	181	82	0	59%
1975	6	514	112	0	69%
1976	12	982	135	0	73%
1977	13	1,052	152	0	83%
1978	14	1,258	171	0	88%
1979	16	1,336	190	0	90%
1980	17	1,550	291	0	91%
1981	16	1,618	300	0	93%
1982	16	1,661	296	2	94%
1983	16	1,758	308	5	96%
1984	16	1,994	361	51	98%
1985	20	2,080	417	58	98%
1986	18	2,078	705	101	99%
1987	17	2,140	739	112	99%
1988	16	2,085	814	160	100%
1989	16	2,176	844	179	100%
1990	17	2,280	931	226	100%
1991	16	2,416	1,091	271	100%
1992	15	2,688	1,349	351	100%
1993	14	2,844	1,535	451	100%
1994	13	2,882	1,654	531	100%
1995	12	2,877	1,648	582	100%
1996	12	2,925	1,929	681	100%
1997	9	3,348	2,486	817	100%
1998	8	3,354	2,899	984	100%
1999	8	3,826	2,785	1,019	100%
2000	8	3,765	2,773	1,169	100%
2001	7	3,703	2,809	1,226	100%
2002	7	3,695	2,789	1,281	100%
2003	6	3,582	2,973	1,394	100%
2004	5	3,548	3,156	1,524	100%
2005	5	3,346	3,054	1,497	100%

A SAMPLING OF SOME OF THE FINEST CARQUEST STORE OWNERS

Don Landon
Michigan

Allen Lyon
New Mexico

Greg Palmer
Minnesota

Wayne Foote
Michigan

Dick Seehase
Michigan

Jimmy Durbin
Alabama

Bruce Camp
New York

Junior Anderson
North Carolina

Bill Carpenter
Indiana

Ed Florida
Tennessee

Craig Martens
Illinois

Slick Gibbons
South Carolina

Larry Sloan
North Carolina

Chuck Murray
Ohio

Chuck Karl
Minnesota

Bill Toy
Indiana

George Amory
Virginia

Dirk Goettleman
Wisconsin

Larry Thomas
Alabama

Mark Peterson
Michigan

Rich Castelli
Utah

Jimmy Liles
South Carolina

Tom Roland
Florida

Mike Washington
Ohio

George Amory
Virginia

Danny Durbin
Alabama

Ralph Lee
Tennessee

Kevin Boozer
South Carolina

Edwin Florida
Tennessee

Blaine Bingham
Arizona

Bob Connor
Arizona

Ed Lightfoot
Georgia

Dave Seehase
Michigan

Mike Morse
Ohio

Jim Miller
Missouri

Marv
Stephens
Montana

Chris Farrell
California

Carl Staat
Michigan

Merle
Bauman
Arizona

J. C. Wright
Mississippi

Marc Beasley
Colorado

Earl Stockford
New
Brunswick

J. J.
Rodriguez
New Mexico

Greg Lawson
Maryland

Bert Knight
Kentucky

Paul Leitle
Missouri

Bob Curtis
Arizona

Henry Horsfall
Ontario

Gerry Young
Colorado

Dan Esse
Arizona

Jerry Curtiss
Montana

Eddy Caldwell
North Carolina

Buddy Kittrell
North Carolina

Tom Fraze
Indiana

Les Hugins
Washington

Mitch
Hampton
North Carolina

Mike Knox
Maine

Pete Bush
South
Carolina

Jim Karl
Minnesota

Manuel
Rodriguez
New Mexico

Ken
Washington
Ohio

Reggie
Stewart
Alabama

Larry
Thomason
Mississippi

Spence Verry
North Dakota

Ron Therien
Quebec

Sandy Oen
Washington

Ron Peck
Illinois

Carl Hestand
Arizona

John Phillips
North Carolina

Glenn
McAdam
Illinois

Harry
Hoffman
Indiana

Tony Michaud
Minnesota

Doug Miller
Missouri

Don
Cunningham
Iowa

Phil Flies
South
Carolina

Jim McGarity
Maryland

Perry Mullis
Maryland

Shelia Duncan
North Carolina

Roy Kittrell
North Carolina

Marc Blanc
Wisconsin

A FishQUEST

ONE OF THE WAYS THAT GENERAL Parts shows its appreciation to CAR-QUEST Auto Parts Store Owners is by inviting them on a four-day fishing trip to Canada. The first trip, in 1988, was to Camp Lochalsh in Ontario. After that, the annual event has been held at Sportsman's Lodge.

Sportsman's Lodge is located on Lake McIntosh, which is part of the Churchill River System in north Saskatchewan, approximately 600 miles north of the Montana border. There are no roads leading to this lodge, making it a Mecca for walleye and northern pike fishing. Those who have been there will testify there are only a few things to do . . . catch fish, eat, establish friendships with other CARQUEST store owners, and lie about the size of the fish they *almost* caught. Since 1988, more than 200 GPI customers have experienced the joys of a Sportsman's Lodge fishing trip.

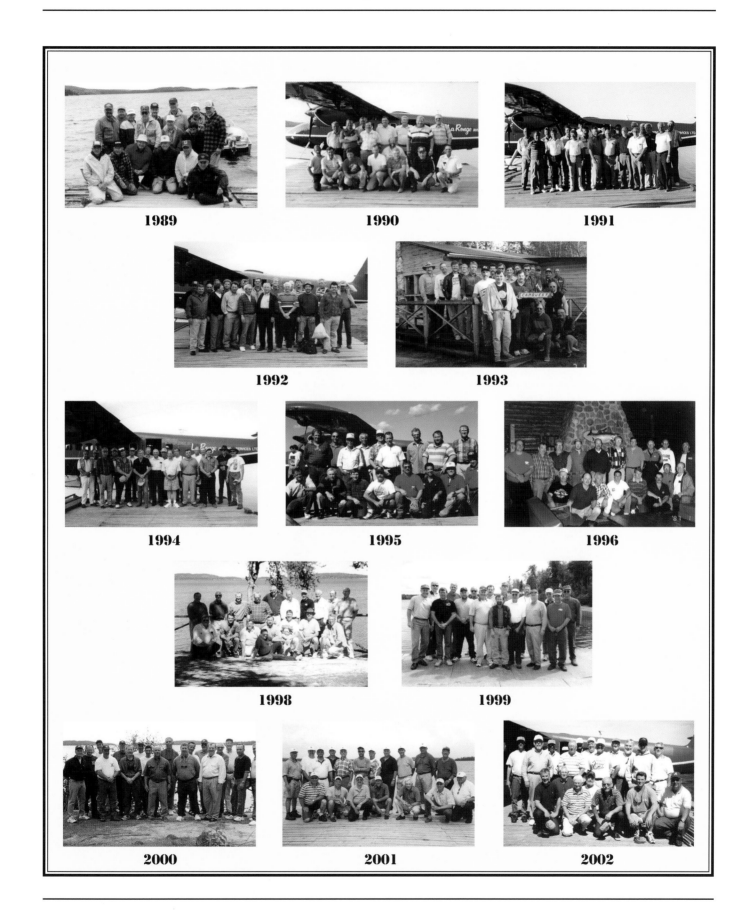

1989 1990 1991

1992 1993

1994 1995 1996

1998 1999

2000 2001 2002

CHAPTER THIRTEEN

A SPECIAL THANKS

THE GPI HISTORY WOULD NOT BE COMPLETE without a special thanks to several people among the suppliers who have made an extra effort to build a unique relationship between their companies and General Parts. These relationships were built on mutual trust and respect. The following deserve mention:

Michael Cardone, Ken Mullen and Ken Rogers at Cardone Industries; Jack Creamer at Distribution Marketing Services; Delight Breidegam and Dan Langdon at East Penn Manufacturing; Joe Magliochetti, Woody Morcott, Larry McCurdy, Bill Herring, and Terry McCormack at Dana Corporation; Ray Peck, Joe Fellechelli, and Bob Egan at Federal Mogul; Byron Pond, Bill Steele, Leon Viars, and Dan Daniel at Arvin; Jack Williams, Bob Holwell, Don Miller, John Riess, Al Stecklein, and Jay Guddat at Gates Rubber Company; Ed Gammie at Victor Gasket; John Collins at Moog; Phil Costello at McQuay-Norris; Bill Samuelson at Murray; John Goerlich, H. C. "Skip" Stivers, and Bud Ackerman at AP Parts; Jim Ledbetter at Arrow; Jim McGovern and Dave Cunningham at Raybestos; John Westling and Jack Giese at Westling Mfg. Co.; Neal Williams and Arthur Page at the N. A. Williams Company; Bill Grote at Grote Industries; and Larry Sills and John Gethen at Standard Motor Products Co.

Bill Herring	Delight Breidegam	Michael Cardone	Joe Magliochetti	Ken Rogers	Larry McCurdy	John Riess
Bill Steele	Ken Mullen	Woody Morcott	Dan Langdon	Larry Sills	Neal Williams	Jack Williams	John Westling
Bill Grote	Ray Peck	Terry McCormack	Don Miller	Arthur Page	Jim Ledbetter	Bud Ackerman	Jack Creamer

SALUTES

It is also appropriate to recognize a number of additional special friends who have played a vital role in the success of General Parts, Inc.

MURF HANDMAKER
Investor
Tucson, Arizona

Murf Handmaker founded two successful automotive parts companies, one in Scranton, Pennsylvania, and the second in Tucson, Arizona. Both companies were sold to Maremont Corporation in the early 1960s. In 1971, Murf joined his friend, Carl Pohlad, a very successful banker, and purchased General Trading Company in St. Paul, Minnesota, from Maremont. In 1977, General Trading joined the CARQUEST Marketing Program. In January 1980, following Murf's heart attack, he and Carl felt they should sell General Trading Company. I met with Murf in the bar at the Atlanta Sheridan Hotel during the CARQUEST Meeting. In spite of 20% interest rates, Murf strongly urged GPI to acquire General Trading. He advised us how it could be financed, protecting us from the record high interest rates. The General Trading transaction changed the direction of GPI from a small regional distributor to the national company it has become. Until his death in 1995, Murf reviewed our financials every month and was an invaluable advisor during the growth of GPI in the 1980s and 1990s. General Parts never had a better friend or more valuable advisor than Murf Handmaker.

—Temple Sloan Jr.

BYRON POND

CEO of Maremont Corporation

CEO of Arvin Corporation

Byron Pond was introduced to GPI by Murf Handmaker, and Byron's confidence and support in the General Trading Company acquisition was critical to our ultimate success. Working with Byron, we were successful in developing a financial program with our largest suppliers, which enabled GPI to not only make the General Trading acquisition, but many other major acquisitions during the 1980s and 1990s. It is debatable whether we could have succeeded in these major acquisitions without the program developed with Byron Pond.

Until his retirement in 2000 as CEO of Arvin, Byron made an annual trip to Raleigh, and during that visit critiqued our operating financials at a level of detail that only he could provide. Byron has a special place in the GPI success story.

—Temple Sloan Jr.

CARL POHLAD
Banker

I met Carl Pohlad when General Trading Company joined CARQUEST in 1977 (Carl and Murf Handmaker had purchased General Trading in 1971). Our relationship strengthened as a result of GPI's purchase of General Trading on July 1, 1980. Carl is an extremely successful banker and ultimately merged his banks with US Bank and Wells Fargo.

Throughout the 1980s and 1990s, Carl was not only an important banker to General Parts but a valuable advisor. In 1983, GPI had agreed to acquire the controlling interest in Valley Motor Supply in Havre, Montana. The transaction was held up by a lawsuit by a former major stockholder. After reviewing the transaction and lawsuit, Carl advised GPI that the risk of a potential loss from the suit was not enough for GPI to stop the transaction. He gave us the confidence to proceed with the transaction that put us into the store business for the first time, doubled the size of the company, and introduced us to employee-ownership, which led to our highly successful joint venture store program. These are huge milestones in our history. In addition, when he merged his banks with US Bank, he personally introduced us to Jack Grundhofer, CEO of US Bank, which has led to a major banking relationship with GPI for many years.

Carl's advice, confidence in GPI, and friendship hold a special place in our history.

—Temple Sloan Jr.

MARTIN LARNER

Founder, Indiana Parts Warehouse

Indianapolis, Indiana

I was fortunate to meet Marty Larner early in my career. Through Marty, I met my good friend and partner in building CARQUEST, Joe Hughes. Marty was our teacher, mentor, and advisor about this industry. He understood customer service, trust, and integrity as well as anyone I ever met. He spent many days and nights, sitting patiently for hours, answering the endless string of questions from two young men who had an insatiable thirst for his knowledge and experience. In 1972, when Joe Hughes, Dan Bock, and I wanted to start CARQUEST, our greatest supporter and advisor was Marty Larner. He made the opening comments at the inauguration of CARQUEST in Chicago, February 1974.

Marty Larner holds a special place in the history of CARQUEST and General Parts.

—Temple Sloan Jr.

CHARLES MCADAMS

CPA for John C. Muse and Company

Sanford, North Carolina

Charles McAdams had a long history with the Sloan family, from Mack's Stores, the finance business, family advisor for more than 40 years, and General Part's accountant and advisor for more than 20 years.

Charlie was famous for being very conservative in whatever subject, but his experience and intelligence made him an invaluable advisor to our company. In every meeting, his focus was on being sure you had thought through all aspects of the transaction, and he was never hesitant to offer his viewpoint. Following his retirement and up until his illness in the late 1990s, he frequently made the trip to Raleigh, and over lunch, he made certain his old clients and friends were on "solid ground."

Charlie McAdams was a true friend to GPI and his advice and counsel were critical during our first 20 years.

—Temple Sloan Jr.

KEN ROGERS
Automotive Aftermarket Veteran

Few people have had a more diverse career in the automotive aftermarket than Ken Rogers. For well over 50 years since graduating from Wayne University in 1951, Ken has held key management positions with a number of the most reputable automotive companies, including General Motors, Chrysler, Kelsey Hayes, McCord, Merit, A.P. Parts, Republic Automotive, Standard Motor Products (SMP) and Cardone Industries. Additionally, Ken has been active in practically all of the aftermarket industry associations including serving as chairman of the Automotive Service Industry Association in 1987.

Ken has also been a friend of General Parts, Inc., since the day it was founded. His integrity has been unquestioned and his supreme respect for the customer has never outweighed his loyalty to the company he represented. A real test of this trait occurred in 1987 when he convinced SMP and the Sills family to private label its product offering under the CARQUEST brand. Ken had just joined SMP as vice president of customer relations. This decision was right for both SMP and GPI.

Ken fully retired in 1999. At about this time, a decision was made at GPI to publish a history of our company, which would also preserve the individual history of every company acquired. To help organize this project, Ken Rogers agreed to assist. He did an excellent job and for that, GPI will forever be grateful.

—Joe Owen
—Temple Sloan Jr.

GERALD THORNTON
Manning, Fulton

In the late 1960s, we were introduced to Charlie Fulton of Manning, Fulton & Skinner. While Charlie was primarily a real estate attorney, he served us well for a few years before turning us over to Gerald Thornton who had joined Manning, Fulton & Skinner as its corporate and tax attorney. Gerald and the Manning, Fulton team have been our general counsel for more than 35 years and have been a significant contributor to our success. Gerald has been our advisor and partner in every significant acquisition and merger transaction since 1980, and we have been the beneficiary of his good business judgment, as well as his excellent tax and legal advice.

—Temple Sloan Jr.

DANA CORPORATION

Many people have contributed to GPI's success, and near the top of the list is the Dana Corporation. It began in the mid-1960s when Ed Ganme and Clyde Hill agreed to sign GPI as a Victor gasket distributor. Victor quickly became GPI's second-largest volume line. In the mid- to late 1970s, Bill Herring took over as head of Dana's aftermarket group. Not only did Dana become our largest supplier, but our relationship with Bill Herring turned out to be very important in the 1980s and 1990s. Through Bill, we got to know the Dana top management.

Stan Gustason, Woody Morcott, and Joe Magliochetti—all CEOs—supported GPI during our major acquisitions. In addition, they became valuable advisors when we were charting new waters. Laird McGregor, a Dana executive vice president, had been a successful entrepreneur in the financial world and was very experienced in acquisitions. By way of Bill Herring's introduction, Laird gave John Gardner and myself sound advice in making acquisitions successful, which we continue to use to this day.

Dana has been our largest supplier for many years, and with the sale of most of their aftermarket companies in 2004 to the Cypress Group, we continue to distribute Dana's Victor gaskets under our CARQUEST brand.

—Temple Sloan Jr.

EAST PENN MANUFACTURING

Because of the nature of the product, the CARQUEST board of directors determined that each member would select his own vendor for automotive batteries using CARQUEST as the brand name.

Shortly after that decision, and following less than positive experiences with two other battery suppliers, GPI sought a battery manufacturer with a passion for quality.

"We looked at several battery suppliers but the search ended with our first visit to East Penn Manufacturing Co., in Lyon Station, Pennsylvania," said Joe Owen. "Not only did we find passion for quality in their product, we also found quality in their people from the founder, Delight Breidegam; the president, Dan Langdon; and others throughout the organization, including Chris Pruitt, Josh Livermore, Frank Cline, and the entire dedicated CARQUEST sales team."

One of the most memorable things about that first visit was being introduced to Chairman and CEO Delight Breidegam Jr. One would expect that the introduction would take place in his office but that was not the case. Delight was in the plant, in a work jacket, working on a new process to improve the product. I later learned that this was routine for him and that he actually spent most of his time in the plant, rather than behind his desk. It certainly spoke volumes of the attitude at East Penn concerning quality.

East Penn Manufacturing is the epitome of success through perfection. Its integrity is second to none as is its desire to be the best. Its willingness to share associate programs and ideas have made it a valuable partner. It is the only manufacturer that has ever been awarded a Plaque of Appreciation by General Parts, Inc. Our association with the company has truly been a pleasure.

—Joe Owen
—Temple Sloan Jr.

CHAPTER FOURTEEN

AWARDING EXCELLENCE

RECOGNIZING ACHIEVEMENT HAS LONG been a practice at GPI. The President's Club was formed in 1977 to honor those annually who achieved pre-set management standards in distribution center sales and operations. In 1985, the President's Club ring became an added incentive awarded to those who achieved President's Club status two consecutive years. Once achieved, a diamond was inserted in the ring for every year thereafter that President's Club standards were met. In 1992, separate President's Club standards were set for GPI's joint venture stores.

202 Different DC Division associates have won the President's Club status at least once over the 28-year period. Of the 96 who have won the President's Club ring, 62 (or 65%) have won diamonds.

1,322 Different JV associates have won the President's Club status at least once over the 20-year period. Of the 482 who have won the Presidents Club ring, 240 (or 50%) have won diamonds.

PRESIDENT'S CLUB RING WINNERS AND TOP PERFORMERS

	Name	X	Name	X	Name	X	Name	X	Name	X
	Abell, Kevin A.		Blanton, Donny	X	Chapman, David	X	Dockter, Dale	X	Gould, David	
	Adams, Dennis	X	Blauer, Steve	X	Charbonneau, Gilles		Doucette, Michael	X	Grabenhofer, Ron	
	Adkins, Ron	X	Bley, Jim	X	Chouinard, Pascal		Dowdle, Charles		Graham, Ron	X
	Ahiborn, Dennis	X	Blue, Allen		Christensen, Bruce	X	Ducharme, Alain		Gran, Jerry	X
	Albert, Peter	X	Boardman, Don		Christensen, Vern	X	Dufour, Michel		Grantham, Marty	
	Allard, Normand		Boatwright, Jerry		Cichocki, Dave	X	Durham, Danny	X	Gray, Mike	X
	Allen, Don		Boberg, Pat		Clark, Jeff		Durran, Steve		Greathouse, Bob	
	Alvarez, Raymon	X	Boltman, Don		Clarke, Bruce		Eichelberger, Greg	X	Green, Sam	X
	Ancel, Skip	X	Bowers, John A.		Clay, Wallace	X	Eichelberger, Jim	X	Greenwood, Al	
	Anderson, Butch		Bowl, Chris		Cobb, Larry		Ellison, Dave	X	Gregory, Art	
	Anderson, Francis		Bradford, Giv		Cochran, Jim	X	Emerson, Daniel	X	Greuel, Mark	X
	Anderson, Jim	X	Braun, Gerald		Cockerman, Jon	X	Engel, Arley	X	Griffin, Rick	
	Anderson, Robert		Braun, Richard		Cole, Larry	X	Erts, Marty		Griffith, Bill	X
	Andrews, Alfred	X	Brian, John	X	Collins, Gerald		Faircloth, David		Griggs, Mark	
	Andrews, Car	X	Briggs, Jerry		Colquett, Charles	X	Farris, Bob		Gross, Steve	X
	Andrews, Keith		Bright, Charlie	X	Compston, Scott		Faust, Arnie	X	Gruenthal, Bill	X
	Archer, Matt	X	Britt, Ron	X	Conover, Glenn	X	Ferguson, Norm	X	Guerndt, Bonnie	X
	Armstrong, Bill		Britt, Wayne		Conroy, Dan	X	Ferguson, Tom	X	Guilford, Mike	X
	Armstrong, Ron		Brost, Chris	X	Cook, Jack	X	Ferland, Jean		Gunderson, James	X
	Ashworth, Steve	X	Browder, Travis		Cook, John		Field, Stan	X	Gushie, Steven	
	Auglis, Arnold	X	Brown, Dan	X	Coone, Donnie		Fischer, Jon		Gutherie, Scott	X
	Ayers, Chris		Brown, Gary		Cooper, Gary	X	Fisher, Don	X	Haerr, Bob	
	Ayres, Chuck	X	Brown, Jon		Cote, Andre		Fisher, Joel		Hale, Jamie	X
	Bailey, Brian		Brown, Tommy		Cote, Tony	X	Fisher, Keith	X	Hall, Rodney	X
	Bailey, Travis	X	Brown, Virgil	X	Coxe, John III	X	Flaherty, Steve	X	Hall, Tucker	X
	Baker, Eddie	X	Bruhn, Gilbert Jr.		Crouse, Bob	X	Fletcher, Jeff	X	Hamilton, Jack	
	Ball, Bill	X	Brummett, Herschel	X	Crump, Gerald	X	Fochtman, Dan		Hamm, Glenn	X
	Banks, Jeremy		Brunkhorst, Doug	X	Cutsinger, Larry		Fortier, Pierre		Hammett, Eugene	X
	Barlage, Mark		Bryant, James	X	Damewood, Myron		Fortier, Simon	X	Hammett, Wally	X
	Barrow, Harold	X	Bubar, David	X	Dantro, Jamie		Fossat, Dave		Hampton, L. J.	X
	Bass, Brent		Budnik, Kevin		Dassow, Michael	X	Foster, Bob		Hanney, Gene E.	X
	Bauer, Phil		Buechlin, Wayne		Daulton, Mark		Fowler, Joan		Hansen, Phillip	
	Baumler, Pat	X	Buntrock, Larry		Davis, Don	X	Fox, Peter R.		Harman, David	
	Beane, Bill	X	Busby, Gary	X	Davis, Gary		Franz, Eric		Harrington, D.	
	Beck, Clarence	X	Buss, Mike	X	De Long, Larry	X	Franz, Rick	X	Hattaway, Henry	X
	Becker, Dan		Buxton, Jeff		DeCosta, Frank	X	Freeburg, Dan		Hauer, Karl	X
	Bedard, Rejean		Cady, Gary		Dedman, Allen	X	Gajewski, Bryan	X	Head, Jim	X
	Belding, Tom		Cain, Robert	X	Deetjen, Chris		Gallet, Gerald	X	Healey, Gerry	X
	Beliveau, Guy		Caldwell, James	X	Dejoy, Tom	X	Garcia, Miguel	X	Heaviland, Larry	
	Bell, Johnny	X	Calhoun, Dean		Dekker, Nathan	X	Gardner, Rex	X	Hedley, Shawn	
	Bell, Steve		Callahan, Tom		Del Toro, Pable	X	Gaudio, John	X	Henderson, David	X
	Bennett, Mike	X	Canaday, Robert W.		Delisle, Normand	X	Gehlmann, Ralph	X	Henderson, Mike	X
	Benson, Don	X	Canterbury, Mike		Desautels, Francois	X	Geiger, Gannon	X	Henderson, Tom	X
	Berdan, Steve	X	Cantwell, Tom	X	Desroches, Rejean		George, Bruce		Henline, Chuck	
	Bergeron, Sylvain	X	Carpenter, Chris		Dewald, Larry		Gibbs, Paul	X	Hensiel, Donnie	
	Berriault, Keith		Carr, Gene		Dewar, Catherine		Gilbert, Laurie		Hertz, Rod	
	Berry, Richard		Casey, Roger		Dickerson, Trey	X	Girard, Ron	X	Hiatt, Kathy	
	Beyer, Rick	X	Castonguay, Gilles		Dilts, Tom		Glenn, John		Hickethier, Pete	
	Biggs, Shelton	X	Cayouette, Christian		DiMatteo, Rocky		Gonzales, Joey	X	Hietala, Morris	X
	Biladeau, Larry	X	Cellini, Nick	X	Dobson, Brian	X	Gould, Dan		Hileman, Mike	

Name		Name		Name		Name		Name	
Hintz, Dale	X	Labbe, Claude		Monsey, James	X	Riley, Thomas	X	Taylor, Brian	
Hogan, Lynn		Lambert, Lane	X	Moore, Greg		Rizor, Ken		Taylor, Grant	
Holder, Buddy	X	Lampy, John	X	Moore, Tim	X	Roa, Octavio		Terrill, Dave	X
Hollenbeck, Mike		Landrum, Jason	X	Morales, Rodney	X	Roach, Gary	X	Terry, Norman	X
Holliday, Paul	X	Langston, Greg		Morris, Dale		Rob Scott		Thibert, Thomas	
Hollingsworth, Mike	X	Lanza, Charlotte		Mortensen, Val		Robertson, Jeff		Thomas, Tommy	
Holman, Ricky		Lappert, Mike		Moxham, Chris	X	Robinson, Dana	X	Titus, Vic	X
Hosea, Richard		Larson, Lonny	X	Mueller, Bill	X	Robinson, Don	X	Tomasiewicz, Rich	X
Hotchkiss, Dana	X	Larson, Tim		Mueller, Gary	X	Roger, Jason		Tomisich, Burke	X
Houser, Dennis		Lavallee, Christian	X	Mutchie, Dave	X	Rose, George		Tompins, Troy	X
Howard, Michelle		Law, Tony	X	Napier, Johnny	X	Roth, Jim	X	Torres, Chris	X
Howard, Ralph	X	Leidholt, Randy	X	Neal, Jerry	X	Roth, Mark	X	Tortorelli, Bob	X
Howell, Brian	X	Lester, Kalvin	X	Newbanks, James		Roy, Kelley		Travis, Glenn	
Hubal, Tom	X	Linerman, Jeff	X	Newman, Perry		Russell, David		Tremblay, Serge	
Hubner, Bruce	X	Loeffel, Clark		Niccum, Ed	X	Rustman, Steve	X	Trommitz, Mike	X
Huffman, Andy	X	Loney, Monty		Nickel, Dave		Rutkowski, Keith		Turner, John	
Huffman, Phillip		Long, Mike		Niedzwiecki, Adam	X	Scheid, Theodore	X	Vallier, Keith	
Hultz, Jeff	X	Long, Wayne	X	Nielsen, Billy	X	Schmokel, Claude	X	Van Alstyne, Joe	
Huslig, Phil	X	Lopez, Noe		Niemiec, Frank		Schmokel, Paul	X	Van Zant, Rick	
Huttman, Doug	X	Lorenz, John	X	Norris, Larry	X	Schnoebelen, Dave		Vandenboom, Mike	X
Hutton, David	X	Lortie, Rejean		Novak, Michael		Schoessler, Roy	X	VanEngen, Gary	
Ihlan, Mark		Lovin, Kurt		Oberlander, Larry	X	Scofield, Steve	X	Vredenburgh, Peter	X
Jackson, Ken	X	Lowman, Steve	X	Ogden, Rod		Scott, Michael	X	Wachs, Art	
Jamil, Pierre		Luttrell, Larry	X	Oliver, Ken	X	Sessions, David		Wade, Phil	
Jay, John		Maclaren, Tim	X	Onorato, Randy	X	Settle, Richard	X	Walling, Jeff	X
Jeffers, Kelly		Macomber, Sandy	X	Ottenbacher, Dean	X	Sharp, Eric	X	Warner, Roger	X
Jenkins, Alton	X	Mader, Wynn	X	Owczarzak, Dan	X	Sharp, Gene	X	Watson, Barney	X
Jensen, Thomas (Roy)	X	Mailman, Sheila		Palmer, Gary	X	Sharp, Kevin	X	Webb, Mike	
Jette, Don	X	Maldonis, Ronald	X	Parker, Keith	X	Shore, Andy	X	Wehrenberg, Dick	X
Jines, Steve	X	Manley, Frank		Parkison, Mark		Shumaker, Dennis		Weinmann, John Sr.	X
Jobe, John		Mann, Mike		Parrack, Doug	X	Simard, Paul	X	Weis, Tom	X
Johnson, Neal		Marks, Stan		Parrott, Ken	X	Sisco, Frank	X	Weldon, Daryl	X
Johnson, Richard		Marquissee, Dave	X	Pattison, James		Sisson, Mel		Wells, Ashton	
Johnson, Robert	X	Martel, Pierre		Pearson, Kevin		Sloan, Hamilton Jr.		Wells, Ralph	X
Johnson, Tim	X	Martin, Fred	X	Peavy, Lackey		Slodowski, Thomas		Wertman, Kren	
Jones, Gary		Martinez, Tony		Pederson, Kevin		Smith, Dan		West, Bradley	
Jones, Ron	X	Mathews, Barry		Perkins, Alan		Smith, Gary		Wheeler, Al	X
Jones, Shawn	X	Mathie, Russ		Perkins, Bob	X	Smith, Randy	X	White, John	X
Jones, Tommy	X	Matthews, Danny		Perry, Dan		Smith, Robby		White, Roger	
Jorgensen, Bruce	X	Mauldin, Jeff	X	Peters, Clint	X	Smith, Stephen	X	Wibben, Dave	X
Jozak, Jim		Mauze, Layton		Peterson, Paul		Smith, Travis		Wiens, Ken	X
Juarez, Maurice		McClinton, Clay		Peyman, Tom	X	Smoot, John	X	Williams, Donny	X
Just, Gerhart		McConnell, Michael		Pfeifer, Tim	X	Snyder, Jerry T.	X	Williamson, Mike	X
Kahut, John	X	McDaniel, Rick		Phillips, Ralph		Snyder, Phil		Willis, Joe	
Katsel, Kenny	X	McDermott, Mike	X	Pike, Mike		Sonsteng, Eric		Willis, Steve	X
Kautsman, Mike		McElheny, Jim	X	Ponder, Garrett		Sparks, Tom		Wilson, Brent	X
Kemmer, James		McFadden, Larry		Porter, Phil	X	Spencer, Jake	X	Wilson, Juan	X
Kerins, Harry		McKnight, Irwin	X	Powell, Dick		Spencer, James		Wilson, Kevin	X
King, Rick		McMichael, Don		Powell, Donnie	X	Spiers, Dennis	X	Wilson, Ron	x
King, Thomas		Meade, Steve		Poynter, Steve	X	Spunaugle, Dave	X	Winders, Hil.	X
Klieforth, Randy	X	Mehalovich, John		Pressley, Donald	X	Stanley, Larry	X	Wischmann, John	
Knaub, Paul	X	Melvin, Tom	X	Pruitt, Roger	X	Steinke, Jeffrey L.	X	Wissmiller, Craig	X
Knewtson, G.	X	Mendoza, Henry		Rabon, Gene		Stephenson, Jack		Woodfill, Bob	
Koenig, Anthony	X	Menke, John	X	Rapp, Brian	X	Stewart, Christopher	X	Wygal, Rob	
Komenda, Joe		Merchant, Rich	X	Ream, Dennis	X	Struif, Bob	X	Yearley, Gordon	X
Kos, Scott	X	Merers, Paul	X	Reather, R.		Struiksma, Jack		Yound, Allen	X
Kosobucki, John	X	Merlino, Peggy		Rebholz, Andy		Subjoc, Gary		Young, Michael	X
Kramer, Andrea		Mettler, Barry	X	Redfern, Michael		Sumerall, Rosina		Zajbel, Tom	
Kramer, Bob	X	Michutka, John		Redmon, Tim	X	Summers, Mike	X	Zeltinger, Mike	X
Kratochvil, Ken	X	Miller, Doug	X	Reese, Tracy	X	Svard, Steig	X	Zibolski, Andy	
Kreesen, Mike	X	Miller, Louie	X	Repak, Jerry		Swanson, Robert		Zinda, Gary	
Kreiger, Walt		Miller, Mark	X	Reymundo, Johnny	X	Sweeney, Kevin	X	Zuanich, Mark	
Krueger, Pete	X	Miller, Ray	X	Rice, Ronnie	X	Sweeney, Tom	X		
Krug, Jim		Minske, Martin	X	Rice, Wes	X	Switzer, Ray	X		
Krus, Bob	X	Molin, Trey	X	Rich, Steven	X	Tanji, Mike	X	**X = Has earned Diamond**	

Top Performers			# P.C. WINNERS	# RING WINNERS	# DIAMOND WINNERS
Jack Cook	Ring + 8 Diamonds	**1977**	4	N/A	N/A
Arnie Faust	Ring + 8 Diamonds	**1978**	2	N/A	N/A
Tommy Jones	Ring + 8 Diamonds	**1979**	7	N/A	N/A
Scott Kos	Ring + 7 Diamonds	**1980**	0	N/A	N/A
Jason Landrum	Ring + 7 Diamonds	**1981**	4	N/A	N/A
Jim Eichelberger	Ring + 6 Diamonds	**1982**	6	N/A	N/A
Henry Hattaway	Ring + 6 Diamonds	**1983**	11	N/A	N/A
Mike McDermott	Ring + 6 Diamonds	**1984**	12	N/A	N/A
Jack Stephenson	Ring + 6 Diamonds	**1985**	4	N/A	N/A
John White	Ring + 6 Diamonds	**1986**	21	1	
Herschel Brummett	Ring + 5 Diamonds	**1987**	22	10	1
Doug Brunkhorst	Ring + 5 Diamonds	**1988**	54	6	5
Jeff Fletcher	Ring + 5 Diamonds	**1989**	45	19	2
Miguel Garcia	Ring + 5 Diamonds	**1990**	46	7	8
Paul Gibbs	Ring + 5 Diamonds	**1991**	28	5	2
Steve Gross	Ring + 5 Diamonds	**1992**	43	3	5
James Gunderson	Ring + 5 Diamonds	**1993**	91	15	8
Chris Moxham	Ring + 5 Diamonds	**1994**	103	24	18
Ronnie Rice	Ring + 5 Diamonds	**1995**	102	13	7
Don Robinson	Ring + 5 Diamonds	**1996**	172	35	27
Jim Roth	Ring + 5 Diamonds	**1997**	142	34	33
Theodore Scheid	Ring + 5 Diamonds	**1998**	258	37	44
Dan Smith	Ring + 5 Diamonds	**1999**	180	56	33
Eric Sonsteng	Ring + 5 Diamonds	**2000**	223	32	60
Gary Subjoc	Ring + 5 Diamonds	**2001**	313	48	82
Ralph Wells	Ring + 5 Diamonds	**2002**	368	58	79
		2003	351	77	82
		2004	336	46	68
		2005	288	53	80
		TOTAL	3,236	579	644

CARQUEST EXCELLENCE AWARDS

GPI and the CARQUEST organization target the professional automotive service technician as its prime customer. It was recognized early on that to be a better supplier, it was important to know the true needs of this prime customer. Starting in the early 1980s, GPI held meetings with small groups of carefully selected professional auto service center owners. Through the CARQUEST professional markets committee, these meetings were elevated to a national scope and evolved to the present CARQUEST Excellence Award.

GPI and CARQUEST are thankful to the many professional auto service center owners who have participated in these annual events and are especially thankful to the following five who have won the CARQUEST Excellence Award and have been extremely helpful assisting CARQUEST additionally in "above and beyond" activities.

Stan Elmore, owner, Stan's Tire & Auto Service Center, Lafayette, CO
Jerry Holcom, owner, S & S Service Center, Kansas City, MO
Lynn Cardwell, owner, Car Care Center, Sacramento, CA
Steve Pokorny, owner, Sun Service Center, Jennings, MO
Joe Marconi, owner, Osceola Garage, Baldwin Place, NY
(pictured below, from left to right)

CARQUEST Excellence Award Winners

2006	John Sawatsky	MJS Automotive	Windsor, Ontario, Canada
2005	Rick Allen	Rick Allen's Auto Repair	Hampton, NJ
2004	Al Duebber	Duebber's Automotive Service	Cincinnati, OH
2003	Don Fowers	Fowers Service Center	Clearfield, UT
2002	Dan Ritchie	Express Auto Service	Fredericksburg, VA
2001	Bob Anderson	A.J.'s Auto Repair	Salem, OR
2000	Lynn Cardwell	Car Care Center	Sacramento, CA
1999	Tom, Terry Keller	Keller Bros.	Littleton, CO
1998	Dan Waskow	Superior Auto Service	Bryan, TX
1997	Joe Marconi	Osceola Garage	Baldwin Place, NY
1996	Steve Pokorny	Sun Service Center	Jennings, MO
1995	Jerry Holcom	S & S Service Center	Kansas City, MO
1994	Lynn Beckwith	Beckwith's Automotive	Humble, TX
1993	Stan Elmore	Stan's Tire & Auto Service Center	Lafayette, CO
1992	Wayne Reed	Computer Tune	Lexington, KY

CARQUEST Technician of the Year Award

In 2001, CARQUEST added recognition of the Technician of the Year to the Excellence Award. Those winners were:

2006	Greg Epsaro	Harriman Auto	Harriman, NY
2005	Jim Rowledge	Broadway Estates Conoco	Littleton, CO
2004	Richard Robb	Tech-Net Auto Service	Elkhorn, WI
2003	Rich Allen	Rich Allen Auto Repair	Hampton, NJ
2002	Thomas Eberly	North Hills Automotive	Greenville, SC
2001	John Shields	Shields' Garage	Dunkirk, IN

CARQUEST Collision Center Excellence Award

In 2003, the CARQUEST Collision Excellence Award originated and the first winner was Rick Booth of Rick's Auto Body in Missoua, MT.

2005	Angela Zenoniani	Classic Auto Collision	Escanaba and Marquette, MI
2004	David Sirois	Zeol's Body and Auto	Meriden, CT
2003	Rick Booth	Rick's Auto Body	Missoula, MT

CARQUEST Vendor of the Year Award

Vendors have played an important role in General Parts' success. Since 1992, CARQUEST has recognized the vendor of the year based on performance. Through 2005, the winners were:

2005	Wells Manufacturing	CARQUEST Sensors/Ignition
2004	East Penn Manufacturing	CARQUEST Batteries
2003	WIX Division of Dana	CARQUEST Filters
2002	Gates	CARQUEST Belts & Hose
2001	Victor-Reinz Division of Dana	CARQUEST Gaskets
2000	Arvin-Maremont	CARQUEST Exhaust
1999	Federal Mogul	CARQUEST Bearings & Seals
1998	Cardone	CARQUEST Remanufactured Products
1997	ARI	CARQUEST Reman. CV Axel Shafts/Driveshafts
1996	Gates	CARQUEST Belts & Hose
1995	WIX Division of Dana	CARQUEST Filters
1994	Moog Manufacturing	CARQUEST Chassis Parts
1993	EIS	CARQUEST Brakes
1992	WIX Division of Dana	CARQUEST Filters

Recognizing Your Contribution To The Success Of CARQUEST Through Quality Products & Outstanding Marketing Support

2004 VENDOR OF THE YEAR
CARQUEST Batteries
East Penn Manufacturing

It is appropriate to also express special thanks to the following people who represented key suppliers to GPI. Their contributions have been vital to GPI's success:

Airtex	Dee Monge
AMS	Chris Jackson, Ron Jackson, and Bob Insalaco
Dana/Affinia	Bruce Blankenhorn, Cathy Gallagher, Mike Harvey, Bob Kaulig, Kirk Minich, Lee Murray, Richard Odom, Dan Rouso, Terry Shively, Wayne Sorenson, John Washbish, Bryan Watson, Keith Wilson, and the entire CARQUEST dedicated sales team
East Penn	Frank Cline, Josh Livermore, and the entire CARQUEST dedicated sales team
Gates	Bob Alderton, Ron Carlson, Clark Wasson, and the entire CARQUEST dedicated sales team
Lisle Corp.	Bill Lisle
NEAPCO	Keith Strickland
Qualis	Marvin Fudalla and Dave Soule
Wells Manufacturing	Bill Allen
N.A. Williams Co.	Rick Griffin, Keyma Harris, Roger McCollum, Chris Williams, and the GENQUEST sales team

GPI SCHOLARSHIP AWARD RECIPIENTS

Education has long played an important role in establishing the GPI culture as well as that of the CARQUEST membership. Since 1985, 494 scholarships have been awarded to children of associates and customers including these awarded by the O. Temple Sloan Jr. Founders Scholarship Fund and the Sam Rogers Northwood CARQUEST Scholarship Fund.

Tonya Abke
John Abner
Brian Addington
Kimberly Dawn Adkins
James Aerts
Karla Afshari
Kyong Aho
Jessica Albert
Matthew Albert
David Albright
Brock Aldrich
Kyle Allee
Kaycie Ammons
James M. Anderson
James Williams Anderson
Andrea Arnold
Mark Atkinson
Michael Atwood
Ryan Ault
Robert Daniel Ayera
Lonny Babin
Matthew Bailey
Michael Bailey
Adam Ballard
Toby Ban
Renee Bandy
Sarah Bange
Tonisha Barksdale
Gretchen Barnes
Mindy Barrow
Bret Barth
Brendon Bartholomew
Laura Bauer
Kevin Bayer
Dana Beasley
Jeffrey Beck
Christine Behn
Amanda Bell
David Bell
Craig Berdan
Tammy Bergeron

Katherine Bernard
Douglas Berndt
Rhonda Beyer
David Bishop
Charles Bissell
Zachary Bittinger
Ernest Blackwell
Buffy Blair
Kenny Borum
Sheila Borum
Jeffrey Bova
Matthew Boyd
Janet Bozeman
Jo Anna Brannon
Kelly Bressler
Melissa Brones
Jace Brooks
Christopher Brower
Jamey Brown
Shannon Brown
Robert Browning
Kelly Bull
Cynthia L. Bunnel
Korrie Butler
Cathy Byorth
Clint Caffey
Cathleen Callahan
Janet Cameron
Erin Camp
Lillie Campbell
Saffron Carew
Lee Carpenter
Melissa Ann Carington
Suzannah Carter
Christain Chadwick
Kristina Chadwick
Laban Chappell
Michael Chavez, Jr.
Eric Cheek
Melinda Church
Matthew Clarke

Keith Clasen
Michael Cleveland
Travis Cloukey
Jeanetta Cochran
Deon Devel Coleman
Jeffrey Compeau
Jennifer Conley
Zachary Cooley
Christopher Corbat
Dawn Cowan
Kristina Cowdrey
Michael Cox
Keith Crocker
Chad Crosby
Tracee Crump
Dionne Cruz
Amanda Curier
Scott Curtiss
Stephanie Cussen
Mark Damveld
Kendra Dance
Shelley Davis
Amber Deal
Joshua Dean
Anna Dearmon
John DeBacco
Daniel Dedman
Christopher Deetjen
Dustin DeFord
Jason DeFord
Dustin DeVries
Antonette Diaz
Nathaniel Diedrich
John Dieterle
Christopher Dillard
Mary Dixon
Jonathan Dockhorn
Levi Doner
Nichole Douglas
Amanda Dunbar
Wade Dunham

Jessica Dunn
Stacy Durland
Rachel Edwards
Chris Eiler
Donna Ekart
Kelly Ekker
Kimberly Eldridge
Billy Douglas Ellenburg
Jason Ellenburg
Dennis Englehardt
Kendra Eulinger
Casey Everett
Chad Evers
Dolores Faas
Gabriel Falcon
Conie Finley
Matthew Flier
Jesse Florida
Monica Forbes
Frances Marie Ford
Shannon Fountain
Danielle Fragala
Thomas E. Fraze
Brian Frazier
John Thomas Freyermuth
Jonathan Mark Gaddy
Melanie Galloway
Christine Gannon
Melissa Garner
Michael Garner
Julie Ann Gebhart
Jason Gibbs
Kyle Gibbs
Gordon Gibson
Monty Gibson
Suzette Gibson
Susan Ginn
Robin Gjeustad
Kristin Glass
Jessica Godzik
Sarah Goodpasture

Shane Gourley
Matthew Graves
Kelly Gray
Theresa Green
Ashley Greenwood
Nay Griffith
Brian Griggs
Melody Gunther
Amy Halvorson
Angela Hamilton
Kayla Hancock
Michelle Hanover
Shane Hansmeier
Susannah Harden
Evan Hardesty
Robert Harrison
Rebecca Hart
William Harvey
Clinton Hatch
Larissa Heanssler
Kristin Heinz
Derek Henderson
Vanessa Hendricks
Jamie Hermes
Anthony Hiess
Robert Hilburn
James Hill
Jay Hillard
Angela Hines
Valerie Hohneke
Stacy Hollantz
Pamela Sue Howard
Ashley Hughes
Paula Kay Humphrey
Justin Humphreys
Seth Hunt
Marla Hunt
Tracy Innello
Heather Jackson
Lori-Jo Jacquette
Mari-Jo Jacquette

Keith Jalbert
Frederick James
Ronald James
Tim Jansen
Bethany Jedlicka
Jeremy Johnson
Matthew Jolin
Angelia Jones
Anita Jones
Heather Jones
Brian Kabat
Joy Lynn Kauffman
Michael Kelly
Melanie Kemp
Millie Kennedy
Angela Kerley
Roxie Kimble
Amanda Kincaid
Justin Kinder
John Kleibocker
Trenton Klein
Michael Klieforth
Daniel Knaub
Christi Kochen
Cory Koliscak
Kyle Krumlauf
Robert Kunze
Stefanie Kuzminski
Angela Kyzer
Jeremy Lade
Kimberly Ann Lahucik
Meagan L. Landers
Sherrie Langston
Jessica LaRue
Timothy Layton
Pamela Lee
Brian Lenhardt
Nancy Lenhardt
Amanda Lesberg
Andrew Lester
Dawn Marie Lewis
Julie Lewis
Lori Lewis
Julia Linderman
Jolynn Therese Litcher
Phillip Lithgow
Andrew Locicero
Ryan Long
Susan Long

Jody Lonning
Christopher Loos
John Lucht
Stephen Lund
Ryan Lynn
Brett Macklin
Paula Mangrum
Robert Mann
Alan Marquardt
Charles Marshall
Jason Martens
Suzann Martin
Claudia Martinez
Jennifer Maskell
Michael Maslowski
Jennifer Mastrovito
Nicolas Mayer
Christine Mazur
Matthew McArthur
Jason McCammon
Amy McDaniels
Diana McDonald
Anthony McGinnis
Kristi McGriff
Jeffery McGuire
Nancy McKenzie
Stephanie McKenzie
Jason McLouth
Mary Metger
Jonathan Middaugh
Carl Miller
Kelli Miller
Matthew Miller
Lathan Mills
Chad Minne
Ashley Monroe
Deanna Moore
Margaret Morgan
Robert Morgan
Jason Mueller
Todd Muench
Aimee Mullis
Mark Munt
Clifford Murphy
Joseph Murray
Sarah Neu
Jonathan Nielson
Kristen Nolan
Edward Norris

Michael Northcutt
Rian Nostrum
Kimberly Nowell
Elizabeth Ann Olson
Damon Palm
Carnie Parker
Asley Kristine Parks
Jennifer Pasco
Bethany Pelletier
Leslie Perdue
Jacqueline Peterman
Brent Petermann
Amanda Peterson
Cliff Peterson
Christine Pflibsen
Angela Phillips
Sherray Pleinis
Lisa Pohl
Christopher Poncelet
Megan Price
Rogetta Prueitt
Shawn Quinn
Renata Raughton
Richard Ravin
Kelly Ray
Jonathan Rearden
Shannon Reeder
Joshua Reese
Matthew Reeves
Kristian Reither
Scott Rhinehart
Robert Richter
Tracy Riedinger
Kristina Rightmire
Brenda Riley
Gregory Rodgers
Jarrod Roger
Michael Rogers
Allyson Rose
Charles J. Runser, Jr.
AmySuzanne Russell
Elizabeth Russell
Matthew Ryder
James Rymer
Joan Sanders
Jill Sartain
Barbara Savoy
Heather Sawyer
Darby Schaffer

Charles Schardein
Jason Schieffler
Adam Schmidt
Nathan Schneider
Kristin Schroeder
Lesly Schulte
Kristi Schuster
Paula Michele Schweiger
Jeffrey Scott
Clint Seegers
Alexander Seger
Greg Sellner
Nicholas Sequin
Julia Shannon
Tricia Shapland
Lauren Sharp
Meagan Shelton
Gordon Shetler
Kevin Shipp
Amanda Shull
Amy Siedschlag
Christian Siegel
Elisa Siegmann
Janice Marie Simmons
Elgie Sims
Lori Slade
Tiffany Slagg
John Sloan
Adam Smith
Michelle Smith
Steve Smith
Tarinn Smith
Rhonda Fay Snow
Joseph Soeder
Thomas Olai Sparks, Jr.
Jaime Spencer
Randy Sproat
Samantha Srp
Staci Staat
Rebecca Stamm
Jennifer Starling
Michelle Steiger
Bonnie Stevens
Heather Stevens
Kerry Stone
Alana Stricker
Rodney Strickland
Christopher Stump
Keith Suazo

Jessica Tamayo
Dereka Taylor
Paul Taylor
Roy Taylor
Angela Tedesco
Thomas Teets
Ashley Thibodeaux
Barry Thomas
Jimmy Thorpe
Jenelle Timmons
Hope Tipton
Michelle Tjugum
Kevin Todd
Katie Toomey
Katie Toomie
John Totenhagen
Amber Towe
Jason Tuntland
Artemio Vazquez
Michael Vick
Mandy Virant
Lori Wabeke
Mindi Wagenblast
Amy Walker
Dancia Wall
Patrick Walrath
Rebecca Walter
Joshua Waltz
Sheila Wanner
Sean Waters
Tonya Watts
Jerod Web
Angela Webert
Kevin Weichert
Drew Allan Weiland
Tami Wells
Sarah Wenniger
Michael Wenniger
Amanda Williams
David Williams
Virginia Williams
Pamela Williamson
Robert Williford
Robert Wilson
Misty Winter
Rebekah Witt
Ashley Nicole Wrasman
Cissy Wright
Jennifer Yakel

Winners of the Sam Rogers Northwood Institute CARQUEST Scholarship Award

Sam Rogers was a former owner, along with his brother Al and his nephew Bobby, of Parts Warehouse Company in Michigan. The company was merged into GPI in 1986. Sam was honored in December 1992 when GPI associates, suppliers, and Michigan CARQUEST store owners gathered for an announcement of the Sam Rogers Northwood Institute CARQUEST Scholarship Fund. Sam continues to be an inspiration to all who knew him. Scholarship winners include:

Jim Abraham	Princess Kirk
Jordan Ashford	Paul Kress
Josh Ashford	Scott Lake
Joshua Benson	Brian Lesiewicz
Elizabeth Ciot	William Lindsey
Arthur Eppler	Bryan Phillips
Nikki Evans	Michael Reedy
Ryan Gillewater	Ryan Spies
Derrick Hudson	Craig Stanton

Founder's Scholarship Award

The O. Temple Sloan Jr. Founder's Scholarship program was established in 2003 in honor of the founder and chairman of General Parts, Inc. This scholarship program recognizes and rewards children (dependents) of CARQUEST associates who excel in their academic performance and who desire to continue their education beyond high school. The following scholarships have been awarded since 2003:

2005	2004	2003
Andrew Camus	Ryan Clawson	Sarah St. Jean
Julie Desautels	Adrienne Hollister	Todd Jensen
Dustin Follen	Katy Mallard	Rebecca Krus
Angela Sharer	Garrett Martin	Rachel Sondag

BIBLIOGRAPHY

Sources

Aftermarket Business,
www.aftermarketbusiness. com.
Automotive Aftermarket Industry
Association (AAIA), www.aftermarket.org
(Editor's note: Automotive Warehouse
Distributor's Association [AWDA] is now
managed by AAIA.)
Automotive Aftermarket Suppliers
Association (AASA),
www.aftermarketsuppliers.org.
Automotive Week, www.auto-week.com.
Counterman Magazine,
www.aftermarketnews.com.
Lang Report, www.langmarketing.com.
Motor & Equipment Manufacturers
Association (MEMA), www.mema.org.
Saturday Evening Post. "Roll Call of
Automobiles Sold in America During the
Past 60 Years," published in 1954.
"The $7 Billion After-market Gets an
Overhaul," *Fortune* March 1962(65):82-
87.
Ward's Reports, Inc. 3000 Town Center,
Springfield, MI, 48075.

Personal Interviews

Allen, Mike, interview by Richard Hubbard,
audio recording, 27 September 2002.
Write Stuff Enterprises.
Blair, Robert, interview by Richard Hubbard,
audio recording, 26 April 2002. Write
Stuff Enterprises.
Bock, Dan, interview by Richard Hubbard,
audio recording, 24 September 2002.
Write Stuff Enterprises.
Bryant, James, interview by Richard
Hubbard, audio recording, 6 June 2002.
Write Stuff Enterprises.
Camp, Bruce, interview by Richard
Hubbard, audio recording, 21 January
2002. Write Stuff Enterprises.
Carpenter, Bill, interview by Richard
Hubbard, audio recording, 23 January
2002. Write Stuff Enterprises.
Carson, R.D., interview by Richard
Hubbard, audio recording, 10 April
2002. Write Stuff Enterprises.
Carter, Brad, interview by Richard Hubbard,
audio recording, 11 June 2002. Write
Stuff Enterprises.

Cellini, Nick, interview by Richard Hubbard, audio recording, 10 June 2002. Write Stuff Enterprises.

Cotton, Bill, interview by Richard Hubbard, audio recording, 24 April 2002. Write Stuff Enterprises.

Couch, George, interview by Richard Hubbard, audio recording, 11 June 2002. Write Stuff Enterprises.

Cunningham, Don, interview by Richard Hubbard, audio recording, 22 January 2002. Write Stuff Enterprises.

Cutsinger, Darold, interview by Richard Hubbard, audio recording, 7 June 2002. Write Stuff Enterprises.

Davis, Clarence, interview by Richard Hubbard, audio recording, 11 June 2002. Write Stuff Enterprises.

Deal, Chris, interview by Richard Hubbard, audio recording, 6 June 2002. Write Stuff Enterprises.

Duerst, Deb, interview by Richard Hubbard, audio recording, 10 June 2002. Write Stuff Enterprises.

Durbin, Jimmy, interview by Richard Hubbard, audio recording, 24 January 2002. Write Stuff Enterprises.

Durbin, Danny, interview by Richard Hubbard, audio recording, 24 January 2002. Write Stuff Enterprises.

Ellis, Chandler, interview by Richard Hubbard, audio recording, 11 April 2002. Write Stuff Enterprises.

Florida, Ed, interview by Richard Hubbard, audio recording, 20 August 2002. Write Stuff Enterprises.

Foote, Wayne, interview by Richard Hubbard, audio recording, 28 January 2002. Write Stuff Enterprises.

Fox, Dennis, interview by Richard Hubbard, audio recording, 10 April 2002. Write Stuff Enterprises.

Gardner, John W., interview by Richard Hubbard, audio recording, 11 April 2002. Write Stuff Enterprises.

Ginsburg, Scott, interview by Richard Hubbard, audio recording, 11 April 2002. Write Stuff Enterprises.

Graham, Malcolm C., interview by Richard Hubbard, audio recording, 10 April 2002. Write Stuff Enterprises.

Guirlinger, Richard B., interview by Richard Hubbard, audio recording, 11 April 2002. Write Stuff Enterprises.

Hall, Jim, interview by Richard Hubbard, audio recording, 3 September 2002. Write Stuff Enterprises.

Huffman, Russell, interview by Richard Hubbard, audio recording, 13 June 2002. Write Stuff Enterprises.

Hughes, Joe, interview by Richard Hubbard, audio recording, 19 June 2002. Write Stuff Enterprises.

Karl, Chuck, interview by Richard Hubbard, audio recording, 23 January 2002. Write Stuff Enterprises.

King, Bill, interview by Richard Hubbard, audio recording, 10 April 2002. Write Stuff Enterprises.

Knight, Bert, interview by Richard Hubbard, audio recording, 3 September 2002. Write Stuff Enterprises.

Kornafel, Pete, interview by Richard Hubbard, audio recording, 23 April 2002. Write Stuff Enterprises.

Kos, Scott, interview by Richard Hubbard, audio recording, 6 June 2002. Write Stuff Enterprises.

Kotcher, Frederic S., interview by Richard Hubbard, audio recording, 10 April 2002. Write Stuff Enterprises.

Kurszewski, Andy, interview by Richard Hubbard, audio recording, 6 June 2002. Write Stuff Enterprises.

Kuykendall, Bill, interview by Richard Hubbard, audio recording, 10 April 2002. Write Stuff Enterprises.

Landon, Don, interview by Richard Hubbard, audio recording, 25 January 2002. Write Stuff Enterprises.

Lavrack, Wayne D., interview by Richard Hubbard, audio recording, 11 April 2002. Write Stuff Enterprises.

Lee, Ralph, interview by Richard Hubbard, audio recording, 23 January 2002. Write Stuff Enterprises.

Long, Randal, interview by Richard Hubbard, audio recording, 11 April 2002. Write Stuff Enterprises.

Lottes, Art, interview by Richard Hubbard, audio recording, 10 April 2002. Write Stuff Enterprises.

Lyon, Allen, interview by Richard Hubbard, audio recording, 21 January 2002. Write Stuff Enterprises.

Martens, John, interview by Richard Hubbard, audio recording, 26 April 2002. Write Stuff Enterprises.

McCurdy, Larry, interview by Richard Hubbard, audio recording, 21 August 2002. Write Stuff Enterprises.

McQuillan, Bud, interview by Richard Hubbard, audio recording, 10 April 2002. Write Stuff Enterprises.

Minnis, Al, interview by Richard Hubbard, audio recording, 24 April 2002. Write Stuff Enterprises.

Northcutt, Shipman, interview by Richard Hubbard, audio recording, 11 April 2002. Write Stuff Enterprises.

Peavy, Lacky, interview by Richard Hubbard, audio recording, 10 June 2002. Write Stuff Enterprises.

Peterson, Dave, interview by Richard Hubbard, audio recording, 25 January 2002. Write Stuff Enterprises.

Pisciotta, Fred, interview by Richard Hubbard, audio recording, 21 August 2002. Write Stuff Enterprises.

Roberts Reed, interview by Richard Hubbard, audio recording, 3 September, 2002. Write Stuff Enterprises.

Roberts, Stan, interview by Richard Hubbard, audio recording, 6 June 2002. Write Stuff Enterprises.

Rogers, Ken, interview by Richard Hubbard, audio recording, 6 June 2002. Write Stuff Enterprises.

Romee, Chuck, interview by Richard Hubbard, audio recording, 10 June 2002. Write Stuff Enterprises.

Russell, Jim, interview by Richard Hubbard, audio recording, 22 April 2002. Write Stuff Enterprises.

Sloan, Larry, interview by Richard Hubbard, audio recording, 12 February 2002. Write Stuff Enterprises.

Sloan, O. Temple III, interview by Richard Hubbard, audio recording, 10 April 2002. Write Stuff Enterprises.

Sussen, Dan, interview by Richard Hubbard, audio recording, 29 April 2002. Write Stuff Enterprises.

Taylor, Jimmy, interview by Richard Hubbard, audio recording, 23 April 2002. Write Stuff Enterprises.

Taylor, John, interview by Richard Hubbard, audio recording, 30 April 2002. Write Stuff Enterprises.

Tenniswood, Ken, interview by Richard Hubbard, audio recording, 6 June 2002. Write Stuff Enterprises.

Thorton, Gerald, Esq., interview by Richard Hubbard, audio recording, 31 May 2002. Write Stuff Enterprises.

Tyson, Deborah, interview by Richard Hubbard, audio recording, 5 June 2002. Write Stuff Enterprises.

Weichart, Tom, interview by Richard Hubbard, audio recording, 7 June 2002. Write Stuff Enterprises.

Wheeler, Al, interview by Richard Hubbard, audio recording, 11 April 2002. Write Stuff Enterprises.

Whirty, Ed, interview by Richard Hubbard, audio recording, 10 June 2002. Write Stuff Enterprises.

Whitehurst, Ed, interview by Richard Hubbard, audio recording, 11 April 2002. Write Stuff Enterprises.

Winters, Chris, interview by Richard Hubbard, audio recording, 10 April 2002. Write Stuff Enterprises.

INDEX

Page numbers in italics indicate photographs.